www.yahoo
Science_and_Nature/
Computer_Science/

A GUIDE TO
Computer User Support

www.instantweb.com/
~foldoc/Dictionary

Fred Beisse
Lane Community College

COURSE
TECHNOLOGY

ONE MAIN STREET, CAMBRIDGE, MA 02142

an International Thomson Publishing company I(T)P®

Cambridge • Albany • Bonn • Boston • Cincinnati • London • Madrid • Melbourne • Mexico City
New York • Paris • San Francisco • Singapore • Tokyo • Toronto • Washington .

A Guide to Computer User Support is published by Course Technology.

Managing Editor:	Kristen Duerr	*Composition House:*	GEX, Inc.
Associate Product Manager:	Margarita Donovan	*Text Designer:*	GEX, Inc.
Production Editors:	Nancy Shea and Melissa Panagos	*Cover Designer:*	Meral Dabcovich
Development Editor/Project Manager:	Barbara Clemens	*Marketing Manager:*	Tracy Foley

© 1999 by Course Technology—I(T)P®

For more information contact:

Course Technology
One Main Street
Cambridge, MA 02142

ITP Europe
Berkshire House 168-173
High Holborn
London WCIV 7AA
England

Nelson ITP Australia
102 Dodds Street
South Melbourne, 3205
Victoria, Australia

ITP Nelson Canada
1120 Birchmount Road
Scarborough, Ontario
Canada M1K 5G4

International Thomson Editores
Seneca, 53
Colonia Polanco
11560 Mexico D.F. Mexico

ITP GmbH
Königswinterer Strasse 418
53227 Bonn
Germany

ITP Asia
60 Albert Street, #15-01
Albert Complex
Singapore 189969

ITP Japan
Hirakawacho Kyowa Building, 3F
2-2-1 Hirakawacho
Chiyoda-ku, Tokyo 102
Japan

Photo Credits: FIGURE 2-5: Job description courtesy of Stream International, Inc. FIGURE 3-2: Photo courtesy of Hewlett-Packard Company. FIGURE 3-3a: Advertisement courtesy of Corel Corporation; p. 54: Photo courtesy of Lane Community College; p. 66: Photo courtesy of Freight Services Incorporated; p. 89: Data courtesy of Freight Services Incorporated. FIGURE 5-5: © 1998 Belkin Components; p. 131: Logo courtesy of Timberland Regional Library.

Trademarks

Disclaimer

ISBN 0-7600-7001-6

Printed in Canada

1 2 3 4 5 6 7 8 9 WC 02 01 00 99 98

Brief Table of Contents

TABLE OF CONTENTS

PREFACE

For the last three years, I have taught a college course on Computer User Support without a textbook that adequately covers this new field. Through this experience, I learned a great deal from my research and from my students, and this book reflects that learning.

As computer use has grown, so has the need for user support specialists. Businesses have increasingly turned toward colleges to supply them with the entry-level staff they need. As a result, many schools have created, or are now creating, courses to meet this need. But instructors are finding a lack of texts that address the necessary user support areas. There are trade books on various aspects of user support and the help desk, but these are usually not written for entry-level support staff. They also lack the learner aids like end-of-chapter review questions, exercises, and projects that help readers practice and apply their new knowledge. As a result, many instructors are teaching without a text and developing their own materials—an arduous task.

With this book, I hope to address the needs of those who want to learn about this burgeoning field and who need resources to help them. *A Guide to Computer User Support* is designed as an overview of the wide range of topics that an entry-level user support specialist will be expected to know. Support positions can vary widely, and with a broad foundation in the topics covered in this book, specialists entering the support industry will be ready to meet employer needs.

THE INTENDED AUDIENCE

This book is primarily intended for three kinds of readers:

- Readers who are considering career opportunities in computer user support and who want an introduction to the user support field. This book describes the kinds of knowledge, skills, and abilities they need to be employable in the support industry.

- Readers who were trained in another field, but find themselves in a job with user support responsibilities. They will be able to use this book to get additional breadth and depth about the user support field. This audience includes programmers, computer operators, network administrators, and computer applications specialists.

- Readers who are taking a course in a user support or a related degree program. They can use this book to tie together knowledge and skills introduced in other courses. These readers will especially benefit from the end-of-chapter activities that provide practical experience and practice skills they will use on the job.

THE USER SUPPORT CURRICULUM

An increasing number of colleges and universities now offer courses and even complete degree programs to prepare professionals for the user support industry. This trend resulted because an increasing number of programming majors who enter the job market are actually employed as user support staff, not as programmers. In addition, many large software vendors outsource their support positions, meaning that support centers are distributed over a wider area of the country, creating job opportunities in more locations. In many areas of the country, an increasing number of small software companies are developing and marketing software packages that will eventually require documentation, training, installation, and other support activities. And finally, many businesses and organizations are expanding their user support operations to support their employees. Across the country, the future demand for employees with user support skills appears to be on the increase.

To help plan its new computer user support degree, Lane Community College in Eugene, Oregon formed an advisory panel of representatives from the computer industry in Lane County. It invited a number of local employers who hire computer support workers to participate on the advisory committee. Their assignment was to help design the second year of the curriculum, which includes the advanced, professional courses for user support specialists.

In addition to the technical content of the program, the most significant message Lane heard from the industry advisory panel was that problem-solving, interpersonal relations, and communications skills for future support workers was of utmost importance. Representatives on the advisory committee emphasized that changes in computer technology influences what they expect their employees to know from one year to the next. What does *not* change from year to year are the interpersonal, communications, and problem-solving skills required in these positions. Many college programs in user support are therefore blends of technical information and communication skills. This book reflects that blend. It aims to represent a balanced mixture of information about the technical aspects of user support with an appropriate emphasis on problem solving and communications skills.

THE APPROACH

A Guide to Computer User Support is designed as a guide to each of the topics covered. The author firmly believes that a user support textbook can do little more than provide concepts and background information, lead the reader into the field, and point in the direction of appropriate knowledge and skills. To derive maximum benefit from this book, the reader must be an active participant in the learning process.

The end-of-chapter activities are specifically designed to develop knowledge and skills, an important percentage of which are gained through interactions with other students. Learning to work with other students in project groups or teams is important preparation for the team-oriented work environment of the 1990s. Many of the end-of-chapter activities are designed to acquaint readers with information resources and technical tools, knowledge that is essential to functioning effectively in support positions.

ASSUMED KNOWLEDGE

This book assumes that its readers have experience in the following areas, either through course work or work experience:

- Basic computer concepts or computer literacy
- Word processor, spreadsheet, and database applications
- Internet and World Wide Web concepts

OVERVIEW OF THIS BOOK

The outline of this book follows from a list of services provided by user support centers. It parallels a list of skills user support staff need to be effective employees in user support roles.

Chapter 1, Introduction to End User Computing, explains the historical context of end user computing, how end users increase their productivity using computer systems, the resources they need, and common problems they encounter.

Chapter 2, Introduction to Computer User Support, describes why end users need help, what kinds of help support centers provide, and how companies have found ways to provide them with this support. It also describes the knowledge, skills, and abilities a successful applicant for a support position needs.

Chapter 3, Product Evaluation Strategies and Standards, describes strategies to evaluate computer products and define company product standards.

Chapter 4, User Needs Analysis and Assessment, provides tools to help user support staff analyze and assess user needs for computer hardware, software, and network products.

Chapter 5, Installing End User Computer Systems, covers the process of installing hardware, operating systems, and applications software.

Chapter 6, Training Computer Users, explains how to plan training activities, how to prepare training materials, and how to present and evaluate training for end users.

Chapter 7, Documentation for End Users, briefly examines the many types of documentation a support specialist might have to prepare, and explains how to plan, write, and evaluate end user documentation. It covers the common strategies and tools technical writers use and how to avoid common writing problems.

Chapter 8, Computer Facilities Management, deals with a number of facilities management tasks user support staff are likely to encounter, including security, media backups, preventive maintenance, and ergonomic issues.

Chapter 9, Help Desk Operation, introduces a multi-level support model, the call management process, and provides an overview of the features of help desk software packages. It also discusses the help desk mission and staffing concerns as they affect an entry-level employee.

Chapter 10, Customer Service Skills for User Support, describes the communication and customer service skills user support staff need. It also outlines ways to develop a call management strategy and handle some difficult support situations.

Chapter 11, Troubleshooting Computer Problems, discusses common tools and methods troubleshooters use to solve computer problems. It also describes seven problem-solving strategies that a user support specialist can apply to any troubleshooting situation.

Chapter 12, Common Support Problems, approaches computer problems from a practical perspective. It describes the types of common computer problems, and shows how to apply problem-solving strategies to six actual computer problems from the experience of user support specialists.

Chapter 13, Information Resources for User Support, describes information resources useful to support staff and search strategies for locating information resources. Organized according to the topics in this text, it recognizes that few of us know everything we'd like to be successful, and that ability to locate information is a critical skill for user support staff.

FEATURES

To aid you in fully understanding user support concepts, there are several features in this book designed to improve its pedagogical value.

- **Chapter Objectives**. Each chapter in this book begins with a list of the important concepts to be mastered within the chapter. This list provides you with a quick reference to the contents of the chapter, as well as a useful study aid.

- **Illustrations and Tables**. Illustrations help you visualize common components and relationships. Tables list conceptual items and examples in a visual and readable format.

- **Notes**. Chapters contain Notes designed to expand on the section topic, including resource references, additional examples, and ancillary information.

- **Bullet figures**. Selected figures contain bullets that summarize important points. They give you an overview of upcoming discussion points and help you review material as you skim through the chapter.

- **CloseUps**. Selected chapters contain CloseUps, which detail real-life examples of the chapter topic. Taken from actual experiences, CloseUps confirm the importance of the topic and often contribute extra related information to give you additional insight into real-world applications of the topics.

- **Chapter Summaries**. Each chapter's text is followed by a summary of chapter concepts. These summaries provide a helpful way to recap and revisit the ideas covered in each chapter.

- **Key Terms lists**. Each chapter contains a listing of the terms introduced in the chapter and a short definition of each. This listing provides a convenient way to review the user support vocabulary you have learned.

- **Review Questions.** End-of-chapter assessment begins with a set of approximately 25 review questions that reinforce the main ideas introduced in each chapter. These questions ensure that you have mastered the concepts and often ask you to provide examples so that you can use the information you have learned.

Hands-on Projects. Although it is important to understand the theory behind user support topics, no amount of theory can improve on real-world experience. To this end, along with conceptual explanations, each chapter provides eight to ten Hands-on projects aimed at providing you with experience in user support topics. Some of these involve researching information from people in the support industry, printed resources, and the Internet. Because the Hands-on projects ask you to go beyond the boundaries of the text itself, they provide you with practice in the real-world research you will most likely perform as part of a user support position.

Case Projects. There are three case projects at the end of each chapter. These cases are designed to help you apply what you have learned to business situations much like those you can expect to encounter in a user support position. They give you the opportunity to independently synthesize and evaluate information, examine potential solutions, and make recommendations, much as you would in an actual business situation.

INSTRUCTOR SUPPORT

The following supplemental materials are available when this book is used in a classroom setting. All of the supplements available with this book are provided to the instructor on a single CD-ROM.

Electronic Instructor's Manual. The Instructor's Manual that accompanies this textbook includes:

- Additional instructional material to assist in class preparation, including suggestions for lecture topics.

- Solutions to all end-of-chapter materials, including the Project and Case assignments.

- A disk containing the following: End-of-chapter review questions, Hands-on projects, and Case projects in Microsoft Word, which can be made available to students. Students can enter their answers in the space provided within the file and submit them to the instructor by disk, by printing out their answers, through the network, or through e-mail.

Course Test Manager 1.1. Accompanying this book is a powerful assessment tool known as the Course Test Manager. Designed by Course Technology, this cutting-edge Windows-based testing software helps instructors design and administer tests and pre-tests. In addition to being able to generate tests that can be printed and administered, this full-featured program also has an online testing component that allows students to take tests at the computer and have their exams graded automatically.

PowerPoint presentations. This book comes with Microsoft PowerPoint slides for each chapter. These are included as a teaching aid for classroom presentation, to make available to students on the network for chapter review, or to be printed for classroom distribution. Instructors can feel free to add their own slides for additional topics they introduce to the class.

UPDATED WEB ADDRESSES

This book contains references to many sites on the World Wide Web. Sooner or later, these sites will be changed or replaced with newer information. In some cases, the URLs you find here will lead you to their replacements; in other cases, they will produce a "File not found" message. As a means of keeping our printed books up to date in the constantly changing Web environment, Course Technology maintains a Web page for this book with updated Web addresses. To view this page, go to **www.course.com** and search by the author's last name (Beisse).

ACKNOWLEDGMENTS

I wish to thank the staff at Course Technology who played vital roles on the team of people who created this book, including Kristen Duerr, Managing Editor, Nancy Shea and Melissa Panagos, Production Editors, as well as Margarita Donovan, who was instrumental in producing supplementary materials.

I want to express my great appreciation to the professional educators who reviewed the draft manuscript and made suggestions that added significantly to the value of the book. Their experiences in both the support industry and in education contributed to the quality of the topics covered and to the content of the book as a learning tool. The reviewers are Wendy Bailey, Wilson Technical Community College; Stephen S. Linkin, Houston Community College, Southwest College; Rajiv Malkan, Montgomery College; John Ross, Fox Valley Technical College; and Jeff Woodruff, Schaumburg Branch of Computer Learning Centers, Inc.

I am also very grateful to the following people for their valuable contributions to the CloseUp sections in several chapters: Dave Callaghan, Course Technology; Valerie Goulds, Wall Data; Fred and Susan Hamlin, Freight Services, Inc.; Mary Ann Shaffer, Timberland Regional Library; and Jonathan Vester, Wilson Technical Community College.

Barbara Clemens served as both the developmental editor and the project manager for this book, but her contributions are so much greater than those titles would suggest. Her editorial suggestions improved virtually every sentence in every chapter. However, it is her experience with computer publications and her insights into the support field that, in so many instances, added immeasurably to the contents of the book. And her pep talks when I needed them kept the project on track. My warmest regards, Barbara!

My wife, Kathleen, who is a computer professional and an educator, also contributed many perspectives from her experiences to this book. She is my closest advisor, friend, and companion, as well as the source of constant encouragement.

Finally, I want to dedicate this book to the over 150 Computer User Support and Network Operations majors at Lane Community College who suffered through CIS 225 End User Computer Support without an adequate textbook or with a pre-publication draft of this book. I hope they learned as much from our joint experiences as I learned from them in our discussions.

Fred Beisse
Eugene, Oregon

CHAPTER ONE

INTRODUCTION TO END USER COMPUTING

Almost everyone who works in business offices, manufacturing facilities, and government agencies today has a computer on their desk, near their work site, or in their cars. Widespread computer use has been much more common over the last 10 or 15 years than ever before. Furthermore, people interact with computers in a much different way than they did in the early years of computing. As the computer industry has grown and changed, so has the way people have used computers.

This chapter provides an overview of end user computing. You'll examine some of the important trends that have influenced computer use over the last 50 years. You will also learn about the different types of end users and the main types of computer applications they use. Finally, you'll examine the problems that have accompanied the growth of end user computing and that threaten the increased productivity end user computing promised in the first place.

AFTER READING THIS CHAPTER AND COMPLETING THE EXERCISES YOU WILL BE ABLE TO:

- Explain the major historical changes in computer use
- Classify end users
- Describe the computing resources end users need
- Describe the major types of end user applications software
- Describe some problems computer end users encounter

Historical Changes in Computer Use

The everyday use of computers by workers, sometimes called **end user computing**, is now commonplace. At every level in businesses and organizations, workers interact directly with personal desktop computers, often connected in a network, to accomplish their work. More and more people have computers in their homes. However, when computers were first introduced in businesses and organizations, most employees did not have computers on their desks and did not use computers themselves—at least not directly.

The 1950s and 1960s: Mainframes

In the 1950s and 1960s, computer systems in business and government were highly centralized. Large **mainframe computers** that processed high volumes of transactions were installed behind locked doors in a secure central location and were operated by computer professionals in a **data processing department**. Only the professional staff that programmed and operated mainframes had direct access to them and could write programs, enter information, perform computations, and produce reports. An employee who wanted to process information with a computer had to request the work from the data processing department.

For example, accounting clerks in 1960 would prepare sales data for input into a mainframe system. Often they would carefully handwrite information in pencil into columns on large sheets of ledger paper. They would then send the sheets to the data processing department, where the computer staff would enter the data, run programs to produce printed reports, and give the reports back to the accounting clerks at a pick-up window. The accounting clerks themselves did not program or operate the computer system. It was not unusual in the early years of mainframe computing for clerical employees to report that they had never actually seen the computer system they relied on in their work.

Between 1950 and 1960, computers were primarily used for transaction processing and management reports. **Transaction processing** is the use of computers to input large volumes of business events or activities, process the business data, and prepare printed reports. Unlike most transaction processing today, transactions were collected in the mainframe for a day, a week, or even an entire month or year. The transactions were then processed in a batch with other transactions, a procedure known as **batch processing**. The goal of transaction processing on mainframe computers was to replace as much manual processing of business information as possible with automated processing. Transaction processing was used to calculate payroll, control raw materials and finished goods inventory, enter product orders and shipments, and perform other high-volume daily record keeping required to operate a business or government agency.

For example, a large organization would have a clerical staff to record, calculate, and file payroll information. It invested in a mainframe computer system in part to automate many of the manual payroll processing steps. The payroll application (software program) could input, sort, match, calculate, print, and store payroll records with little or no manual processing by clerical employees. Mainframe computers could process payroll transactions much more rapidly and with fewer errors than clerical workers. Because of their speed and accuracy, mainframe computer systems were often justified as a cost-saving productivity tool for businesses.

Another common use of mainframe systems during this period was management reporting, in which detailed data stored on a computer disk or tape by transaction processing systems could be summarized and printed as a report for management. Management reporting systems, sometimes called **management information systems (MIS)**, dramatically reduced the manual labor required to summarize data and to type lengthy reports for managers.

For example, a supervisor of a maintenance shop could request a weekly printed report that showed the number of hours worked on each project, projects that were over budget, or projects that required substantial employee overtime. An MIS programmer could access payroll data from the transaction processing system and prepare the necessary management reports. A computer operator would schedule the reports for printing at regular intervals to meet the maintenance supervisor's need.

Because mainframe computers were centralized, data for input had to be delivered physically (in the form of punched cards, paper tape, or magnetic tape) to the central system location. Output (in the form of payroll checks, for example, or printed reports) had to be delivered back to the department where it was used or distributed.

Figure 1-1 summarizes mainframe computer use in the 1950s and 1960s.

- Located at a central site in the company

- Programmed and operated only by computer professionals

- Used primarily to automate manual transaction processing and to prepare management reports

Figure 1-1   Characteristics of mainframe computer use

As you can see from this brief overview, computing in the 1950s and 1960s was very different from what it is today. Although it may seem cumbersome by today's standards, mainframe computers met many of the objectives of that era. Early mainframes provided a substantial increase in productivity over manual processing methods. However, the first steps toward end user computing did not occur until the 1970s.

THE 1970S: FIRST STEPS TOWARD DECENTRALIZED COMPUTING

During the 1970s, computer use gradually became decentralized as terminals became common. A **terminal** included a keyboard and a display screen and was connected to the mainframe computer system. Terminals permitted clerical employees to interact directly with the mainframe computer from their own desks. Although the data was still stored in the mainframe computer at a central site, employees who were computer users could run programs and input and retrieve data themselves, without leaving their desks. An accounting clerk, for example, could run a program to prepare a payroll report directly from a desktop terminal. The payroll report could be printed on a printer located in the accounting department. Because users didn't have to rely on a central operator to enter and obtain information, terminals produced a significant increase in clerical worker productivity.

However, not every employee had access to a terminal. One reason was cost: terminals were expensive at the time. In addition, some mainframe professionals regarded terminals with skepticism because direct computer access by clerical workers meant that the central computer staff had lost a degree of control over the mainframe and the information stored in it. The data processing department staff often expressed the concern that errors and mistakes made by users in the accounting department could offset any productivity gains due to terminal access to the mainframe.

In addition to the use of terminals to connect to mainframe systems, another early step toward decentralized computing was the growth in the use of minicomputers during the 1970s. A **minicomputer** is a small computer, less powerful than a mainframe, but that costs much less. Because mainframe systems cost $1 million and up, they were affordable only by large corporations and government agencies. Minicomputers could be purchased for $100,000 to $500,000 and were therefore affordable by small businesses and individual departments in large companies and organizations.

CAUSES OF DECENTRALIZED COMPUTING GROWTH

It was not until the 1980s and 1990s that large numbers of employees in many companies began to use computers directly, ushering in the era of end user computing. Several trends converged in the 1980s that made the widespread transition to decentralized, end user computing possible. These trends are summarized in Figure 1-2.

> The unmet backlog in requests for new mainframe applications
>
> An increase in the number of knowledge workers
>
> The availability of inexpensive microcomputers
>
> The availability of inexpensive productivity software

Figure 1-2 Major causes of decentralized computing growth

The following sections briefly discuss each of these trends.

The Applications Backlog. First, it became increasingly clear to businesses in the 1970s and 1980s that the programmers and analysts who created programs for the central computer could not keep up with the demand for their services. Managers in many organizations began to think of new ways to use computer technology. They wanted analysts and programmers to design and write computer programs to solve specific business problems to make employees even more productive. For example, a marketing and sales manager might want analysts to create a sales contact and tracking system to help sales reps organize the large amount of customer and product information they work with every day. However, mainframe computer staffs could not grow fast enough to meet the increasing demands on their time. This situation became known as the **applications development backlog**.

The problem was widespread and well known during this period, and it was a source of frustration for both the professional data processing staffs and the business departments that needed new applications. A marketing representative, for example, might develop an idea for a computer application that would increase sales and make the marketing department more productive, only to be told that the analysts and programmers wouldn't be able to start on it for another two years.

More Knowledge Workers. A second trend that contributed to the growth of end user computing was a dramatic increase in the number of **knowledge workers**, or employees whose primary job is to work with information. The growth in the number of knowledge workers has corresponded with shifts in the U.S. economy from mechanical to electronic ways of working. Whereas factory workers need industrial equipment to do their jobs, knowledge workers need access to information. The most efficient way to obtain information is through computers; so more and more knowledge workers needed to interact directly with computers to do their jobs.

Declining Microcomputer Cost. Another reason for the growth of end user computing was that the cost of providing computer power to employees dropped dramatically, even as the capabilities of the technology (especially semiconductor power and capacity) was increasing exponentially. Mainframe systems cost $1 million or more and some companies invested in several mainframes. Even when the purchase and operating cost of a mainframe is spread over a large number of employees, mainframe computer power is expensive. However, low-cost desktop microcomputers with price tags of around $2,000 were more affordable, especially for small and mid-sized businesses and organizations. In fact, the first microcomputers appeared in some companies when employees made purchases on their own, despite warnings by the data processing department that money should not be wasted on these "toy" computers.

The cost of computer hardware is somewhat deceiving. A basic personal computer system configuration cost about $2,000 to $2,500 in the early 1980s. Today, many systems still sell in that price range. If the price for a typical system has not dropped significantly in 20 years, what has changed? What a user gets for $2,000 to $2,500 has changed dramatically. A typical 1980s-vintage personal computer had a 1 MHz speed processor, 64 KB of RAM memory (that's *kilo*bytes, not megabytes; a factor of 1,000 difference), a 5 MB hard drive (that's *mega*bytes, not gigabytes; again a factor of 1,000 difference), a monochrome (one color) display screen, and a 300 baud modem. A popular rule of thumb in the computer industry is that the capabilities of the technology double every few years. Recently, the pace of change has made the old rule obsolete. The doubling of computer capabilities may be measured in months, in some cases, not in years.

Inexpensive Productivity Software. Finally, the development of inexpensive applications software contributed to the rapid expansion of desktop computers in many businesses and organizations. If mainframe computer hardware was expensive, programming the applications software to run on a mainframe was even more expensive. Many companies reported that they spent more on software development than on hardware. The availability in the early 1980s of inexpensive software packages such as Visi-Calc, WordStar, Lotus 1-2-3, and dBASE meant that employees could not only afford microcomputer hardware, but they could also afford the software that would make them more productive users. End users were no longer dependent on the schedules and backlog of in-house program developers. Software development companies that specialized in mass-market productivity software for microcomputers were more than happy to supply general-purpose programs that met user needs. Many of these programs incorporated pull-down menus and **graphical user interfaces** (GUIs), or screen images that let users interact with the program, which made them much easier to use than command-oriented mainframe software. Generic operating systems, such as MS-DOS and Windows also contributed to the rise in end user computing. In the next section, you'll learn about several types of productivity software.

Centralized mainframe computing and today's end user computing share a common goal: to make employees more productive. However, the way users interact with computers, as well as the size and cost of the computers used to reach that goal, has certainly changed. Other innovations in the way computers are used are still underway in the 1990s. Widespread use of computer networks (both local area and wide area networks), even in small businesses, and the phenomenal growth in the use of the Internet as a communication and information resource will have significant impacts on future business and home computer users. These changes are illustrated in Figure 1-3.

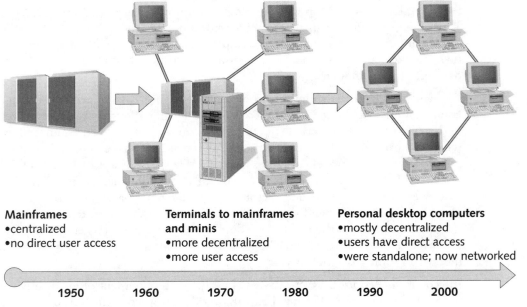

Mainframes
•centralized
•no direct user access

Terminals to mainframes and minis
•more decentralized
•more user access

Personal desktop computers
•mostly decentralized
•users have direct access
•were standalone; now networked

1950   1960   1970   1980   1990   2000

Figure 1-3   From centralization to decentralization

Although end user computing has changed the way many people work with and obtain information, mainframe computing still plays, in the late 1990s, a significant role in most corporations and government agencies. Many organizations own modern mainframe systems that still process transactions and management information. Corporate need for these mainframe applications has not diminished and often cannot be met with desktop systems.

The era of mainframe computing has not been totally replaced by end user computing; rather, the two have been joined together through the technology of computer networks. The term **distributed computing** describes an environment where the needs of the organization determine the location of computer resources in the organization. Organizations frequently need both centralized, organization-wide record keeping and transaction processing as well as tools to increase personal productivity at each employee's workplace. Distributed computing relies on network technology to link mainframe systems and personal computers (PCs) in an attempt to meet both corporate and individual employee needs.

Yesterday's data processing department has changed its name to **Information Systems** or **Information Services (IS)** to reflect a change in its mission and to improve the tarnished image it earned earlier. The IS department now operates mainframe systems that frequently act as hubs of corporate computer networks. These networks often include mainframe, mid-size, desktop, and portable systems.

Table 1-1 summarizes the main events that occurred in the decades between the 1940s and the present.

Table 1-1   Milestones in the Adoption of Computer Technology

Decade	Primary Types and Uses of Computer Systems
1940s	Invention of computer processing units and mainframe peripherals
1950s	Early use of mainframe computers in large corporations
1960s	Widespread use of mainframes Early use of work group minicomputers
1970s	Widespread use of minicomputers in work groups Terminal access to mainframe and minicomputers Early use of microcomputers
1980s	Widespread use of home and business microcomputers Availability of mass market applications software and personal computer operating systems Early use of data communications and networks to connect micro-to-micro and micro-to-mainframe
1990s	Widespread use of data communications, local area and wide area computer networks Distributed computing Rapid growth of the Internet as a global network

CLASSIFYING END USERS

To understand the environments and situations in which businesses provide technical support, it is helpful to recognize the different types of end users. Who are end users? Where are they located? How do they use computers in a business or home environment? One way to classify end users is by skill level. End users range from novice, unskilled employees who have little or no computer experience at one end of the spectrum, to highly skilled users at the other extreme.

Another way to classify end users is by location, viewed from a company's perspective: are the users internal (in-house company employees) or external (company clients or customers)? Whether users are internal or external usually determines the type of support that a business offers.

INTERNAL USERS

It is difficult to think of a department in a business or organization today that does not use computer technology in some way. Clerical and administrative employees, whose manual tasks were the target of the first attempts at automation on early mainframe computers, continue to be a significant category of end users. However, managers, professional workers, engineers, marketing representatives, and factory workers also make extensive use of personal and corporate computer systems today to get their work done. Employees at any level within a company that use computers to do their work are called **internal users**. Internal users need technical support as they use their computers to perform their daily work tasks.

What about information technology professionals, such as programmers and analysts? Are these employees internal users, too? Computer professionals often use the same kinds of personal computers and software as other employees. Just because employees are computer professionals does not mean that they do not need support services. A highly skilled software programmer in a company, for example, may know little about how to diagnose and repair a hardware or network problem. Information technology professionals are end users who, because they work within a company, are also classified as internal users.

EXTERNAL USERS

End users also include customers of hardware and software companies, known as **external users**. Home computer users who have purchased personal computer hardware and software from a company or retail outlet are external users. When they have problems, they contact the hardware or software company (the vendor) for help.

End users can be both internal and external users. For example, people may have a computer at home, where they are external users to the company where they purchased their system. When they work at their business and use software and hardware products as part of their jobs, they are internal users to the company where they are employed.

Internal and external users both require technical support services, but the environment in which they work affects the support services they need and how those support services are delivered.

RESOURCES END USERS NEED

People who want to use computers at home, on the job, or in school often buy their first computers based on media advertising. Computer ads sometimes tout complete systems for under $1,000. These are usable, but fairly basic, hardware systems that may or may not include a monitor and/or a printer. New users are often surprised that the full cost of owning a personal computer system is more than the purchase price of the initial hardware.

To become truly productive and to successfully automate routine tasks, end users need more than just computer hardware. They also need software and other resources so that their computers will continue to help them solve problems over time. These resources have implications for the kinds of services users need, as you will see in the next chapter.

HARDWARE

The original cost of the hardware is only a starting point in budgeting for a computer system. In addition to the central processing unit (CPU), a display screen (monitor) and a printer are necessary for even a basic task such as word processing.

PERIPHERALS

In addition to basic hardware, end users frequently need **peripheral devices**, or add-ons that plug into the system unit, either externally or internally. For example, anyone who wants to connect to the Internet will need a modem. Office users who want to connect to a local area network need a **network interface card (NIC)** that connects their PCs to the network. Users who work with graphics and images will want to purchase a peripheral such as an image scanner or a digital camera. Those who want to make convenient media backups may invest in a removable disk drive. The list of available peripheral devices is long and can add a considerable amount to the total cost of a system.

HARDWARE UPGRADES AND MAINTENANCE

During the two- to four-year life of their computer systems, users might need to upgrade the amount of memory, the CPU speed, the amount of hard disk drive space, peripheral speed (such as a modem or a printer), or other system components. Some users upgrade their systems at the time of their initial purchase, especially if they know they will run a software package that requires more than the minimum amount of memory. Although a high-end word processor may operate on a system with 16 MB of RAM, it often performs better with 32 MB. As new technology comes on the market, users want to take advantage of devices such as an improved sound system or a readable/writeable CD-ROM drive. Hardware upgrades help keep systems fully functional as larger, more complex software packages with higher memory and disk space requirements become available, and as new, more capable hardware devices are developed.

Although end user computer systems are generally reliable, hardware service organizations seem to keep busy diagnosing and repairing a multitude of malfunctions. Most organizations with a sizable investment in computer equipment need to budget a realistic amount for occasional hardware repairs. Although an individual home user may escape the odds and never have to pay for hardware repairs, it is likely that users, at some time, will experience a burned-out power supply or a crashed hard drive.

SOFTWARE AND SOFTWARE UPGRADES

Many hardware packages are bundled (sold) with preconfigured operating systems. However, some users want to run one of the several alternatives to industry standard operating systems, such as OS/2, instead of Windows. For these users, the operating system is an added cost.

In addition to operating system software, users can spend a considerable part of their computer system budget for applications software, especially if they purchase one or more special purpose packages. Some businesses require a specialized package, such as a computer aided design (CAD) program, or a software package tailored to a specific business, such as a legal system. Although mass-market software is not expensive, specialized software often adds thousands of dollars to the cost of a complete system. In the next section, you'll review some common software applications.

Besides the initial purchase of the operating system and applications software, users need to budget for software upgrades. Although some software upgrades are free for users willing to download them from the Internet, many new software versions must be purchased. The price can vary depending on the extent of the upgrade and the type of software. For example, a virus protection package may have frequent, inexpensive upgrades, whereas a tax preparation program may require yearly replacement at the same cost as the original.

SUPPLIES

When estimating the total cost of systems, end users should be sure to include consumables such as printer paper, mailing labels, ink jet or laser cartridges, cleaning supplies, media (floppy disks, removable cartridges, or tape cartridges), cables, and other supplies they will need to operate their system. Laser cartridges and high-capacity disk media can be very costly.

DATA AND INFORMATION

As end users communicate more with other users and get information from outside sources, they can incur costs for information services. Internet services fall into this category, as do the costs of downloading stock market, financial, or economic data from a service such as America Online. Although many information vendors and brokers initially offer free access to their data, over time more information providers will charge for information access. Proprietary information and expert opinion, in particular, will cost more as awareness grows that information has a value to consumers.

TECHNICAL SUPPORT

As end users buy and learn new programs and discover new uses for programs they already have, they often need technical support. Support can include installation assistance, training courses, training materials, books, and magazines. Inevitably, users must contact a software help

desk to solve a problem. When they do, they often have to pay for long distance charges in addition to the cost of the support call itself. Some computer vendors sell support packages for a fixed fee. In a large organization, personal computer support is a major budget item.

FACILITIES, ADMINISTRATION, AND OVERHEAD

Both home users and businesses should budget for the cost of facilities they will need to house and operate a computer system. Facilities include furniture, ergonomic devices (such as keyboard wrist rests and antiglare screens), electricity, air conditioning, power conditioners, space, and other workplace components that are necessary to operate a computer system.

In many businesses and organizations, overhead and supervisory costs are associated with the management of end user computing systems. These costs include acquisition assistance, purchase order processing, shipping, inventory control, insurance, and related costs of doing business. The cost of end user computing must include a proportional share of overhead costs. The list of cost categories for an end user computing system is long. Of course, not all costs apply to each user or to every system installed. But what does it all cost, bottom line? Several organizations have studied the **total cost of ownership**, or the total expenditures necessary over the life of an end user's computer. For example, one estimate indicates that the total cost of ownership for a personal computer system in a five-year period is about $40,000, or approximately $8,000 per year. Hardware costs account for only about 20% of the total cost of ownership, while software and support make up a substantial portion.

As you can see from this brief listing, end users need many types of resources to make their computers true productivity tools. End users who are attracted by the ads for $1,000 computer systems should be aware that there are other ownership costs that they should include as part of the total package.

DOES COMPUTER TECHNOLOGY REALLY INCREASE PRODUCTIVITY?

Businesses believe that employees who use technology are more productive. But productivity for an individual worker is often difficult to measure. Is there evidence that investments in technology actually do result in an increase in worker productivity?

The U.S. Labor Department measures the productivity of all nonfarm workers in the U.S. economy. It calculates the total dollar value of all goods and services produced each year. It divides that figure by the number of hours worked by employees to produce those goods and services. The result is the dollar value of worker productivity per hour worked.

According to figures released by the Labor Department for 1997, the value of worker productivity increased by about 1.7% during 1997. That increase compares with a similar increase of 1.9% in 1996. The productivity gains of the two most recent years are significant because the average annual increases in worker productivity during the previous two decades (before 1996), averaged about 1% each year.

Economists and financial analysts think the increase in productivity is due to investments in computers, cellular phones, facsimile machines, copiers, and other technology products. Alan Greenspan, Chairman of the U.S. Federal Reserve Board, says the notable pickup in productivity is due to U.S. business making investments in technology that are now paying off. Why hasn't the increase in worker productivity been more obvious before the last couple of years? Greenspan thinks the delay is because it takes time for investments in technology and for worker training to use new technology to result in increased productivity.

One example of increased worker productivity is occurring in the banking industry. Some banks have doubled the number of ATM machines available to customers in the last two to three years. The result is an increase in the number and speed of transactions for both the customer and the bank. However, automated transactions take fewer hours for bank employees to process. Bank employees can spend more time on customer services now that they spend fewer hours processing transactions. The banking industry is gearing up for what is expected to be the next big productivity gain in the industry: the use of personal computers to process bank transactions.

END USER APPLICATIONS SOFTWARE

Among the resources end users require, applications software is one that has a significant impact on user productivity. End users run a variety of software applications, which fall into the following categories.

WORD PROCESSING

Word processing software permits users to enter, edit, format, store, and print text information. Many newer word processors also allow the integration of graphics, numbers, and reference information into a document. Because most clerical, administrative, and managerial employees produce letters, memos, papers, reports, and other printed documents, word processing is the most frequently used type of software application among end users.

ELECTRONIC MAIL

Electronic mail (e-mail) allows employees to communicate with others, both inside and outside a company. It is closely related to word processing, because the goal of electronic mail is to enter, modify, format, transmit, and receive text messages. In order to send and receive e-mail, a computer must be connected to a network, either directly or via a modem.

SPREADSHEETS

Because clerical, administrative, and managerial employees frequently work with numeric information in addition to text, electronic spreadsheets are second in popularity to word processing and e-mail as end user applications. Spreadsheets are used to prepare budgets, sales reports and forecasts, financial statements, and other reports in which numeric information is organized into a row and column format and where calculations are necessary to produce meaningful results.

DATABASE MANAGEMENT

End users frequently need to track information that relates to business activities and projects. A database management program allows an end user to enter, update, store, format, and print reports containing information that is stored as a series of records that share a common format in a database. Client lists, mailing lists, personnel records, office supply inventories, and class rosters are examples of common database applications.

GRAPHICS

Users often need to organize and summarize information in the form of pictures, charts, or drawings. Graphics software lets a user create illustrations and charts that analyze trends, show relationships, and summarize large amounts of data. **Presentation graphics** programs let users create attractive electronic slide shows for training and sales presentations. Although some software packages are specifically designed to prepare graphical images on a computer, many word processor, spreadsheet, and database packages sold today include some graphics capabilities.

PLANNING AND SCHEDULING

Office employees spend considerable time planning and scheduling their individual work as well as team projects. Software packages for planning and scheduling include **personal information managers**, which allow an employee to maintain an electronic calendar, to-do list, and address book. For group projects, some scheduling and calendar software can schedule meetings at a convenient time for all members in a group. In addition, **project management programs** allow managers to plan, schedule, and monitor the status of project tasks.

DESKTOP PUBLISHING

Desktop publishing software combines the features of a word processor and a graphics program. It permits end users to prepare, at a relatively low cost, brochures, newsletters, posters, and other printed material that would otherwise need to be designed and typeset by a printing professional.

EDUCATIONAL SOFTWARE AND COMPUTER GAMES

Educational software provides students with learning experiences to supplement the materials a teacher provides. Educational software can also test and give students feedback on their understanding of concepts or on their ability to solve problems. Tutorial software is also available to help computer users learn new software packages. Computer games are, of course, a significant portion of the entertainment industry.

MAINFRAME APPLICATIONS

No list of end user applications would be complete without mentioning that many end users today also use their personal computers as terminals to connect to company mainframes. Once connected, they can run programs on the mainframe much as they did 25 years ago, or download information from the mainframe to their personal computer. Transaction processing and management reports are tasks end users can now run on their personal computer systems with data extracted from a corporate mainframe.

Because personal computers are much more powerful than the terminals of the 1970s, they can process some information locally, on the PC's processing unit. **Client–server computing** is a form of distributed computing that shares processing tasks between a mainframe system or powerful microcomputer (the server) and a local personal computer (the client).

The preceding categories encompass the most common personal computer applications and include many of the primary applications employees use in business, government, education, and other organizations. New types of applications emerge when a need develops. For example, Internet browser software applications have flooded the market in recent years, ever since the Internet and the World Wide Web experienced a meteoric rise in popularity. Whether for home or business use, almost all these applications are designed to increase users' productivity. In fact, most companies justify their computer purchases on the basis that they help make employees more efficient. To accomplish this objective, computers should either increase the amount of output (product or service) an employee can produce based on a given amount of input (effort), or reduce the amount of input required to produce a given amount of output. In general, end user computing has accomplished this ambitious goal, but not without problems along the way.

PROBLEMS IN END USER COMPUTING

Judging from the widespread acceptance of end user computing, you might assume that it has met its objectives and solved every problem. However, end user computing often is accompanied by a set of problems that organizations must address. Although not necessarily unique to end user computing, the problems listed in Figure 1-4 can result from an environment where powerful hardware and software tools are used (and can be easily misused) by a large number of employees.

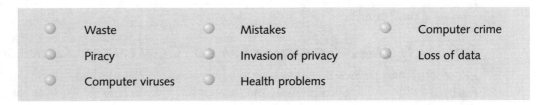

Waste	Mistakes	Computer crime
Piracy	Invasion of privacy	Loss of data
Computer viruses	Health problems	

Figure 1-4   Common problems with computer technology

There is a good chance that end users will experience one or more of these problems in the course of their work or home computing.

WASTE

End users who are not trained as computer professionals may lack the expertise and experience to make cost-effective purchase decisions about hardware, peripherals, software, and networks. For example, end users who are not knowledgeable about the relationship between hardware and software capabilities may purchase software that does not operate (or operate efficiently) on their hardware configurations. If the software an end user purchases operates inefficiently or causes the user's system to crash frequently, the result is often frustration and lower user productivity. Another example of waste occurs when end users purchase software that does not meet their needs as well as a competing program, but that costs more.

MISTAKES

End users who are careless or not properly trained can easily make mistakes as they use sophisticated software. For example, an end user that prepares a spreadsheet to provide an estimate of a project's cost may use the wrong formula to make critical calculations. The user may not understand the importance of testing even simple spreadsheet formulas for correctness and fall victim to a common assumption: "If the results are output from a computer, they *must* be correct."

 A well-publicized example of a computer mistake occurred in the early days of spreadsheets when a bidder failed to get a job contract because of a spreadsheet miscalculation. The user didn't realize that adding a row to a spreadsheet in that particular program meant that he had to revise the formula to include the added row. Consequently, the total amount bid was unrealistically overstated. A lawsuit followed, but the spreadsheet software company won. The court ruled that the spreadsheet user was responsible for mastering documented features.

Computer mistakes can be extremely costly, especially in high-stakes business situations. All computer users need to build in safeguards and double-checks to ensure that computer errors are detected before they do significant damage.

COMPUTER CRIME

Although waste and mistakes are usually unintentional, computers are also used to commit intentional crimes. For example, an employee may have access to company information that would be potentially valuable to a competitor and try to profit from the sale of the information. Information theft, fraud, sabotage, and embezzlement can be committed with the aid of a computer. These crimes are not unique to end user computing; they emerged very early in the use of mainframe computers. However, the number of personal computer users, the lack of security measures, and the easy access to information multiply the potential for computer crimes among end users.

PIRACY

Another form of computer crime is software theft, or **piracy**. Because floppy disks are easy to copy, software theft is frequent. For example, an employee may copy the installation disks for a software package purchased by his or her company, take the disks home, and install the program on a home computer. Legal or illegal? It depends on the software vendor's license agreement and on company policy. Some companies either do not have a specific policy about software piracy, or look the other way when this kind of theft occurs. Piracy costs software companies billions in lost sales and in effect raises the price that software developers must charge to cover their costs.

INVASION OF PRIVACY

Another form of computer crime is invasion of privacy. This problem occurs because vast amounts of information about employees, clients, patients, and students (both current and former) are stored in computer systems today. Without adequate company policies and security safeguards to define who has authorized access to which pieces of information, the potential for invasion of individual privacy is substantial.

LOSS OF DATA

Many (perhaps most) end users do not make frequent or effective backups of important information stored on their workplace or home personal computers. Consequently, when hardware, software, or a network fails, loss of data is a significant risk for end users and the companies for which they work. Loss of critical data can be expensive because lost data is sometimes impossible to replace. In contrast, restoring lost data from a backup disk or tape is an almost trivial operation.

COMPUTER VIRUSES

A **computer virus** is a program that can destroy information, erase or corrupt other software, or adversely affect the operation of a computer. Virus programs are transmitted from computer to computer via networks (including the Internet), or through exchange of media between computers (including floppy disks, removable hard disks, and cartridge tapes). In a networked environment, such as an instructional computer lab at a school or a training department in a business, the spread of computer viruses is a frequent problem for computer facilities managers. Virus protection software can be costly because it must be updated frequently to defend against new versions of viruses.

HEALTH PROBLEMS

Every tool that can be used can be misused. A common source of misuse that may not even be apparent to end users is the physical workplace environment where a computer is operated. Without proper lighting, space, furniture, and environmental safeguards, physical injury to computer operators can result. Without proper operating procedures and techniques, an appropriate work environment, periodic breaks, and correct eyewear, employees may subject themselves to a variety of physical ailments. Common ailments include headaches, nausea, eyestrain, wrist pain (often the result of **carpal tunnel syndrome**, an inflammation of the tendons), and back and neck aches. In addition, there is stress due to the frustrations of working with technology and possibly longer-term health impacts the medical profession doesn't yet fully understand. **Ergonomics** is a field that studies how to design a workplace that promotes employee health, safety, and productivity. Many common ailments can be avoided by attention to workplace ergonomics.

You'll learn more about some of the preceding problems later in this book, as they are problems that often confront employees who perform technical support for end users. A technical support job description will likely include providing end users with solutions to many of these problems, as you will see in the next chapter.

CHAPTER SUMMARY

- Early computer systems in businesses and organizations were primarily large, centralized corporate mainframes. They were used mainly to automate transaction processing and management reports. The first step toward decentralized computing was the use of terminals to connect employees directly to a mainframe system and the availability of less powerful, but less expensive minicomputers.

- The development of end user computing was due to several industry trends during the 1970s and 1980s: the backlog of requests for new mainframe applications, an increase in the number of employees who work primarily with information, the availability of inexpensive microcomputers, and the availability of inexpensive productivity software.

- End users can be categorized according to skill level (novice, semi-skilled, highly skilled) or location (an internal employee or an external client). End users run a variety of software packages on their personal computers, including word processing, electronic mail, spreadsheets, database management, graphics, planning and scheduling, desktop publishing, educational software, and computer games, as well as traditional mainframe applications.

- Resources that end users need to use a computer system include hardware, hardware upgrades and maintenance, operating system and applications software, software upgrades, supplies, data and information, facilities, and support. These resources significantly affect an individual or a company's budget for end user computing.

- A primary goal of end user computing is to make employees more productive in their jobs. However, productivity is not without costs because end users can misuse their personal computers. Common problems include waste, mistakes, computer crime, piracy, invasion of privacy, loss of data, computer viruses, and health problems.

- In the next chapter, you will learn about the kinds of support services end users require to make effective and productive use of their personal computer systems.

KEY TERMS

- **applications development backlog** — The accumulation of project work orders for development of new computer applications in the data processing department; the backlog of requests for software development was often measured in years of staff effort.

- **batch processing** — The processing of transactions that had been collected in a mainframe computer over a day, a week, a month, or a year.

- **carpal tunnel syndrome** — Severe hand or wrist pain due to an inflammation of the tendons in a user's hand and wrist; often a result of overuse in combination with a work environment that is not arranged according to ergonomic principles.

- **client-server computing** — A form of distributed computing where processing tasks are shared between a mainframe system or powerful desktop system (the server) and a local personal computer (the client). In a client-server system, some data is stored and processed on a central system; other data storage and processing occurs on a local system, such as a personal computer.

- **computer virus** — A computer program created with malicious intent that can destroy information, erase or corrupt other software, or adversely affect the operation of a computer that is infected by the virus program.

- **data processing (DP) department** — A department or division in a company that programs and operates the company's mainframe computer system; Information Systems (IS) is a more modern name for the DP department.

- **desktop publishing software** — Software that combines the features of a word processor and a graphics program. It permits end users to prepare, at a relatively low cost, brochures, newsletters, posters, and other printed material.

- **distributed computing** — An organization of computer equipment and resources in which systems are physically located where processing is needed. Distributed systems often include a centralized system, such as a mainframe computer or network hub, and decentralized systems, such as individual personal computers located on employee office desks.

- **end user computing** — The use of computer technology in businesses and organizations to increase the productivity of employees, managers, students, and users of home computers.

- **ergonomics** — The study of ways to design a work environment that promotes employee health, safety, and productivity.

- **external user** — An end user who is a customer of a hardware or software manufacturer or vendor; a company's external users are those who purchase its computer products or services.

- **graphical user interface** — Images on the screen that provide the user with a means of accessing program features and functions, using a mouse or other input device.

- **Information Systems** or **Information Services (IS)** — The modern name of the department in a business or organization that designs, programs, and operates a company's mainframe computer system. The IS department may also have responsibility for a company's network and distributed systems, such as employee personal computers, as well as user support services.

- **internal user** — An end user who is an employee of a company; compare with external user.

- **knowledge worker** — An employee whose primary job function is to work with and use information; contrast with factory workers who work primarily with industrial equipment, and service workers who provide services to customers.

- **mainframe computer** — A large, powerful computer system used by a business or organization to process sizable volumes of transactions, store databases with thousands or millions of records, and serve as the hub of a corporate network.

- **management information system (MIS)** — Computer systems that automate the preparation of reports based on summary data. MIS reports provide information for managers and employees.

- **minicompute**r — A smaller, less powerful computer system than a mainframe, but more powerful than a microcomputer; minicomputers were popular in small businesses, departments, and work groups during the 1970s and 1980s.

- **network interface card (NIC)** — An adapter card located within a computer's system unit that connects a PC to a computer network. The network cable plugs into the NIC, which sends and receives signals to and from a network server.

- **peripheral device** — A hardware device that connects to a computer's system unit. Computer peripherals include input (keyboard or scanner), output (display screen or printer), both input and output (modem, network interface card, or touch screen display), and storage (magnetic tape or disk drive) devices.

- **personal information manager** — A computer program that helps users with time management tasks, such as meeting and appointment schedules and reminders, to-do lists, contact lists, and expense records.

- **piracy** — A form of computer theft that involves illegal copying, distribution, or use of computer programs or information.

- **presentation graphics** — A type of computer program used to prepare text, pictures, charts, and diagrams for use in project proposals, sales presentations, and other events where the appearance of visual information is important.

- **project management program** — A type of computer program that helps supervisors and project leaders manage the tasks in a group project. Resources such as time, money, staff, and vendor schedules can be planned, coordinated, and monitored with project management software.

- **terminal** — A computer peripheral connected to a mainframe computer and used to enter and access information in a mainframe system. A terminal includes a keyboard and a display screen.

- **total cost of ownership** — All of the accumulated costs to purchase, upgrade, and support a personal computer system over its expected useful lifetime. The total cost of ownership includes hardware, software, network, information, training, and support costs.

- **transaction processing** — Computer processing in which business events or activities are entered into a computer system and processed, usually at the time each business event occurs. Banking systems that process deposits and withdrawals from customer accounts are a familiar example of transaction processing.

REVIEW QUESTIONS

1. Describe the important changes in the way computer systems are used in businesses and organizations today, compared with the 1950s and 1960s when they were first used for business purposes.

2. What kinds of applications run on mainframe computers? How do these applications differ from those that run on personal computers? Are some applications run on both large and personal computer systems?

3. Why is access to a computer with a terminal considered a first step toward computer decentralization?

4. Why are minicomputers considered a step toward decentralization of computer resources?

5. What were the principal causes of the growth in end user computing?

6. What is distributed computing?

7. Describe the primary goal of end user computing as described in this chapter.

8. Why has the name of the data processing department changed to Information Services in many organizations today?

9. To what extent has end user computing replaced mainframe computing in today's businesses?

10. Who is an end user? Describe two different types of end users.

11. Describe the types of resources end users need in addition to computer hardware.

12. Describe how each of the resources needed to perform end user computing plays a role to help knowledge workers collect, process, store, and manage data and information.

13. List several types of end user applications software packages and briefly describe the purpose of each.

14. Describe some common problems that arise from end user computing. Are these problems inevitable?

15. Describe a computer virus and the effects it can have on a computer system.

16. What is one of the major causes of waste in end user computing?
17. Name four types of computer crime.
18. If you were concerned about software piracy, where would you look to find out if a particular use of a software package was illegal?
19. What is the principal reason people are able to invade others' privacy with computers?
20. What is the most important strategy to avoid the loss of computer data?
21. In what ways are computer viruses transmitted?
22. Name three common health problems that can result from using computers.

HANDS-ON PROJECTS

PROJECT 1-1

Talk to an employee in an Information Systems department at the company where you work, at the school you attend, or interview a friend or acquaintance who works in an IS department. Find out whether the employee is a programmer, systems analyst, computer operator, or supervisor.

1. Ask about the kinds of computer equipment she or he works with.
2. Ask the purposes the computer system(s) serves in the organization. What tasks does it perform? Who uses the output from the systems?
3. Ask how mainframe computing has changed since his or her company first used computers.
4. Write a one-page summary of the information you obtain.

PROJECT 1-2

Find a coworker, instructor, acquaintance, friend, or neighbor who worked with computers in the 1960s or 1970s.

1. Interview the person to learn the following:
   a. The type of business
   b. The type of computer equipment she or he worked with
   c. The principal tasks the computer performed and who used the results
   d. The relationship between the computer professionals and the end users of the information
   e. Whether terminals were used

f. Whether he or she was involved with application programming; if so, ask if he or she experienced any of the difficulties mentioned in this chapter

g. What changes she or he experienced while working there, and over what time period

2. In a one-page report, summarize the results of your interview and compare this person's experience with the information in this chapter.

 ## PROJECT 1-3

1. Based on your knowledge of current trends in the computer industry, add a line to the decade milestones shown in Table 1-1 for the next decade (2000-2009).

2. Make some predictions about the size of computers, their cost, ease of use, and primary uses in businesses and homes during the next decade.

 ## PROJECT 1-4

Locate a technical support person at your school, your business, or a company you know.

1. Find out:

a. Whether he or she supports internal or external users

b. What resources she or he works with (i.e., hardware, software, peripherals, networks, information)

c. What types of applications end users work with the most in their jobs

d. Do any users or applications present particular problems for a technical support person?

e. Which of the problems described in this chapter does he or she most often encounter?

f. Does the school or business have a policy on software piracy, invasion of privacy, or virus protection?

2. Write a one-page summary of the information you collect.

 ## PROJECT 1-5

Find out if your organization or school has a computer use policy or guidelines that apply to end users. Make a list of activities that are permitted under the policy and another list of activities that are not permitted.

PROJECT 1-6

Find a mail-order computer catalog (in your computer room or library) or an Internet site that sells applications software packages of the types described in this chapter.

For each application such as word processing, electronic mail, spreadsheets, database management, graphics, planning and scheduling, desktop publishing, educational software, and computer games, make a list of some packages that are representative of each category. Include in your list the price range for a typical package in each category.

name of pkg + price

PROJECT 1-7

Interview two to three students or coworkers in your school or workplace about their health concerns related to their use of computers. Make a list of their health, safety, and productivity concerns as students or as workers.

CASE PROJECTS

1. THE $1,000 COMPUTER

Your friend Ron, has approached you for help buying a home computer system. He is skeptical of ads for computers that cost less than $1,000. He intends to use the computer for word processing, e-mail, entertainment, and Internet access, and he would like your advice about a realistic budget for a home personal computer system. What is a realistic amount your friend might expect to spend, both at the time of initial purchase, and over the next four years of ownership? Use catalogs, computer magazines, or the Internet to obtain current price information. Draw up a sample budget, showing your recommended initial expenditure, and the yearly cost for the next four years. Break the costs down by categories described in this chapter. Show the total cost of ownership over the four years that Ron plans to own the computer.

2. THE WILEY CORPORATION

The Wiley Corporation has just relocated to a town near you and is actively seeking technical support employees. At a local job fair, you meet Cynthia, a recruiter for the company, and decide to learn more about the technical support function there.

Based on what you have learned in this chapter, write a list of questions you would ask Cynthia to get a realistic profile of end user computing and technical support at Wiley.

INTRODUCTION TO COMPUTER USER SUPPORT

As you learned in Chapter 1, the widespread use of computer technology by employees and home users has created a new industry called end user computing. End users are not computer professionals, yet they need to use a computer to get their work done. In the course of their work, they frequently encounter situations where they need some form of help and assistance. They need someone to turn to when they have a question or problem, need advice or information, want training, or are just plain frustrated because they can't get done what they want or need to get done.

Many companies recognize the need for a user support function for employees or customers who use a computer at work or at home. To fill this need, companies have formal or informal structures to provide user support. Although you may think of user support as a software company employee at the other end of a telephone line or as a problem solver at a school help desk, user support actually can include a variety of tasks. In this chapter, you will become familiar with many of these tasks. You should then be able to understand and evaluate a few sample job descriptions that represent the recent explosion in the number of jobs in the user support area.

AFTER READING THIS CHAPTER AND COMPLETING THE EXERCISES YOU WILL BE ABLE TO:

- Explain why the need for user support employees is growing
- Describe the common ways companies organize the user support function
- Describe and explain the services that user support centers provide
- Understand position descriptions for user support staff members
- Describe the knowledge, skills, and abilities needed to qualify for an entry-level user support position

THE NEED FOR USER SUPPORT EMPLOYEES

The need for user support employees is greater now than at any time in the past. With the growth of end user computing in offices and homes, along with the growth of the Internet as a way to obtain information, companies find themselves unable to fill support positions. To fill them, they have formed partnerships with community colleges and have developed extensive training programs to prepare employees to meet the demand for support services.

HOW COMPANIES ORGANIZE THE USER SUPPORT FUNCTION

A manufacturing, service, or consulting company usually provides computers to its knowledge workers, but the company's job does not end there. The company must provide ongoing help to these workers so that the computers become tools that increase their productivity, instead of sources of frustration. Similarly, a hardware or software company provides products to its customers, but in spite of rigorous testing, there are inevitable problems that end users will surely encounter and that the company must help them solve. **Computer user support** provides information and services to customers to help them successfully use computers in their jobs. Computer user support is the spectrum of all services provided to computer users to help them resolve problems that arise and to help them be more productive when they use computer technology. **Technical support** is a level of user support that focuses on high-level troubleshooting and problem solving. In some organizations, user support is called technical support, especially if the support staff consists of people who are technicians or who have high-level technical skills. In other situations, user support may be called tech support for marketing or public relations purposes. Despite different naming conventions, what is important are the tasks user support performs in an organization.

Companies provide support to their employees or customers in a variety of ways. Figure 2-1 provides a brief overview of the most common methods, which are described in more detail in the following sections.

- Informal peer support
- Combine user support with another position
- Form a user support group
- Establish a help desk operation
- Organize an information center
- Assign the responsibility to the Information Services department
- Outsource the support function

Figure 2-1   Common ways companies organize the user support function

The method(s) that companies choose varies a great deal, depending on the company size, location, financial situation, type of business, goals for computer support services, and skill level and support needs of employees and customers.

INFORMAL PEER SUPPORT

Some organizations, especially small companies, provide support for computer users informally. One or more employees whose job titles have nothing to do with computers (such as Office Manager, Administrative Specialist, Accounting Department Head) are generally recognized as *the* person to turn to when users have computer questions. This form of support is sometimes called **peer support** because employees look to their colleagues, or peers, when they need computer help. These employees often have no special training or preparation for the computer support role. They accept the responsibility because they have greater interest or more experience than other employees, because they enjoy showing off their skills and having their expertise recognized, or simply because no one else will provide help when it is needed.

In a large organization with no formal organizational structure to provide computer support, there may be several support "specialists," each in a different department. For example, a sales rep with a special interest in computers may become the "guru" when problems arise in the marketing department. An informal network of peers who provide user support often precedes the formation of a more formal organizational structure.

Informal peer support also occurs in schools and colleges, where students quickly learn who among their classmates is a good source of information and assistance. You may have provided informal peer support in a computer or training lab, when the person next to you asked for your help to solve a hardware or software problem.

COMBINE USER SUPPORT WITH ANOTHER POSITION

The first step in formally recognizing the need for a support function may occur when user support is written into an existing employee's position description. This step formalizes a responsibility that may have existed informally for some time. The combination of user support with other responsibilities is a good way for very small companies to meet the need for technical support when they cannot cost-justify a full-time support employee. For people who are assigned official user support responsibility in this situation, the designation can be a positive step because their expertise is formally recognized, and perhaps rewarded financially. On the down side, this person can become overloaded because user support can make significant demands on an employee's time and can compete with other assigned tasks. As the number of computers and employee users increases, or as the company adopts new software that may increase the number of problems to solve, a part-time person may not be able to handle all the responsibilities and still do the job well.

Because this level of support is informal, communications with users in this situation are often informal, as well. Often information about computer technology is exchanged during coffee breaks or in brown bag sessions where those interested get together to discuss problems and issues of mutual concern.

FORM A USER SUPPORT GROUP

When companies find that they have several employees who provide technical support, they may decide to form a user support group. Depending on the needs of the company, a **user support group** can consist of employees who provide part-time support in addition to other job responsibilities. Alternatively, it can consist of one or more full-time employees whose primary job function is to provide user support. The group may provide support either internally to company employees or, in the case of a hardware or software company, to external clients.

ESTABLISH A HELP DESK OPERATION

Members of a user support group may go to individual employees to provide them face-to-face assistance, or they may operate a help desk facility. A **help desk** provides a single point of contact for users in need of technical support, whether they are internal employees or external customers. A help desk manages customer problems and requests and provides solutions-oriented support services. The help desk may be

- A physical location where internal employees or external customers can go or telephone with a question or problem or to request an office visit or a field service call

- A telephone number (sometimes called a **hotline**) that an external client can call for assistance with a purchased hardware or software product

- An e-mail address to which an employee or customer can write for assistance

Regardless of their location, the help desk staff will try to resolve problems as soon as possible, and if they cannot, they will take responsibility for seeing that the problem is resolved by someone else to whom they may refer the problem.

ORGANIZE A USER SUPPORT CENTER

Another organizational model for user support services is a user support center. A **user support center** (also called an **information center**) provides a wide range of services to a company's computer users. These services can include consulting on computer purchases (it may even sell computer products to employees), training and documentation on supported hardware and software products, and a help desk for information, troubleshooting, and assistance. The user support center in some companies provides hardware repair services as well.

ASSIGN SUPPORT RESPONSIBILITIES TO THE IS DEPARTMENT

The responsibility for technical support of end users may rest with the Information Services department. In this arrangement, either the technical staff in the IS department provides user support services directly, or a separate group within IS provides them.

On the one hand, because the IS department's primary responsibility is to design and develop programs and operate the company's mainframe systems and telecommunications networks, some companies have found that the IS department is not a good location for the end user support function. The IS staff is busy working on other priorities, such as the development of new mainframe computer applications and the maintenance of existing ones. For example, IS staffs in the late 1990s are preoccupied with modifications to mainframe systems to deal with the Year 2000 date conversion problem. On the other hand, some organizations believe that all corporate computing activities should be organized under one umbrella (the IS group) in order to provide a single point of contact for all users, mainframe and personal computer users alike. Whether end user support is organized separately or combined with other computer activities probably depends on an organization's history, its experience with computer support, its company culture, and the needs of its users. Either structure can be successful and, similarly, either structure can fail to meet user expectations.

OUTSOURCE THE SUPPORT FUNCTION

Outsourcing is a relatively new alternative for companies that want to provide support services to their employees and clients. In **outsourcing** user support services, a company contracts with another company that specializes in user support to handle support calls about its products. Companies can outsource support services for both internal and external users. For example, employees may contact a support provider via a direct line from a company telephone. Alternatively, an internal help desk operation may handle some calls itself and refer difficult or technical calls to an external support provider.

Outsourcing can be an attractive option for a company that wants to control its costs or take advantage of expertise it does not have among its existing support staff. There are at least three disadvantages of outsourcing computer user support.

1. Access is usually via telephone, because on-site assistance can be prohibitively expensive and is usually not included in an outsourcing agreement

2. Although support costs are predictable, they are not necessarily lower than internal support

3. A company relies on another business for an important business function and does not develop in-house technical support expertise; there is little transfer of knowledge from the support provider to internal staff about computer use issues

Companies discover there is no one, obviously correct organizational structure for end user support that works well in every situation. More often than not, a company's approach to user support evolves over time, depending on the company's goals, resources, and needs.

Services User Support Centers Provide

User support centers in organizations provide a variety of services. The range of services provided depends on the goals of the company, the specific needs of the employees or customers, and the resources the organization decides to devote to the support function. Some common user support services are summarized in Figure 2-2.

- Evaluate hardware and software products
- Coordinate company standards for product support
- Perform needs assessment and purchase assistance
- Provide system installation assistance
- Provide training on the use of computer systems
- Prepare documentation on computer use
- Perform computer facilities management tasks
- Provide a help desk or hotline for problems
- Provide technical troubleshooting assistance
- Locate information to assist users
- Assist users with applications development problems

Figure 2-2   Common user support services

Figure 2–3 shows the relationship between user support and the individual support services that, taken as a whole, define user support.

Not every company provides all these services to its employees or customers, but most companies that provide user support offer at least some services to respond to employee or customer demand.

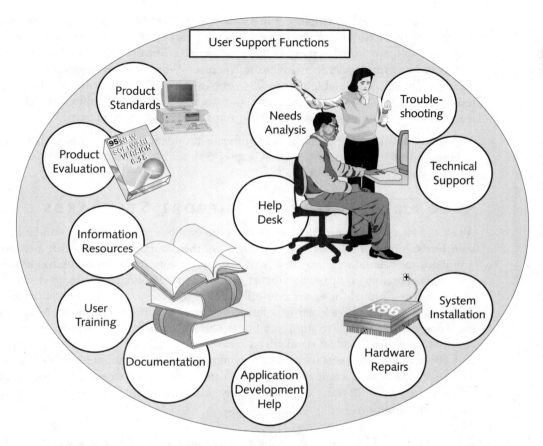

Figure 2-3   Common user support functions in organizations

EVALUATE HARDWARE AND SOFTWARE PRODUCTS

Because employee productivity is an important objective for businesses, most organizations are constantly on the lookout for new technologies that will help them enhance productivity. Consequently, the user support center must continually research, compare, and evaluate new technology products and services, including hardware, software, and network products, against existing products. User support must find answers to such questions as

- Is there a product that will make employees more productive?

- Will product X meet employee needs better than product Y?

- Should some or all users upgrade from version 97 to version 98? Or wait until version 99?

- What characteristics are important in the purchase of a new system?

- Will a particular system or software package be cost-effective?

In cases where individual employees make these decisions, companies can encounter compatibility, cost, usability, and productivity issues that can be difficult to resolve. For example, employees in the editorial department of a publishing company might use Microsoft Word 97, and its production department might use Microsoft Word 95. Consequently, the production department will not be able to use files sent to it by editorial, unless editorial personnel remember to save files in the earlier version format. This compatibility problem can cause wasted time and communication, and can impact employee productivity.

The evaluation of new hardware and software products is an important, challenging, and ongoing task for user support staffs. Chapter 3 describes some tools to help support staffs with product evaluation tasks.

RECOMMEND COMPANY SUPPORT STANDARDS

A task closely related to product evaluation is the establishment of support standards. **Support standards** consist of a listing and explanation of the computer products that a company recommends to its employees and that it will support. Support standards are important because it is impossible for a company to support every hardware configuration marketed by all hardware vendors. Similarly, it is not cost-effective for a company to try to support all software packages, not even all packages in a limited category such as spreadsheets. Most companies and organizations choose to support a limited list of hardware and software options, and they communicate these product standards to their employees. Such a list of supported products is cost-effective, because most user support centers do not have unlimited resources. To arrive at a set of standards for a company, a company's user support center evaluates competing products and consults with users and management. Chapter 3 describes the role of support standards in organizations.

PERFORM NEEDS ASSESSMENT AND PURCHASE ASSISTANCE

In addition to evaluating products and establishing support standards, the support center staff matches supported products with the needs of each user. If the matching task is not obvious, they may perform a user **needs analysis**, or assessment, to determine the characteristics of hardware and software (from among those supported) that will best meet a user's needs. Based on the needs analysis, the support staff are then in a position to recommend the purchase or upgrade of a system to meet the user's needs and improve employee productivity. Most support centers that offer this type of needs assessment service also assist users with the paperwork required to purchase a system. This might include how to justify the purchase, how to place an order, and how to pay for the system. Chapter 4 describes how to perform a needs analysis for an end user.

PROVIDE SYSTEM INSTALLATION ASSISTANCE

Once a company has purchased a system or upgrade, the support center may offer to unpack, set up, install, and configure the system for an end user. The purpose of this service is efficiency: the support center staff have the tools and expertise to make sure the installation is done correctly and can identify and solve many common installation problems that would frustrate an inexperienced user. The support staff can make sure the appropriate network software is installed and configured to connect a system to the company network. They can also install and configure peripheral devices such as printers and printer driver software. End users might be able to perform these tasks, but a support staff member can often get the work done faster and with fewer errors. Chapter 5 describes the system installation process.

PROVIDE TRAINING ON THE USE OF COMPUTER SYSTEMS

Users who have new hardware or software may require training in order to make effective use of a new or upgraded system. One role user support centers play in many organizations is to provide end user training. The support center may have periodic training sessions, provide one-on-one training, or at least point to ways to learn a new system that will meet a user's learning needs and style. Training programs can include basic, introductory classes to help users get started quickly with a new system or with new software. Training can also provide experienced users with the knowledge and skills they need to use advanced features of hardware and software. Chapter 6 provides some guidelines on how to prepare user training materials.

PREPARE DOCUMENTATION ON COMPUTER USE

Although end user training is a necessary and often effective way to learn to use a computer system, documentation is an equally important aid for many computer users. Whereas training is a one-time event, documentation is always available to answer questions or to remind a user how to perform a task she or he may do only occasionally.

User documentation includes introductory, "how-to" manuals for new users, explanations of company computer use guidelines, as well as tutorial and reference manuals on specific software products. It can also include online documentation in the form of help files. Chapter 7 provides some pointers on how to write documentation for end users.

PERFORM COMPUTER FACILITIES MANAGEMENT TASKS

Mainframe computer installations have a professional staff of computer operators, maintenance engineers, and facilities managers whose job it is to ensure that the computer systems run on a daily basis. In a PC environment, there is no less need to keep the computers operational. To accomplish this, support centers perform **computer facilities management** tasks such as maintaining security, making media backups, preventing viruses, dealing with ergonomics, purchasing supplies, performing preventative maintenance, and the like. Chapter 8 describes some guidelines on facilities management challenges in an end user environment.

PROVIDE A HELP DESK OR HOTLINE FOR INFORMATION AND PROBLEMS

Users who encounter problems with the use of a computer system need a place to turn for answers. A help desk or hotline serves this need and is the most common type of service provided by a user support center. A help desk or hotline can provide several types of services, such as

- Responding to requests for product information

- Marketing products and services

- Providing solutions to problems

- Receiving user complaints about product features

Chapter 9 describes the operation of a help desk from the perspective of a support center staff. Chapter 10 describes the customer service and communication skills support staff need in a help desk environment.

PROVIDE TROUBLESHOOTING ASSISTANCE

Although a help desk or hotline can handle common kinds of user problems and questions, occasionally problems arise that go beyond the immediate services the help desk can provide. Many organizations recognize the need for a level of technical troubleshooting assistance that can deal with the really intractable problems that do not occur every day but that need a high level of expertise when they do occur. These problems can include hardware diagnosis and repair or replacement and fixes or workarounds for difficult applications software and network problems. Chapter 11 describes some strategies for troubleshooting difficult technical problems, and Chapter 12 provides examples of common user support problems.

LOCATE INFORMATION TO ASSIST USERS

A challenge that continually confronts user support workers is the need to locate information to resolve a user's question or problem. Although companies provide their employees with computers and software, they often do not supply manuals or other useful materials that will help workers get their job done. Though online help is excellent in many software products, it often does not go far enough to help users solve every problem. Therefore, the ability to access, search for, locate, and work with information is a critical skill for user support staff members. This information can exist in a variety of locations: printed manuals from vendors, trade and text books, online help, CD-ROM databases, Internet Web sites, interactive fax services, and automated telephone voice-response units. User support workers need to understand the characteristics of each of these resources and be able to use them effectively. Chapter 13 describes and gives you experience with several information resources.

Assist Users with Applications Software Development

2

In some organizations, the support center staff may help users develop software applications to solve specific problems or meet specific requirements. Software development has long been considered the domain of the Information Services (IS) department. However, with ever more powerful application development tools, such as scripting languages, spreadsheets, and database management packages, end users are able to develop applications independent of the IS department. But end users often encounter problems during the development process and frequently turn to the support staff for assistance. Yet supporting end users with applications development is a potential source of conflict between the IS department staff and the support center staff. User-developed applications may not include compatibility, design standards, documentation, security, and other controls that the IS department feels are necessary in a well-designed application. Most user support centers do not provide software development or programming as part of their regular services to users. Instead, they see their staff as *assisting* users with some aspects of applications development, such as the most effective way to program a difficult task with a spreadsheet. In fact, software development is the least common activity for user support centers.

Although the missions of user support centers differ considerably, the tasks they perform define their service profile in a company. Whereas most support centers provide help desk services and troubleshooting assistance, a smaller percentage provides documentation or product training. A job applicant for a position in a support center can ask about the amount of emphasis placed on various user support tasks to obtain a well-rounded picture of user support at a particular company.

Dave Callaghan
Course Technology (Publisher)
Director of Information Technology

The internal support function at Course Technology (CT) is part of the IS department, and since the company's creation in 1991 has evolved from a technical support focus to a customer support focus. We now think of CT employees as clients, and we act as consultants to them. Our goal is to produce 100% client satisfaction.

Organization: We have three workstation support specialists who support 110 employees. In the past, employees experiencing hardware or software problems would call one of these specialists for help. This worked in many cases, but not all. If a specialist was away from his or her desk, on the phone, or on vacation, the employee didn't know when the problem would be solved. Now we operate as a Help Desk that provides a single point of contact for all employees. The contact person either handles the call or passes it off to one of the other available specialists. Recently, we've provided the contact person with a portable phone, so he is not tied to a desk all day. He is free to respond to users himself, and still make sure that other calls are handled immediately.

Tasks: Our support specialists evaluate hardware and software and make purchase recommendations to management. They install hardware and software and help employees troubleshoot and solve problems. Specialists sometimes provide documentation. For example, if there is a new virus going around the office, a specialist will write instructions on how to identify and get rid of it, and will circulate the instructions to our clients. Their facilities management responsibilities include managing user accounts on servers, as well as backup and recovery tasks. Recently, one support specialist began holding office hours to offer one-on-one help with standard applications or other issues. This is very popular with our clients.

We also have two business analysts who help individual departments who have software needs and conduct group training. Most applications they develop are custom database solutions.

Standards: We have company standards for hardware and software, and we aim to maintain them. But having strict policies can sometimes conflict with getting the job done. Sometimes we find we have to be flexible in order to meet client requirements and to be prepared for future needs.

POSITION DESCRIPTIONS FOR USER SUPPORT STAFF MEMBERS

Positions in the user support industry often include some combination of the tasks outlined in the previous section. Position descriptions reflect how a company structures its user support function. For example, a company with a full-fledged support center is more likely to offer employees consultation about the purchase of home computers. A company that provides only informal peer support is much less likely to have company hardware and software standards or to be able to locate information to assist users. A company that provides a hotline service to its external customers rarely provides other support services to customers.

To understand in more detail what the specific job of a user support center staff member entails, it is useful to look at three position descriptions of actual support positions. The first position description, shown in Figure 2-4, describes the duties and responsibilities of a class of Oregon state government employees called User Support Analyst 1. The "1" is a level designation to signify that this position is the first in a series of positions that feature increased responsibility and opportunities to work independently.

Although User Support Analyst 1 might look like an extremely difficult job, in reality, no one employee hired under this position description does all these tasks. A person hired for this position in a specific state agency in Oregon would perform only a subset of the tasks in the description. However, the hiring agency does want someone who *is able* to perform all these tasks, to provide maximum flexibility. The description does provide a good picture of the range of activities you might encounter in user support positions in today's job market. If you are a prospective user support center employee, you should know managers would probably look for these kinds of capabilities.

USER SUPPORT ANALYST 1

Duties and Responsibilities
The User Support Analyst 1 provides training, technical support, diagnostic help, and operating instructions to users of microcomputers, minicomputers and/or mainframe systems to enable them to use their systems more effectively.

Major Duties
- performs analysis and troubleshooting to resolve moderate problems for users;
- analyzes users' application requirements;
- may design and program user applications;
- assists technical support analyst with development and provision of formal training and provides formal training to users and trainers;
- directs and schedules activities of co-workers to meet deadlines and complete tasks based on a project timeline;
- tests new hardware and software for integrity and usability;
- analyzes special project requirements and support needs and recommends hardware and software options;
- recommends system-wide or agency standards;
- serves as project leader for various information processing support projects;
- conducts feasibility and cost/benefit analysis studies and writes proposals for justification or consideration of new acquisitions;
- prepares technical reports to be used by management in automation decisions for planning, acquisition and development;
- analyzes networking of systems, procedures, data flow requirements, and line traffic;
- installs communications software and system configuration to support a variety of communications;
- diagnoses performance failures and analyzes performance to suggest improvements to existing systems;
- links new systems to established networks;
- performs pre-site visits to determine environmental and electrical requirements for new and existing installations and installations that need to move across a room or across the state;
- installs components of newly acquired micro-, mini-, or mainframe computer systems; sets up and installs configuration files; installs software; and
- documents application programs, user instructions, hardware and software installation procedures, software versions, operational procedures, and maintains documentation to ensure accuracy.

Figure 2-4   State of Oregon position description for User Support Analyst 1

The second description of a user support position, shown in Figure 2-5, is from Stream International, a private company that provides a range of information services to other companies and organizations, including contract end user support. Companies that outsource their support function would consider a company like Stream International. The position description describes a Software Support Representative. Employees in these positions provide primarily telephone support to clients who have purchased Stream International's help desk support services. Because this position focuses on telephone support, the list of responsibilities is shorter than Oregon's description of the User Support Analyst classification.

SOFTWARE SUPPORT REPRESENTATIVE

Objective
Provide responsive and competent telephone support to customers in areas of product features, installation, use, and usability for the specified software product (s).

Responsibilities
- Provide a high level of professional, competent support to all customers in pre-sales and post-sales situations.
- Insure that the department goals of problem response and problem duration are met by keeping your assigned open call queue current.
- Maintain customer satisfaction according to the current levels of measurement for this position.
- Maintain a high level of technical knowledge in the specified software products and become knowledgeable in new products as assigned.
- Act in a mature and professional manner toward customers, vendors, and other IS employees at all times.

The purpose of this job description is to provide a concise statement of the major responsibilities of this position in a standardized format. It is not intended to describe all the elements of the work that may be performed and should not serve as the sole criteria for personnel decisions and actions.

Figure 2-5   Stream International position description for Software Support Representative

The third position description represents a recent trend in the user support industry: a position that combines network support with user support. The position description, shown in Figure 2-6, is for a Computer Network Support Technician at Richard Blank College in Petersburg, Virginia.

Although many of the job duties in the Network Support Technician position description are similar to other user support positions, some of the duties are more like those you would find in a position description for a Network Administrator. This example emphasizes the wide variety of tasks user support specialists may be expected to perform, depending on the specific needs of the company or organization in which the support position is located.

Job Description: Computer Network Support Tech

Agency: **Richard Blank College**
Salary Range: **$24,337 -$37,995**

Job Duties:
- Assist faculty with hardware and software problems
- Set up new PCs for academic users with proper hardware and software, LAN and TCP/IP access
- Coordinate academic computer equipment repair and perform periodic maintenance
- Train faculty in Web and LAN software utilization
- Perform software and hardware upgrades on PCs in faculty office and library
- Administer student E-mail accounts
- Maintain user software located on the LAN servers
- Cooperate in the administration of a complex local area network (LAN)/wide area network (WAN) of academic and administrative PC users with several critical links to external computer centers
- Troubleshoot and correct network and connectivity problems
- Backup the administrative computer network support technician

---

Figure 2-6   Richard Blank College Computer Network Support Tech

KNOWLEDGE, SKILLS, AND ABILITIES

One way to understand job requirements better is to analyze them in terms of the knowledge, skills, and abilities (**KSAs**) needed to perform the job. Human resource personnel often break down a position description into a checklist of KSAs to use to screen applicants.

Knowledge. Each position includes a description of what an employee needs to know in order to do the job. The knowledge component may be stated in terms of a specific number of years of education or a degree in a specified field.

Examples of knowledge required for the User Support Analyst position described in Figure 2-4 include:

- Knowledge of basic computer operation
- Knowledge of systems analysis and design methods

Skills. Each position requires some job skills or tasks a support specialist needs to be able to perform well. Positions may require expertise in one or more areas. One difference between an ability and a skill is that an ability is a characteristic a person either has or does not have, whereas a skill is something that one can get better at with training or experience.

Examples of skills required to do the User Support Analyst position described in Figure 2-4 include:

- Skill in troubleshooting hardware and software
- Skill in network administration procedures

Abilities. Each position requires some minimum level of job skills or tasks a support specialist must be able to perform. Abilities are tasks an applicant can either do or not do. Sometimes the ability component is stated as the specific number of years' experience in a field. Some positions may specify abilities such as the ability to lift 50-pound boxes or the ability to communicate in Spanish.

Examples of abilities required to do the User Support Analyst position described in Figure 2-4 include:

- Ability to work as a supervisor or project leader
- Ability to write documentation

If you have difficulty with the difference between skills and abilities, don't worry. People often use the terms interchangeably in everyday use. For example, is *write documentation* an ability or a skill? It is probably a task one can either do or not do, but it is also something one can get better at with more education or practice.

How do you ever learn to do all the tasks described in these position descriptions? Few employees start in an entry-level position on day one with all the knowledge, skills, and abilities to perform every task listed in the description. Most user support positions include a training program before a support employee ever answers an actual telephone call or installs and configures a piece of network hardware. Most user support positions also include a significant amount of continuing education or on-the-job learning. So don't get discouraged if you can't do everything in these job descriptions today.

If you compare the list of services offered by user support centers and the job duties in the position descriptions in this chapter with the table of contents of this book, you will find that this book is organized around these job duties—many of the primary tasks of a support staff member are described in this book. There are chapters devoted to each of the major topics to help give you exposure to the many and varied responsibilities that are required of user support staff in today's job market.

CHAPTER SUMMARY

- End users who are not computer professionals often need help when they encounter problems with their computer system. Help can be organized in several ways, including peer support from a coworker, a user support group, a help desk/hotline operation, a user support center, directly from the technical staff in the Information Services department, or from a vendor who contracts to provide support services.

- Users need a variety of support services, depending on how they use their computers and their level of expertise. Services frequently provided by user support centers include: evaluating new hardware and software products; establishing company-wide product support standards; analyzing and assessing user needs; installing systems; training users; writing user documentation; managing computer facilities; staffing a help desk or hotline; troubleshooting difficult problems; locating information; and assisting with software development projects.

- The job description for support staff members reflects the variety of services a support center offers. Many jobs require a combination of knowledge, skills, and abilities in hardware (microcomputers and mainframes), operating systems, applications software, networks, interpersonal communications, problem solving and analysis, and supervisory or leadership skills.

KEY TERMS

- **computer facilities management** — Support services to help users with information and questions about security, media backups, viruses, ergonomics, purchase of supplies, preventative maintenance, and other tasks required to keep a computer system operational.

- **computer user support** — A job function or department in a company that provides information and services to employees and/or customers to help them use computers more productively.

- **help desk** — A single point of contact for face-to-face, telephone, or e-mail access for customers or employees; provides information and problem-solving services.

- **hotline** — A telephone number an internal or external user can call to reach a help desk service.

- **information center** — An older name for a user support center.

- **KSAs** — The knowledge, skills, and abilities required to perform a job; every position has minimum requirements for what applicants must know, what they must have the ability to do (or perform), and the skills they must have (tasks they can do well).

- **needs analysis** — An investigation to determine the features and configuration of hardware and software that are the best match to a user's specific task needs; also called needs assessment.

- **outsourcing** — An arrangement or agreement to provide support services for employees or customers in which a company contracts with another company that specializes in support services.

- **peer support** — An informal level of user support where coworkers in a company or department exchange information and provide assistance about computer use and problems encountered by users.

- **support standards** — A list of computer products that a company recommends to its employees and for which it will provide support services; support standards limit the hardware and software products a support staff must be able to support and reduce support costs.

- **technical support** — A level of user support that focuses on higher-level troubleshooting and problem solving; whereas user support deals with a broad spectrum of support issues, technical support deals with advanced and difficult problems users encounter.

- **user support center** — A group or department in an organization that provides a wide range of services to a company's computer users, including a help desk, consulting on product purchases, training, documentation, and troubleshooting.

- **user support group** — A formal work group that is organized to provide computer user support services.

REVIEW QUESTIONS

1. Why do organizations and their employees need end user support?

2. Describe the current industry need for end user support employees.

3. What are industries doing to help fill open positions in the user support industry?

4. Describe some ways companies have met the need for end user support for their employees.

5. In your own words, describe informal peer support.

6. Name two ways companies have formed user support groups.

7. What are some differences between a help desk operation and a user support center?

8. What are some advantages to assigning the user support function to a company's Information Services department? What are some advantages to a user support function that is independent of the Information Services department?

9. Describe outsourcing, and list the advantages and disadvantages of outsourcing the user support function.

10. List and describe the services a user support center might provide to an organization's employees. Which of these services are more important than other services?

11. Why do companies limit the hardware and software choices their employees can purchase with a product standards policy?

12. Why is it necessary to provide end users with documentation if they have been well trained?

13. Discuss the following statement: "Facilities management is more of a problem with mainframe computer systems than it is in an end user computing environment." Do you think the statement is true or false? Explain your position.

14. What services can a help desk or hotline service provide beyond troubleshooting and problem solving?

15. Why is learning a programming language for a user support staff member not necessarily as important as learning to use applications software?

16. Describe some common duties a user support staff member would need to be able to perform.

17. What are examples of knowledge, skills, and abilities a user support specialist needs to perform the duties of a support specialist?

18. List some ways that someone interested in a user support career can learn the knowledge, skills, and abilities support specialists need.

HANDS-ON PROJECTS

 ## PROJECT 2-1

Find out whether the company where you work or the school you attend has a user support function. Use the categories listed in this chapter to learn about the support organization, the location of the support function within the company or organization, and the services it provides. See if you can learn from users whether they feel the user support function is responsive to their needs. Write a summary of your findings.

 ## PROJECT 2-2

If you work for a company or attend school, find out if the organization has one or more position descriptions for user support staff members. How do the duties and responsibilities compare with those described in this chapter? What are some similarities? What are some differences?

 ## PROJECT 2-3

Use the Internet or the Human Resources department at your place of employment to locate position descriptions for user support positions in your company or in other business and government organizations. How do the duties and responsibilities compare with those described in this chapter? What are some similarities? What are some differences?

Some Internet sites you could visit include:

http://www.cns.state.va.us/~dpt/	A description of jobs in the state of Virginia
http://www.texas.computerjobs.com	Access to job information for computer jobs in Texas with links to other sites
http://www.carolina.computerjobs.com	A similar site for the Carolinas
http://www.PositionWatch.com	Contains information about job openings; search on "help desk"
http://www.usajobs.opm.gov	A job bank of positions with the federal government

PROJECT 2-4

Based on the position descriptions for user support staff in the chapter:

1. Would you classify the position of user support staff member as primarily a technical position or a people-oriented position? Why?

2. Do you think a user support staff position requires a person who is a specialist (one with depth of knowledge) or a generalist (one with breadth of knowledge)? Why?

3. What other qualities do you think would be necessary for someone to be successful in the user support field?

4. Locate a user support staff member and ask him or her to describe the most important qualities for someone in his or her position.

5. If you are a member of a project group, meet with the other members and discuss their answers to the previous four items.

Write a one-page summary of your conclusions.

PROJECT 2-5

Sometimes people use the term "power user" to describe users who have extensive experience, excellent breadth and depth of knowledge, and well-developed skills. If you are a member of a project group, discuss the following with the members of your group:

- What are some characteristics of a power user? Be as specific as possible.

- Are you a power user? Is anyone in your group?

- Is it necessary to be a power user, according to your or your group's consensus definition, in order to be a user support staff member?

- How can an organization make maximum use of a power user to assist with support functions within a department?

Write a one-page summary of your conclusions.

PROJECT 2-6

Choose a position description for a user support position. You may use the examples in this chapter if you'd like. List the knowledge, skills, and abilities (KSAs) you would need to perform the duties in the position description. Don't worry too much about the differences between skills and abilities. Compare your list of KSAs with those of other students or your co-workers.

If you are taking courses or are working toward a degree, or if you have taken courses in the past, how do the KSAs you listed correspond to the courses you are taking now or have taken in the past? Are there additional courses you could take to satisfy the knowledge areas on your list?

PROJECT 2-7

Find two ads in the help wanted section of a newspaper (the Sunday edition usually carries the most help wanted ads). See if you can find one for a position that supports internal users in a company and one for a position that supports customers of a hardware or software company. For each ad, make a list of the knowledge, skills, and abilities that each position requires.

CASE PROJECTS

1. FRED'S PAINT STORE

Fred's Paints is a company in your town that manufactures and sells paint. It employs a staff of about 80 and currently sells close to $4 million in paint and related products. The company sells paint to hardware and building materials stores and directly to the public through a factory retail outlet.

Fred, the owner of the company, says that the 80 employees are organized into 4 groups:

- Manufacturing (the largest group)
- Marketing and retail sales (second largest in size)
- Accounting
- Administration and Human Resources

The Manufacturing group operates the equipment that mixes and packages paint products for retail and wholesale use. The Marketing group consists of both outside sales representatives who call on hardware and building materials stores and inside sales representatives who work in the retail store. The other groups are fairly small, but the size of the company and dollar value of sales has grown considerably in recent years and is expected to continue to grow.

Fred reports that the company currently has about 50 computers, mostly in the Accounting and Administration and Human Resources departments but a few in Manufacturing and Marketing. They are primarily standalone PCs the company has purchased over the last 15 years, although there is a point-of-sale minicomputer system in the retail store that is networked to several cash registers.

The PCs range from 286s to Pentiums and run a variety of software that includes WordPerfect for DOS and for Windows, Microsoft Word (several versions), and even WordStar, a word processor that was popular in the early 1980s, which is used by the executive secretary. She learned WordStar over ten years ago, says she is used to it, that it meets her needs very well, and that she doesn't want to learn to use a new word processor. She has told Fred that she would rather retire than learn a different word processor.

Fred says he is aware of a growing frustration among his employees. During the last six months, he has talked with several of them about the computer situation at Fred's Paints. They are particularly concerned about how hard it is to get help when they need it. Several employees said they felt like they are on their own whenever problems occur with the use of their computer systems.

Fred says that most departments have a person who everyone recognizes as the computer "expert." For example, the head of the Accounting department is very knowledgeable and willing to help people in her department when they have problems with Lotus 1-2-3 or with the accounting program Fred's purchased to prepare financial reports. However, employees in the Accounting department say she is not always available when they need help.

Examples of some of the complaints Fred hears from employees include:

- They can't find manuals when they want to look something up.
- Department computer experts are frequently busy so employees have to wait for help with a problem.
- Employees occasionally lose data because of hardware or software problems and lose time when they have to re-enter the data.

When an employee needs new hardware or software at Fred's, the employee usually talks to one or more of the computer experts or other employees who have computers to learn how they like their systems and what they would recommend for purchase. This procedure seems to have worked well in the past.

Fred has approached you for advice on dealing with the frustrations he hears from his employees. He is concerned about what appears to be both a productivity and morale problem among his employees. Either by yourself or working with your project group, brainstorm these questions:

1. List the problems you hear Fred describe.
2. Which of these problems are technical and which ones are organizational?
3. What recommendations would you make to Fred about alternative solutions he should consider to address the problems you heard him describe?
4. Are some alternative solutions more feasible than others?

Write a report that summarizes your analysis of the situation and your recommendations to Fred.

2. CASCADE UNIVERSITY

2

Mary Ann Lacy is the coordinator of Cascade University's computer training facility. The facility offers courses in computer applications software to Cascade's regular students and faculty and to employees of local companies that send their employees to Cascade's Continuing Education division to upgrade their computer skills.

The computer training facility consists of two rooms: a training room where scheduled classes are conducted and an open lab facility where students can work on assignments outside of class time. The training lab facility is open from 8 a.m. to 5 p.m., Monday through Friday. Each room is equipped with 24 Pentium-class computer systems. Mary Ann operates a Novell NetWare operating system so that students can access software on the Novell server, store data files on the server, and access e-mail and the Internet. She also teaches some of the continuing education classes in the training room. Cascade University's computer faculty members teach in the training room when it is not in use for continuing education classes.

Mary Ann recently conducted a user satisfaction survey to learn how Cascade students, faculty, and continuing education students rated the training lab facility. She was pleased that lab users were very satisfied with the equipment because she tries to keep the systems properly maintained and gets units serviced as soon as a problem arises. The Electronics Shop at Cascade maintains the systems. The users also expressed satisfaction with the operation of the network server and with the selection of software that is available to them. However, Mary Ann was less than pleased about some of the comments users wrote on their survey forms. Here is a sample of some comments she was willing to share:

- "I am an advanced user of the lab. Some of the inexperienced students have discovered that I know a lot about the hardware and the network. They ask me a lot of questions. I don't mind answering them, but when I have a class assignment due, I can't take time out to help everyone who has a question. After a while, some of the questions get pretty repetitious."

- "The lab runs smoothly when the coordinator is in the room. But when she is next door teaching a class in the training classroom, there is no one to ask for help. I feel badly when students have to interrupt her training session to report a problem or to get a new ink cartridge put in the printer."

- "The software manuals are in a locked cabinet. When I need one, I have to track down Mary Ann to get the key. Why can't the documentation cabinet be left unlocked?"

- "Last year, there was seldom a wait to get a computer. This year, with more classes in the lab, the wait is longer. It would be nice if the lab was open more than 8 to 5. Some evening and weekend hours would be great."

Mary Ann has decided to ask a small group of lab users, consisting of students, faculty, and continuing education students to meet to discuss the responses to her survey. If you were a member of the group, what advice would you give Mary Ann that would address the concerns described about the operation of the training facility? What support issues have lab users raised? What are some alternative ways Mary Ann could address the issues raised? Are some alternatives more expensive than others?

3. STATE OF NEW YORK

In the fall of 1996, the state of New York conducted a survey of help desks in New York state agencies. The purpose of the survey was to develop a profile of help desk staffing, functions, and common problems. The results of the survey are at the Web site www.irm.state.ny.us/helpdesk/helpdesk.htm. Study the data collected about help desks in New York state government. Write a short paper that summarizes your conclusions from the study. Use the following questions as a guide to your conclusions.

1. What is the relationship, if any, between the size of the agency and the kinds of help desks that are used? (Compare large versus small agencies.)

2. What are the most common functions performed by the help desks? What are the least common functions performed?

3. Compare the most important functions performed by help desks in agencies that have a formal help desk with those agencies that do not have a formal help desk. Are there similarities? Are there significant differences?

4. What are the two or three biggest concerns of help desk managers?

5. Were you surprised by any of the findings in the study?

CHAPTER THREE

PRODUCT EVALUATION STRATEGIES AND STANDARDS

As you learned in Chapter 2, support organizations often evaluate computer products and services and help set product standards for end users in their companies. There are several reasons user support groups spend time and resources on these activities, which you'll learn about in this chapter. You'll also learn about several of the most commonly used methods and strategies analysts use to evaluate computer products and services and how product evaluations contribute to the definition of product standards. At the end of the chapter, you'll examine one organization's product support standards.

AFTER READING THIS CHAPTER AND COMPLETING THE EXERCISES YOU WILL BE ABLE TO:

- Explain how product standards emerged
- Describe the most common tools and methods analysts use to evaluate and select computer products
- Explain how companies develop and implement product standards

How Product Standards Emerged

In the early years of end user computing, there were few product standards. In the early 1980s, it was not unusual for users within the same department to use several different hardware platforms. There were often hardware products from Apple, KayPro, IBM, RadioShack, Commodore, AlphaMicro, Atari, and other manufacturers on users' desks. Each of these manufacturers touted the advantages of their systems for users in specific applications areas where their hardware had competitive strengths. Because manufacturers felt that the differences between competing products had significant marketing advantages, there was little pressure to move toward industry standards. For example, on the one hand, Atari hardware was designed to emphasize graphic displays and computer games; its market appeal was primarily to the home market. KayPro, on the other hand, built one of the first portable computers and aimed it at students and businesspeople for whom portability was important. These two hardware products were incompatible; neither became an industry standard, except perhaps in their niche markets.

If incompatible and competing hardware platforms were widespread, the problem was worse in the software market. Among owners of IBM PCs, for example, users with identical hardware models chose a word processor from a long list that included WordStar, Microsoft Word, DisplayWrite, WordPerfect, PerfectWrite, PFS Write, and several others. Because word processing was the leading application in businesses, there were many products that competed for market share. The list of competing spreadsheet and database software was not as long, but there were several popular choices in those software categories, as well.

It might appear that product incompatibility and competition simply reflected a healthy, competitive market environment. However, from the perspective of a business or organization that purchased hardware and software products, the lack of product standards caused several problems, which are summarized in Figure 3-1.

> - Incompatible systems
> - Excessive parts inventories
> - Lack of skills transfer
> - Increased support costs

Figure 3-1   Problems caused by product incompatibility

Incompatible systems. Because there were few industry-wide hardware standards in the early 1980s, compatibility between hardware platforms was low. For example, a floppy disk written on one manufacturer's system frequently could not be read or modified on another manufacturer's hardware. Even hardware products from the same manufacturer were occasionally incompatible. Incompatible products meant that two employees might have difficulty sharing data, because the primary method of exchanging information was by transfer on a floppy disk.

3

Excessive Parts Inventories. Companies often repaired their own hardware during the 1980s. Consequently, they needed to maintain a large inventory of different and incompatible components. There were few industry standard power supplies, disk drives, motherboards, CPUs, or memory chips. For example, each hardware manufacturer made its own central processor and memory chips. Memory chips for a RadioShack computer could not be used in another manufacturer's system, and vice versa. Hardware incompatibility substantially increased the cost to an organization to make even simple component repairs.

Lack of Skills Transfer. Employees knew how to operate their own desktop systems but often knew little about the systems on their colleagues' desks. The lack of standard operating system and applications software meant that employees could not fill in for each other if one was absent, reducing overall employee productivity. Furthermore, the cost to train and retrain employees to use several different software packages was substantial. For example, an employee who transferred from a department that used the VisiCalc spreadsheet to another that used Lotus 1-2-3 represented an additional cost to the company for applications software retraining.

Increased Support Costs. Finally, and perhaps most important, incompatible computer systems dramatically increased user support costs. In the late 1970s and early 1980s, information centers in large companies were confronted with the task of providing training, documentation, troubleshooting assistance, hardware problem diagnosis, and software upgrades for a very large number of incompatible hardware and software products. A user calling a help desk might well reach someone who knew little about Microsoft Word on the Macintosh, but who instead specialized in WordPerfect on an IBM PC. If training sessions were offered at all, they often did not meet the needs of a significant number of employees who worked on different hardware platforms, operating systems, or applications packages.

During the 1980s, companies with large investments in computer hardware and software began to realize that permitting employees to purchase the computer systems of their choice imposed a significant cost on the company. Incompatible systems clearly caused computer technology and its related support costs to be more expensive than necessary.

To help cut costs, companies began to develop **product standards**: first, they standardized a few selected hardware platforms selected to meet their users' needs. Second, they adopted standard operating systems, and in the 1990s, standard network operating systems. Third, they limited the choice of applications software to a few standard applications packages in each software category. You'll learn more about product standards later in this chapter. But first you'll look at how companies evaluate products so they can set effective standards.

METHODS FOR EVALUATING AND SELECTING COMPUTER PRODUCTS

In many businesses and organizations, the responsibility for establishing and enforcing computer product standards falls on the user support staff. To establish standards, the staff evaluates products. In the **product evaluation** process, the support staff collects product information; tests, compares, and evaluates competing products; and publishes the results of its work. Decisions about which specific products to support are often joint decisions with input from the user support staff, technical staff, end users, and management.

The support staff, with access to information resources and input from end users and others, continually evaluates new hardware and software products and upgrades of existing products to answer questions such as:

1. Does the product or upgrade work as advertised?

2. Is a competing product significantly better than one the company already uses?

3. Is a product compatible with existing hardware, network, and operating system configurations the company currently uses?

4. Is the product cost-effective to acquire and maintain, and will it help maintain or increase user productivity?

5. Will the product reduce the total cost of ownership to the company?

6. Is the product likely to become an industry standard?

7. Is it better to upgrade now or to wait for a future release?

Members of a support staff who are knowledgeable about computer products and industry trends can research these and related questions. They collect relevant information, conduct product tests, and ask critical questions to identify the advantages and disadvantages of competing products. Product testing often takes place under controlled conditions, as shown in Figure 3-2. It would not be cost-effective for end users to perform these tasks because there are thousands of new computer products and upgrades that come on the market every year. End users could lose focus on their primary jobs and would duplicate the efforts of others.

Figure 3-2   Support staff evaluates products under controlled conditions

The user support staff has several tools and information resources at its disposal to help evaluate computer products. These resources include:

- Vendor literature, marketing information, Web sites, and user manuals
- Product demonstrations and evaluation versions
- Product reviews and comparison articles in computer periodicals
- Opinions from industry experts available in trade publications and Internet news groups

Some of these resources are shown in Figure 3-3. Although all of these are useful information resources, articles in computer periodicals that provide side-by-side comparisons of several competing products are among the most effective.

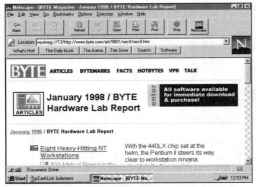

Figure 3-3   Sources of product information

Several popular industry trade publications provide comprehensive, up-to-date product comparisons, including those shown in Table 3-1.

Table 3-1   Computer Industry Periodicals that Publish Product Comparisons

Periodical	Web Site
Byte	**www.byte.com/views/lablst.htm**
InfoWorld	**www.infoworld.com/cgi-bin/displayTC.pl?/comp.htm**
MacWorld	**www.macworld.zdnet.com/buyers/**
Mobile Computing	**www.mobilecomputing.com**
Network Computing	**techweb.cmp.com/nc/core/index.html**
PC Today	**www.pctoday.com/editorial/headtohead98.html**
PC Magazine	**www.zdnet.com/pcmag/pclabs/pcs/index.html**
PCWorld	**www.pcworld.com/hardware** **www.pcworld.com/software**

(If any of the Web addresses in this chapter have changed since the publication of this book, you can find an updated link in the Student Online Companion for this book title at **www.course.com**.)

Following are examples of articles that compare and evaluate computer products.

- "Buyer's Guide: Ultrathin Is In," in *Mobile Computing & Communications*, January 1998; view this article on laptops and a product comparison chart at **www.mobilecomputing.com/articles/1998/01/9801bg.htm**.

- "Web Search Solutions: Too Much Information," in *InfoWorld*, May 12, 1997; view this article on Web search tools at **www.infoworld.com/cgi-bin/displayTC.pl?/970512comp.htm**.

- "Head-to-Head: 36-bit Scanners," in *PC Today,* February 1998; view this article at **www.pctoday.com/editorial/hth/980229.html**.

- "Virus Killers 1998," in *PCWorld,* March 1998; view this article on virus utilities at **www.pcworld.com/software/utility/articles/mar98/1603p189.html**.

Each article describes the evaluation criteria, rates competing products against the criteria, and explains the pros and cons of each product. Some articles provide numerical evaluation scores or "best buy" designations for products the evaluators prefer.

In addition to reviews in periodicals about new and competing products, support staffs can frequently request or download demonstration or evaluation copies of software products. An evaluation copy permits a support staff to conduct its own independent evaluation of a software product with actual company data. Evaluation copies may be available on a CD-ROM disk, via a toll-free telephone number, or, if the size of the demo version is not prohibitive, they can be downloaded from a vendor's Internet Web site. Evaluation copies may have fewer features than the full commercial version, or they may operate only for a limited trial period (often 30 or 60 days).

Although demonstration and evaluation copies of software packages are common and freely distributed, vendors do not usually offer evaluation copies of hardware products. However, some vendors will provide evaluation components, or even complete systems, if the potential order has a substantial dollar value. In these cases, many support groups routinely and successfully request evaluation copies of hardware products they are seriously considering.

When decision makers need to decide which of several products they will select to support or purchase, they can use several tools, methods, and strategies as decision aids. These decision tools are summarized in Figure 3-4.

- Industry standard or best-selling products
- Products used by competitors
- Benchmarks
- Weighted point evaluation method
- Acknowledged subjective criteria
- A request for proposal (RFP)

Figure 3-4   Product decision-making tools

The following sections briefly describe each decision-making tool.

INDUSTRY STANDARD OR BEST-SELLING PRODUCTS

When support staffs need to choose administrative and office automation applications, they often select **industry standard products**, those that have a large market share in their respective categories. The support staff may decide not to spend substantial time evaluating word processor or spreadsheet software; many feel this would be reinventing the wheel. However, when an organization has specialized needs, such as a significant volume of legal document preparation, for example, the support group evaluators often look beyond market leaders. Product evaluators will probably research features available in less well known products that are specifically targeted at users with specialized needs. Mass-market products may lack these features.

Similarly, evaluating accounting software may be a simple task for a small business, because a relatively small number of products dominate the market. One of the mass-market accounting systems for small businesses will probably meet its needs. However, medium-to large-scale businesses often undertake a more extensive evaluation of accounting packages, because off-the-shelf products vary considerably in how they handle such situations as multiple divisions, different geographical locations, global operations, and tax issues that smaller businesses do not encounter. Most very large businesses develop their own accounting systems or modify an off-the-shelf package to get the level of customization they need to meet their unique circumstances.

Selecting industry standard hardware and software products can reduce a company's support costs. Popular software products are more likely to be targeted by trade book publishers, training material developers, and support service vendors. However, selecting market-leading products does not guarantee that they are a good match with the specific and perhaps unique requirements of end users. Furthermore, market leadership changes over time. A product that appears to be a safe purchase and support decision today may become obsolete, and therefore a poor choice, within a short period. For example, during the late 1980s, WordPerfect would have been an obvious choice as a word processor, Lotus 1-2-3 was a frequently selected spreadsheet, and dBASE IV was often the database manager of choice. None of those packages is a best-seller in its category today.

When selecting application software to recommend for company-wide purchase and support, a support group should always get user input before making a software selection decision. Product evaluators should find out which products end users have experience with, the advantages and disadvantages of competing products for specific tasks, and whether users have preferences among products. Support organizations that do not seek user input during the selection process might make an expensive mistake if the software they select is not a good match with user needs or is too difficult to learn and use.

PRODUCTS COMPETITORS USE

In addition to industry standard and best-selling products, support specialists who do product research and evaluation should consider products used by a company's competitors, especially within niche or vertical markets. A company's competitors may have thoroughly researched the market and identified strategic reasons for adopting the computer products they use, even if they are not market leaders. If the information can be obtained legally, a product evaluator should analyze the strengths and weaknesses of products the competitors use. Evaluators who consider the products used by the competition are not simply "followers." Their decision is based on the knowledge that companies that operate in the same industry often have very similar technology needs.

BENCHMARKS

A **benchmark** is an objective test or measurement that evaluators use to compare two or more competing products. Benchmarks are a popular way to compare hardware products, but they are also useful for software packages or even entire systems. In comparing products using benchmarks, an analyst begins by defining one or more criteria that are critical factors in the product selection. Examples of benchmark criteria include speed, storage capacity, or user productivity. These are **objective evaluation criteria**, meaning that they are measurable and are not influenced by an evaluator's personal opinions. The evaluator uses a controlled test environment to measure how competing products compare on the same objective criteria, such as speed. In the test, the evaluator attempts to control all extraneous variables that do not relate to the product being evaluated. For example, if software performance is the measurement criterion, two or more competing software products are operated on identical hardware, in identical operating environments, by the same user. Observed differences in test performance are most likely due to real differences in product capabilities.

An evaluator who wants to use benchmarks to compare the speed of competing modems, for example, defines a constant unit of work, such as a file transfer of 1 MB of data. Then, using competing vendors' modems that should run at the same speed, the evaluator runs a series of tests in which 1 MB of data is transmitted and received in several trials of modem models. (There can be performance differences among modems that have the same speed designation.) As part of the test, the evaluator attempts to eliminate other variables that could affect the benchmark results. The evaluator uses the same computer system, the same operating environment, and the same modem communications software. The only variable that changes from trial to trial is the modem itself. In this controlled test environment, an evaluator can determine whether one brand of modem is significantly faster than others.

An evaluator can also use benchmarks to evaluate software. As with hardware benchmarks, the evaluator defines a constant unit of work, for example, the time it takes a data entry clerk to enter and process 100 typical accounting transactions. Then the evaluator measures the amount of time it takes a typical data entry operator to perform the same unit of work using competing accounting packages. Finally, the evaluator compares the benchmarked times for each package.

 In addition to evaluator-defined benchmarks in product evaluations, vendors use several common industry standard benchmarks to evaluate their products against the competition. If you would like to know more about benchmarks, see the article, "Behind the Benchmarks," in *Byte,* April 1998. The author, Michael Hurwicz, describes several industry standard benchmarks used to evaluate hardware and software, and he describes problems associated with their use.

Companies that provide hardware and software benchmarks include:

- Business Applications Performance (BAPCO) **www.bapco.com**

- Symantec **www.symantec.com**

- Ziff-Davis **www.zdnet.com/zdbop**

Benchmark comparisons are popular because they are objective, and because they provide an unbiased evaluation of a hardware or software product.

WEIGHTED POINT EVALUATION METHOD

Some articles in computer periodicals use a weighted point evaluation method, a strategy that support staff evaluators can also use in their own evaluation projects. The **weighted point evaluation method** uses several evaluation criteria of predefined importance to arrive at a numerical score for each product. As with benchmarks, the goal of the weighted point method is to make the evaluation and selection process as objective as possible. It attempts to treat competing products equally, to eliminate possible favoritism or bias among evaluators, and to force evaluators to specify in advance the important factors in the evaluation of competing products. Because weighted point evaluation is an objective procedure that requires the use of well-defined criteria, public agencies are often required to use this method, or a variant of it. The mechanics of the weighted point evaluation method are discussed in a later section of this chapter.

ACKNOWLEDGED SUBJECTIVE CRITERIA

The evaluation tools and methods just described are based primarily on objective criteria, where a neutral observer should be able to reach the same conclusion as the evaluator. Either a product performs as well on a benchmark comparison as another product, or it doesn't. Although product evaluators base many hardware and software purchase decisions on objective criteria, they sometimes use criteria that are known to be subjective. **Subjective evaluation criteria** are those that are based on personal relationships, convenience, personal product preferences, tradition, and on other factors that are not directly related to the match between the needs of users and the features of products. (Comments such as "We've always bought from them" are good indicators that subjective criteria are in use.) Subjective criteria are neither measurable nor repeatable, and two evaluators may well disagree on the result.

There may be legitimate reasons to base a purchase decision on a personal relationship between a company official and a computer products vendor. Or, a company and its supplier may have a partnership arrangement that overrides all other evaluation criteria. Or an evaluator might express the opinion that he or she would never, under any circumstances, recommend a product from a particular vendor because the evaluator does not respect the vendor's product designs, marketing ethics, or customer service standards. These are examples of acknowledged subjective criteria. However, subjective criteria often do not give much weight to the match between end user needs and the features of the hardware or software. In extreme cases where subjective selection criteria are used, a company won't even consider competing products. It might have traditionally bought its power supplies from a particular company, for example, perhaps based on past experience, reputation, location, or a personal contact. Other factors, including price, are irrelevant in this situation, and the company will probably not even consider looking elsewhere.

Large, privately held companies often use an objective evaluation or selection procedure for computer products, but smaller companies often use more subjective criteria.

THE REQUEST FOR PROPOSAL (RFP)

By law, many public organizations and agencies are required to use an objective evaluation process. They use a bidding process, or request for proposal procedure. A public agency may issue a **request for proposal** (**RFP**) that invites competing vendors to submit product and price proposals on a particular system. Employees of public agencies are often required to select products from vendors who win a bidding competition or who submit the most competitive response to an RFP. As a result of an RFP process, a public agency may designate the successful bidder as the sole authorized vendor for computer products covered in the RFP. There are eight primary steps in the RFP process.

1. An agency or organization conducts a user needs analysis (which you will read about in Chapter 4).

2. Based on the needs analysis, the agency develops a procurement specification for the equipment or software. The specification describes the technical characteristics of the hardware or software it will acquire or recommend.

3. The agency defines the decision criteria and the importance of each criterion in advance. Many criteria are based on mandatory or desirable product features; others include support, vendor stability, product costs, and compatibility with existing systems.

4. The agency writes the RFP document, which describes the user requirements, bidding procedure, and decision criteria.

5. The RFP document is sent to prospective vendors (some companies and agencies maintain a list of vendors who are prescreened to meet acceptable financial criteria).

6. Interested vendors respond to the RFP with a written proposal that addresses how their products meet or exceed the user requirements; the response also includes a bid price at which the vendor can supply the products or services to the agency.

7. The agency analyzes the responses to the RFP and its user support staff evaluates them, often using weighted point evaluation tools.

8. The company or agency chooses a vendor and awards the contract.

The RFP process is one of the most common and most objective decision-making tools.

MECHANICS OF THE WEIGHTED POINT EVALUATION METHOD

The weighted point evaluation method is a popular evaluation tool that an evaluator can use formally, as in the RFP process, and informally. Product comparison articles in trade journals frequently use this method, as well. In this section, you will learn some of the mechanics of the process. You can apply this method equally well to selecting a 1,000-user computer network or to a home personal computer.

To perform a weighted point evaluation, evaluators follow these steps:

1. Decide on the evaluation criteria.

2. Decide on the importance of each criterion.

3. Rate each competing product on all the evaluation criteria.

4. If more than one evaluator rates products, compute the average rating for each product for each criterion.

5. Weight the product ratings for each criterion by the importance of the criterion.

6. Compute the total rating for each product.

7. Compare product ratings.

The evaluation criteria selected in the weighted point method are based on several important factors, including:

- The specific type of hardware or software product to be evaluated
- The needs of end users
- Support issues
- Cost

Evaluation articles in periodicals are an excellent source of ideas for criteria to use to evaluate specific products. Table 3-2 provides some examples of criteria in each of these categories.

Table 3-2 Examples of Criteria in Weighted Point Evaluation Method

Category	Examples of Criteria
Hardware or software	▪ Processing or access speed ▪ Storage capacity ▪ Capabilities ▪ Transaction volumes ▪ Compatibility with existing systems ▪ Upgradability (scalability)
End user needs	▪ Ease of learning ▪ Ease of use ▪ Mandatory features ▪ Desirable features
Support issues	▪ Technical support ▪ Installation assistance ▪ Training ▪ Documentation ▪ Troubleshooting ▪ Maintenance
Cost	▪ Total cost of ownership (see Chapter 1)

As an example of the weighted point evaluation method, suppose your company wants you to evaluate two computer systems for purchase. The company wants you to use the criteria and weights shown in the first two columns of Table 3-3.

Table 3-3 Criteria and Weights for Evaluating Two Computers

Criterion	Criterion's Importance (Weight)	System X Evaluation	System Y Evaluation
Hardware configuration	25%		
Software bundled	35%		
Vendor reputation	10%		
Vendor support	30%		
TOTALS			

After they select the criteria, evaluators decide on the relative importance of each one, usually based on the significance of the criteria to the company, to its users, and to the support group. For example, a relatively unimportant criterion might receive a weight of 10%. The sum of the criteria weights should total 100%.

After assigning weights, the evaluators review the capabilities of each system and assign a number of points, usually between 1 and 100, for each product on each criterion. For example, for the criterion "Vendor reputation," an evaluator could discover that a particular vendor is very well regarded and might assign that vendor a 95 out of 100 on that criterion.

Each of three evaluators rates each system independently. The three evaluations are averaged to compute the points earned for each criterion. Or the three evaluators might discuss their preliminary ratings to identify and negotiate any large discrepancies and arrive at a consensus rating. For example, if one evaluator rated the hardware for System X at 40 on a criterion and another rated the same hardware at 100 on the same criterion, the two evaluators should discuss the issue to determine why there was such a significant difference and to arrive at a mutually acceptable rating of perhaps 80 out of 100. In this example, after discussion, the evaluators agreed that the hardware configuration for System X was worth 90 points (out of 100), and the competing system was worth only 70, as shown in Table 3-4.

Table 3-4   Weighted Point Evaluation Method with Points Assigned to Criteria

Criterion	Criterion's Importance (Weight)	System X Evaluation	System Y Evaluation
Hardware configuration	25%	90	70
Software bundled	35%	70	70
Vendor reputation	10%	50	95
Vendor support	30%	60	90
TOTALS	100%		

In the next step, the weight of each selection criterion is multiplied by the number of points assigned to each system for each criterion. The resulting points for each system for each criterion are then added together to arrive at a total number of points, as Table 3-5 shows. The system with the higher number of total points is the preferable system.

Table 3-5   Weighted Point Method Example with Evaluation Points

Criterion	Criterion's Importance (Weight)	System X Evaluation	System Y Evaluation
Hardware configuration	25%	90 × 25% = 22.5	70 × 25% = 17.5
Software bundled	35%	70 × 35% = 24.5	70 × 35% = 24.5
Vender reputation	10%	50 × 10% = 5.0	95 × 10% = 9.5
Vendor support	30%	60 × 30% = 18.0	90 × 30% = 27.0
TOTALS	100%	70.0/100	78.5/100

3

In this example, System Y's higher scores on vendor reputation and support offset its lower score on hardware configuration. The weighted point method can be used to evaluate more than two products, and it can accommodate as many criteria as evaluators think are important.

The advantage of the weighted point evaluation method is that it forces evaluators to address two important questions early in the evaluation process: 1) What do we think are important criteria in the product purchase decision or recommendation, and 2) How important is each criterion in relation to the other criteria? Some argue this method applies numeric points to criteria where the points have little meaning. However, the weighted point method forces evaluators to ask important questions when they might be tempted to use more subjective criteria. It uses measurable criteria in place of subjective beliefs. Sometimes the objective results of a weighted point method conflict with an evaluator's subjective feelings. If you finish the process and it gives you the "wrong" result according to your "gut" feelings, you can reexamine the criteria and the weights and ask why you got the result you did. Sometimes it's your "gut" that's wrong.

 For another, more extensive example of an objective evaluation strategy, see the article by Patrick McNeil, "Avoid Service Nightmares!," in *Support Management*, November/December 1997, pages 24-42; view portions of the article at **www.supportmanagement.com/goldbuttons.map?63,196**. (The printed version contains worksheets not available in the Web version). The article describes a method for selecting a hardware maintenance and repair company.

Support specialists who evaluate and select computer products can use objective or subjective methods, but the purpose of all evaluation and selection strategies is to arrive at the right products for a particular user situation. Once a company has researched products, the next step is often to develop computer product standards, which you'll learn about in the next section.

COMPUTER PRODUCT STANDARDS

As you learned in the first part of this chapter, companies control support costs by establishing computer product standards to limit the number of hardware and software options users can choose. Although the decision to adopt product support standards may sound like a "one-size-fits-all" approach, it doesn't have to be. Within a company standard, options and alternatives are often permitted. Most companies try to strike a reasonable balance between the two extremes of "Select only this product" and "Select anything you want."

Lane Community College, in Eugene, Oregon, is typical of many organizations that struggled with computer product support issues. In 1995, it adopted a policy that says, in part:

> The college shall maintain a list of supported computer hardware and software. Purchases of products on the college's list will be supported by Computer Services and Electronic Services in terms of compatibility, installation, training, maintenance, troubleshooting, and upgrades. Computer Services and/or Electronic Services may decline to provide support for products not on the list. Staff who wish to purchase products not on the college list may submit those products for review and possible inclusion to the committee charged with maintaining the list.

Lane's list of support products includes both PC-compatible systems and Macintosh computers. The CPU and memory requirements for each platform ensure that the minimum configurations will run current versions of popular operating system software and applications programs.

The list of approved products specifies selected software packages in several categories. Part of Lane's Computer Support Standards Policy is included in this chapter's CloseUp.

Some organizations do not spend time to research and evaluate products and develop standards as described in this chapter. However, larger organizations with a substantial investment in computer technology tend to spend staff resources to evaluate products and set purchase standards because the potential for waste is so large. Because of their ongoing research and investigation into new products, support specialists can make effective use of a list of approved products to answer questions such as, "What kind of computer should the company buy?" and "Is this printer model compatible with company systems?"

HOW COMPANIES DEVELOP COMPUTER PRODUCT STANDARDS

A company's product and service standards can come from a variety of sources. In some companies, product standards arise over time as a company "computer culture" develops. For example, the early adopters of technology in a company may be predominantly Macintosh users. The company may adopt a standard that primarily Macintosh systems are supported, unless there is good reason to deviate from the standard. Alternatively, companies that adopted WordPerfect as their preferred word processor during the 1980s may be reluctant to change to a different one, even though WordPerfect is no longer the most popular word-processing product sold today.

Whereas company culture and traditions are one source of product standards, some companies assign the task of developing and maintaining standards to the user support group or to a product standards committee. A **product standards committee** is a committee composed of support specialists and end users whose task is to define the current company standards and coordinate their use in the company. Once established, standards must be effective—that is, they must help users get their work done. They must be evenly administered and enforced. When users have to work around the standards to get the equipment, software, and services they need to do their jobs, this is an indicator that computer standards are ineffective.

HOW COMPANIES IMPLEMENT COMPUTER PRODUCT STANDARDS

In many companies, two forces often influence the adoption and implementation of product and service standards. One force is the company's existing inventory of hardware and software products. It is very difficult for a company, unless it is very small or has a very large computer budget, to discard its entire investment in computer systems and adopt a new standard overnight. Product support groups often take into account the predominant kinds of hardware, software, and network architecture that currently exist in the organization as they define product standards. To deviate substantially from what employees are currently using can result in a large, one-time expense to a company as employees convert to the new standard.

A second force that drives changes in product and service standards is the continual arrival of new products, services, and product upgrades. An important task of the product support group is to learn about and evaluate new products that have potential to replace existing company standards. The decision to modify existing product standards is usually based on criteria such as the following:

- New products offer technical improvements over current products.

- New products have features with the potential to improve employee productivity compared with existing products.

- Employee tastes in products change over time.

- New products and services are available at a lower cost than existing products, which makes them financially more attractive.

- New products may be more compatible with changes in industry standards than older products.

- New products become more popular than products they replace.

However, the decision to replace an existing product or service is often difficult to make because a company may have a sizable investment in the existing standard. Similarly, employees may have invested the time to learn how to use existing products and may be reluctant to change because the conversion means retraining and a possible temporary loss in employee productivity. For these reasons, companies that want to move to a new standard may decide to phase in new product standards over time. A transition period occurs when both old and new products are permitted and supported under the standards policy. Of course, transition periods are difficult for the support staff, because they must provide support for both old and new products. The transition period is often a period of increased support costs, as support and maintenance of existing hardware, software, and network products continues for some users, while other users convert to and get trained in the use of new products.

For example, when Windows 95 first became widely available in 1995, many companies were reluctant to convert from MS-DOS or Windows 3.x to Windows 95. They were not convinced that the advantages of the new Windows 95 operating system were worth the conversion costs, and they had a substantial existing investment in MS-DOS or Windows 3.x applications. Consequently, some companies stayed with the Windows 3.x operating system standard for several years. Other companies included both Windows 3.x and Windows 95 as standards for an extended transition period, because they relied on applications software that ran primarily under Windows 3.x. Windows 95 lacked support for a small percentage of existing MS-DOS and Windows 3.x applications. However, as more applications software that specifically required Windows 95 came on the market, more companies felt pressure from their employees to convert to it and to support the emerging industry standard. Some companies are only now, several years later, dropping MS-DOS and Windows 3.x as supported operating system standards.

Product and support standards will continue to change in the future. In the late 1990s, companies are struggling with decisions about when to adopt, convert, and support hardware and software based on the new version of Windows 98, the latest version of Windows NT, new devices based on the Universal Serial Bus (USB), rewritable CD-ROM disks, Digital Video Disks (DVDs), and voice recognition input technology. Every decision to modify an existing technology standard or adopt a new one requires analysis and evaluation of products and services by the user support group. It also triggers potential support cost increases for installation, upgrades, training, documentation, troubleshooting, and help desk services.

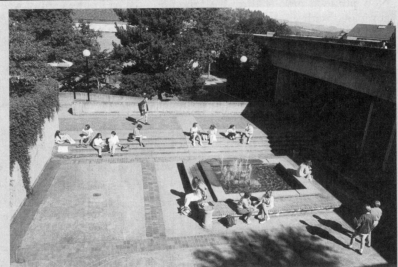

Courtesy of Lane Community College

LANE COMMUNITY COLLEGE'S COMPUTER SUPPORT STANDARDS
COMPUTER SUPPORT STANDARDS
(EFFECTIVE MARCH 31, 1997)

CRITERIA FOR SELECTING SUPPORT HARDWARE AND SOFTWARE

The Computer Support Committee began meeting in February 1995. Over the course of many discussions, the members of the committee reached consensus on criteria for selecting software and hardware standards. The criteria strongly reflect the purposes of developing and maintaining standards, as set out by the initial Computer Standards Task Force and approved by the Executive Cabinet. The purposes include:

a. To provide the best support services possible to college computer users
b. To provide college computer users with a list of products that are compatible with existing college systems and portable across departments
c. To provide college computer users with a list of products that are of high quality and the best values available
d. To maximize the resources available for technical support through Computer Services and Electronic Services

3

Key criteria are listed below. No ranking is implied.

- Supported software and hardware options are limited to one or two choices to ensure economies of scale, that is, the most efficient use of limited resources for support.

- Supported software and hardware are state-of-the-art, providing staff with increased computing capabilities.

- Supported software and hardware are compatible with the college network.

- Supported software has cross-platform compatibility and similarity (Mac and PC versions are similar), resulting in ease of transferability among staff and ease of training on either platform.

- Supported software is or will be used by a proportionately high number of staff across several departments.

- Supported software requires a relatively low learning curve (avoid supporting high-end, specialty software which has a high learning curve).

- Supported hardware is acquired under purchasing contract guidelines, including hardware built in-house.

- Supported hardware makes use of the existing training base, technical support library, parts inventory, and parts ordering links maintained by Electronic Services for repair and maintenance.

Software Standards			
Software	Macintosh	PC—Windows 3.x	PC—Windows 95
Operating system	Mac OS 7.x	Windows 3.1x	Windows 95
Integrated packages	MS Office*	MS Office* Corel WordPerfect Suite 6.1	MS Office 95/97 Professional* Corel WordPerfect Suite 7
Word processing	MS Word 6.x, 5.x	MS Word 6.x* WordPerfect 6.x	MS Word* 95/97 WordPerfect 7.x
Spreadsheet	MS Excel 5.x	MS Excel 5.x* Quattro Pro	MS Excel* 95/97 Quattro Pro
Database	FileMaker Pro	MS Access 2.0*	MS Access* 95/97
Internet	Netscape 2.x, 3.x	Netscape 2.x, 3.x	Netscape 2.x, 3.x
E-mail	BeyondMail Vines Mail	BeyondMail Vines Mail	BeyondMail Vines Mail
Presentation	MS PowerPoint	MS PowerPoint	MS PowerPoint 97

*Recommended

Software Standards (continued)			
Software	**Macintosh**	**PC—Windows 3.x**	**PC—Windows 95**
Desktop publishing (Basic level)	N/A	MS Publisher	MS Publisher 97
Virus protection	Symantec Antivirus for Macintosh (SAM)	McAfee* Norton AntiVirus	McAfee for Windows 95* Norton AntiVirus
Utilities	Norton Utilities	Norton Utilities	Norton Utilities

*Recommended

GUIDELINES FOR HARDWARE ACQUISITIONS AND UPGRADES

Hardware support standards take into account connecting CPUs to the college network and providing maintenance and repair through Electronic Services. Many older computers are not suitable for connection to the college network. For this reason, *buying "hand-me-down" or other used computers is discouraged.* Buying computers outside of the college's purchasing contract also is discouraged because internal components may not be compatible with the network or may not meet the specifications determined by Computer Services and Purchasing in the requirements contract. The standards listed here assure ease of connectivity and operation on the college network.

For newly acquired systems (new or used), the minimum system that will be supported must conform to the specifications of the current purchasing contract. Specifications are updated periodically and published in *The Daily* and on the Purchasing Department Web page.

The minimum configurations will be able to do the current operating system, Beyond Mail e-mail, Netscape 2.x, and Microsoft Office at an acceptable speed, but not necessarily all at once. To run several applications at once, additional MBs of RAM are required. Multimedia applications will need additional RAM and more hard disk capacity as well. *Call the Help Desk for assistance* in identifying the best system configuration for your needs. Call the Help Desk and Bookstore for information on site licensing and possible cost savings on software and hardware purchases.

UPGRADING TO WINDOWS 95

Computer Services has resolved the incompatibilities between Windows 95 and Lane's wide area network. Windows 95 can be used on networked computers on campus and may also be used for remote access to Lane's wide area network. Training for remote access from Windows 95 systems will be offered; watch *The Daily* for training announcements. Because of the complexity of Windows 95 and the need to maximize resources available for technical support, the Computer Support Committee is recommending that users carefully consider the decision to upgrade to Windows 95. Many computer users will not need or want to upgrade to Windows 95. Windows 95 will be most effective when used with Windows 95 application software (designed to run on Windows 95) and when used with a sufficiently powerful hardware configuration.

Running software designed for Windows 3.x or older operating systems on Windows 95 will not be supported. Upgrading to Windows 95 and appropriate applications software may require increasing RAM or hard disk capacity. Consult the Help Desk if you have any questions about the suitability of Windows 95 for your particular needs.

3

Hardware Standards			
Hardware	Macintosh	PC—Windows 3.x	PC—Windows 95
Computers–Desktop The standards are not intended as a buyer's guide! Consult the Computer Services Help Desk for assistance in buying or upgrading any computer.	Electronic Services is an Apple Authorized Service Provider (AASP) and will service all makes and models of Apple equipment both in warranty and out of warranty.	Models purchased from LCC Applied Engineering Dept. or contracted vendor according to purchasing contract specifications	Models purchased from LCC Applied Engineering Dept. or contracted vendor according to purchasing contract specifications
Computers–Laptop	Upgrade modifications only. For repairs, take unit to dealer for shipment to manufacturer. Recommend Toshiba TC2400c series. PowerBooks will require special cards to be Ethernet-ready.		

Peripherals: All Platforms	
Laser and inkjet printers	HP and Apple printers
Impact printers	Okidata, Panasonic, Epson
Scanners	HP flatbed
Monitors	Models purchased from contracted vendor or Apple monitors
Tape drives	Conner or Colorado; recommend Conner (internal or external)
Zip drives	Iomega
Keyboards, mice	Models purchased from LCC Electronics Dept. or contracted vendor according to most recent purchasing contract specifications

©1997 Lane Community College.

Updates to LCC's standards are posted at **www.lanecc.edu:1080/webpages/lcc/ instadv/csspage2/.htm**.

CHAPTER SUMMARY

- During the 1980s, companies and organizations with a substantial investment in desktop computer technology recognized the need to evaluate computer products and set purchasing and support standards. Because there were few acknowledged industry standards, incompatible hardware and software made the cost of computer technology higher than necessary and reduced productivity among users. Today, companies lower their support services costs by restricting purchases to a limited list of approved products.

- User support employees spend time evaluating computer products and services so they can make recommendations to users and departments in an organization about what will and will not meet their needs. Support employees often help a company set standards for computer hardware and software products. Standard products help increase the compatibility among various hardware and software components and help to reduce the resources (costs) required to support end user computer systems.

- Support staff members use a variety of information resources to evaluate hardware and software products, including vendor literature, Web sites and user manuals, product demonstrations and evaluation versions of software, product reviews and comparison articles in computer periodicals, and opinions of company or industry experts.

- Several decision aids are available to help support specialists make selection decisions among competing products and services. These aids include:
  - Industry standard or best-selling products
  - Analysis of products used by competitors
  - Product benchmarks
  - The weighted point evaluation method
  - Acknowledged subjective criteria
  - The request for proposal (RFP) procedure

- Many companies adopt industry standard and best-selling products. They are in widespread use and make the selection decision look easy. However, because a product is a best-seller does not mean it is the best fit with a specific user's needs. Another less popular product may have features not found in the best-sellers that are actually a better match with a particular user's needs.

- Benchmarks are an objective way to compare two or more products by observing them perform a standard, predefined task or workload. The weighted point evaluation method forces a product evaluator to make a list of important criteria and assign a weight to each criterion that reflects its importance. Competing products are evaluated against the criteria, and the product that best matches the criteria is selected. Common criteria include product features, ease of learning, ease of use, compatibility, product technical support, and total cost of ownership.

- Hardware and software standards are important to companies because standards help control the user support costs. Whereas some support standards are based on company culture and tradition, many standards are the result of systematic analysis and evaluation of new products. The decision to adopt or modify a standard is often made by a group or committee with representatives from user support, end users, technical support, and management. Implementation of new standards can be affected by the investment in existing hardware and software and loss of employee productivity during the conversion to the new standards.

KEY TERMS

- **benchmark** — An objective test or measurement that can be used to evaluate the speed, capacity, capabilities, or productivity of competing products.

- **industry standard products** — Hardware, software, and accessories that are market leaders in sales; standards in the computer industry are not standards in the traditional meaning (no industry group may have participated in their design) but are often standards based on sales and market share.

- **objective evaluation criteria** — Factors used in a product selection procedure that are relatively unbiased; a neutral observer should ideally be able to use objective criteria to reach the same conclusion as another evaluator.

- **product evaluation** — A process of researching and analyzing computer product features, capabilities, and suitability to solve a specific user need.

- **product standards** — A list of hardware, operating system, network, and applications software products that have been selected to meet the needs of users in an organization; product standards are often enforced to reduce the cost of acquiring and supporting computer systems.

- **product standards committee** — A group of user support staff, end users, technical support, and managers who are assigned the task of developing and maintaining a list of company-wide standard products; standards are then recommended for purchase by employees and supported by the user support staff.

- **request for proposal (RFP)** — A product selection or competitive bidding procedure that uses objective criteria to distinguish among products proposed by vendors; often used as the basis for awarding a contract to provide computer products.

- **subjective evaluation criteria** — Factors used in a product selection procedure that are not directly related to the fit between a product's features and a user's needs; subjective factors include personal relationships, convenience, personal preferences, and traditional practices.

- **weighted point evaluation method** — A product comparison method that uses several evaluation criteria of predetermined importance to grade competing products and arrive at a numerical score as a basis for selection.

Review Questions

1. Explain why there were few standards in the early years of small computer use in businesses and organizations.

2. What impact did the lack of industry-wide hardware and software standards have on companies and their employees that used small business computers in the 1980s?

3. What impact did the lack of industry standard products have on user support?

4. List examples of questions a user support staff might want answered as it researches and evaluates whether new computer products and services should be adopted as company standards.

5. Describe the information resources available to support staffs who research and evaluate new hardware and software products.

6. List and briefly describe several decision-making tools and methods that support staff use to help evaluate and select computer products.

7. Where can product evaluators obtain demonstration or evaluation copies of software packages?

8. Who should be involved in the decision to adopt a hardware platform or software package as a company standard? Why?

9. What are the advantages and disadvantages of adopting best-selling, popular, or industry standard computer products to support?

10. Explain why a company may want to consider computer products that are known to be used by its competitors.

11. Describe a benchmark and give an example.

12. What are the steps in the weighted point evaluation method?

13. Why is the weighted point method popular among product evaluators?

14. List four examples of criteria that are often used in a weighted point product evaluation.

15. What can product evaluators do when they disagree on the points awarded to a selection criterion during a weighted point evaluation procedure?

16. What is the difference between subjective and objective evaluation criteria? Give three examples of each.

17. Describe briefly the advantages and disadvantages of both objective and subjective selection criteria.

18. What is an RFP? Is it an objective or subjective procedure? Explain why.

19. What are the important steps in the RFP process?

20. Describe how a company that does not have computer product standards can develop and maintain them.

21. What two forces are at work in many companies that impact the implementation of product standards?

3

22. Explain why setting product standards is an ongoing process and why companies may need to periodically modify their standards.

23. List some product standard decisions that will confront companies within the next 12 months.

HANDS-ON PROJECTS

 **PROJECT 3-1**

Locate a magazine that contains articles that present a side-by-side comparison of two or more products.

- What criteria are used to compare the products?

- Can you think of additional criteria that could have been used?

- What evaluation method was used to do the product comparisons?

- Did the method(s) produce an objective or subjective result?

- Do you agree with the result? Why or why not?

Write a summary of your findings.

 PROJECT 3-2

If you work for a company or attend a school, find out if it has computer product support standards. Write a comparison between those you find and those in this chapter's CloseUp.

 PROJECT 3-3

Use the Internet to locate computer product support standards for two companies or organizations. Write a comparison between those you find and those described in this chapter's CloseUp.

PROJECT 3-4

Choose a category of computer products from among the following: hardware, peripherals, operating systems, applications software, and local area networks. Make a list of some computer products you think fit the description "industry standard." Compare your list with the list of a colleague or others in your project group. Do the members of your group agree or disagree about the industry standards? Write a short paper that lists the agreed-on standards, products over which there are disagreements, and your explanation of the reasons for any disagreements.

PROJECT 3-5

Find two Internet users, one who uses Netscape Navigator as a Web browser and the other who uses Microsoft Internet Explorer. Ask them why they prefer their browser choice to the other. What criteria do they use? Are they subjective or objective criteria? Write a summary of your findings.

PROJECT 3-6

Suppose you were selected to lead a product standards committee where you work or go to school. The committee's assignment is to develop a product standard for your business or organization. Write an agenda for the first committee meeting that lists the highest priority tasks the committee should undertake. *Hint:* Think about the information the committee will need, the decisions it will need to make, and what the end result will look like.

PROJECT 3-7

Use spreadsheet software to develop a worksheet that product evaluators can use for the weighted point evaluation method. Set up columns and formulas that will make the worksheet easy to use. To test your worksheet, enter the data from the example in this chapter. Design your worksheet to be as general as possible so it is easy to add more products or more evaluation criteria. Print your worksheet.

CASE PROJECTS

1. FRED'S PAINT STORE

Fred's Paint Store plans to purchase each of its outside sales representatives an inexpensive, portable laptop computer to prepare narrative notes and summaries of their sales calls. Because the sales representatives are not skilled computer users, one goal is to make the computer system as easy as possible to use. Another goal is to keep the cost of the laptops as low as possible.

The manager of the sales staff does not want the sales reps to spend time learning a full-featured word processor. So Fred's Paints plans to teach each sales rep to use WRITE, NOTEPAD, or WordPad to prepare their sales summaries. None of these simple Windows accessories, however, includes a spell checker. In your role as a Computer User Support Specialist, you are assigned to help the marketing department research and recommend a spell checker that can be used in the Windows environment.

Your first task is to develop evaluation criteria for a Windows spell checker program. As resources for an evaluation checklist, you can use your personal knowledge and experience with spell checkers in popular word-processing programs, product evaluation articles in trade periodicals, and discussions you have with others in your project group. Then, create your own criteria checklist for a spell checker. Develop as complete a list of criteria as you can, but limit your criteria to spell checker features you think the sales reps at Fred's Paints would be likely to use, and not on infrequently used features. You can also consider any software support issues you think are relevant.

If your computer location allows you to download shareware, and with the help of your instructor if necessary, obtain two Windows shareware spell checkers you can evaluate against the criteria you developed. Install and test each one. Then evaluate each program in terms of the criteria you established. If you add other criteria based on your test of the spell checkers, identify the additional criteria you used in your evaluation.

Finally, write a summary of your evaluation of the two spell checker packages and your recommendation to the marketing department at Fred's Paints.

2. COLUMBIA SAND & GRAVEL

Mark Allen, owner and operator of Columbia Sand & Gravel, needs some computer advice and wants to hire you to consult with his company. Due to several large construction projects and subdivision developments, Columbia has grown dramatically in recent years, and it needs to replace its soon-to-be obsolete computer billing system. The existing software runs on an IBM PC system and was purchased over 12 years ago. The hardware and software no longer have the capacity and speed to process invoices and record payments for Mark's customer base. Unfortunately, the company that originally sold the software to Mark is no longer in business, so an upgrade of the existing system is not an option.

Mark is aware of two software companies in your state that sell invoicing applications that are specifically tailored for use in the sand and gravel industry. Both Digital Rock and Extractasoft claim to have the best-selling software available for sand and gravel invoice applications. Mark wants your help in evaluating these two competing products and in making a recommendation on which software the company should adopt as its standard.

Mark Allen is also aware that his company will have to purchase new hardware to run whichever software is selected. In recent years, Columbia Sand & Gravel has developed a good working relationship with The Modular PC, a local company that sells and services computer hardware products. The owner of Modular PC is a close personal friend of Mark's, but does not sell invoicing software as specialized as he needs. Although Mark has decided that he will probably purchase a small networked computer system to run the invoicing software, he would like to hire you to evaluate the software products.

Based on this information from Mark and on what you learned in this chapter:

1. Describe any concerns you have about the product evaluation approach and methods at Columbia Sand & Gravel.

2. List any changes or suggestions you would make in Columbia's approach to select a replacement invoicing system to use in its business.

3. Write a letter to Mark Allen that discusses your concerns and suggestions.

3. NATSUKO'S INDOOR GARDEN

Natsuko's Indoor Garden has been growing and selling plants since its owner, Natsuko Hayashi, graduated from college several years ago. Natsuko says that her company slogan is "We're in a growing business." Thanks to Natsuko's hard work and good management, her sales volume has more than doubled in the last four years; but her accounting system is no longer adequate to handle the sales volume. Natsuko has three sales locations: one downtown and two in suburban shopping centers. The store managers in each sales location use a slightly different calculator-and-paper method of record keeping. Natsuko recently read a trade publication for nursery and flower shop owners about accounting programs for small businesses like hers but has not yet had time to investigate any of them.

She would like to convert from the manual systems currently in use to an automated accounting system for each store. She would like you to help evaluate some small business accounting packages. Her goal is to standardize all the sales locations on one accounting package, which should make consolidating her financial reports and statements much easier at the end of the month and at tax time.

To get started, Natsuko has made a tentative list of features she needs in a computer accounting system.

- Invoicing
- Accounts receivable
- Accounts payable
- Payroll
- Inventory
- Purchase orders
- Cash reconciliation (to bank statement)
- Customer records and lists
- Vendor records and lists
- General ledger financial statement

As an accounting software evaluator for Natsuko, you are to use various information resources to research the features of some small business accounting packages. She would like to know whether existing programs measure up against her list of needed features, or whether she needs to consider a custom programming project. She would also like to know whether there are other criteria in addition to her list that she should consider when making a selection decision. Based on your research, write a product evaluation summary for Natsuko that compares the features of at least three small business accounting packages. You can use any information resource or consider any packages you'd like; you can also include the following product web pages in your research:

Accpac	**www.accpac.com**
DacEasy	**www.daceasy.com**
Great Plains Accounting	**www.gps.com**
PeachTree	**www.peachtree.com**
QuickBooks	**www.intuit.com/quickbooks**

User Needs Analysis and Assessment

You learned in Chapter 2 that user support specialists are often asked to help users select computer products. Sometimes there are limited products from which to choose, especially when an organization maintains lists of standard, supported products, which you learned about in Chapter 3. This chapter describes how to analyze and assess user needs and help users decide among competing products. It is targeted primarily to user support specialists who work with internal users; it does not apply to support specialists who work mainly on help desks or provide telephone support to external users.

If you have ever taken a course in computer systems analysis and design, you will probably recognize many of the issues, resources, and tools described in this chapter. In some degree programs, students are required to study systems analysis before they take courses in end user computing support. Experience in systems analysis and design provides a good background for this chapter and for user needs assessment. However, the tools user support specialists use are not always the same as the tools used by a systems analyst, who designs an applications program for a programmer to code. This chapter focuses on analysis and assessment tools that support specialists use to match a user's needs to available products and services.

AFTER READING THIS CHAPTER AND COMPLETING THE EXERCISES YOU WILL BE ABLE TO:

- Explain some basic information about needs analysis and assessment
- Explain the major steps an analyst uses to analyze and assess a user's needs
- Describe the most common tools that aid a support specialist in a user needs analysis project

OVERVIEW OF USER NEEDS ANALYSIS AND ASSESSMENT

As you learned in Chapter 2, the support staff often analyzes and assesses user needs to determine the hardware and software products that will best meet those needs. Once analysts understand a user's environment and work situation and investigate alternatives, they can then decide on a solution to the user's needs and on whether to purchase or build the solution.

A user needs analysis and assessment project can take many forms. It can be informal, such as a friend or business acquaintance asking for help with the purchase of computer hardware or software for home or business. A project can also be formal, as when a supervisor assigns a user support specialist or a support group the task of working with users in a department to select a new network configuration or new applications package. It can also be just about anything in between.

The steps in the needs analysis and assessment process are summarized in Figure 4-1 and explained in detail in the discussion that follows.

I. Preparation

    1. Understand the business goals

    2. Understand the decision criteria and constraints

    3. Define the problem clearly

    4. Identify the roles of stakeholders

    5. Identify sources of information

II. Investigation

    6. Develop an understanding of the existing system

    7. Investigate alternatives to the existing system

III. Decision

    8. Develop a model of the proposed system

    9. Make a build-versus-buy decision

Figure 4-1   Steps in the needs analysis and assessment process

Analysts don't always perform every step in every needs assessment situation, and not all steps are always equally important. But analysts need to start with a list like this one to guide a needs analysis project. Similarly, an experienced support person knows that user needs analysis and assessment is not a perfect process or a science with obviously right and wrong answers. For example, users are rarely certain of their exact needs or know how to put their needs into words. However, it is important for a support specialist to begin with the right list of questions—even if the answers are sometimes inexact.

USER NEEDS ANALYSIS STEPS AND TASKS

Each step of a user needs analysis project can be grouped under one of three phases: preparation, investigation, or decision. In the **preparation phase**, analysts try to understand the business goals as well as the decision criteria and constraints; they try to define the problem, identify the roles of stakeholders, and identify sources of information. In the **investigation phase**, analysts try to understand the present system and alternatives to it. Finally, in the **decision phase**, analysts develop a model of the proposed system and decide whether to build or buy it. Within each phase, analysts take specific steps that allow them to obtain information and propose a solution in an orderly fashion. By performing certain tasks for each step, analysts ensure that they have considered all relevant sources of information in order to arrive at an appropriate solution for that particular situation. The following sections describe the major tasks of each step of the analysis and assessment process.

STEP 1: UNDERSTAND THE BUSINESS GOALS

Before support specialists can make a recommendation about new computer products, they must get an overall perspective of the business goals (or a purchaser's objectives for a home system). Medium- to large-size businesses often have a written strategic business plan or a mission statement that describes the business goals and objectives. These plans are often a good way for a support analyst to learn about the business goals. If these documents are not available, it is usually possible to interview managers or supervisors to learn about their vision, goals, and future plans.

Analysts should learn the answers to the following questions:

1. What are the purposes of the business or business unit (department)?

2. Is the business for-profit or not-for-profit?

3. Does the company have plans to grow or expand?

4. What is the business's attitude (or culture) about technology?

5. What is the business's budget for computer systems and services?

6. Does the business's staff have the expertise to operate and maintain a computer system?

The purpose of these questions is to learn the big picture—the environment into which the future system will fit. Growth or expansion plans are an especially important input to the assessment process. The solutions analysts might recommend to a company that is growing 5 to 10% per year would probably be very different from solutions that they would recommend to a company that plans to grow 25 to 50% per year. A smaller company may not be able to maintain or support a sophisticated application with a lot of features and flexibility; it might be better off with a more straightforward package.

STEP 2: UNDERSTAND THE DECISION CRITERIA AND CONSTRAINTS

Another question a support analyst needs to ask up front involves the criteria the business will use to make a decision. User support specialists often recommend solutions to users or managers rather than decide on a solution themselves. However, the more support specialists understand about the criteria a user or manager will eventually use, the more they can focus their analysis on realistic alternatives.

It is important to know what is feasible, or possible, in terms of time, money, or technology. There are several kinds of **feasibility**:

- Economic feasibility: What budget constraints will influence the final decision on the project?

- Operational feasibility: With what other systems or procedures does this system need to interact?

- Technological feasibility: Are there limitations due to the state of technology that impose constraints on possible solutions?

- Timeline feasibility: What time constraints immediately rule out some possible alternatives?

A user support analyst also needs to understand the factors that will influence the final decision. For example, is the company sensitive to cost, so that only low-cost solutions should be considered? Does the company pride itself on doing business with only well-known, reputable vendors, so that the analyst should consider systems from established vendors more seriously than those offered by relatively new, unknown companies? Does the company try to stay on the leading edge of technology, or does it take a relatively conservative view of new, and perhaps untried, products? What priorities does the company place on vendor support? For example, some companies rely on their own support staff and don't need vendor support. The answers to all these questions will form criteria and constraints that the support analyst must consider in order to recommend an appropriate solution.

STEP 3: DEFINE THE PROBLEM CLEARLY

Problems come in a variety of shapes and sizes. Some are well formulated; others are not. User support specialists who work on user needs assessment projects have to clearly define the problem they are trying to solve. Furthermore, not all problems are technical; some "computer" problems actually turn out to be organizational, work flow, political, management, or company resource problems.

"Do I really understand the problem I'm trying to solve for this user?" should be a question that guides the needs analysis from beginning to end. For example, a user may complain that the accounting application he is using does not work correctly and that he wants to replace it with one that is more robust—that doesn't hang up the system like the current one does. The problem may, in fact, be the accounting program, and the user may have correctly deduced that he needs a new one. However, the problem may actually be related to the way the existing program is configured to operate on the user's computer system or in a network environment. To recommend replacing expensive hardware or software when the real problem is something else can be a costly mistake. Therefore, clearly defining the problem is critical to any user needs analysis.

It is also important for support specialists not to assume at the outset that the user has correctly analyzed the problem. The user may understand what is wrong but not understand the array of possible causes or the variety of options available to fix the problem. So a support analyst needs to ask many questions, observe as the user operates the existing system, and consider solutions other than the obvious ones.

STEP 4: IDENTIFY THE ROLES OF STAKEHOLDERS

Stakeholders are those who have a substantial interest in the successful outcome of a needs assessment project. They usually participate in one or more steps of the project. Four kinds of stakeholders are important in a needs analysis project.

Users: First, a support specialist should learn who the end user is, or who the users are, if there are several. What are their job responsibilities? What computer experience do the users have? What is their business background? How long have they worked for the organization?

Manager: Second, the user probably has a manager who will be involved in any final decision to purchase a computer system or implement another solution. The support specialist should determine the following: Who will make the final decision? How knowledgeable about the application are the managers who will participate in the decision? What business and computer experience do they bring to the process? Sometimes the final decision makers lack technical expertise, and a support specialist needs to devote time to educate them so they can make an intelligent decision.

In some cases, the owner of a small company provides the management perspective. In other situations, a department manager, supervisor, or project leader may provide the management perspective that is important input to an assessment project. Experienced support analysts know that one of the biggest mistakes they can make in a needs assessment project is to ignore the management perspective.

Support Specialist: Third, the support specialist him- or herself who coordinates and conducts the needs analysis project is a key participant in the process. It is just as important for analysts to clarify their own role in the needs assessment process as it is to understand the roles of other participants. Is their role to assist existing staff with the needs analysis, to perform the analysis and describe the pros and cons of various alternatives, to make a recommendation, or to make the final decision? What time and resources has the company allocated to the project, and how do these affect their work?

Information systems or technical support staff: Finally, if an organization has an existing information systems or technical support staff, they may be important participants in a needs assessment project. These staff members may ultimately be responsible for installing, configuring, maintaining, and troubleshooting the system an analyst recommends. It can be a mistake not to consider their input.

Needs analysts who work on a project that involves several users, managers, and IS or technical support staff may want to develop a written profile that summarizes information about each participant in a project. A profile can include contact information, position title and description (if appropriate), background, primary job functions, and interests in the outcome of the project.

STEP 5: IDENTIFY SOURCES OF INFORMATION

In addition to understanding the roles of various participants in a project, a related step is to learn about sources of information that will be available during the project. Some common sources of information a support analyst should investigate are:

- Interviews with end users or managers
- Surveys or questionnaires sent to end users who will be affected
- Procedure manuals that detail how to operate the existing system
- Direct observation of the existing system
- Forms used for input into the existing system
- Reports output from the existing system
- Problem reports or help desk logs for the existing system
- Reports and recommendations from consultants or auditors who have studied the existing system

This list seems like a lot of information to consider. Obviously the amount of time analysts spend on various information resources depends on the size of the project, its budget, and timelines. Not all information resources are equally useful. Analysts often use this checklist of resources to help them gather information about the system they have been asked to analyze.

STEP 6: DEVELOP AN UNDERSTANDING OF THE EXISTING SYSTEM

During the investigation phase, a support analyst must learn as much as possible about the existing system, whether it is manual or computer-based. In this step, the analyst collects and examines important papers (examples of forms, reports, and documentation), interviews key participants (end users, managers, and technical support staff), observes the operation of the existing system, and develops a clear understanding of what the existing system does and how it works.

If the project is large, analysts should organize the information they collect so they can easily locate what they need. Analysts often use a project notebook or a set of file folders to keep records of various forms, reports, and interviews. One way to organize information is according to the steps in the analysis process described in this chapter. Some analysts organize project information by grouping it according to the input, processing, storage, and output functions.

The goal or outcome of this step is to build a model that describes the existing system. The **model** is a plan that represents the current system. It can be in narrative form or in the form of a diagram, such as a flowchart. The analyst can also create a model using analytic and planning tools, such as software designed especially for systems analysts. After constructing the model, the analyst can show it to other project participants to make sure it accurately represents the system. Sharing a model with users, managers, and other staff often uncovers misunderstandings about the capabilities or features of the existing system.

There are three key questions a support specialist needs to ask at the end of this step:

1. Do I understand the existing system well enough to explain how it operates to other participants?

2. Do I understand the features of the existing system that users like?

3. Do I understand what users think is wrong with the existing system?

Without an understanding of each of these aspects of the existing system, an analyst is not yet prepared to consider alternatives to replace or repair it.

STEP 7: INVESTIGATE ALTERNATIVES TO THE EXISTING SYSTEM

In previous steps in the analysis process, the analyst's goal has been to understand as much as possible about the existing system: its purpose, features, users, advantages, disadvantages, problems, and other important characteristics. In this step, the analyst now tries to resolve the problems with the present system.

During this step, a support specialist considers several alternatives:

Changes. The existing system may continue to meet the needs of the organization if changes are made to it. For example, the configuration of a software package may be the cause of low user productivity and dissatisfaction with a system. If the software is reinstalled or reconfigured, the software may continue to meet the company's needs. Another common problem is that users may require additional training to use the features of a system effectively.

Upgrades. The company may need to upgrade hardware or software components to resolve the documented problems. Upgrades may improve processing speed, storage capacity, compatibility, or offer new features that address identified problems.

New hardware. New hardware may be necessary to address capacity constraints, run software efficiently, or operate new software with features that solve user problems.

New software. New software may be necessary to address issues analysts identified in the needs assessment project. Software alternatives include packaged, off-the-shelf software or custom-developed software that can be designed to meet specific, and perhaps unique, user requirements. An alternative solution might be a new software package that can be modified to meet specific user requirements.

When developing options, analysts often investigate what users who perform similar tasks in other organizations use. Before they recommend replacing an entire system to meet a user's needs, analysts should investigate the successful options others use in similar situations. Solutions others have found may not solve the problems an analyst has identified, but it is better to ask than to risk spending resources to arrive at an already known solution.

Trade magazines targeted at a specific industry are a good source of ideas and products that address specific business needs. Articles in trade magazines often report on successful computer systems in similar organizations. Some trade magazines publish articles that evaluate and compare technology options. Finally, advertisements in trade periodicals often identify vendors who supply hardware and software products aimed at a specialized market niche. The Internet is yet another resource for locating products and solutions for particular businesses. For example, a support specialist looking for software tailored to a video rental store or a veterinarian clinic could find leads with a search engine on the World Wide Web. See the examples of industry-specific software shown in Figure 4-2.

STEP 8: DEVELOP A MODEL OF THE PROPOSED SYSTEM

Once they have completed the preparation and investigation phases, analysts begin the decision phase. With a clear description of the problem, an understanding of the current system, and a list of possible alternatives to the present system, analysts can then develop a model of the proposed new system to recommend to users and management.

The model a user support analyst builds often includes a narrative description of the proposed system and one or more graphic aids to help users and managers understand the model. The narrative should include a description of the alternatives the analyst considered, as well as the pros and cons of each alternative. The model should answer the question, "Why is the proposed solution an improvement over the present system and the best of the available alternatives?"

The decision on which of the various alternatives to recommend may be obvious. There may be only one feasible solution, or one solution may stand out from among the others as superior. Where the solution is not obvious, or where it is a legal requirement, an analyst may do a cost-benefit analysis of several options to help chose from among the alternatives. A **cost-benefit analysis** is a balance sheet (a sheet of paper divided into two columns) with the costs of a proposed system on one side and the benefits on the other. Later in this chapter, you will look more closely at the factors to consider in a cost-benefit analysis.

Experienced support analysts recognize that a cost-benefit analysis is not an exact science. For such an analysis to be most useful, it is important to compare alternatives in the same general category and with the same features. For most small projects, a detailed cost-benefit analysis is not necessary, but even an informal cost-benefit analysis can increase the likelihood that the analyst has considered the significant advantages and disadvantages of each alternative.

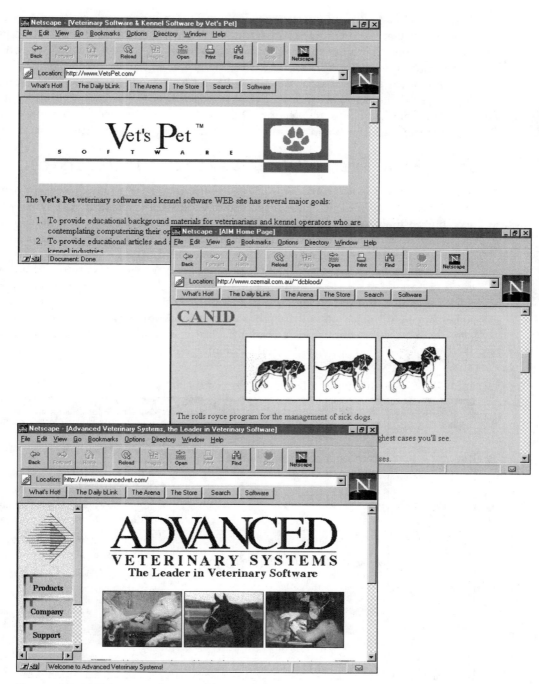

Figure 4-2   Web pages for veterinary software

When a needs assessment project results in a decision to purchase a new computer system, it is important that the user's needs drive the specifications for the new system. End users frequently consider hardware to be the most crucial component of a system. They often focus on the hardware specifications to the exclusion of more important components. What can be more important than hardware? When a user's needs determine the specifications, it is more important to consider applications software solutions first. The software requirements should then determine the hardware selection. Only when software is specified for an already existing hardware platform should the software selection depend on the hardware configuration.

STEP 9: MAKE A BUILD-VERSUS-BUY DECISION

A significant decision for many companies and organizations is whether to build a new system or purchase one off the shelf, known as a **build-versus-buy decision**. The build-versus-buy decision can apply to hardware, software, and even complete systems. For example, many organizations have employees who have the skills to assemble a PC from components. Whether it is cost-effective to do so and who maintains an assembled system are important issues. In most cases, however, the build-versus-buy decision applies primarily to software. Although many needs assessments result in a decision to purchase off-the-shelf software, custom-developed software can have advantages because it is designed to suit the user's exact needs. For other companies, buying turnkey solutions are more appropriate. A **turnkey system** includes hardware, software, and support from a single vendor. Table 4-1 summarizes some of the advantages and disadvantages of building versus buying a system.

Table 4-1   Advantages and Disadvantages of Building versus Buying a System

	Building a New System	Buying an Off-the-Shelf System
Advantages	▪ System can be designed to meet special needs ▪ System may provide strategic advantages over competition	▪ Lower cost due to larger market ▪ Quickly becomes operational ▪ Better documentation ▪ Standard user interface ▪ Fewer bugs due to more exhaustive testing
Disadvantages	▪ Higher development costs ▪ Longer timelines to develop and get operational ▪ Software bugs more likely in custom-developed software ▪ Diverts programming resources from other projects ▪ Higher maintenance costs	▪ Fewer opportunities to customize to meet special needs ▪ One-size-fits-all approach to capabilities and features ▪ Upgrades may not contain needed features

Developing a complete custom system may be prohibitively expensive for many companies, especially those that do not have an in-house programming staff. And even for organizations with staff members who have programming expertise, the cost of custom software development generally outweighs the benefits when there are reasonable preprogrammed (off-the-shelf) alternatives.

Each needs assessment project is a unique situation, meaning that the steps in this chapter need to be tailored to the specific situation. In some instances, budget constraints may mean only a few options are possible. In other situations, political issues, such as a long-term relationship with a vendor, may outweigh other factors and make a cost–benefit analysis of little use.

4

Do you know where your railroad cars are?

Freight Services Incorporated (FSI) is headquartered in Oregon, but it serves companies nationwide that use railroad freight cars to ship several kinds of raw materials and commodities. FSI provides railcar management services to companies that mine or manufacture cement, coal, rock, gypsum, petroleum, and other commercial and industrial products.

Among other services, FSI manages fleets of rail freight cars that travel from where products are mined or manufactured to where they are distributed and used. FSI's fleet management services rely on its ability to provide customers with accurate, up-to-date reports on where railcars are located as well as their current status: are railcars moving from shipper to consumer on time, are they sidetracked or delayed, are they in need of repair? When a railcar shipment is delayed, the cost to suppliers and consumers can be significant if, for example, a highway project is delayed because it is out of cement. The location of railcars is information that has an economic value to FSI and its clients.

The computer system at FSI uses a modem communications program to call each of the major national railroads and download data about the current location of each railcar under FSI management. The system then uses a custom-written BASIC program to sort and organize the data on railcar locations and print reports that are then faxed to FSI clients in several states.

By 1996 the system FSI had relied on during the early 1990s had two significant problems: 1) it was not as reliable as FSI needed to provide its clients with the car location information they needed, and 2) the existing system took too many hours of valuable FSI staff time to operate, which impacted FSI employee productivity.

FSI hired a consultant to help analyze and assess its needs and advise it about ways to improve the reliability and employee productivity of its railcar tracing system. The consultant interviewed Fred and Susan Hamlin, president and treasurer of Freight Services, respectively; and Carol Franson, the FSI employee who operated the existing railcar tracing computer system. During the interview with the key stakeholders, the following points were covered:

- The developer of the original car tracing system was no longer available to maintain, upgrade, or support it.

- The system had previously operated on one computer. As FSI's business grew, however, software limitations required the use of a second system for car tracing.

- The system required an excessive amount of data entry by Carol Franson to prepare and manage the lists of cars to trace.

- The modem communications program frequently downloaded no data or data that contained invalid characters.

- The report preparation software had a variety of problems, including creating reports with missing or duplicate cars or inaccurate car location data.

- The manual on how to operate the system was poorly organized and hard to use; other FSI staff had difficulty operating the system without Carol Franson's help.

As a result of these factors, FSI staff routinely spent extra evening and weekend hours to work around the problems with the computer system in order to prepare accurate reports their customers needed.

FSI's consultant analyzed the car tracing problems from four critical perspectives:

1. Communications software

2. Report preparation software

3. Staff productivity

4. Documentation and staff training

The consultant considered several options that might solve the problems FSI described.

- **Communications software** One option was to upgrade the existing communications software to a newer version to improve its reliability. A second option was to switch to a different communications program. The staff at FSI also knew about a communications program supplied by one of the national railroads that was specifically designed for use in railcar tracing.

■ **Report preparation software** The consultant considered whether the existing BASIC report preparation program could be modified to increase its reliability, its capacity to handle more data, and to add new features FSI needed. The consultant also investigated whether there were commercial report writer programs available at a reasonable cost that had the flexibility to output a report in the format needed by FSI and its clients. Another option was to design and write a new program to replace the existing BASIC program.

■ **Staff productivity** A factor that affected any decision about the software was the need to address FSI staff productivity. Whichever software options were selected, the amount of data entry required to manage the lists of railcars had to be reduced.

■ **Documentation and staff training** The new system needed user documentation on its operation that other FSI staff members could use when Carol Franson was not available. Several staff said they would like to have online documentation in addition to a printed manual.

FSI's consultant analyzed and assessed each of the software options and weighed the costs and advantages and disadvantages of each. Some options turned into dead ends. For example, modifications to the BASIC report writing program were not possible because FSI did not have access to the source code for the program. Other options were considered and discarded. For example, none of the report writer software investigated had the flexibility necessary to produce the special report format FSI needed. However, tests showed that the modem communications program provided by the national railroad could be a useful tool to download car location information.

After researching each option and additional discussion with the FSI owners and staff, the consultant prepared and presented the results of the needs assessment and a recommendation to address the problems. The consultant proposed a system that uses: 1) the modem communications software provided by the national railroad, 2) a custom-developed report preparation program written in FoxPro (see the sample report on the next page), 3) several scripted command language files to make the system user-friendly and provide online help, and 4) a user manual and training so that other FSI staff can back up Carol Franson when she is out of the office or needs to work on other projects. The needs analysis solution proposed combined some packaged software (the buy option) and some custom-developed software (the build option).

The system FSI's consultant proposed was developed and is operational today. President Fred Hamlin thinks FSI's next big railcar tracing challenge is just down the tracks, however. He sees the Internet as an increasingly important tool to locate railcars and deliver information on their whereabouts to FSI and its clients.

```
Freight Services, Inc.
Eugene, OR

FROM:   Carol Franson

DATE:   05-17-1998

S U M M A R Y:     FSIX cars
COUNT  L/E           STATUS        LOCATION   DESTINATION
=====  ======  ====================  ========   ===========
   1   load    arrived destination   BARSTOW    BARSTOW   CA

   1   load    arrived intermediate  CASGRANDE  CASGRANDE AZ
   1   load    spotted               CASGRANDE  CASGRANDE AZ
   1   load    departed              EAGPASS    CASGRANDE AZ
   1   load    pulled from industry  EAGPASS    CASGRANDE AZ
   2   loads   arrived intermediate  TUCSON     CASGRANDE AZ

   1   load    arrived intermediate  COFFEYVIL  KECHI     KS

   1   load    departed              WAYCROSS   KINGSLAND GA

   4   loads   spotted               MURRAY     MURRAY    UT
   1   load    departed              ROPER      MURRAY    UT

   1   load    constructive placemt  NEWNAN     NEWNAN    GA

   1   empty   spotted               OROGRANDE  BARSTOW   CA

   3   empty   junction delivered    EAGPASS    EAGPASS   TX
   2   empty   arrived intermediate  HOUSTON    EAGPASS   TX

   1   empty   spotted               MICHOUD    MICHOUD   LA
   3   empty   released              NEWNAN     MICHOUD   LA

   3   empty   junction delivered    BARSTOW    OROGRANDE CA
   2   empty   departed              BARSTOW    OROGRANDE CA
   3   empty   arrived intermediate  OFFICER    OROGRANDE CA

   1   empty   arrived intermediate  KANCITY    PRYOR     OK
   1   empty   arrived intermediate  OKLCITY    PRYOR     OK
   1   empty   spotted               PRYOR      PRYOR     OK
-----
 36 cars reported.

            E N D   O F   R E P O R T
```

NEEDS ANALYSIS AND ASSESSMENT TOOLS

In the needs analysis steps described in the previous section, you learned about several tools that analysts often use as aids in the assessment process. The latter part of this chapter describes some of these tools in more detail. The tools you will learn about are summarized in Figure 4-3.

- Project charter
- Cost-benefit analysis
- Data collection instruments
- Charts and diagrams
- Prototyping software
- Other tools

Figure 4-3   Needs assessment tools

Some of these tools are relatively easy for an analyst to write or create, whereas others require more extensive work and, in some cases, special software. An analyst can create some of these tools independently. Other tools require the cooperation of users, managers, and support staff, as well as an extended timeline.

PROJECT CHARTER

In needs analysis and assessment projects that involve more than a few participants, it is important that all stakeholders understand some basic information about the project. One way to ensure a common understanding is to develop a project charter. A **project charter** is a short narrative that answers basic questions such as:

1. What are the objectives of the project? What will be achieved if this project is successful?

2. What is the scope of the project? What is included in the project and, sometimes more important, what is excluded?

3. What methods will be used to achieve the result? What tools and resources will be used?

4. Who are the key project participants? What are their roles?

5. What are the project deliverables? (A **deliverable** is the end result of an analysis project, such as a recommendation to purchase, modify, upgrade, or build a system.)

6. What are the steps in the assessment project?

7. What is the project timeline? What are significant project milestones that indicate whether the project is ahead of or behind schedule?

8. How will the project's success be measured?

The form shown in Figure 4-4 is an example of a project charter that you can use or modify.

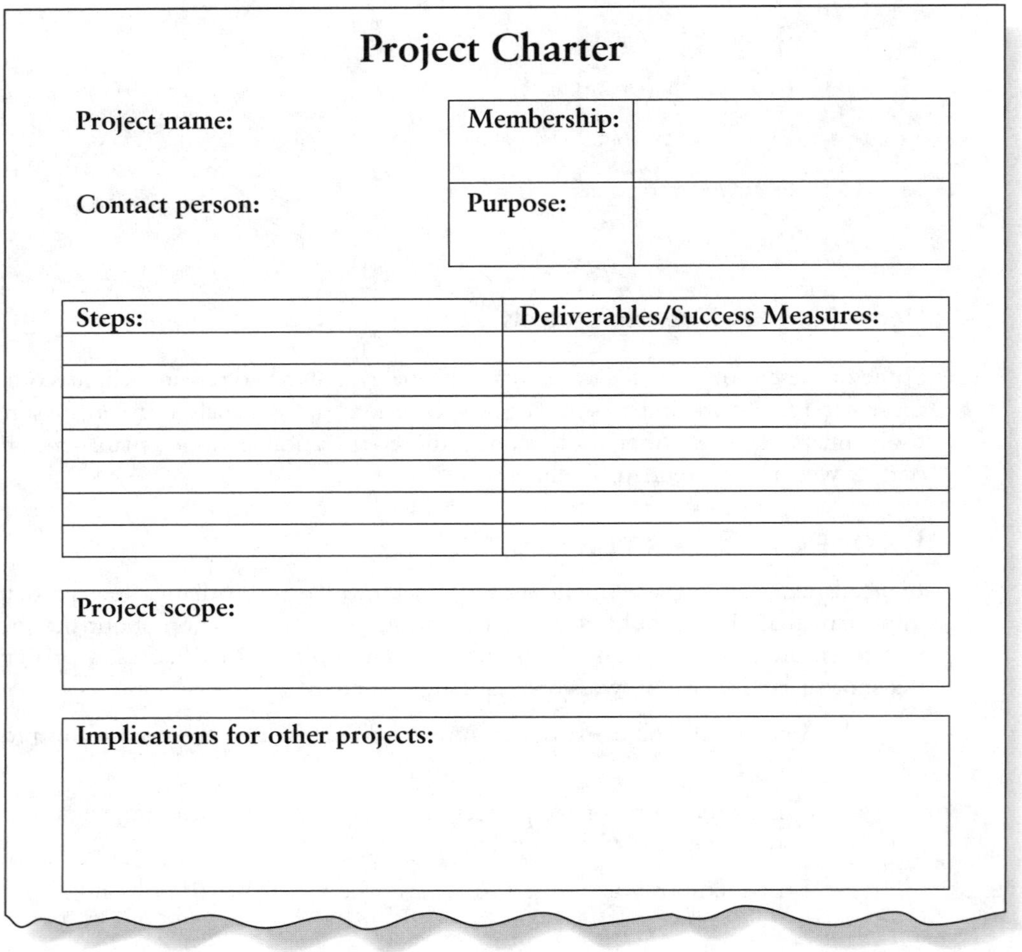

Project Charter

Project name:	Membership:	
Contact person:	Purpose:	

Steps:	Deliverables/Success Measures:

Project scope:

Implications for other projects:

Figure 4-4   Project charter

Note that the project charter is only about a page long. It should not be a detailed document but instead a high-level overview of the project. Some organizations use a project request form (more like a work order) instead of a charter, but its contents are similar to a charter, and it serves a similar purpose.

COST-BENEFIT ANALYSIS

As you learned earlier in this chapter, a cost-benefit analysis is a tool to help identify the costs and the corresponding benefits of a proposed solution. A cost-benefit analysis is often in the form of a side-by-side comparison, or balance sheet, that lists costs on one side of the sheet and benefits on the other.

Table 4-2 shows examples of items that might appear in a cost-benefit balance sheet. It shows that costs can be categorized as acquisition costs (whether built or purchased) and operating costs (ongoing costs). Benefits can be reduced expenses, increased revenue opportunities, or intangible benefits.

Table 4-2   Cost-Benefit Balance Sheet

Costs of Alternative	Benefits of Alternative
Acquisition costs	**Reduced expenses**
■ Purchase computer equipment	■ Less expensive hardware and software
■ Purchase software packages or licenses	■ Fewer personnel required to operate system
■ Software development costs (programming)	■ Lower manufacturing or inventory costs
■ Time to implement alternative	■ More efficient use of staff time or equipment
	■ Faster response to customer needs
Operating costs	**Increased revenue opportunities**
■ Lease or rental equipment	■ New products or services to customers
■ Personnel (salaries and benefits)	■ Expanded markets
■ Computer supplies	■ Increased business volume
■ Hardware and software maintenance	■ Higher prices due to better quality
	Intangible benefits
	■ Improved image of company
	■ Improved service to customers
	■ System easier to learn and use
	■ Higher employee morale

The goal of a cost-benefit analysis is to weigh the benefits of each alternative against the costs of each alternative. However, cost-benefit analyses are not always easy to do because some of a project's benefits might be difficult to quantify. **Intangible benefits**, benefits that don't lend themselves to direct measurement, are particularly difficult to calculate. For example, what is the dollar value of "improved image of company"? Analysts should always try to estimate intangible benefits of various alternatives. However, experienced support analysts recognize that if most of the benefits of an alternative are intangible, and if there are few quantifiable benefits that reduce expenses, improve productivity, or increase revenue, then they should seriously consider other alternatives.

DATA COLLECTION INSTRUMENTS

Several steps in the needs analysis process depend on an analyst's ability to collect relevant information. When analysts gather information, they often use the sources summarized in Figure 4-5.

- Input forms
- Output forms
- Procedure documentation
- Interviews with users
- User questionnaires
- Direct observation

Figure 4-5   Data collection instruments

The sections that follow contain a brief overview of each data collection instrument.

Input forms. The purpose of an **input form** is to collect information about a business transaction. Information on the input form is then entered into a business system. These forms are often called **source documents**. For example, a copy shop might use a form like the sample in Figure 4-6 to collect information about a copy order for a customer.

The form in Figure 4-6 contains spaces for the basic order information the copy shop collects manually. If a needs assessment project for the copy shop includes automating the order form, a needs analyst should understand how employees use the form. Who fills out the form and when? Does the form serve as a receipt for the customer? Is the customer's address or phone number ever included? Are there problems with the form? For example, are there types of orders for which it doesn't work very well?

Output forms. Output forms contain the results of a business transaction. Examples include a sales receipt from a grocery store or restaurant, a paycheck stub, and a report card at the end of a school term. In this case, once a copy shop employee fills in the input form from Figure 4-6, it becomes an output form; the information on it might get processed manually or in a computer system and printed on a customer receipt.

ORDER   Date _____

🖨 **the print works**
1473 Main St.
Stamford, CT 06902
PHONE 555-2697
FAX 555-2698

Sold to _____

Paid By   ☐ Cash   ☐ Check #_____

FAX Send _____ pgs/Receive _____ pgs	
Photocopies	
Taken By: **TOTAL**	

Figure 4-6   Sample input form for a copy shop

Procedure documentation. Written instructions about how to perform a business trans-action or handle a routine business procedure are called **procedure documentation**. In the copy shop example, procedure documentation would describe how to fill out the order entry form for various kinds of copy orders, what to do with the form after it is filled out, or where to file the form when the transaction is completed. Procedure documentation is often used to train new employees or to answer questions about processing problems that arise infrequently.

Good procedure documentation is rare, because procedures are often communicated verbally instead of in writing. Procedures change frequently, and the documentation that describes them may not get updated. However, even out-of-date or handwritten procedure documentation can be a useful tool to help an analyst collect information about transactions and how they are processed.

Interviews and questionnaires. Analysts use interviews and questionnaires to collect relevant information from users about the work they do and how an existing or proposed computer system might affect their work. The advantage of face-to-face interviews is that the interviewer can probe, where appropriate, to learn the details of issues that are of special interest. The ability to probe is especially useful because it is often difficult to anticipate every possible question one might like to ask on a printed questionnaire. However, interviews take more of an analyst's time than a questionnaire, and when analysts need information from many users, they often use a questionnaire to save time. When there are many users, a combination of face-to-face interviews for a few users and a questionnaire for the remainder is often a good compromise.

Interviews and questionnaires need to be structured to extract the appropriate information. There are two kinds of questions that an analyst can ask in either an interview or a questionnaire format: open-ended and forced-choice. In an **open-ended question**, the answer can be any response the respondent thinks is appropriate. For example, to the question "How many copying orders do you process in a typical day?", the answer might be anywhere from 5 or 10 to 100 or more, and each copy shop employee might respond with a different number. Employees could respond with a range.

In a **forced-choice question**, a respondent must choose from among several predetermined options. A forced-choice version designed to obtain the same information as the previous example might be:

How many copying orders do you process in a typical day?

❏ none   ❏ 1-5   ❏ 6-10   ❏ 11-15   ❏ more than 15

Both open-ended and forced-choice questions are appropriate in various situations. An analyst needs to consider at least three issues when she or he designs a question. First, what information do I want to get? Second, how am I going to analyze the information when I get it? Third, how can the question be asked so it makes sense to users and helps them respond accurately?

Both the open-ended and forced-choice question examples elicit information on the number of orders processed. However, the open-ended question may require the analyst to take the additional step of grouping (or coding) the responses into meaningful categories for later analysis.

Forced-choice responses are usually easier to tabulate. The analyst would simply count the number of responses in each category. However, some respondents do not like to be forced to fit their answer into fixed response categories. Additionally, forced-choice answer categories must reflect each user's experiences, or the choices are meaningless. For example, consider the following question:

How many hours per day do you spend on e-mail messages?

❏ none   ❏ 1 hour   ❏ 2 hours   ❏ 3 hours   ❏ more than 3 hours

Which box do respondents check if they spend 1.5 hours per day on e-mail messages? This question might be improved if the response categories used ranges to accommodate partial hours.

How many hours per day do you spend on e-mail messages?

❏ less than 1 hour   ❏ 1-2 hours   ❏ 2-3 hours   ❏ more than 3 hours

Although the ranges handle responses of fractional hours, which box can a user who spends exactly 2 hours check? Construction of questionnaire items is challenging and takes practice.

Open-ended responses have the advantage that they do not force a respondent to pick a category; however, they often take longer to complete because a respondent must write out the answer, rather than check a box. Also, open-ended responses are often more difficult to tabulate than forced-choice responses.

Questionnaires and interviews are very useful tools to acquire information from users. However, they require care to design so that they extract information that is clear, unambiguous, and so that they elicit the information the analyst needs. Most textbooks on systems analysis and design contain a chapter on interview and questionnaire methods that provides suggestions on and examples for interview and questionnaire design.

To ensure that they have high-quality questions, needs analysts who participate in a project with many users—where more formal interviews or questionnaires are used—often ask other analysts to help with question design. Questions designed by a team are often better than those written by one analyst. Another strategy to produce better questions is to field-test them on a small group of respondents who can give feedback on which questions were difficult to answer.

Direct observation. Needs analysts can often gain critical insight into user needs by simply watching users work. Direct observation can be a powerful method of data collection in situations where questionnaires, interviews, procedure documentation, and other forms of data collection aren't possible.

One key to successful direct observation is to plan sufficient time with a user for the activity. It is useful to take notes on what the users do, when they do it (the sequence of tasks), what tools and strategies they use, with whom they interact, and where they store information.

Data collection instruments help analysts collect useful, relevant information about the existing system that they can use to evaluate not only how the system functions but also its strengths and weaknesses.

CHARTS AND DIAGRAMS

A chart or diagram can show the flow of information in an organization, relationships between employees, or the parts of an information processing system. Or it can show a system, part of a system, or a work flow. Charts and diagrams are often easier for users to read and understand than lengthy narratives written in technical language.

Analysts create charts and diagrams either manually or with a variety of graphic design tools. Some of these tools are highly specialized and take considerable training; books on systems analysis describe these tools in detail. Other graphic design tools are more accessible and allow analysts with a minimum of experience to create charts and diagrams. Analysts can use relatively simple tools to create two common types of charts: flowcharts and I-P-O charts.

Flowcharts. A **flowchart** is a schematic drawing that uses symbols to represent the parts of a system. Figure 4-7 shows a flowchart of the process in a computer repair shop.

In a flowchart, rectangular boxes might represent departments in a company, nodes on a network, or processing steps an employee performs. Diamond-shaped symbols often represent decision points or questions that need to be answered. Lines connect various symbols in a flowchart to illustrate how the parts in the diagram are related or the sequence of processing steps.

I-P-O charts. Most manual procedures or computer processing tasks can be described as some combination of Input, Processing, and Output steps. An **I-P-O chart** represents the Input, Processing and Output steps required to perform a task. An I-P-O chart answers three fundamental questions about a procedure that a user or computer performs:

- **Input**: Where do I get the information with which to work?

- **Processing**: What do I do to transform the information?

- **Output**: What do I do with the information when I'm done?

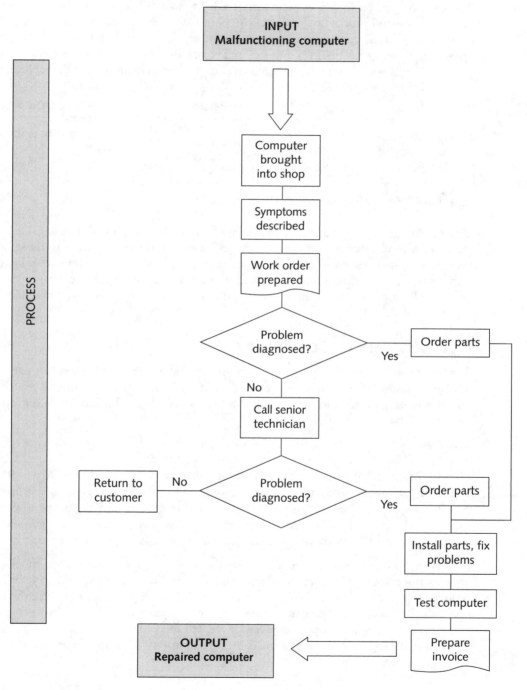

Figure 4-7   Flowchart showing the PC repair process

The example in Figure 4–8 shows a simple I-P-O chart that describes a procedure in a brokerage firm to prepare a stock portfolio report for a client. A related chart is an H-I-P-O chart, which can be used to describe more complex processes. The *H* in H-I-P-O stands for <u>H</u>ierarchy. It represents the idea that a complex task may be made up of a hierarchy of input, processing, and output steps, where each level in the hierarchy shows a different level of detail.

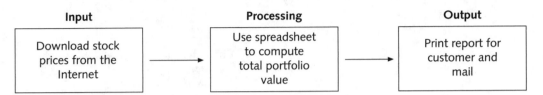

Figure 4-8   Example of an I-P-O chart

Analysts use a variety of analytic and design tools as aids in a needs analysis. Dataflow diagrams, entity-relationship diagrams, and CASE tools are used in addition to those previously mentioned. However, these more complex tools are probably of greater use to systems analysts who design custom computer applications that will be developed by programmers. A textbook for a course on systems analysis and design describes these and other tools in considerable detail.

PROTOTYPING SOFTWARE

A **prototype** is a working model a support analyst builds to let users evaluate how the finished product of an analysis project will actually work. The purpose of a prototype is to provide an easy, quick, low-cost way for a user to view the characteristics the operational system will have when it is built.

When an application design project involves software development, prototyping tools can be used to build a working model. For example, programming and database languages such as Microsoft Access, Microsoft Excel, FoxPro, and dBASE can be used to build a working prototype of the menus, data input screens, processing steps, output forms and reports, and the user interface for a system. Figure 4-9 shows a data entry form for a database of event sponsors created with Visual Basic for Applications in Microsoft Excel. Once a model is built, users can try out the prototype and evaluate whether or not it meets their needs.

Prototyping has become an increasingly popular tool for support analysts. It is much faster and less expensive to develop a prototype in a database language than to write a program in a procedural language such as C, COBOL, or Fortran. For small processing systems, the prototype may actually become the production system after users are satisfied it meets their needs. For larger processing systems, once users have accepted the prototype, it is usually translated into a procedural programming language. Although prototype systems can give users a realistic preview of how a new system might operate, prototypes usually operate slowly or have limited capacity for data storage. These limitations can be reduced or eliminated when a programmer converts a working prototype into a production system written in a procedural programming language.

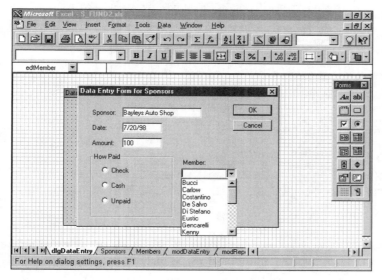

Figure 4-9   Data entry form for a database of event sponsors

OTHER NEEDS ASSESSMENT TOOLS

Two tools you learned about in Chapter 3 are also useful to support analysts: benchmarks and weighted point comparisons. These are especially useful when an analyst needs a decision aid to compare two or more products or approaches to solving a user problem.

For larger scale analysis projects, a **project management software** package such as Microsoft Project can help project leaders organize the steps in a large project, set priorities, establish and monitor project costs, and schedule staff and activities. Figure 4-10 is a Microsoft Project screen showing the steps involved in a project and how the relationship of the steps affects the staff, time, and resources needed to complete the project.

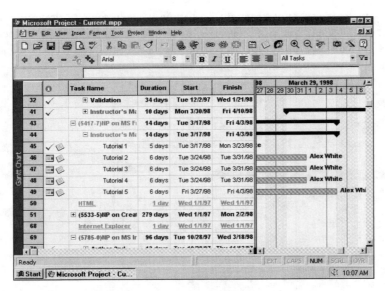

Figure 4-10   A Microsoft Project schedule

Project management software is most appropriate for large-scale needs assessment and development projects that will involve a number of users, analysts, and steps.

The needs analysis tools described in this chapter are among those that support analysts find useful when they undertake needs assessment projects. However, the tools described here just scratch the surface of the resources and tools available. New tools, especially automated ones, become available every year.

Not every needs assessment requires all the steps and the use of every resource or tool described in this chapter. In an actual project, a support analyst would choose from among the approaches described here to make the resources fit the task. User support analysts who spend a significant amount of time on user needs assessment may benefit from a course on systems analysis and design such as those offered in many two- and four-year schools. The most important fact to remember about user needs analysis and assessment is that it is a process, and the process and tools an analyst chooses for one particular situation will be different from the process and tools for another situation.

CHAPTER SUMMARY

- User support specialists who undertake a needs assessment for end users follow a sequence of steps designed to obtain relevant information and help the user make an informed decision. In the needs assessment process, analysts may use one or more tools and information resources to aid their task.

- Typical steps in a user needs assessment include:

Preparation

Before an actual analysis and assessment begins, the analyst should:

1. Understand the business goals.

2. Understand the decision criteria and constraints.

3. Define the problem clearly.

4. Identify the roles of participants.

5. Identify sources of information.

Investigation

In the investigation phase, the analyst examines the current system and evaluates possible choices for a new one.

1. Develop an understanding of the existing system.

2. Investigate alternatives to the existing system.

Decision

In the decision phase, the analyst creates a model of what the proposed system will look like and decides how the new system will be obtained.

1. Develop a model of the proposed system.

2. Make a build-versus-buy decision.

- Several tools are available to user support analysts who work on needs assessment projects. Some of the popular tools include a cost-benefit analysis to weigh the costs of an alternative against its payoffs; several data collection instruments (including input and output forms, procedure documentation, interview and questionnaires, and direct observation); graphic design tools to draw flowcharts, I-P-O charts, and related schematic representations of systems; and prototyping tools to model software systems.

Key Terms

- **build-versus-buy decision** — The decision an organization makes about whether to build a new system itself or purchase one off the shelf; can apply to hardware, software, or complete systems, but it is most often applied to software.

- **cost-benefit analysis** — A comparison between the expenses a project will incur and the payoffs to the organization; organizations are reluctant to spend resources on projects where the costs outweigh the benefits.

- **decision phase** — The third phase of a user needs analysis and assessment project, in which analysts develop a model of the proposed system and decide whether to build or buy it.

- **deliverable** — The end results of a needs analysis project; a deliverable can be an assessment report, a recommendation; or a decision to build, buy, or upgrade a system.

- **feasibility** — An investigation into the economic, operational, technical, and timeline constraints during a user needs analysis and assessment process.

- **flowchart** — A schematic drawing that uses symbols to represent the parts of a system or the steps in a procedure.

- **forced-choice question** — A question on a questionnaire or in an interview with predetermined response categories; on a test, a multiple-choice question is forced-choice.

- **input form** — A paper document or display screen image used to collect information about a business transaction. Also called a source document.

- **intangible benefits** — An expected result from a computer acquisition that is difficult to quantify; although increased user productivity may be measurable (tangible), increased employee morale is intangible.

- **investigation phase** — The second phase of a user needs analysis and assessment project, in which analysts try to understand the present system and alternatives to it.

- **I-P-O chart** — A diagram that represents the Input, Processing, and Output steps.

- **model** — A narrative or graphic plan that approximates an aspect of a business (such as work flow) or a computer system component.

- **open-ended question** — A question on a questionnaire or in an interview where respondents use their own words, instead of predetermined responses, to answer a question.

- **output form** — A document that contains the results of a business process.

- **preparation phase** — The first phase of a user needs analysis and assessment project, in which analysts try to understand the business goals, decision criteria, and constraints; they define the problem, identify the roles of stakeholders, and identify sources of information.

- **procedure documentation** — Written instructions about how to perform a business transaction or handle a routine business procedure.

- **project charter** — A short narrative statement that describes the objectives, scope, methods, participants, deliverables, and timeline for a needs assessment project.

- **project management software** — An applications software tool to help project leaders organize the tasks in a project, set priorities, monitor project costs, and schedule activities.

- **prototype** — A model a support analyst builds to help users experience and assess the finished product; a prototype contains enough of a representation of an actual system that users can operate the model to evaluate its features.

- **source document** — Any form used to collect information about a business transaction for input into a business or computer system; examples include payroll timecards, a problem log, a membership application, and an expense account record.

- **stakeholders** — The participants in a user needs analysis and assessment project who might gain or lose from its success or failure; includes end users, managers, technical support, and the needs assessment analyst.

- **turnkey system** — A packaged solution that provides hardware, software, and support from a single vendor.

REVIEW QUESTIONS

1. Describe the major steps a user support specialist follows to analyze and assess an end user's needs for a computer system.

2. What are the differences between a formal and an informal needs assessment?

3. What should a support analyst learn about the mission, goals, and objectives of a business during a computer needs assessment?

4. Why is it important for a support specialist to learn about who will make the final decision on a project and what decision criteria they will use?

5. If a new system is feasible, what tests must it pass?

6. What is wrong with this statement: The end user completely understands the problem a support specialist is asked to investigate.

7. Describe the four important stakeholders in the needs assessment process and the role of each one.

8. Describe several sources of information available to a support analyst investigating a user's computer needs.

9. List three key questions support specialists should be able to answer if they understand an existing system that they are considering for replacement.

10. Explain several common alternatives to address problems identified with an existing system that an analyst should consider.

11. What is a model of a system? What does a model look like?

12. What are the primary advantages and disadvantages of the build option versus the buy option in an acquisition decision?

13. List several tools support specialists can use during the needs assessment process.

14. What is the purpose of a project charter?

15. What information does a project charter contain?

16. In a cost-benefit analysis, what are some examples of costs that are often included for a computer system? What are some examples of benefits?

17. Why are benefits more difficult to measure than costs?

18. If the goal of a needs assessment project is to replace the current system, why is it important to collect information about various forms and reports that are part of the current system?

19. What is the difference between input and output forms?

20. What is procedure documentation? Why is it necessary? Why is it sometimes difficult to find?

21. Describe the advantages and disadvantages of questionnaires and interviews as methods to collect information from end users.

22. Explain the difference between an open-ended and forced-choice question. In what situations is one kind of question more effective than the other?

23. What is direct observation, and how is it useful in the needs analysis process?

24. What is the advantage of charts and diagrams over narratives in user needs assessment projects?

25. What is a prototype, and how is a prototype used as a needs assessment tool?

HANDS-ON PROJECTS

PROJECT 4-1

Think about how you would modify the steps described in this chapter if you were recommending a personal computer system to a friend for home use. Which steps would you omit? Which steps would be most important? Write a two-paragraph summary of your conclusions.

4

 PROJECT 4-2

Some systems analysts have written that the steps in a needs assessment project really should be described as:

1. Unbridled euphoria
2. Questions about the feasibility of the project
3. Growing concern about the project results
4. Unmitigated disaster
5. Search for the guilty
6. Punishment of the innocent
7. Promotion of the uninvolved

It is said that behind each piece of humor is some grain of truth. Discuss ways a support specialist can prevent the steps in a needs assessment project from turning into those described.

 PROJECT 4-3

Design an input form that could be used to record information about a computer system problem in an instructional lab or a training facility. Include spaces on the form to record information such as:

- System identification
- Date and time problem was reported
- Who reported the problem
- Description of the problem
- Who was assigned to work on the problem
- Problem resolution (how was it fixed)
- Date and time problem was fixed

 PROJECT 4-4

Study the categories included in a cost-benefit analysis in Table 4-2. Think about the purchase of a home computer system. List the cost categories you think are most important in the purchase of a PC for home use. Are the benefit categories you listed tangible or intangible benefits? Explain why.

PROJECT 4-5

If you have purchased a PC or have ever helped a friend or relative purchase one, write a project charter that describes the purchase process you followed. Use the project charter form in the book as an example or use a word processor to make a project charter form of your own.

PROJECT 4-6

Select a common sales transaction, such as a video rental or a grocery store purchase. Analyze the transaction and make a list of the items of information that are input, the processing that takes place as part of the transaction, and the resulting output. Record your analysis in the form of an I-P-O chart as shown in this chapter. Then sketch a flowchart of the transaction. Compare the information communicated in the I-P-O and flow diagrams. Which do you prefer? Explain why.

CASE PROJECTS

1. FRED'S PAINT STORE

In a Case Project for Chapter 3, you examined a decision to purchase laptop computers for the outside sales representatives of Fred's Paints. The owners were considering buying the laptops because of a specific problem the outside sales reps encountered.

Fred's sales reps currently create their orders and sales reports as they call on customers. Some prepare them manually, and a few use portable typewriters they carry for that purpose. When the orders and sales reports are completed, and if the sales reps plan to return to Fred's factory in the next two or three days, they just bring the orders and sales reports back with them. If they will be on the road for more than three days, the sales reps usually mail them to the factory. Consequently, there can be about a week lag between when the orders are taken from a customer and when Fred's staff can process the information about the order.

This lag means the sales staff, including other sales reps, do not have up-to-date information on sales volumes, commitments of inventory to customers, and changes in the popularity of various types and colors of paints. Furthermore, there is a lag between when the sales department receives information about the order and when that information is transmitted to the manufacturing division where the paint is formulated.

In addition to the time lag, the manual processing of sales orders and reports by the sales reps introduces errors. On one occasion, ten pallets of latex paint were shipped to a customer when the customer actually ordered oil-based paint. The problem was traced to an error on a handwritten sales order.

What factors would you consider in a cost-benefit analysis for the laptop computers for Fred's outside sales representatives? Describe some of the major costs Fred's Paints would encounter and some of the major benefits that might accrue to Fred's if it purchases the laptop systems. Do you think the benefits to Fred's will outweigh the costs? Write a one- to two-page analysis.

2. QUICK SPLICE VIDEO

You are a consultant for Kathleen Marsh, a recent community college graduate planning to open a video rental store in the next couple of months. Kathleen majored in small business management but also took a number of computer courses as electives in her community college degree program, including:

- Introduction to Business Information Systems
- Operating Systems
- Spreadsheets (Excel)
- Database Management (Access)
- Integrated Software (Microsoft Office)
- Introductory and Advanced Visual BASIC
- Systems Analysis
- Introduction to Computer Networks

Kathleen did well in these courses and feels very comfortable with computer technology, but she would like an independent perspective on the feasibility of a computer system for her video rental business. That's why she has asked for your advice.

Although this is her first real venture as an entrepreneur, Kathleen has considerable part-time work experience in video rental stores during high school and college.

The video rental store, Quick Splice Video, will be in a new shopping center. Kathleen chose the location because there is no major competition nearby, and there is a sizable bedroom community in the area, which is about 15 miles from the nearest large town. She has arranged to rent 1,500 square feet of space in the shopping center.

Kathleen has located a video distributor who can supply her with a start-up inventory of 3,000 to 3,500 popular videos. The distributor can also serve as a one-stop supplier for new videos as they are released to the video rental market.

Kathleen has identified her major expenses, both start-up and ongoing, which are shown in Table 4-3.

Table 4-3   Quick Splice Video's Expenses

Start-up Expenses	Ongoing Expenses
Furniture	Rent & utilities
Counters	Payroll & taxes
Video racks	New video releases
Popcorn machine	Advertising
Initial video inventory	
Computer system (?)	

Kathleen's initial thinking about a computer system is that she probably cannot afford one in her start-up budget. Instead, she had worked out a simple manual system for keeping track of videos and customer rentals. Each video would have an ID number recorded on the video case and on a card she would keep in a video card file on top of the counter. In a separate file on the counter, she would keep a card for each customer. The customer cards would be filed by telephone number, which she would use as a customer ID number. When a customer rented one or more videos, she would clip the video card(s) to the customer card, and put them together in a third file labeled *Rentals*. When the videos were returned, Kathleen would unclip the video and customer cards and return them to their respective card files. At 6 p.m. the next day, if there were cards in the rental box from the previous day, Kathleen would contact the customer and assess a late charge.

Kathleen thinks this simple manual system would work until her business volume grew and she could afford a computer system. But she wonders whether a computer system would be feasible when she opens the doors in a couple of months. She even thought she could rent a computer and write a simple program in Access or Visual BASIC for Applications or Excel to replace the manual card system. Kathleen would appreciate your advice.

1. Prepare a list of interview questions you would like to ask Kathleen that would help you make a recommendation.

2. After you have a list of potential questions to ask in an interview, compare your questions with others in your project group. Prepare one list of questions for your entire project group. Try to group the questions into categories with other, similar questions.

3. When you have completed the list of interview questions, your instructor will provide you with Kathleen's responses to several of the questions from the interview with her. Based on her responses, answer these questions:

a. If Quick Splice decides to purchase a computer system, what are the major decisions the owner will need to make?

b. Would you recommend that the owner of Quick Splice build her own software system or purchase one? Why?

c. Make a list of the software Quick Splice will need to meet the needs the owner described in the interview.

d. In order to build or buy a transaction processing program to handle rentals and returns, Quick Splice would probably need a database of videos and a database of customers. Select either the customer or video table and list the fields you think Quick Splice will need.

e. A word processor or a database language such as Access can be used as a tool to build a prototype (model) of a report. Use one of these tools to design a prototype of the video rental agreement that would be printed for customers to sign when they rent a video.

f. Given what you know of Quick Splice's business plan and needs and its financial situation, do you think a computer system for Quick Splice is feasible? Why, or why not?

3. RECOMMENDING A COMPUTER FOR AMY LEE

Amy Lee was recently hired as a personnel assistant in the Human Resources department where you work. Because you are the user support specialist, she has contacted you for some help with a computer she will use in her job in employee benefits administration. You want to make sure that she gets the computer tools she will need to be productive.

Amy says that she wants an office suite and that her boss gave her a choice of Microsoft Office 97 or Corel Office Professional 7. Because she has previous work experience with WordPerfect, which is part of the Corel suite, she would like to use it. The Corel suite includes most of the tools Amy needs, so her other software requirements are minimal. In addition to CorelPerfect, Amy needs the Windows 98 operating system. She also needs a Web browser to access the Internet, because there is an increasing amount of company information about benefits and employee compensation on the Web.

Where she needs your help is with hardware. Amy's boss said that she doesn't have much left in this year's Human Resources equipment budget for hardware. So she suggested that Amy try to find a basic starter system, but one that could be upgraded next year when there will be more equipment money available. Amy would like you to recommend a hardware configuration that would meet her immediate needs now, would be reasonably priced, and could be upgraded next year. It needs to be able to run the software Amy has selected. Whatever hardware she buys also needs to be compatible with the local area network in Human Relations. It operates from a Novell NetWare 4.1 server. The network server can provide Amy with access to one of two laser printers, so the hardware system she buys does not need to include a printer. However, Amy would like to be able to scan documents into her system, and no scanner is available on the network.

Your task is to analyze Amy's situation and recommend a hardware configuration that will meet her immediate needs. In addition, see if you can find equipment for sale in a trade magazine, advertised in a local newspaper, or on the Internet that you believe is the appropriate configuration for Amy. When you are finished, prepare a recommended list of hardware specifications (and prices, if available) that Amy could take to her boss.

INSTALLING END USER
COMPUTER SYSTEMS

After you have evaluated computer products (Chapter 3), conducted a needs assessment (Chapter 4), and perhaps even helped justify and purchase an end user system, the next step is to install the system. Installation can include hardware, peripherals, operating systems, utility software, and applications software—either packaged together or sold individually. During the installation process, you may also need to deal with some user training and site management issues. This chapter introduces training and site management, and you will also learn more about these activities in Chapters 6 and 8.

It is not unusual for new computer users to be intimidated by the system installation process. Support specialists can often set up and get a system running in a fraction of the time it would take a user to figure out the procedure and work around the pitfalls. This chapter describes some of the typical tasks of many personal and office computer installations, although every installation poses different challenges. You will learn about site preparation, as well as the tools and steps necessary to install hardware, operating systems, and applications software.

AFTER READING THIS CHAPTER AND COMPLETING THE EXERCISES YOU WILL BE ABLE TO:

- Describe the major site preparation steps for computer installations
- Perform the major tasks to prepare an installation site
- Understand the purpose and contents of a site management notebook
- List tools needed to install hardware
- Explain the steps to install hardware
- Explain the steps to install and configure an operating system
- Explain the steps to install and configure applications software packages
- Describe the wrap-up tasks that installers often perform

OVERVIEW

As you learned in Chapter 2, a user support specialist is often responsible for installing end user systems. With adequate preparation, the proper tools, and a well thought-out procedure to track important details, system installation should run smoothly and efficiently so that end users can be up and running with a minimum of interruption to their work. This chapter emphasizes the importance of installation checklists and system documentation. Whether the installation is for a single home computer, a small office system, or for hundreds of networked systems, experienced system installers know that it is easy to forget important details— whether at the time they install a system or later when the system needs to be repaired or upgraded.

The major installation steps are summarized in Figure 5-1 and discussed in detail in the sections that follow.

Site preparation

Hardware installation and configuration

Operating system installation and configuration

Applications software installation and configuration

Site management

Figure 5-1   Overview of system installation steps

User support specialists may not be involved in all the system installation steps listed in Figure 5-1. For example, they might not need to install or configure an operating system if one is pre-installed. The checklists in this chapter are generic; you should modify them to fit specific situations. In some cases, you may need to add steps; in other cases, certain steps will not directly apply to your situation.

SITE PREPARATION

Before installing a system, a support specialist often visits the location for a pre-installation inspection. The purpose of the site visit is to anticipate any problems that may arise so the installer can address them before the installation. Many installers use a written checklist to make sure that they address certain critical questions during the visit. A typical site installation checklist would contain the following:

1. What are the space requirements for the workstation?

2. Are there space constraints at the user's site?

3. What materials need to be stored near the workstation?

4. Are there ergonomic issues that the installation should address?

5. Do special ADA (Americans with Disabilities Act) or OSHA (Occupational Safety and Health Administration) issues apply to this installation?

6. Is the power supply accessible to and adequate for the system?

7. Is power conditioning required?

8. Where is the nearest telephone and/or network access?

9. Is air conditioning required?

10. Are there potential lighting problems?

11. Is there a fire suppression system installed?

An experienced installer may not need to carry an actual checklist. Observation of the site may be sufficient to determine what problems exist, if any. However, if there are many installations to perform at numerous sites, a checklist may be necessary to keep track of conditions at each location.

LOCATING SYSTEM COMPONENTS

When a user support specialist installs a computer system, he or she must determine the best location for the system unit, monitor, printer, keyboard, mouse, and other peripherals and accessories. A system that has properly located components will be easy and efficient to use, will not cause discomfort for the user, and will ensure the physical safety of the system itself. Each installation site presents unique challenges, and the installer must adapt the installation to the space and layout constraints of each site.

Ideally, a computer system should be installed in a work area where the table or desktop height is 26 to 28 inches from the floor, a comfortable keyboard height for most users. A typical office desk surface is 30 inches from the floor; a keyboard used on a regular office desk or table at this height can cause user discomfort because the angle of the wrists at the keyboard is unnatural. To prevent wrist and finger pain, make sure that when a user's hands rest on the keyboard, they extend in a relatively straight line, or slightly downward, from the forearms. If an office desk or table is the only possible keyboard location, it may be possible to shorten the desk or table legs to get the keyboard to a comfortable height. If a keyboard must be located on a standard-height office desk, it may be possible to adjust the chair height so the user's wrists are in a comfortable position. However, the solution to one problem can cause another: a chair seat that is too high can cause leg problems; a footrest may help. In some offices, users want systems installed on furniture that was never intended for computers, such as older or antique furniture or a credenza. In these cases, furniture may need to be significantly adapted to avoid ergonomic problems later. Be sure there is adequate knee room, especially if the user is tall.

As laptop computer models increase in popularity, support specialists need to be aware of special ergonomic challenges they present. Because laptops are designed to be transported from one location to another, the height of a laptop keyboard will vary according to the location. A laptop should ideally be used on a surface that is at the lower end of the 26-to-28-inch high recommended range, because the thickness of the laptop itself can add 1 to 2 inches to the keyboard height.

There should be sufficient space for the system unit near the keyboard and monitor. If a system unit is a desktop model, the table or desktop is often the most logical location for it, especially for users who frequently access the peripherals inside the system unit case (such as the floppy disk drive, removable hard drive, or CD-ROM drive). However, the **footprint** of a desktop case, which is the number of square inches (length times width) of usable space the computer case occupies, is relatively large. Mini-tower cases, which are popular because they have a smaller footprint, can be set on the work surface, on a bookshelf, or even on the floor. However, be sure that mini-tower cases located on the floor cannot be accidentally kicked or get in the way of foot traffic. For some users, frequent bending to reach a floor unit can cause back strain. Wherever possible, floppy and tape drive peripherals should be located within arm's reach of the worker in a normal working position.

Locate the monitor so the user can look straight ahead or slightly downward at it, as if reading a book held up on the desktop. The user should not have to look up at the monitor. Tilt the display screen so the user can view it with a natural head position, without neck strain. On desks that do not have much available space, or in a situation where a user wants to maximize the desk space, it may be possible to install a monitor arm that attaches to the tabletop or to the wall. A monitor arm holds the monitor 3 to 4 inches off the desktop. Some monitor arms have a storage area for the keyboard when it is not in use, which frees up additional desk space. With careful planning, it is possible to free up desk space by locating the system unit and monitor close to the desk area but not actually on it. Several vendors also manufacture furniture specially designed for computer equipment that can save desktop space.

Both system units and monitors produce heat when they operate. The vent holes in the cases of these units should not be blocked by office or bookcase walls or by shelves. Air should be able to circulate around the cases of all computer peripherals.

Many ergonomic desks have keyboard shelves built in under the work surface, and these shelves can often be added to nonergonomic desks and workstations. Keyboard shelves are often adjustable. In addition to saving desk space, adjustable keyboard shelves allow the user to position the keyboard at a comfortable height. They are especially useful where a workstation will be used by more than one user, such as a shared desk or in a computer lab or training facility.

A printer does not have to be placed on the desktop but can instead be on a printer stand or, where available, on a worktable or bookshelf. A printer should be in a convenient location where users have easy access to load paper and ribbons or cartridges and where the case can be opened to remove paper jams.

Users usually want various supplies near their computer equipment. These supplies include printer paper, mailing labels, ribbons or ink or toner cartridges, magnetic media (floppy disks, tapes, cartridges), computer manuals and books, cleaning supplies, extra cables, and other accessories. They can be stored in an office file drawer, bookcase, or closet. For some supplies, it is critical that their location avoid storage problems. For example, paper should not be stored where it can draw excessive moisture. Magnetic media should not be stored near motors, generators, or electrical or telephone equipment that can generate a magnetic field.

ERGONOMIC CONCERNS

5

As you learned in Chapter 1, ergonomics is the study of how to design computer equipment and workspaces to minimize health problems and maximize employee safety, productivity, and job satisfaction. Some large companies employ a safety engineer whose job responsibilities include office and factory floor ergonomics. In a small company, a user support specialist is often the main source of advice about ergonomic issues.

There are several common ergonomic problems that a proper computer installation can help users avoid:

Back or neck muscle pain. Pain in the back or neck muscles can have one or more sources. The user may be straining neck muscles to see a monitor that is placed too high; the chair may be too low, which also forces the user to look up to view the monitor. The chair may not be well designed for computer use. Poorly designed chairs can cut off circulation in legs or force the user to use back and neck muscles that should be relaxed. The keyboard may be too high so the user's arms are held in an unnaturally high position. It is also possible that the user, despite a correctly designed workspace, works too long without adequate breaks or without changing body position.

Solutions to back or neck muscle pain can include keyboard height adjustments, a chair with both back and seat adjustment levers, sufficient back support and adequate cushioning, and a "waterfall" seat design that takes pressure off the backs of a user's legs and promotes better circulation. Advise users that they should take "stretch" breaks at least once an hour. Frequent finger, hand, wrist, and neck stretches during breaks can be very effective to prevent and sometimes cure pain, as can isometric exercises.

Leg pain. Leg pain can result from a chair that is too high for the user's feet to touch the floor or that is improperly designed and impairs leg circulation. Leg pain can also result from a work area with too little knee room.

Solutions to leg pain include ergonomically designed office chairs with back and seat adjustment levers, sufficient back support and adequate cushioning, and a "waterfall" seat design. A footrest placed at a 15–degree angle may be necessary to support the legs and reduce strain.

Eyestrain and headaches. Eyestrain and headaches can result from screen glare. The monitor may reflect sunlight or room light, which is one of the primary causes of eyestrain. (Also see the section on Lighting Problems later in this chapter.) Users' glasses or contact lenses may not be appropriate for the distance they are sitting from the computer screen.

Solutions to eyestrain and headaches include changing the orientation of the computer or using window shades to reduce glare. The level of lighting in the computer area may need to be reduced. Antiglare screen filters are available from office and computer supply stores. Users can ensure that eyeglass prescriptions are correct and that they take breaks at least once an hour. Encourage users to look at distant objects periodically to minimize eyestrain.

Wrist and finger pain. Wrist and finger pain is usually the result of a keyboard that is too high or too low. Hand and wrist muscles and tendons should not be tense or strained at the keyboard; the arm and wrist should have support.

Solutions include placing the keyboard at the optimal 26 to 28 inches from the floor, an adjustable keyboard shelf, a keyboard wrist rest, a chair with arms, and "stretch" breaks at least once an hour.

Figure 5-2 illustrates some of the important dimensions that will ensure user comfort and avoid many of the potential ergonomic problems that can arise.

Figure 5-2   Workstation ergonomics

These ergonomic problems and possible solutions are summarized in Table 5-1.

Table 5-1   Ergonomic Problems and Solutions

Ergonomic Problem	Possible Solutions
Back or neck muscle pain or numbness	▪Replace office chair with one than can be adjusted ▪Adjust keyboard height ▪Install adjustable keyboard shelves ▪Recommend frequent breaks and exercises to reduce stress
Leg pain or numbness	▪Replace office chair ▪Place footrest on floor
Eyestrain Headaches	▪Reorient computer to reduce display screen glare ▪Adjust office lighting ▪Install display screen antiglare filter ▪Check for proper glasses and prescription ▪Recommend frequent breaks and exercises to reduce stress
Wrist and finger pain or numbness Carpal tunnel syndrome	▪Adjust keyboard height ▪Install adjustable keyboard shelf ▪Supply keyboard wrist rest ▪Recommend frequent breaks and exercises to reduce stress

Support specialists should treat ergonomic concerns seriously. Some computer users have experienced painful repetitive stress injuries that can require medical treatment and can virtually disable users for an extended period, or even require a job change.

POWER REQUIREMENTS

Most small computer systems do not require special electrical power. They plug into standard three-prong outlets. However, there are several situations where you should check electrical power before installing a computer.

1. **Outlets.** If the installation is in an old building with two-pronged outlets (that is, without a ground), special wiring may be necessary. Avoid "cheater" plug adapters, which convert two-pronged plugs to three-prong, because they defeat the ground feature that protects electronic circuits.

2. **Outlet Wiring.** Test three-prong outlets to make sure the hot, neutral, and ground prongs were correctly wired when the outlet was installed. Incorrect wiring is not common, but it can cause problems if a computer system is plugged

into an outlet that was improperly wired. A simple tester with LED lamps to test each outlet is available from most electrical suppliers.

3. **Circuit Amperage.** If a system is installed in an environment with a significant amount of other office equipment (copiers, typewriters, coffeepots, fax machines, or calculators), determine the amperage of the circuit to see whether it can handle an additional load. Most appliances, including computers, monitors, and printers, display the number of amps of current they draw on an information plate. If the circuit breaker at the electrical distribution box is 15 amps, and the total amperage of devices on the circuit is even close to 15, then use a separate electrical circuit. Note also that some appliances draw more amps than their rating during start-up.

4. **Shared Circuits.** A computer system should not be installed on an electrical circuit that services devices with heavy motors or generators. These devices can, at times, draw large quantities of power from a circuit, which may reduce the available amps on a circuit to less than required for proper operation of computer devices. For example, hard disk drives rely on electrical current for timing during read and write operations. Inadequate power during one of these operations could cause loss of data on the media in a drive.

5. **Power Stability.** In some parts of the country the electric supply varies considerably, even during normal operation. When installing computer equipment in areas with unstable power, consult with the local electric company to determine whether special equipment is recommended to protect computer hardware. The electric company may recommend a power conditioner device for the circuit where the computer equipment will be installed. A **power conditioner** is a device placed between the computer and the power source that regulates the electrical power to keep it within acceptable limits. Power conditioner prices vary; it is important to purchase a unit that has the capacity to condition power for the total load it must service. For example, the load on a circuit may include the system unit, monitor, printer, scanner, other computer peripherals, and perhaps other office equipment. Electrical contractors or electricians can usually advise about the need for a power conditioner. They can connect a special metering device to a circuit to monitor it for a 24 to 48 hour period. Metering devices print out a statistical summary of electrical quality and the number of spikes, surges, or brown-downs that occurred.

6. **Multiple Computers.** In any situation where multiple computer systems will be installed, such as an office, training room, or computer lab facility, the total electric power requirements need to be planned in advance and an electrical contractor consulted to verify that the power is adequate and well-conditioned. The need to get specialized help with electrical power also applies to minicomputer installation and high-end workstations where the power requirements may be unusual.

Power strips are convenient because the user has only one switch to turn on a system. The system unit, monitor, printer, and other peripheral devices can all be plugged into the power strip. However, power strips should not be used as electrical extension cords. Each power strip should be plugged into an electrical outlet and not another power strip. This requirement is part of the electrical code in many areas and makes good sense where it is not. The best power strips include protective circuits that help prevent damage to computer equipment due to power surges and spikes. They may also include filters that protect against radio frequency interference.

Electrical power and peripheral signal cables should be installed so they cannot be damaged or stressed during regular use. When computer wires are installed in an existing building, surface-mounted cable conduits can be installed along an office or computer lab wall. These conduits provide access to the cables if they need to be upgraded or repaired, but they protect the cables from potential problems due to shorted or broken cables. Avoid running power cables or signal cables over a tile office floor or under a carpet. If power or signal cables must run over or under any kind of flooring, purchase protective rubber conduits to protect cables from the wear and tear of traffic. Plastic cable ties can be used to bundle cables and secure them to furniture to get them off the floor, out of the way, and avoid stress on the cable runs.

TELEPHONE AND NETWORK ACCESS

Few computer systems today are standalone installations. Most systems require access to a telephone line for modem dial-up connections with other computers. Some telephone companies offer ISDN (Integrated Services Digital Network) services that provide very fast voice and data connections over the same line. Many computer systems today require connection to a local area network in an office or computer lab. Determine the location of the nearest telephone and network access points before installation in case telephone or network extension lines are necessary to reach the installation site.

AIR CONDITIONING

Just as many computer installations do not require special electrical work, most do not require air conditioning beyond what is necessary for employee comfort. However, in locations where a large number of computer systems will be installed close together, such as in a small office, training room, or computer lab facility, additional air conditioning may be required. An engineer or consultant who specializes in heating, ventilating, and air conditioning (HVAC) can help determine the requirements. HVAC specialists use a formula that considers the total wattage of electrical devices and the heat generated by people and computes the number of BTUs (British Thermal Units) of air conditioning capacity required to maintain the temperature within a predetermined range.

Minicomputer and high-end workstations are more likely to require air conditioning than office computer systems. However, it is the total wattage within a space that determines air conditioning requirements. Even a few computers in a small office can create a need for air conditioning, especially during summer months.

LIGHTING PROBLEMS

As you learned earlier in this chapter, incorrect office lighting can cause significant ergonomic problems. The lighting level can be too intense, from the wrong source, or the wrong type of lighting. The result can be lower employee productivity due to eyestrain or headaches.

Many offices were designed primarily for paper-and-pencil activities and are overlit for computer use. It may be possible to turn off some light fixtures to reduce the amount of glare on the display screen. In cases where there are four florescent bulbs in a fixture, an electrician may be able to remove two of the four bulbs by making a simple modification to the fixture. Where it is not possible to adjust the amount of light, purchase an antiglare filter that covers the entire display screen area and reduces or eliminates glare from light sources.

In addition to the amount of light, the source of light may cause problems. For example, if there are windows in an office or training room, position display screens so they are at a 90-degree angle (perpendicular) to the light source. This position is preferable to the light source hitting the screen directly, which will happen when the screen is positioned directly opposite the light source. A user should not usually face a light source directly, because this could cause the user discomfort.

Finally, the type of lighting may cause problems for the display screen and ultimately the user. Some florescent bulbs flicker at the same frequency as the refresh rate on a display screen. The result is a noticeable flicker or visible moving scan line on the computer display screen. In these situations, an electrician or lighting consultant may be able to recommend a florescent bulb with less flicker, or one that flickers at a different rate than the monitor.

FIRE SUPPRESSION

Fortunately, computer systems rarely burst into flames. However, computer equipment is electrical and mechanical, and electromechanical equipment can cause fires, primarily due to power supply problems. Devices that have moving parts, such as disk drives or printers, can also cause fires, although fires from these sources are unusual. Although it is difficult to forecast when a fire may occur, it is possible to be prepared for a fire. If an office does not have a fire suppression system, place portable fire extinguishers near the equipment. Look for fire extinguishers that are rated for electrical fires, because extinguishers that are designed for wood or paper fires contain a dry chemical that can further damage computer equipment. The most effective fire extinguishers for use on and around computer equipment contain Halon gas. Unfortunately, the Environmental Protection Agency (EPA) has made the manufacture of new Halon systems illegal. It is legal to continue to use an existing Halon system, and a few are still available for purchase. Manufacturers have invented substitute fire extinguisher gases that are effective, such as a 3M product called CEA 614.

 For additional information about Halon, see the EPA Web site at **www.epa.gov/region4/air/cfc/q&ahalon.htm**.

Figure 5-3 is a checklist of questions to resolve during the installation planning stages.

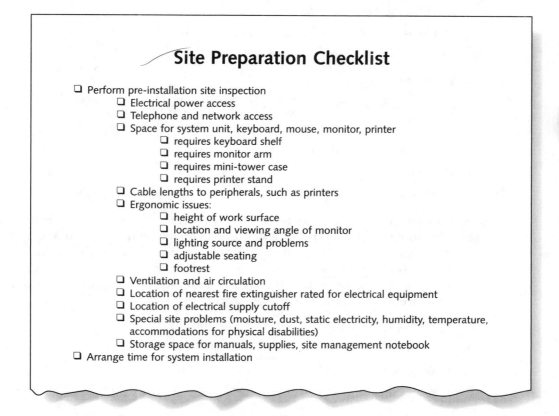

Figure 5-3   Site preparation checklist

SITE MANAGEMENT NOTEBOOK

The primary goal of any installation is, of course, to achieve an operational system. However, there are other goals you may want to accomplish at installation. One of those is to build a **site management notebook** that contains important information about the system, all in one location. An installation management notebook contains all the information a support specialist might need in the future to operate, diagnose, troubleshoot, reconfigure, upgrade, and repair the system and its components.

The site management notebook documents important details about the system, including:

- The hardware configuration
- The operating system configuration
- The network configuration
- Software licenses
- The configuration of applications software
- Special operating procedures
- Warranty and repair information
- A problem log
- A backup media log

A site management notebook may be "overkill" for a simple installation of a single home or small office computer; however it is usually a necessity for systems installed in offices, training facilities, and computer labs. A site management notebook is especially critical in situations where a large number of computers are installed and multiple support staff are likely to work on various components of the systems from time to time. The notebook acts as a one-stop source of information to answer questions such as:

1. What kind of bus does this system contain?
2. What is the speed of the internal modem?
3. What software is legally licensed to be on this system?
4. Who should the user call when the monitor doesn't work?
5. Where are the media backup disks and when were they created?
6. Is this the first time this printer has had problems?

Support technicians build and maintain a site management notebook as they install and work on a system. They know from experience that maintaining the notebook is preferable to spending hours trying to patch together the information when they need it later.

Figure 5-4 contains examples of the kinds of information that is often included in a site management notebook, including hardware and software configuration sheets and configuration details.

Other sheets that may be included in a site management notebook include software licenses, operating procedures, a list of contacts (phone number and e-mail addresses) for problems, warranties, a problem log, and a backup media log. Operating system utility software, such as MSD, Magic Solutions, and CheckIt, often print a report that includes some of the information in the sample pages shown in Figure 5-4.

PC Hardware Configuration Sheet

SYSTEM: _____ Serial # _____

1. **System unit:** ☐ desktop ☐ mini-tower ☐ full-tower
   ☐ laptop/notebook   Power supply (watts) _____

2. **CPU:** ☐ Intel ☐ NEC ☐ AMD ☐ Cyrix
   ☐ 386 ☐ 486 ☐ Pentium ☐ Pentium II
   ☐ math co-processor ☐ MMX-compatible
   Clock speed, megahertz (MHz) _____
   Bus: ☐ ISA-16 ☐ MCA-IBM ☐ EISA-32 ☐ VESA-32 ☐ PCI-32

3. **Internal memory** (RAM), megabytes _____ MB ☐ 30-pin SIMM
   Memory access speed, nanoseconds _____ NS ☐ 72-pin SIMM
   Cache memory _____ KB MB   Chip capacity _____

4. **Storage:**
   Controller card ☐ IDE ☐ EIDE ☐ SCSI-2
   Hard drive (megabytes) _____ MB GB
   Hard disk access, milliseconds _____ ms
   ☐ 5.25" floppy drive: ☐ DSDD 360 kb ☐ HC 1.2 mb
   ☐ 3.5" floppy drive: ☐ DSDD 720 kb ☐ HD 1.44 mb
   ☐ cartridge tape: ☐ 1/4" (QIC) ☐ 8mm ☐ 4mm DAT
   ☐ CD-ROM speed: _____ × ☐ MPC ☐ MPC-2
   ☐ Removable hard drive: _____ MB GB capacity

5. **Input:** Keyboard: ☐ 84 keys ☐ bus mouse ☐ trackball
   ☐ 101 keys ☐ serial mouse ☐ keyboard pointer
   ☐ 104 keys ☐ touch pad pointer

6. **Output:**
   Graphics adapter: ☐ EGA ☐ VGA ☐ SVGA
   Video memory (VRAM): _____ KB MB Accelerator card: ☐ Yes ☐ No

   Display screen (monitor): ☐ monochrome ☐ color
   ☐ CRT: dot pitch: ☐ .28 ☐ .39
   pixels: ☐ 640x480 ☐ 768x640 ☐ 1024x768 ☐ 1280x1024
   colors: ☐ 16 ☐ 64 ☐ 256 ☐ 16.7 mil
   ☐ LCD: ☐ dual scan ☐ active matrix
   pixels: ☐ 640x480 ☐ 768x640 ☐ 1024x768 ☐ 1280x1024
   colors/gray scale: ☐ 8 ☐ 16 ☐ 64 ☐ 256
   Printer: ☐ 9-pin dot matrix, _____ cps draft _____ cps LQ
   ☐ 4-pin dot matrix, _____ cps draft _____ cps LQ
   ☐ inkjet: _____ pages/min (ppm) ☐ B/W ☐ Color
   Ribbon or cartridge number: _____
   ☐ laser printer: _____ (ppm) _____ dots per inch (dpi)
   Toner cartridge number: _____

7. **Communications:** ☐ modem, error correction: _____
   speed (baud): _____ ☐ FAX
   ☐ NIC card ☐ NE2000-compatible
   ☐ BNC coaxial connector (10 BASE-2)
   ☐ RJ-45 twisted pair connector (10 BASE-T)

8. **Expansion:** Ports: ☐ serial ☐ parallel ☐ mouse ☐ game
   Slots: ☐ 8-bit ☐ 16-bit ☐ 32-bit
   PCMCIA slots, type: ☐ I ☐ II ☐ III

Figure 5-4 Sample pages from a site management notebook

5

Software Configuration Sheet

SYSTEM: _____ Serial # _____

1. Applications needs analysis:

- ❑ accounting
- ❑ CAD/CAM
- ❑ database management
- ❑ decision support
- ❑ desktop publishing
- ❑ e-mail
- ❑ expert systems
- ❑ _____

- ❑ financial
- ❑ forecasting
- ❑ graphics
  - ❑ analytic
  - ❑ presentation
  - ❑ draw/paint
- ❑ groupware
- ❑ _____

- ❑ Internet access
- ❑ multimedia
- ❑ project management
- ❑ spreadsheets
- ❑ statistics
- ❑ word processing
- ❑ _____

2. Operating systems/environments and networks:

- ❑ MS-DOS v. _____
- ❑ Windows _____   ❑ WFW   ❑ Windows 95   ❑ Windows 98
- ❑ OS/2 (Warp)   ❑ XENIX   ❑ Linux
- ❑ Novell NetWare v. _____   ❑ Windows NT v. _____

3. Tools and utilities:

Programming language: ❑ QBASIC   ❑ Visual Basic   ❑ C   ❑ C++   ❑ JAVA
❑ COBOL   ❑ Fortran   ❑ Pascal   ❑ _____
Utilities: ❑ Symantec/Norton   ❑ PC Tools   ❑ Backup _____   ❑ Anti-virus

4. Applications software :

Word processing: ❑ Word v. _____   ❑ WordPerfect v. _____   ❑ AmiPro
Spreadsheet: ❑ Excel v. _____   ❑ 1-2-3 v. _____   ❑ QuatroPro
Database: ❑ Access   ❑ dBASE IV   ❑ FoxPro   ❑ Paradox
Accounting: ❑ QuickBooks   ❑ DAC Easy   ❑ ACCPAC
Financial: ❑ Quicken v. _____   ❑ Microsoft Money
Integrated: ❑ MS Works   ❑ Claris Works
    ❑ MS-Office (Excel, Word, Access, PowerPoint)
    ❑ SmartSuite (AmiPro, 1-2-3, Paradox)
    ❑ PerfectOffice (WP, QuatroPro,)
Draw/paint: ❑ CorelDRAW   ❑ PowerPoint   ❑ Freelance
    ❑ Harvard Graphics   ❑ Print Shop
Desktop publishing: ❑ Adobe PageMaker ❑ Adobe Illustrator   ❑ Quark Xpress
Communications: ❑ Delrina v. _____ (terminal emulation)
    ❑ PC Eudora (e-mail client)
    ❑ Navigator   ❑ Internet Explorer
Info utilities: ❑ CompuServe   ❑ Prodigy
    ❑ America OnLine   ❑ Microsoft Network (MSN)

5. Supplies:

- ❑ desk (26–28" height)
- ❑ diskettes/cartridge tapes
- ❑ power strip
- ❑ books and manuals
- ❑ wrist rest
- ❑ anti-glare screen
- ❑ cleaning supplies: ❑ air

- ❑ chair (ergonomic)
- ❑ diskette/cassette case
- ❑ surge suppressor
- ❑ bookshelf/rack
- ❑ mouse pad
- ❑ footrest
- ❑ vacuum   ❑ wipes   ❑ alcohol

- ❑ printer stand

Figure 5-4   Sample pages from a site management notebook (continued)

Configuration Details

SYSTEM: _____ Serial # _____
CMOS settings: CMOS setup key _____ Password _____
Date battery last replaced: ___/ ___/ ___
HDD type # _____ HDD: Cyl_____ Head _____ Sector _____ Size _____
HDD: Other settings: _____
Floppy drives: _____ Boot sequence: _____
Display type: _____
Memory: base _____ extended _____
Power management notes: Device   Time Delay

IRQ use (note changes from standard):
_____ IRQ Status _____

IRQ	Address	Description	Detected	Handled By
0	___:___	timer click	yes	win386.exe
1	___:___	keyboard	yes	block device
2	___:___	Second 8259A	yes	default handlers
3	___:___	COM2: COM4:	COM2:	default handlers
4	___:___	COM1: COM3:	COM1:	default handlers
5	___:___	LPT2:	no	
6	___:___	floppy disk	yes	default handlers
7	___:___	LPT1:	yes	system area
8	___:___	real-time clock	yes	default handlers
9	___:___	redirected IRQ2	yes	BIOS
10	___:___	(reserved)		default handlers
11	___:___	(reserved)		default handlers
12	___:___	(reserved)	mouse	default handlers
13	___:___	math coprocessor	yes	BIOS
14	___:___	fixed disk	yes	default handlers
15	___:___	(reserved)		default handlers

[ ] Attach printout of AUTOEXEC.BAT
[ ] Attach printout of CONFIG.SYS
[ ] Attach printout of SYSTEM.INI
[ ] Attach printout of WIN.INI
[ ] Attach printout from MEM/C
Port use: LPT1: _____ LPT2: _____
COM1: _____ COM2: _____ COM3: _____

Figure 5-4   Sample pages from a site management notebook (continued)

HARDWARE INSTALLATION TOOLS

User support specialists who work frequently with hardware should purchase or assemble a tool kit with the basic tools to perform simple tasks with computer equipment. Computer, electronic supply, and mail order companies sell kits, which start at about $10 for a few basic tools. Most basic kits contain the following:

- **Screwdriver set.** Should include both regular and Phillips head; heads should be smaller than general use screwdrivers, because computer screws are often small. Some hardware repairers prefer a socketed screwdriver with interchangeable heads.

- **Nut driver.** Useful for removing the case from a system, because the screws are often six-sided nuts. (Nut drivers come in several sizes; get one designed for computer equipment.) Note that some socketed screwdrivers are the correct size for a nut driver when the screwdriver heads are removed.

- **Pliers.** Should include both regular pliers and needle-nose pliers for working with small parts.

- **IC chip extractor/inserter.** A useful tool if you work with older types of memory or ROM BIOS chips.

- **Parts-picker.** Useful for picking up small screws, nuts, and bolts in a tight work space; some kits contain tweezers and a magnetic parts grabber for small parts.

In addition to these common tools, support specialists who work frequently on hardware installations or problems may want to augment a basic tool kit with one or more of the following:

- **Pocketknife.** Sometimes when no other tool will do the job, a pocketknife will.

- **Small parts container.** Useful for keeping track of screws, nuts, washers, and other small parts while working on a computer system. An empty plastic film canister makes a good parts container.

- **Mirror.** Useful for viewing in tight spaces and behind components that are difficult to move.

- **Small flashlight.** Useful for hard-to-see places.

- **PC Pocket Reference.** Contains useful information in a compact form about PC hardware.

- **Isopropyl alcohol.** Useful for cleaning electrical components, display screens, keyboards, and mouse parts. (Isopropyl alcohol should be handled with care, like any chemical; it should not be consumed or inhaled under any circumstances.)

- **Lint-free cloth or foam tip brush.** Used to apply isopropyl alcohol for cleaning; antistatic wipes are also recommended.

- **Antistatic wrist strap.** Used to ground a technician to the computer power supply or case whenever there is a need to handle components inside the computer case. Reduces the risk of damaging a device with an accidental static charge. Inexpensive antistatic wrist straps sell for $6 to $10.

- **Electrician's tape.** For simple repairs or in lieu of tie-wraps.

- **Compressed air.** Cans of compressed air are useful for blowing dust out of computer cases, keyboards, and other equipment. A small vacuum cleaner designed for electronic equipment, available in many parts supply catalogs, is an alternative.

- **Circuit tester.** Simple electrical plug-in device determines whether an electric outlet has been properly wired (tests hot, neutral, and ground).

- **Multi-meter.** Sometimes called a VOM (volt-ohm meter), this device can be used to determine whether an electric circuit is active, whether a cable has a short, or whether a battery still has a charge. Inexpensive multi-meters can be purchased for $10 to $15.

Figure 5-5 shows a typical tool kit you can obtain from an electronics supplier.

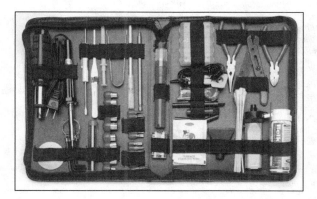

Figure 5-5   A typical hardware installation tool kit

Once you have inspected the installation site and are sure you have the proper equipment, you can proceed with installing the hardware components.

COMMON HARDWARE INSTALLATION STEPS

Installing computer hardware for most users in businesses and organizations today includes unpacking, connecting, and testing the basic components, usually a system unit, monitor, keyboard, and mouse. It can also include installing additional memory or expansion cards for peripheral devices.

An important first step in the installation process is to plan the installation. In addition to the pre-installation site checklist and steps described earlier in this chapter, planning also includes a review to make sure you have all the components and tools you will need. It is also important to arrange an installation time that is convenient for the user. Technicians who install many systems usually build a checklist to use on-site to make sure they perform all the steps required and bring all the necessary components with them. The checklist later becomes a form of documentation that they did so. Figure 5-6 shows a typical hardware installation checklist. The purpose of this checklist, and the others in this chapter, is to provide a starting point for support specialists who want to develop their own checklists and procedures that are specific to each company and situation.

Hardware Installation Checklist

- ❏ Review safety checklist (see Figure 5-7)
- ❏ Get tool kit and spare parts container
- ❏ Unpack hardware components and note any missing or damaged parts
- ❏ Save boxes and packing in case components need to be returned
- ❏ Connect basic components, power and signal cables, and test basic system operation
- ❏ Remove case and inspect components for proper installation
    - ❏ Fill out hardware configuration sheet in site management notebook
    - ❏ Record serial numbers in site management notebook; file warranty information
    - ❏ Install any memory upgrade and expansion cards:
        - ❏ Multi-function I/O   ❏ Sound card
        - ❏ Graphics adapter   ❏ Network interface
        - ❏ Internal modem   ❏ Other:_____
    - ❏ Connect peripherals (monitor, keyboard, mouse, printer, external modem, telephone, ZIP drive, speakers, scanner, microphone)
    - ❏ Connect power and signal cables
- ❏ Install power strip, surge suppressor, or UPS power unit, and connect power cables
- ❏ Power up system and adjust monitor
- ❏ Run diagnostic tests on hardware devices
- ❏ Install ergonomic devices (screen glare filter, copy holder, wrist rest)
- ❏ Attach network cable to NIC card
- ❏ Attach security cables for theft prevention
- ❏ Record vendor contact numbers and e-mail addresses in site management notebook

Figure 5-6   Hardware installation checklist

Support specialists don't perform all these steps at every installation. For ease of future reference, installers can delete steps they do not perform, or add additional steps they do perform.

 The checklist in Figure 5-6 assumes that the support specialist is installing a pre-assembled system. In some hardware installations, the installer assembles a system from basic components, which include a case with power supply, CPU, memory, disk drives, and adapter cards. Trade books on installing or upgrading a computer system describe the detailed steps to assemble a system at the individual component level.

Whenever an installer removes the case from a computer system, she or he should follow the basic safety precautions described in Figure 5-7.

Guidelines for Work Inside the System Unit

Before you begin...

❏   1.   Understand what you are going to do and how you are going to do it. What are your goals?
❏   2.   Get documentation on how to do what you are going to do.
❏   3.   Clear an adequate work space. Remove food or beverages from the work area.
❏   4.   Get the hardware components, tools, and software you will need to do the task (include paper and pencil for notes.)
❏   5.   Get a collector container for small parts, such as screws.

Before you remove the case...

❏   6.   Turn off the power switch. Is there more than one power switch?
❏   7.   Unplug the power cord. Is there more than one power cord?
❏   8.   If in doubt, check for electric current with a tester or turn off the power at the breaker box.
❏   9.   Work with at least one other person in the vicinity where you are working.
❏ 10.   Remember: you should not take the case off the power supply or the monitor, or try to repair those devices.
❏ 11.   Avoid loose clothing while working around mechanical parts, such as printers.

After the case is removed...

❏ 12.   Observe proper handling procedures and warnings for chemicals, such as isopropyl alcohol and printer ink.
❏ 13.   Before you begin work, attach an antistatic wrist strap, especially if you are working on memory components, IC chips, the motherboard, or adapter cards.
❏ 14.   Before you unplug any components, make notes or a diagram of how they are mounted and how cables are connected to any components you work with.

Before you restore power to test a component or system...

❏ 15.   Double check signal connections and especially power connections to make sure they are secure.
❏ 16.   Before you test the system, check inside the system case and around the work area to make sure you can account for all components and tools.
❏ 17.   Before you complete installation or troubleshooting, thoroughly test both the components you worked on, as well as other system components.

After you have tested a component or system...

❏ 18.   If you restored power to the system to test the components, turn the power switch off and unplug the power cord before you resume work inside the case.
❏ 19.   Don't assume that if components worked before the system case was re-installed, they will work after the case is installed; re-test the system with the case on.

After you are finished...

❏ 20.   Put away your tools.
❏ 21.   Document any changes you make to the system or its components in the site installation notebook.

Figure 5-7   Hardware installation safety precautions

MARY SWAZEY
EDITOR, WRITER
SWAZEY PUBLICATIONS
WATERTOWN, MA

As an editor of computer books, I thought that installing my new computer system would be easy. How difficult could it be to set up a portable computer on a docking station in my home office? The challenges proved to be greater than I had expected.

LOCATING THE COMPUTER

My home office is rather small, and the only place to put the desk and computer is in front of a window. This worked fine in the spring, but as the summer progressed, the office received an increasing amount of sunlight, increasing the amount of heat around the computer. One day the computer screen faded to white. I called tech support and learned that laptops are particularly sensitive to heat. Apparently, their components are small and close together, and it's more difficult to dissipate heat than in a desktop computer. The fading screen meant that the computer had overheated. The support technician told me that I should work out a solution to the heat in the office, or risk serious damage to the computer. I used window coverings and fans as a temporary solution, but air conditioning will be the only good long-term solution.

AM RADIO INTERFERENCE

Heat was not the only challenge to this seemingly simple installation. I began having trouble connecting to my Internet Service Provider, especially outside of regular business hours. Sometimes if I pinched the modem cable, just outside the PCMCIA card modem, the connection was successful. But I could connect without any problems if I brought the computer to another location. My dealer said that the problem was AM radio interference, and by pinching the cable, my body was acting as a filter on the line. I added line filters, but still had connection problems.

I contacted the FCC, which said that telephone users themselves are responsible for solving interference problems, not the FCC. I located and contacted the radio station that broadcasted the signal, and their engineers did what they could to help. They said that the PCMCIA card is much more susceptible to AM radio interference than a standard-size external modem, because it does not have the same filtering a larger modem has. They also said that their signal was indeed stronger outside of regular business hours.

They recommended that I try a combination of line filters and a power supply with filters. They also suggested that I try coiling up the modem cable to make it as short as possible, because the cable itself was probably acting as an antenna for the radio signals. If all this failed, they recommended that I purchase an external modem with internal filtering.

Looking for a low-cost solution, I found that two line filters from an electronics store combined with coiling and tying the modem cable allow me to connect most of the time. I sometimes have to pinch the line as well, but I can usually connect. This is fine for now, but the next item on my equipment investment list will probably be a new modem—right after a good air conditioner.

COMMON OPERATING SYSTEM INSTALLATION STEPS   5

There are many situations in which a support specialist does not need to install an operating system. Many pre-assembled computer systems have an operating system pre-installed on the hard drive. Some systems today have both Windows 3.1 (or Windows for Workgroups) and Windows 95 pre-installed. When users boot up the system for the first time, they are asked to select which operating system they want to keep, and the other is automatically erased.

For situations that do require the support specialist to install the operating system, most are supplied on a CD-ROM. Some operating system suppliers provide floppy disk distributions by special request. Others provide operating system updates, patches, and special drivers that users can download from an Internet site. If a system does not have a CD-ROM drive, the installer will need to order the operating system on floppy disks in advance. In cases where a support specialist installs identical operating system configurations on a large number of machines, an image of the system can be written on a removable hard drive, such as an Iomega ZIP disk. An external ZIP drive can then be moved from machine to machine and the image can be copied onto each to speed up the installation process. The installation process is usually not complicated but can take 30 to 45 minutes from beginning to end, or longer if from floppy disks.

The steps to install operating system software include partitioning the hard disk if necessary, installing the operating system software and any device drivers required, and installing the network operating system. After the operating system and network operating system have been configured for hardware peripherals and to meet site-specific standards, the support specialist installs other necessary software, including virus checkers, screen savers, and security and utility software.

As more computer systems use Windows 95 or Windows 98 as an operating system, there is less need to install device drivers, because Windows 95/98 automatically recognizes devices that conform to the Plug and Play standards. In these cases, Windows may install a default device driver for devices it recognizes during the boot process. However, Windows may not recognize peripheral devices manufactured prior to 1995, and device drivers may need to be installed manually in those cases. Installers of Macintosh systems usually have an easier task, because MacOS automatically recognizes many peripheral devices, but some peripheral devices are sold with specialized device drivers for MacOS, as well.

Vendor manuals are a good resource of specific information about how to install an operating system. However, the process has been highly automated in recent releases, so little printed documentation may be available. Trade publications also cover how to install and configure popular operating systems.

Figure 5-8 is a checklist an installer can use when installing an operating system.

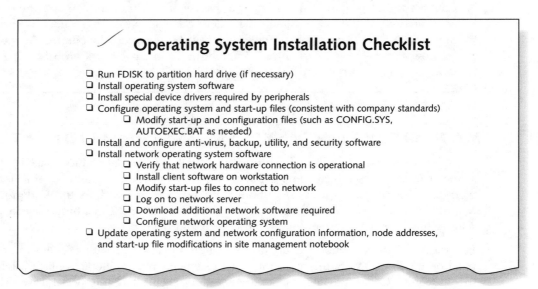

Operating System Installation Checklist

- ❑ Run FDISK to partition hard drive (if necessary)
- ❑ Install operating system software
- ❑ Install special device drivers required by peripherals
- ❑ Configure operating system and start-up files (consistent with company standards)
  - ❑ Modify start-up and configuration files (such as CONFIG.SYS, AUTOEXEC.BAT as needed)
- ❑ Install and configure anti-virus, backup, utility, and security software
- ❑ Install network operating system software
  - ❑ Verify that network hardware connection is operational
  - ❑ Install client software on workstation
  - ❑ Modify start-up files to connect to network
  - ❑ Log on to network server
  - ❑ Download additional network software required
  - ❑ Configure network operating system
- ❑ Update operating system and network configuration information, node addresses, and start-up file modifications in site management notebook

Figure 5-8   Operating system installation checklist

The steps to install and configure network software are specific to each type of network. A typical network installation involves the steps described in Figure 5-8. Usually a network administrator builds a disk that contains preconfigured network client software so it can be copied to a computer easily during installation. Vendor manuals and trade books are available to describe the details of network client software installation.

COMMON STEPS TO INSTALL APPLICATIONS SOFTWARE

Before installing an applications software package, a support specialist needs to determine whether the software is compatible with the hardware and network on which it will be installed. Determine the following:

- The CPU types the software runs on
- The amount of memory the software requires
- The amount of hard drive space the software requires for a full installation
- Whether the software is compatible with hardware peripherals
- Whether the software operates in a network environment

Software vendors usually distribute applications software on **distribution media** such as CD-ROMs or floppy disks. However, applications software packages are increasingly available for users to download, in compressed format, from a network server or the Internet. Whatever the distribution media, the installation steps for most applications packages are generally simpler than they were several years ago. Application programs often automatically update registry and configuration files maintained by the operating system. Most packages auto-install after the user double-clicks an install icon. Some systems equipped with CD-ROM drives that have an AutoPlay feature enabled can recognize that a software installation CD has been inserted in the drive and will automatically begin the installation process.

Immediately before installing a new program, close all open programs as a precaution. The first step in software installation is often the execution of a special installation program, such as InstallShield. The install program guides the installer through the process and pauses to ask questions on the screen if there are user options. When the distribution media is floppy disk, the install program prompts the installer to insert disks identified by name or number as the install program needs them.

The most common options allow a user to select from among the following installation types:

1. **Express installation.** Sometimes called a typical installation; installs the most common features and asks the fewest questions.

2. **Custom installation.** Sometimes called a special installation; lets a user select components or features to install; be prepared to answer more questions than in an express installation.

3. **Minimal installation.** Sometimes called a laptop installation; for users with little free hard drive space available; installs the smallest set of functions and features possible.

4. **Full installation.** Sometimes called a maximum installation; installs all program features, asks few questions; takes the maximum amount of disk space.

It's a good idea to consult the end user on the type of installation required. However, users are generally not familiar with the terms *express* or *minimal* and may not understand the implications of the installation choices. An installer may need to translate these options into lists of specific features for the user. Users often need specific software functions or features that are not included in a minimal installation. Installing applications software may also include installing company-specific applications, templates, or device drivers.

Support specialists are also responsible for checking to make sure that the company has the appropriate software licenses to support an installation. Some companies maintain a database of software licenses that needs to be updated as part of the installation process. After installation, specialists should test the software and make sure it runs properly. Figure 5-9 is a sample checklist that a support specialist can use to track software installations.

Applications Software Installation Checklist

❑ Install standard applications software packages (such as office suite)
❑ Install special-purpose software (such as accounting, marketing, manufacturing, or other company-specific applications)
❑ Install any special device drivers required by applications software (printer drivers are common ones)
❑ Configure applications software to meet the user's needs and conform to company standards
❑ Create desktop shortcut or add to start-up menu as appropriate
❑ Add any company-specific templates for word processing or spreadsheets
❑ Fill out software configuration sheets in site management notebook
❑ File software licenses in site management notebook
❑ Register software with vendor (via mail-in card or online registration)
❑ Verify that user knows how to start the application
❑ Verify that the user is satisfied with the installation and knows how to get help if needed

Figure 5-9   Applications software installation checklist

WRAP-UP TASKS

In the previous sections of this chapter, you learned some of the common steps and problems in the hardware, operating system, and applications software installation process. Depending on the kind of installation and on company policy, support specialists (or home users) might undertake several additional steps. These are steps in which a support specialist can document file settings, back up critical files, create rescue disks, fill out warranty and registration cards, document problems, address ergonomic concerns, and make sure the user will be able to use the system once it is installed. A support specialist can also include "housekeeping" tasks such as storing documentation and shipping containers. Some of these tasks can be classified as facilities management or installation documentation, whereas others are user training. Most installers think of these as "wrap-up tasks," because they are generally performed at the end of the installation.

It is important to keep in mind that an installation doesn't end as soon as the hardware or software is installed. A support specialist who installs or upgrades a system should always check with users to make sure they are capable of using the new system correctly. Go over any new equipment with users; ensure that they can start it up and shut it down properly. Alert them to training opportunities and alternatives. Then check to see that the users are satisfied with the installation and have had their questions answered.

Figure 5-10 is a checklist for some of these wrap-up tasks. Not every step in the checklist applies to every installation. The tasks vary depending on the type of installation and the needs of the user.

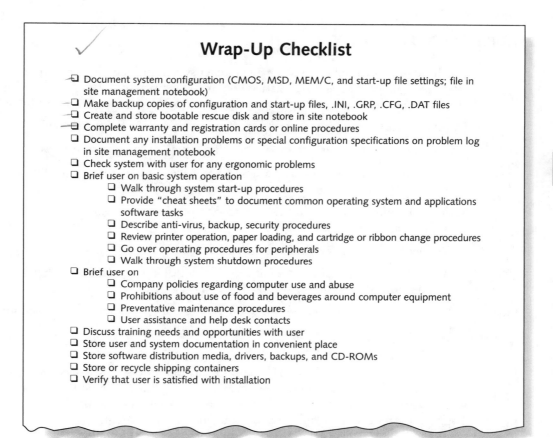

Figure 5-10   Wrap-up checklist

On the one hand, installing systems can be a smooth and error-free process that serves its main purpose: to get the end user up and running as soon as possible. On the other hand, system installation can be frustrating for both installer and user, because an unexpected incompatibility or defective hardware or software can suddenly terminate an installation before it is complete. In some instances, an installer may have to uninstall or reinstall components to get them to work correctly. However, installers must be sure that they plan carefully for each installation, have the appropriate tools, are organized in their procedures, and are alert to the issues and potential problems that each installation presents. Although proper advanced planning does not guarantee a smooth and successful installation, poor planning almost always guarantees the opposite.

CHAPTER SUMMARY

- The basic steps involved in installing a computer system include site preparation, hardware installation and configuration, operating system and network installation and configuration, installation and configuration of applications software, and several wrap-up tasks.

- During the site preparation step, a support specialist deals with several issues:

  - Locating the computer system and devising strategies to conserve space

  - Ergonomic concerns, including ways to adapt the computer system and work environment to maximize user productivity and health

  - Power requirements that address the need to provide a convenient and reliable electric power supply

  - Connectivity issues that deal with telephone and network access

  - Air conditioning, usually not a concern for standalone personal computers, but an issue in offices and training facilities

  - Lighting problems, which are the source of several productivity and ergonomic problems

  - Fire suppression precautions

- One of the secondary goals of the system installation process is to collect a notebook of information about the computer system. A site management notebook is a convenient way to organize information that a support specialist will need in the future to operate, diagnose, troubleshoot, reconfigure, upgrade, and repair a system.

- Tools needed to work with computer hardware include a variety of screwdrivers, a nut driver, pliers, an IC chip extractor/inserter, a parts-picker, a pocketknife, small parts container, mirror, isopropyl alcohol, and a lint-free cloth or foam tip brush, an antistatic wrist strap, compressed air or a vacuum cleaner, a circuit tester, and a multi-meter (VOM).

- Installation of hardware and related peripherals includes unpacking the system, connecting power and signal cables, installing any upgrades, and testing the system. Installing an operating system includes the installing software, usually from CD-ROM or floppy disk, and device drivers if needed, configuring various options and start-up files, and installing network software if necessary. Applications software installation usually involves a choice of the kind of installation from express, custom, minimal, or full system. A support specialist may also install company-specific utilities, templates, or style sheets.

- The final steps in the installation process include briefing the user on various operational aspects of the system and other activities that wrap up the installation. These steps often include updates to materials in the site management notebook. The wrap-up tasks also include a transition into the user training process that is the topic of the next chapter. Finally, the ultimate installation question is, "Is the user satisfied?"

KEY TERMS

- **custom installation** — A software installation option that lets the installer select which modules and features to install; sometimes called a special installation.

- **distribution media** — The original copies of operating system or applications software; common examples include CD-ROMs, floppy disks, and Internet downloads.

- **express installation** — A software installation option that installs the most commonly used functions and features as determined by the manufacturer; sometimes called a typical installation.

- **footprint** — The amount of desktop space a system unit occupies; measured in square inches (length of case times width).

- **full installation** — A software installation option that installs all functions and features of software; sometimes called a maximum installation; usually requires the most disk space of any installation type.

- **minimal installation** — A software installation option that installs predetermined modules and features designed to minimize the system resources required to run the software; frequently called a laptop installation.

- **power conditioner** — An electrical device that connects between a power source and a computer system; it inputs electrical power, makes sure that the frequency, voltage, and waveform are within acceptable specifications, and then outputs power to the computer system.

- **site management notebook** — A binder that consolidates important information about a computer system's hardware, operating system, network, and applications software configurations, as well as facilities management information, that would be needed to upgrade, maintain, diagnose, or repair the system.

REVIEW QUESTIONS

1. Explain why system installation is often a task performed by support specialists instead of end users.

2. Briefly describe the basic steps in a system installation.

3. Explain the purpose of a pre-installation site visit.

4. Describe the factors that determine where a computer system should be located.

5. What is the recommended desktop height for the placement of a keyboard?

6. Describe the difference in footprint between desktop models and mini-tower cases. Why does the footprint make a difference to the user?

7. Describe the proper viewing angle for a computer system monitor.

8. Discuss some ways a support specialist can minimize the amount of desk or table space a computer system occupies.

9. Describe some precautions a support specialist should observe when locating a printer or computer supplies.

10. Describe several ergonomic problems users may experience. For each problem, list some recommended ways a support specialist can address the problem.

11. Describe some electrical supply problems an installer may encounter in the installation of a computer system. For each problem, list some recommended ways a support specialist can address the problem.

12. Explain the purpose of a power conditioner. Under what circumstances is a power conditioner necessary?

13. List some situations where air conditioning may be required in a computer facility.

14. Describe some problems that can occur due to improper lighting of a workspace where a computer is used.

15. Describe the kind of fire extinguisher that is recommended for use around computer equipment.

16. List common tools that a system installer would use and describe the purpose of each tool.

17. Explain the purpose of a site management notebook. Describe the kinds of information that are recorded in a site management notebook.

18. List the main steps to install computer hardware. Briefly explain what tasks occur during each step.

19. List the main steps to install an operating system. Briefly explain what tasks occur during each step.

20. Describe some common media used to distribute computer software.

21. Describe the basic tasks to connect a personal computer to a network and make it operational.

22. List the main steps to install an applications software package. Briefly explain what tasks occur during each step.

23. Describe the four common types of software installation options. Explain when an installer would select each type.

24. Describe the wrap-up tasks normally performed at the end of a system installation. What is the involvement of the end user during the wrap-up tasks?

25. Explain the use of installation checklists described and illustrated in this chapter.

HANDS-ON PROJECTS

 ## PROJECT 5-1

Choose one of the installation checklists in this chapter. Based on your experience, what steps would you add to the checklist? What steps would you leave out? If you have access to a machine-readable version of the checklist you selected, make the modifications you recommend.

5

 ## PROJECT 5-2

If you are familiar with a computer installation in your home, office, or school, compare that installation against the site preparation checklist in Figure 5-3. Were any steps described in this chapter omitted in the installation with which you are familiar? Which ones were they, and what was the result?

 ## PROJECT 5-3

If you use a home, office, or school computer, conduct an ergonomic analysis of the site from the perspective of an end user. List any problems a user would identify with the site, using the ergonomic issues described in this chapter. As a support specialist, what recommendations would you make to address the ergonomic problems you identified? Write a summary of your recommendations.

 ## PROJECT 5-4

Find two mail-order catalogs for computer equipment or supplies, such as Tiger, PC Mall, Compaq Direct, MEI Micro, Lyben, or Global. Look at the supplies sold. What products are available to address specific ergonomic problems such as those described in this chapter? Make a list of examples of ergonomic products and their prices.

PROJECT 5-5

Find a mail-order catalog for computer equipment or supplies. Does the company sell tool kits for working on hardware? How do the contents of the tools kits differ from the list of tools in this chapter? Write a list of the tools you would want to add to the kits you found.

 PROJECT 5-6

Write a detailed table of contents for a site management notebook. Think about the best way to organize the information so a support specialist who needs to quickly find information about a specific system can locate it easily.

 PROJECT 5-7

If facilities are available at your company or school, observe or participate in the set-up of a typical system. Make a list of the steps you observe. Be sure to ask about steps you don't understand, and find out why they are necessary.

 PROJECT 5-8

Checklists of hardware and software components such as those included in this chapter quickly become outdated as hardware technology changes, and as new software is marketed. Look over the hardware and software checklists in this chapter. Describe how you would update the lists based on changes in technology since these lists were created for this book.

 PROJECT 5-9

The checklists in this chapter contain some technical material and product descriptions. Because of your previous experience in the computer field, you have probably encountered some of the technical terms, product names, and specifications used in the chapter. Make a list of any words used in the chapter that are unfamiliar to you or that you would like to know more about. Select five terms to research further. Use whatever information resources are available to you (for example: friends, coworkers, magazines, books, the Internet) to prepare a short definition of each of the five terms you selected.

CASE PROJECTS

1. FRED'S PAINT STORE

You were introduced to Fred's Paint Store in the case studies in several previous chapters. Because computer systems are widely used at Fred's Paints in a variety of office, marketing, and manufacturing locations, the employees at Fred's Paints encounter a number of challenging computer installation problems. Several of Fred's employees have received or will get new computers in the next month. They need your advice about how to deal with the problems described by each of these employees:

- Jose Fonseca, production scheduler: the desk space for his workstation is very limited

- Ralph Emerson, accounting specialist: static electricity is a problem in the office area where Ralph's computer will be installed

- Anna Liu, marketing database coordinator: reports eyestrain, headaches, back strain, and sore wrists

- Roberta Green, employee benefits coordinator: the fluorescent lighting in the office causes a noticeable flicker on the computer screen

- Dale Marcus, engineering supervisor: wants to minimize the number of power switches required to turn on computer and peripherals (system unit, monitor, printer, fax modem, scanner)

- Lou Campanelli, pallet manufacturing: installation is in an unusually dusty cabinet-shop environment

Write a memo to Fred's Paint Store that recommends how you would deal with each of these specific problem areas.

2. BRIANNA MISHOVSKY'S TRAINING FACILITY

Brianna Mishovsky is the training coordinator for a large national insurance company. The company has recently agreed to purchase a new software package that will substantially increase employee productivity in its claims processing department. Although the new software is not yet operational, it is a major change for the company and is scheduled to come online in a month. The implementation schedule poses several problems for Brianna's training group because several week-long training sessions on the use of the new software must be scheduled to accommodate all the employees in the claims processing department. In order to meet the need for additional training classes for employees, Brianna has to install computers in a training room where none exist now.

Brianna has located 20 computer systems that can be used for the training activity, but, unfortunately, they are currently equipped with Windows 3.1 as an operating system. She learned that the new claims processing software runs on Windows 95. Although the hardware configuration on the computers Brianna found is sufficient to run Windows 95, it was never installed on these systems.

Brianna would like your assistance with the installation of Windows 95 on the 20 training systems. She thinks the first task is for you to design some installation procedure notes to install Windows 95 on the training machines. First, research the steps in the Windows 95 installation procedure. (If possible, go through an actual Windows 95 installation to identify the steps in the procedure, the key decision points, and the installation options available.) Next, write a first draft of the installation procedure notes for Windows 95. As you work on your draft, make a list of some questions you will need to ask Brianna to clarify how she wants Windows 95 configured on the training machines. Brianna would like you to make your procedure notes brief, but as complete as possible, because one of her training assistants will probably do the actual installation steps based on your notes. Write a draft of the Windows 95 installation procedure notes and a list of questions for Brianna that you need answered to complete the assignment.

3. THE UPS AND DOWNS OF ELECTRICAL POWER AT CASCADE UNIVERSITY

In a previous chapter, you met Mary Ann Lacy, the training facility coordinator at Cascade University. Mary Ann has plans to install a new network server for her training facility. She has been advised by the electric utility that provides power to Cascade University that she probably also needs to install an uninterruptable power supply (UPS) for whichever brand of server she eventually installs. The idea that a UPS would help protect the university's investment in server hardware and reduce user frustration if there is a power outage appeals to Mary Ann. She would like your help with the UPS part of the installation project.

The consultant at the electric utility mentioned that there are articles in computer periodicals that describe UPS equipment. The consultant also said that the Internet is a good source of information on UPS systems. Many of the companies that sell UPSes for computers have Web pages that describe their products. The consultant also pointed Mary Ann to a recent article in *PC Magazine* as a starting point: "Uninterruptable Power Supplies: The Power Brokers," *PC Magazine*, September 23, 1997. The article is available on Ziff-Davis's Web site at **www.zdnet.com/pcmag/features/ups/_open.htm**.

Mary Ann would like you to 1) learn about some of the important features to consider when purchasing and installing UPS systems, and 2) write a 1 to 2-page summary of the issues the university needs to consider in the purchase and installation of a UPS for its new network server.

CHAPTER SIX

TRAINING COMPUTER USERS

Many organizations that provide user support find that it is expensive. Because of the high costs of support, it is usually in an organization's best interest to try to make users as self-reliant as possible to reduce their need for support. Every problem a user can solve by himself or herself, every question a user can find the answer to without asking the help desk, reduces the burden on the support department and ultimately reduces an organization's total support costs.

Training is one of the best ways to make users self-reliant. There is an old saying, "Give a person a fish, and you have provided a meal; teach a person to fish, and you have provided many meals." That principle certainly applies to the relationship between a user and a user support center: "Answer a question for a user, and you have solved a problem; teach users to find their own answers, and you have solved many problems."

AFTER READING THIS CHAPTER AND COMPLETING THE EXERCISES YOU WILL BE ABLE TO:

- Define training
- Explain the main steps in the training process
- Plan a training session
- Prepare a training session
- Present a training module

WHAT IS TRAINING?

Training is a teaching and learning process that aims to build skills. Some people use the terms *training* and *education* interchangeably. Although training and education are related, there are differences between them.

Education is a teaching and learning process that aims to provide conceptual understanding. Especially in introductory courses, the goal of education is to build a basic vocabulary and understanding of general principles. In education, it is common to test learners' understanding by measuring their ability to explain concepts and principles. The effects of education are intended to be long lasting.

Training focuses on performing activities and building expertise. Trainers often test the success of a training session by measuring a learner's ability to perform a task. Although some training may be long lasting, training can also be very short term. A person could be trained to perform a task she or he will only do once or a few times.

People sometimes associate education with a school environment and training with an industrial or business environment. However, there are schools whose mission is training, such as vocational-technical schools and community colleges. Furthermore, education often occurs outside a school environment, because skill training is usually based on a firm foundation of conceptual knowledge. For example, it is often necessary to educate users in basic vocabulary and understanding of a computer system before they can become skilled users. An understanding of computer vocabulary and general computer operating principles is certainly necessary if users are ever to see a computer as anything more than a black box, where the inputs will somehow yield the correct outputs regardless of how it happens. Users' abilities to troubleshoot and solve problems for themselves are often closely related to how much they understand about a computer system and how well their general knowledge can take them beyond the specific tasks they were trained to perform. Although this chapter focuses primarily on user training, it assumes that training must be based on a solid foundation of vocabulary and concepts.

THE TRAINING PROCESS

Successful training is a three-step process. The three Ps of training are summarized in Figure 6-1.

1.	Plan
2.	Prepare
3.	Present

Figure 6-1   The training process

In the planning step, the trainer gathers information about the objectives of the training process. In the preparation step, the trainer gathers and prepares materials and organizes them into modules. In the presentation step, the trainer presents the training modules to end users, who then evaluate the training process.

STEP 1: PLAN THE TRAINING

Before a trainer begins to prepare materials, it is important to plan for the training sessions. Experienced trainers know that planning is essential to a successful training session. Trainers must learn who the trainees will be, their current skill levels, and what skill levels they need to achieve through the training. Once trainers have this information, they can set learning and performance objectives.

6

WHO ARE THE TRAINEES?

First, determine who the trainees are. Are they novices, intermediate users, or users with advanced skills? Are they adults or children? Adult employees who need specific job-related training require different content and training techniques than school children. Employees are often highly motivated because they may already understand the benefits of applying new technology to their jobs. Adults often bring prior experience to a training session, which can be very useful because a trainer can build on prior experiences and use analogies and metaphors to introduce new material. For example, the trainer might point out that a program feature is similar to one in a program the users already know. Although all adult employees are not equally motivated, the characteristics of adult learners can often be used to good advantage in a training situation. For example, adults are better able to form generalizations and articulate what they do and do not understand. Also, adults are often less willing to put up with a poor trainer than are younger people.

Trainers should be aware that some trainees are not attending training voluntarily but as a job requirement. Required attendance can affect a trainee's motivation level, and trainers may have to spend more time convincing trainees of the benefits of the training and find ways to involve them in the training to help them get past their initial resistance to being there.

WHAT ARE THE TRAINEES' NEEDS?

Second, determine what the trainees need to know, which may require some research. Trainers usually try to discover the kinds of jobs or tasks users will be asked to perform, what specific skills they will need, and how expert the trainees need to be at these skills. Trainers can sometimes locate information about the job, task, or skill objectives in employee position descriptions. In other cases, they must interview the employees or their supervisors to determine the training objectives. They can also administer a pretest to determine more precisely trainees' baseline skill levels.

WHAT DO THE TRAINEES ALREADY KNOW?

As part of the planning process, it is important to establish what trainees already know, so the trainer does not waste learners' time. For adult trainees, the training can begin with a review of how the training material fits with what they already know, but it should move quickly to the new material.

It is also important to know what the trainees "bring to the training table." If there is a wide disparity in backgrounds among a group of trainees, trainers run the risk of covering introductory material too fast for some and too slow for others, thereby aiming the training at a level that misses both groups. Both novices and more advanced users may be equally dissatisfied because the training is not at the level they need. Where different interest or ability levels exist among a group of trainees, background material can sometimes be provided before the training session to help those with less experience feel more comfortable with the basic vocabulary and concepts. It may be possible to arrange an introductory session for some trainees before the actual training session begins. For example, for a training session on Microsoft Word, the trainer should make sure that trainees who participate have basic keyboarding, mouse, and Windows skills, or they will be unable to benefit from the training. They will also slow down other learners with their questions.

Even with extra preparation to bring novice users up to the class level, trainers find that there is almost always a range of skill levels in any given training group. One of the biggest challenges in any training situation is to find an "average" level of instruction that addresses the needs of as many students as possible. Different trainers handle this in different ways. Some try to teach to the majority of the class, with occasional asides to give extra explanation for those below the mean and with extra questions that challenge those above the mean. Practice and experience are the best teachers in handling this classic training challenge.

In any training group, there is not only a diversity of levels, but a diversity of cultural and language backgrounds. Trainers need to recognize these situations and be sensitive to the audience needs. For example, if there are learners who are non-native speakers of English, limit the use of idioms and jargon terms, and instead use clear, concise speech, and use as basic a vocabulary as possible. A trainer also needs to be sensitive to cultural mores. For example, in many cultures, it is unacceptable to touch another's arm in a friendly way, as one might with a colleague in the United States. When you have a chance to talk with trainers, ask them about their experiences with cultural differences and benefit from their background.

Armed with a knowledge of who the trainees are, what they know, and what they need to know, trainers can then plan the training session. At this point, trainers often find it useful to ask "How do I efficiently and effectively move the trainees from where they are now to where they need to be? How do I teach them to perform the tasks outlined in the training objectives?"

WHAT SKILL LEVEL DO TRAINEES NEED?

Trainers first need to determine the skill level that trainees need. To determine an appropriate target skill level, trainers need a basic understanding of skill levels and how they are classified.

There are several ways to classify skills in education and training. One skill level classification is the following:

1. Concepts — the ability to use basic vocabulary

2. Understanding — the ability to explain

3. Skills — the ability to use basic skills to perform a task

4. Expertise — the ability to perform a task well

In this skill classification, the first two levels, concepts and understanding, are conceptual. Training begins with vocabulary, and trainees must learn to use the language necessary to communicate about the topic. They need to know the meanings of the words others use to exchange information about the subject. Then they can begin to build an understanding of how things work and why they work the way they do. Once they understand the topic, trainees can build a mental model of how things work and explain it to others. It is during vocabulary and conceptual learning steps that analogies are especially useful.

Once they build conceptual understanding, trainees can then build skills and abilities to perform tasks. At the lowest level, users first learn the steps to perform a task. Task performance at the basic skill level may take a long time, and trainees may not get it exactly right at first. Each trainee needs to develop the ability to perform a task at a basic level before becoming proficient.

At the highest skill levels in this classification scheme, trainees build speed, accuracy, and expertise. For example, a trainee can not only embed a graphic object in a document (a basic ability or skill), but he or she can do so quickly, without any prompting, and can easily control the placement, size, and design appeal of the result (expertise). Based on these four levels of conceptual knowledge and skills, a trainer can define the vocabulary and level of understanding trainees need, the basic tasks they need to be able to perform, and how much expertise the trainees need to develop.

WHAT ARE THE TRAINING PERFORMANCE OBJECTIVES?

In the final planning step, trainers should specify the learning or performance objectives for the training. **Learning objectives** answer the question, "What do the trainees need to learn?" For example, a learning objective for this chapter is *Explain the main steps in the training process*. **Performance objectives** answer the question, "What should trainees be able to do as a result of this training?" For example, a performance objective for this chapter is *Plan a training session*. Performance objectives may also include objectives that specify how well the trainees need to be able to perform a task. A training session on Internet search engines, for example, might include a performance objective such as *Use Alta Vista to locate a specific piece of information on the World Wide Web within five minutes*. Training objectives should begin with action verbs, which makes them easier to evaluate later on. Avoid training objectives that begin with the word *understand*, because understanding can be more difficult to evaluate. Be as specific as possible about the tasks learners will be able to perform as a result of the training.

Trainers summarize the results of the planning step in a goal statement. See if you can identify the concepts, understanding, abilities, and skills objectives in the training plan shown in Figure 6-2. Does the plan include learning and performance objectives?

Notice that the training plan describes the objectives in general terms. It does not describe *how* the training will be presented (self-guided tutorial, classroom demonstration, face-to-face tutorial, televised demonstration) or list specific topics (for example, which "basic Explorer operations" will be included and which won't). The details of training topics, methods, and organization occur during the second step: training preparation.

Windows 95 Introduction Training Objectives

The goal of this training session is to provide employees who are new computer users with an introduction to the Windows 95 environment. The session is designed for computer users who have no previous experience with Windows 95 but who have keyboarding skills and a basic understanding of office computer system principles.

At the end of the session, trainees will be prepared to take a basic spreadsheet course and know enough about the Windows 95 operating system that they can perform basic tasks such as the following:
- Start the system
- Start an application program
- Store and use files on a disk
- Use a printer in the Windows environment
- Locate and manage disk files
- Use the Windows 95 help system

The session will introduce terms used frequently in the Windows 95 environment including: desktop, window, menu, icon, shortcut, dialog box, cursor, mouse keys, and Recycle Bin. Trainees should be able to define 70% of common terms in a simple test. The session will not emphasize a complete understanding of the organization and operation of Windows 95, but will emphasize the use of Windows 95 to run applications and the use of the Windows Explorer to manage files and disk storage space. Trainees should be able to explain the role of the Start Menu to run applications and the role of the Explorer and Recycle Bin to manage files.

The session will include hands-on experience with basic Windows 95 operations to give trainees the ability to use the Windows 95 interface. Exercises will include mouse operations, window management, use of the Start Menu, and basic Explorer operations useful to locate files. With practice, trainees should be able to perform basic Windows 95 tasks with little help or prompting. Since this is intended to be a short training session, no attempt will be make to build skills or expertise in Windows 95 beyond a basic level.

Figure 6-2   A training plan

STEP 2: PREPARE FOR THE TRAINING

During the training preparation step, a trainer develops more detail about the specific topics that will be covered and how these topics will be organized. This step addresses the specifics of training methods and how the training will be accomplished.

WHAT SPECIFIC TOPICS WILL BE COVERED?

Based on the learning and performance objectives defined in Step 1, a trainer next decides which specific topics must be covered. Even with very clear learning and performance objectives, deciding specific training content is not easy.

Most trainers do not start from scratch, however. They begin with a list of possible topics. Usually this list comes from several sources, including the trainer's own knowledge of what is important, the learning and performance objectives defined earlier in Step 1, and at what level other trainers and writers have covered these topics previously. It is important to discover which topics have been successfully covered elsewhere. Many successful trainers rely heavily on material in vendor manuals, trade books, industry training packages, and other resources. Why reinvent the wheel if there are good ideas already around? And there usually are. Examples of successful training materials can provide a useful starting point as trainers develop their own materials. However, trainers should respect copyrighted material and avoid copying verbatim from a single source.

The list of topics to cover in a training session is one of the most critical decisions in training preparation. First it is just as important to decide what *not* to cover as it is to decide what to cover. The process of selecting topics is like setting priorities. Based on their knowledge of what is important to the audience, trainers have to select the topics that are most useful to the trainees. Second, especially for new trainers, it is preferable to try to cover a little less material than to attempt to cover too much. Most trainees prefer a session with adequate time devoted to fewer topics than a rush job that tries to present two hours of material in a one-hour session.

HOW SHOULD THE TOPICS BE ORGANIZED?

To organize training topics, begin with lower level skills and progress to higher level skills. Introduce concepts and terms first, followed by explanations to build understanding. Then focus on building basic skills and abilities, and finally build expertise. Following this strategy, a generic template for a training session might look like the following:

1. Introduce trainer
2. Review previous topics
3. Introduce new topic
4. Establish motivation
5. Present new material
    - Concepts
    - Explanations

6. Perform training activity
   - Teach basic skill ability
   - Build skills and expertise
7. Summarize the main points
8. Describe next steps
9. Obtain evaluation and feedback

In this generic outline, the trainer plans in advance to review and summarize the material. Trainees remember better how to do tasks they have heard about and performed more than once. There is an old adage among military trainers that describes how to organize training. "Step 1: Tell them what you're going to tell them. Step 2: Tell them. Step 3: Tell them what you told them." While this advice, taken too literally, could lead to repetitious training sessions, it underlines the importance of introducing, presenting, and summarizing training material.

In Step 4 of the generic training outline, where the trainer establishes motivation, it is important to review with the trainees why they are there and what they will achieve at the end of the training. Once trainees are clear on the need for and the objectives of the training, they are more likely to feel motivated to follow the training steps. Step 8 in the outline, in which the trainer describes the next steps, is an opportunity to provide pointers to additional information and resources, to other training opportunities that would logically follow and build on this one, or to suggest how to build expertise, if that is a user's goal.

WHAT ARE THE MOST EFFECTIVE TRAINING ENVIRONMENTS?

Training occurs in a variety of environments, depending on the type of training, its objectives, the needs of the trainees, and the available facilities. The most common training environments are:

- Classes
- Small groups
- One-to-one training
- Self-guided tutorials

Each environment has advantages and disadvantages. Classroom training is more cost-effective because the ratio of trainees to trainers is high. A large group of trainees can be trained by a single trainer, sometimes in a special training facility that includes a computer projection system, an overhead projector, audiovisual equipment, and even computer workstations for hands-on activities. Classroom training can also take advantage of the social learning that takes place during trainee-to-trainee interactions.

Some trainees don't perform as well in large training group settings, however, because they are uncomfortable asking for help in a large group. If the trainer stops to help a couple of trainees, the rest of the trainees may be idle. If some trainees learn at a different pace than others, they are either left behind or slow down the rest of the session. With practice, trainers can learn to effectively handle a large group in a classroom environment, present material at a comfortable pace for everyone, and provide adequate feedback to trainees.

Small groups of trainees have an advantage over classroom sessions in that more individual assistance is available to trainees. Small group training also permits more trainee-to-trainee interaction and social learning. But the more trainers there are for a given group of students, the higher the cost of the training.

One-to-one training is the ultimate small group. It is the most effective environment for trainees because their learning curve can be closely monitored, and help and feedback can be provided in a timely way. Obviously, the cost of one-to-one training is higher than other environments. Then too, social learning among peers is not possible in a one-to-one environment.

Self-guided training, in which a trainee works alone, without a trainer, would appear to be the most cost-effective training environment, because there is no trainer cost. Trainees can cover material at an individualized, comfortable pace. However, trainees in self-guided tutorial programs may not be able to obtain necessary assistance and feedback from a trainer, so self-guided training is more like the classroom training environment in this respect. If help can be provided when it is needed during self-paced training (a possible role for a user support center), then self-guided training can be among the most effective learning environments.

HOW DO LEARNERS LEARN?

In order to choose an effective training method, a trainer needs to consider how learners learn. Unfortunately, there is no one, single learning style that works well for everyone. All learners do not learn effectively and efficiently in the same way and in the same time. Each trainee has a preferred learning style. Some learners are self-motivated and self-reliant and can learn new material best by reading about it or by taking a self-guided tutorial. Others need prodding and the structure that a formal training session can provide. Some learners learn best when they read or listen; others are visual and need to see a diagram in order to retain information. Some people learn concepts easily; others need examples to understand a concept thoroughly.

In general, information retention and learning performance improves with activity and repetition. Figure 6-3 shows several learning methods and how they relate to retention.

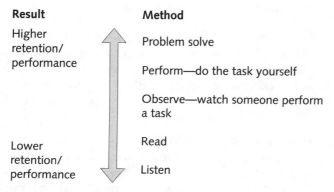

Figure 6-3 Learning methods and retention

Training methods toward the top of the continuum increase the likelihood that information presented will be retained and that job skill performance will improve. In other words, the more that trainees are active participants in the learning process—rather than passive recipients of information—the better they will retain information. What does this continuum say about classroom education experiences based on listening to lectures and reading a textbook?

Learning is often a social phenomenon. The trainer–trainee relationship is usually a human relationship, as is the trainee–trainee relationship. Learning from peers in a group can help the learning process and is also a good way to learn teamwork skills. The ability to work with a team is excellent practice for today's business world, where the size and complexity of projects often requires group effort.

WHAT ARE ALTERNATIVE DELIVERY SYSTEMS FOR TRAINING MATERIALS?

When they decide how to present training materials, trainers can consider a large number of alternative delivery systems. A **delivery system** is a method of presenting information. Most presentations use a combination of the delivery systems shown in Figure 6-4.

Lecture method	Product demonstrations
Reading assignment	Tutorials
Online reading assignment	Hands-on activities
Group discussion	Case studies
Visual aids	Collaborative or group learning
Multimedia materials	Computer-based training (CBT)
Handouts and cheat sheets	Web-based training (WBT)

Figure 6-4   Commonly used training delivery systems

Lecture method. The lecture method is a tried-and-true way to communicate information from an instructor to a learner. It makes effective use of an instructor's time, which is one reason it is popular in higher education. However, the learner's role is very passive, which is why some experts question the effectiveness of this method. Lectures can be used effectively in combination with other delivery systems to introduce topics and materials, motivate trainees, and guide trainees toward a useful learning experience.

Reading assignment from a textbook, trade book, or vendor manual. Some people feel that reading is a preferable delivery method to lectures because the trainee is more actively involved in the learning process. Reading materials need to be planned carefully so that the amount of material to be read is reasonable given the time available. Reading materials should be selected to match the reading ability of the trainees. Some textbook materials are written at too high a reading level for trainees to understand.

Trade books may cover materials thoroughly but are often not organized well for use in training sessions. Also, trade books usually lack learning objectives, chapter summaries, glossaries, comprehension self-tests, and hands-on activities or projects that both instructors and learners need.

Vendor manuals usually seem very authoritative because product manufacturers publish them. However, vendor manuals vary considerably in quality. Some are well organized and well written; others are so poorly written that they actually hinder effective learning. Vendor manuals are often organized as reference manuals, rather than in a tutorial style that makes the most sense to learners.

In addition to giving trainees specific reading assignments, train users to access a variety of supplementary resource materials. Let them know where the materials are located and ensure that they know how to use them effectively.

6

Online reading assignment. An increasing number of hardware and software vendors provide online tutorials and help systems with their products. Online reading assignments can be an effective delivery method. Online materials today tend to be better designed and written than many printed vendor manuals. Furthermore, online materials with hyperlinks can be interactive so that users can search for the information they need and locate answers to questions, which promotes more effective learning.

Group discussion. For some types of training, group discussion is an improvement over the lecture method because it more actively involves trainees. Group discussion is most effective when it is beneficial to share experiences, as in user needs assessment training, help desk call handling procedures, design issues in desktop publishing, or ethical issues.

Visual aids. Visual aids are a popular supplement to lectures and readings because they take advantage of the old adage that "a picture is worth a thousand words." Pictures, charts, diagrams, and other images are useful training aids because most trainees tend to retain visual information better than information they have only heard. Visual aids should be large enough to be visible to the entire audience. The most effective visual aids have simple designs with judicious use of color for emphasis.

Multimedia materials. If visual aids are effective presentation tools, multimedia materials can be even more effective. **Multimedia materials** include a combination of text, still images, animation, and sound. Each form of media can reinforce others to provide a powerful presentation to increase the amount of material learned, as well as the ability to recall material at a later time. However, the cost to develop effective multimedia materials is greater than the cost of many other delivery systems. The cost may be especially prohibitive for a one-time training session; but when the cost of development can be spread over multiple sessions, multimedia materials can be very effective learning aids.

Handouts and cheat sheets. As effective as training can be, training sessions are, by their nature, generally a one-time event. What happens when users return to their workstations, time passes, and they've forgotten important parts of their training? Training sessions, especially short ones, are more effective if they include printed materials users can take with them. Handouts and cheat sheets should contain enough information that users can recall important facts or steps in a procedure. They should not contain extensive detail, because then they become documentation, which is less likely to be read and used.

Product demonstrations. Although hands-on product use during a training session is usually desirable, the lack of equipment, lack of sufficient copies of software, lack of time, or other logistical problems occasionally dictate that the training include only a product demonstration. Liquid crystal display (LCD) projection technology has improved so dramatically recently that it is now possible for even large groups of 50 to 75 trainees to effectively "look over the shoulder" of trainers as they demonstrate an operating system or applications software package.

Product training demonstrations should be carefully designed to adjust the pace of the demonstration. A trainer should be careful not to overwhelm users by going so fast that trainees cannot follow or understand the material. The pace of a demonstration is especially important in a GUI (graphical user interface) environment where it is possible for a trainer to point and click so rapidly that trainees cannot follow the sequence of steps in a procedure. Experienced trainers learn to pause between mouse clicks to give each trainee's eyes and brain an opportunity to assimilate the procedure.

Tutorials. Self-guided **tutorials**, which permit trainees to work through an interactive learning session at their own pace, are one of the most effective ways for computer users to learn new topics. In some tutorials, trainees use hardware or software products as they go through the tutorial. Some on-screen tutorials merely simulate hardware or software products. In either case, a trainee has an opportunity to learn new materials in an environment that is very close to the one he or she will use when the training is completed.

Trainees like the self-paced nature of tutorials, as well as the opportunity to repeat difficult lessons or take a refresher course. Although the cost to develop tutorial materials is very high, once they are developed, hundreds or thousands of users can benefit from a good tutorial at little additional cost per user.

Hands-on activities. Because performance leads to skill development and higher information retention, hands-on activities are an especially effective delivery method for many kinds of computer training. Hands-on activities (sometimes called lab exercises) and practical projects let trainees try out what they have learned, build skills and expertise, and learn to become independent. They can be a significant step toward user self-reliance.

Hands-on activities and projects should begin with easier tasks and progress to more difficult ones so that trainees can experience initial success before trying more complex tasks and projects. It is useful to provide immediate feedback during hands-on activities, as it is difficult to unlearn a skill once the trainee has learned an incorrect or counterproductive way to perform a task. How many readers have watched a user meticulously move the cursor across an entire line of text to the end when a single keystroke or mouse click would accomplish the same result?

Case studies. Larger projects, sometimes called case studies, are designed to encourage trainees to make the transition from the artificial environment of the training room to the realities of the business world. Usually based on actual business situations, case studies are a popular method in higher education to simulate in a training environment the kinds of experiences users will encounter on the job. Case studies are usually more involved than a hands-on activity or a small project and require trainees to apply the skills they have learned. The Case Projects at the end of the chapters in this book are examples of this integrative method of skill testing.

Collaborative or group learning. Collaborative learning activities may involve group discussions, collective hands-on activities, group problem solving, or participation in a joint case study team. Once called group learning, collaborative learning is based on the experience that learning is a social phenomenon and that trainees can learn a great deal from other trainees. Collaborative learning groups can also include a role for the trainer as a learner in the joint learning experience.

Computer-based training. A growth industry in the technical training field is computer-based training. **Computer-based training** (CBT) includes a combination of tutorials, multimedia, product demonstrations, and hands-on activities that use a computer system as an automated training system. Some CBT systems provide features that handle administrative tasks, such as registering trainees, controlling access, presenting information, assessing trainee learning, and monitoring trainee progress. Most CBT products today are distributed on CD-ROM, but older systems used audiocassettes and VCR tapes as delivery media. CBT training can be cost-effective for large groups, but high-quality, instructionally sound CBT materials are extremely expensive to develop.

Web-based training. The latest development in automated training systems is use of the World Wide Web as a vehicle to deliver training. Web-based training (WBT) is very similar to computer-based training, except the Internet replaces CD-ROMs as the delivery media. WBT is likely to make low-cost training modules readily available anywhere in the world. Unfortunately, there is currently little quality control for Web-based training, so a support staff member needs to preview training modules for quality, relevance, and cost-effectiveness. Education and training institutions are just beginning to study and understand the use of the Internet to deliver distance learning in an effective way.

Does the growth in popularity of self-paced training materials such as online tutorials, computer-based training, and Web-based training mean human trainers are obsolete? Is this another instance where human employees have been replaced by a computer system? Probably not. Although it is fairly clear that a delivery system revolution may be under way in the training industry, it is unlikely that the trainer's role will disappear completely. Training will continue to be a responsibility of the user support center and part of the job description of user support specialists, even though the popularity of various delivery systems changes over time. It is more likely that the training role will change. In the future, trainers are more likely to

- Assess training needs of employees
- Design training programs
- Evaluate and recommend training materials
- Help trainees make transitions between modules

- Assess training performance and effectiveness
- Assist trainees when individual attention is needed

These are not tasks CBT or WBT delivery systems can perform very well. Future trainers are less likely to design, develop, and present training materials, except where specialized materials are needed for small training audiences. The mass market is probably headed in the direction of automated training delivery systems.

MARY ANN SHAFFER
REFERENCE LIBRARIAN
TIMBERLAND REGIONAL LIBRARY
OLYMPIA, WASHINGTON

Mary Ann Shaffer is a good example of a professional whose primary job is not computer user support, but who occasionally gets involved in a user support function in her work. Mary Ann is a Reference Librarian. However, part of her job involves training computer users. In this CloseUp, Mary Ann describes an assignment to provide training to other library staff members on Internet use.

I have been running training sessions for new Timberland Library staff in the basics of using the Internet. Based on the kinds of Internet questions librarians frequently get from patrons, I prepared an outline of the topics I want to cover in each training session. Most of the trainees have never used the Internet before, so I start out at a very basic level. I use Netscape Navigator as a browser, although I briefly touch on Microsoft's Internet Explorer. The training session lasts 3 hours. We start with the Timberland home page (*www.timberland.lib.wa.us*). I discuss and demonstrate the various subject links, search engines, information about Timberland, Internet tutorials, and an online catalog, all of which are accessible from Timberland's Web site. We spend most of the training time on how to use subject indexes and search engines because they are excellent library research tools. I use my personal favorite search engine, Metacrawler, to demonstrate how to do effective and efficient World Wide Web searches. I also demonstrate how to use specific URLs to access sites of interest to library staff and patrons.

For the last hour of the class, I give the participants a hands-on assignment sheet. It contains a prepared set of URLs and some Internet searches to try out their skills with a search engine. There is never enough time to finish everything, but I send them back to work with the opportunity to try more search questions when they have time.

I encourage the participants to practice their new skills immediately when they go back to work—or at home—because that reinforces what they have learned. They will need reinforcement so they will be able to answer patrons' questions or show patrons how to access the Internet for themselves. Timberland has Internet work stations in all 27 branches in our service area, so our staff gets lots of questions from patrons about Internet use. The trainees in my classes very quickly become Internet *trainers* when they get back on the job.

For the first time I recently incorporated a PC connected to a projection unit in the training session. It made the whole task much easier for me and for the librarians I trained. They could look over my shoulder, so to speak, while I demonstrated various aspects of Internet use.

I do enjoy the training opportunity, but from time-to-time I still run into librarians who have never sat down at a PC before and have never used a mouse. It is often difficult to teach a group with such a wide diversity of previous experience. Fortunately, in the last class I taught, all the participants had some previous experience because they all have PCs at home. That always makes the training sessions easier for everyone.

6

How is Training Evaluated?

The last training preparation task is training assessment. All training should be evaluated to ensure that it meets the goals it was intended to meet. There are two separate assessment activities that trainers should plan during the preparation steps. The first is feedback to the trainees on how well they met the learning objectives. Feedback can be in the form of a test or quiz that covers concepts and vocabulary. Trainee feedback can also include activities or exercises that use a computer to perform a task that measures mastery of the performance objectives.

Just as trainees need to assess their performance, trainers need feedback as well. Trainees' performance on tests and hands-on activities also provide feedback to the trainer. If trainees don't do very well on the tests and hands-on activities, does that say more about the performance of the trainee or the trainer? Trainers should analyze the results of tests, quizzes, activities, and exercises to see where trainees succeeded and where they didn't. Armed with that knowledge, trainers can adjust training modules to correct problems.

Evaluation forms for trainees to use are another way to obtain trainer feedback. Evaluation forms provide an opportunity for trainees to give their perspective on the strengths and areas that need improvement in the training session. The form in Figure 6-5 is a training evaluation form that can be filled out by both the trainee and the trainer (as a kind of self-evaluation).

Training Evaluation

☐ Trainer: _____   ☐ Trainee: _____

Place a check mark (√) in the column that represents your reaction to each statement.

	Agree	Somewhat Agree	Somewhat Disagree	Disagree	Does Not Apply
1. The objectives of the training were clear.					
2. Terms used in the training were defined.					
3. The training was organized in a step-by-step approach.					
4. The training included useful examples.					
5. The trainer made effective use of time, and the pace was about right.					
6. Training aids were useful.					
7. Overall, the training was done well.					

What was the best part of the training?

What could be improved?

Figure 6-5　An evaluation form

To analyze feedback on trainer evaluation forms, look for response patterns. Although trainees may not agree in their responses to all questions, there may be one particular item to which many trainees assign lower ratings. Trainers should pay particular attention to these items because they represent areas that are the most obvious candidates for improvement.

Training evaluation is a useful tool to help trainers constantly improve their skills at planning, preparing, and presenting training sessions.

STEP 3: PRESENT THE TRAINING

If a trainer has done a good job in the planning and preparation steps, the actual presentation of the training is more likely to be effective and satisfying to the trainee. Figure 6-6 summarizes the top ten list of training presentation guidelines that trainers should observe:

1.   Practice the presentation.

2.   Arrive early to check the facility.

3.   Don't read notes.

4.   Don't try to cover too much material.

5.   Teach the most important skills.

6.   Use humor sparingly.

7.   Stop for comprehension checks.

8.   Monitor the training environment.

9.   Provide frequent breaks.

10. Obtain professional feedback.

Figure 6-6   Training presentation guidelines

Each of these guidelines is explained in more detail in the following paragraphs.

1. **Practice the presentation**. Most trainers find it helpful to practice their training sessions to work out any trouble spots. Some trainers call this a **beta test run,** similar to software beta tests, where companies distribute prereleases of their software to potential users and ask them to use it and note any problems they find. If possible, find a colleague who will act as your audience as you present the training. A beta test gives you feedback from a neutral perspective and is an opportunity to see how the materials work, whether they can be delivered in the allotted time, if the transitions between topics are smooth, and whether overheads and handouts are effective.

2. **Arrive early to check the facility**. Arrive at the training facility early enough to check the physical arrangements for the training. Experienced trainers always do a dry run to make sure their equipment works (including trainer and trainee computers, projection and overhead equipment, lights, sound, and other aspects of the training environment). Make sure participants can see you and your materials from everywhere in the room. You may need to reconfigure the room setup, such as the table and chair layout, or the equipment location, so that it meets your needs and is more comfortable for trainees.

3. **Don't read notes**. If you have prepared detailed notes to use during the training, avoid reading them or reciting statements from memory. It's better to have a general familiarity with what you want to say and use your own words to present the material. Most successful trainers find that it is more effective to work from an outline than to write out or memorize what they want to cover.

4. **Don't try to cover too much material**. A trainer who has too much material for the time allotted should not try to cover everything. When trainers try to review too much material, they rush through it, which makes the pace of the training too fast and therefore difficult for trainees to keep up. Experienced trainers find that it's preferable to reduce the number of topics and cover fewer topics thoroughly.

5. **Teach the most important skills**. When trainers know a piece of hardware or a software package thoroughly, they are sometimes tempted to augment the training with "bells and whistles," features of hardware or software that may be interesting but are infrequently used, especially by beginning users. Bells and whistles might impress the audience with the trainer's knowledge, but they distract from the primary training objectives. They may even confuse new users who are struggling with what is important among all the new material with which they are confronted. Remember to focus on the needs of the learners, not on the trainer.

6. **Use humor sparingly**. Humor during a training session can make the session more enjoyable for trainees, but trainers should be careful about the amount and type of humor they use. The best humor is self-directed because it shows trainees you are human. Ridicule, which is humor directed at someone else, is never acceptable. Avoid making negative comments about vendor products, even in jest. If you are a naturally humorous person, you may need to reign in your talent and recognize the difference between training and entertainment. Some trainers, mindful that the trainees will evaluate them, cross over the line from training into entertainment. Use humor effectively, but recognize that the tradeoff between short-term entertainment and long-term training results should err on the side of training.

7. **Stop for comprehension checks**. During the presentation, stop periodically and ensure that trainees are following the material. Many trainers find it useful to stop for a series of "quick check" questions using a variety of questioning styles. These can include direct questions about the material that has been covered (such as "What are the two ways to select text?"), open questions (such as "What is the best way to locate a file using Windows Explorer?"), or group questions (such as "Get together with your group and take two minutes to list the most important features of the spelling and grammar checker."). Periodic questioning will help keep trainees alert and involved because they know they might be called on to discuss what was covered.

8. **Monitor the training environment**. Trainers should always keep an eye on the training environment to make sure that users are comfortable and focused on the training. Is the temperature in the training room too hot or too cold? Is the room too noisy because a door or window is open? Learn to read your audience. Watch for signs they are uncomfortable, interested, bored, or attentive. Successful trainers can check their perception with the trainees. "It seems like there is a lot of noise coming from the hallway. Can you all hear the presentation?"

9. **Provide frequent breaks**. In a long session, recognize that trainees can become tired, which can affect their concentration. Plan the training to include frequent breaks. Trainers usually find that it's better to have more short stretch breaks than to have fewer long breaks.

10. **Obtain professional feedback**. After a new trainer gets initial experience with the training process, it is useful to get some professional evaluation from other trainers. They often can spot even very small mannerisms that may be distracting to trainees. Another excellent training improvement tool is to videotape a training session. Although a videotape of your own training session can be difficult to watch, every trainer can learn something from the experience that will improve her or his training proficiency.

The training presentation should follow the structure the trainer planned during Step 2. It should include time for questions and both kinds of feedback where appropriate: a test and/or hands-on activity for trainees and a trainee evaluation of the trainer. The purpose of the trainer evaluation, of course, is primarily to improve one's skills and capabilities as a trainer.

 For more information on presenting successful training sessions, see Geoffrey Moss, *The Corporate Trainer's QUICK Reference*, Homewood, IL: Irwin Publishing, 1993. Moss's book contains a wealth of good ideas about training.

After each training session, trainers usually review any feedback they receive and evaluate their own performance. They then modify their presentation style or materials if necessary to correct any problem areas. Trainers usually find that there is always room for improvement to present training that meets learners' needs, helps them become self-reliant, and reduces the company's overall user support costs.

CHAPTER SUMMARY

- User training is an important part of user support because it makes users more self-reliant. A well-trained user is more productive and less likely to generate a call for assistance than one who has not been adequately trained. Though this chapter focuses on training, it assumes that an understanding of vocabulary and conceptual explanations are an important educational base on which to build training modules.

- The training process described in this chapter is a three-step approach:
  1. **Planning**. This step includes identification of who the trainees are, what they need to know or be able to do as a result of the training, the background the trainees bring to the training, the level of skills the trainees need (how well do they need to be able to perform), and the specific learning or performance objectives for the training. Plans should address several levels of training skills including concepts (vocabulary), understanding (explanatory ability), skills (task performance), and expertise (highly skilled performance).

2. **Preparation**. Preparation for training answers several questions.

   - What specific topics will be covered

   - How the topics will be organized

   - Selection of a training environment from among classroom, small group, face-to-face, and self-guided.

   - How the training will be delivered (lectures, readings, discussion, visual aids and media, handouts, demonstrations, tutorials, hands-on activities, case studies, group learning, and automated learning systems like CBT and WBT are popular alternatives)

   - How the trainee and the trainer will be evaluated

3. **Presentation**. A successful training presentation depends on adequate planning and preparation. Ten guidelines help new trainers make more effective presentations. Evaluation of training is an important way trainers improve their future presentations.

KEY TERMS

- **beta test run** — A practice training session to evaluate materials and identify problem areas; this term borrows from the software industry, where prerelease software is distributed to end users who then look for problems.

- **collaborative learning** — Learning that occurs in a group and can include group discussions, collective hands-on activities, group problem solving, or participation in a joint case study team.

- **computer-based training** — Training that occurs as learners use a computer system that provides tutorials, multimedia presentations, demonstrations, or hands-on activities.

- **delivery system** — A method of presenting information in a training session, such as lecture, group discussion, group learning, or hands-on activities.

- **education** — The teaching and learning process that aims to provide conceptual understanding and whose goal is to provide basic vocabulary and understanding of general principles.

- **learning objectives** — A statement of the knowledge and skills trainees need to learn.

- **multimedia materials** — A presentation that includes a combination of text, still images, animation, and sound.

- **performance objectives** — A statement of what a trainee should be able to do at the end of a training session; usually starts with an action verb, such as plan, change, explain, evaluate, or prepare; performance objectives should be measurable.

- **training** — The teaching and learning process that focuses on performing activities and building expertise; can be short term and is often tested by measuring a learner's ability to perform specific tasks.

- **tutorials** — An interactive learning technique where trainees go through step-by-step material at their own pace.

REVIEW QUESTIONS

1. What is education? What is training? How are education and training similar? How are they different?

2. Is the following statement true or false? "Schools provide education, and businesses provide training." Explain your answer.

3. What are the three steps in the training process? Briefly explain the general tasks a trainer performs in each step.

4. In planning a training session, what information should a trainer obtain about the trainees?

5. How does training adults differ from training children?

6. What factors can affect trainee motivation?

7. How should a trainer determine trainees' needs?

8. What are two ways of dealing with a group of learners with different levels of knowledge?

9. What classification of learning levels is presented in this chapter? List the four components and how they differ.

10. What is a performance objective? Give an example.

11. What is a training plan, and what does it include?

12. What are the four main training environments? Describe each one.

13. Name three learning methods and briefly discuss how each one relates to the amount of information learners retain.

14. What is a delivery system? Name ten common delivery systems for training.

15. Describe an advantage and a disadvantage of the lecture method.

16. What are visual aids? What is their role in the learning process?

17. What are multimedia materials, and what is their advantage over printed materials?

18. What is the main advantage of handouts in a training session?

19. What are tutorials, and what is their main advantage?

20. How do hands-on activities help the learning process? How should hands-on activities be organized?

21. What are case studies and how do they help trainees learn?

22. What is collaborative learning? Give two examples. How does collaborative learning help trainees learn?

23. What is computer-based training. Give three examples of media on which computer-based training is delivered.

24. What are two ways to evaluate a training session?

25. What are the ten guidelines to successful training presentations?

HANDS-ON PROJECTS

 ## PROJECT 6-1

If you are taking a class or you work for a company or organization, describe your work or school colleagues in terms of their knowledge and experience as end users. Do your colleagues have similar experience levels, or are they from diverse backgrounds? If there are considerable differences in education or experience among your work or school colleagues, what problems would the differences cause a trainer who was planning a training module for the group? Write a one-page summary of your findings.

 ## PROJECT 6-2

Choose a software package you know well, such as Windows 95 or one of the Microsoft Office 97 applications. Identify an important: 1) concept, 2) point of understanding (explanation), 3) skill, and 4) expertise that a user of the package would be expected to have. Summarize the information in a one-page report.

 ## PROJECT 6-3

Suppose that a trainer has identified as a general goal for a training module *Ability to format printed output according to a specification sheet*. Rewrite this goal statement so that it specifies a measurable performance objective. Write three additional measurable performance objectives for Windows 95 or one of the Microsoft Office applications.

PROJECT 6-4

Discuss this statement with your project group: "Using existing materials from a user's manual, textbook, or trade book as a source of training ideas may violate the original author's copyright, and therefore should never be done." If you need more information on copyright, use a search engine to search the Web. Discuss the information you find. Write a summary of your reaction to the statement after your discussion. Note any points of disagreement among your group.

PROJECT 6-5

Do you personally prefer classroom training, small group sessions, one-on-one training, or self-guided tutorials? Why? Are there circumstances under which you feel one form of training is more effective than another? Write a short summary of your response.

PROJECT 6-6

Locate a training module that uses computer-based or Web-based training. It can also be a video or a CD. Try out the CBT or WBT approach, either alone or with your project group. Write a critique of the module. How well does it achieve its goals? What are the advantages and disadvantages of CBT or WBT delivery systems for training modules in that subject area?

PROJECT 6-7

What other training characteristics could be evaluated in the training evaluation form in Figure 6-5? If your school or work organization uses a training evaluation form, get one and compare it with those described in this chapter. What are the biggest differences? Describe the changes you would make to the evaluation form in Figure 6-5 based on your research.

PROJECT 6-8

Based on your personal experiences as a trainee or student (as a recipient of training), what are some common mistakes trainers or instructors make that you would add to the top ten suggestions for trainers in Figure 6-8? Write your personal top ten list that includes presentation skills you would like to improve on.

CASE PROJECTS

1. FRED'S PAINT STORE

Andrew Spitz is a user support specialist at Fred's Paint Store. In his work with employees over the last year, he has seen many instances where employees are wasting time formatting their Microsoft Word documents inefficiently. Sometimes employees write long reports, client summaries, or presentations, and they manually format each heading. Andrew has noticed that this is very time-consuming and feels that they would save a lot of time if they knew how to use Word's style feature.

He has discussed the situation with the director of user support, Miguel Rodriguez. Miguel has authorized Andrew to hold a two-hour training session with interested employees who sign up. Andrew has asked you to design a training module. Plan and prepare a training module on Word styles. The training module you prepare should include all of these elements:

PLANNING

1. Analyze job skills required
2. Analyze the trainees (make assumptions where necessary)
3. Assess the needs of the trainees
4. Set training objectives

PREPARATION

5. Select and organize training content
6. Select training methods, techniques, aids
7. Prepare training modules
8. Decide how to evaluate the training

Make sure that the training module you design can be used by another trainer. If you have experience with PowerPoint, create a slide presentation that can be used during the training presentation. Then draw or describe the ideal room configuration for this training. Show or describe the location of chairs, tables, presentation equipment, computers, and chalkboard or flip charts.

2. DESIGN YOUR OWN TRAINING MODULE

Choose a topic that you know something about. Plan, prepare, and present a training module on the topic. Some examples of possible topics include:

- How to use basic Novell NetWare commands
- How to write MS-DOS batch files
- How to do a mail merge in a word processor
- How to install a CD-ROM drive in a PC
- How to use a switchboard in Microsoft Access
- How to use one or more basic features of a help desk software package, such as Remedy, Support Magic, or Clientele
- How to use a Macintosh, intended for Windows 95 users

The training module you prepare should include all of these elements:

PLANNING

1. Analyze job skills required
2. Analyze the trainees
3. Assess the needs of the trainees
4. Set training objectives

PREPARATION

5. Select and organize training content
6. Select training methods, techniques, aids
7. Prepare training modules
8. Decide how to evaluate training

PRESENTATION

9. Present training module
10. Evaluate the training
11. Review and revise training process

First, work on the plan for a sample training module for the topic you selected. Cover Steps 1 through 6 in planning and preparation first. For some of these steps, such as the training audience, your instructor may ask you to make some assumptions. If you are in a class environment, work with other class members to brainstorm what could be included and what would be omitted from your training module.

Next, based on the results of brainstorming with class members, work individually to prepare a training module for delivery (Step 7). Your module should be prepared for one-to-one delivery in about 30 minutes. The module should include a hands-on component if possible, a short quiz, and time for a brief evaluation. If you have experience with PowerPoint, create a presentation that can be used during the training presentation.

Then, during the next class session, give each class member an opportunity to be a trainer for another class member (Step 9). Class members who were trainers during the first 30 minutes can be trainees during the second 30 minutes, and vise versa. At the end of the training session, both the trainer and the trainee should fill out a short evaluation (a self-evaluation for the trainer). Use an evaluation form from this chapter, the one you developed in Project 6-7, or write one of your own specifically for this training session. If you are working alone on this book, ask a friend or work colleague to volunteer to help you evaluate your training module as a kind of beta test.

When your training beta test is finished, write a short summary of what you learned from the experience that would improve the training module, or your presentation of it, the next time you present it.

3. PRESENT SOMEONE ELSE'S MODULE

In corporate training, a trainer is often provided with preplanned and prepackaged training materials to present. If you'd like additional practice in presenting training materials, repeat presentation Steps 9 through 11 listed in case 2, Design Your Own Training Module. But this time, do the presentation for a training module a colleague has planned and prepared.

DOCUMENTATION FOR END USERS

As you learned in the last chapter, training users is important to make them self-reliant and reduce their need for user support. However, training is usually a one-time event. That is why a successful training session should include handouts, cheat sheets, and other documentation that users can take back to their workplace as a reminder of what they learned. In addition to printed documentation, online documentation such as help systems and README files are an increasingly popular way to communicate information effectively to end users.

AFTER READING THIS CHAPTER AND COMPLETING THE EXERCISES YOU WILL BE ABLE TO:

- Describe the types of end user documentation
- Explain how technical writing differs from other writing
- Explain how technical documents are organized
- Plan effective documentation
- Describe the technical writing process
- Use formats effectively
- Explain some technical writing strategies
- Describe some common problems in technical writing
- Describe some technical writing tools
- Evaluate documentation

To create any form of documentation, printed or online, you need a basic knowledge of technical writing. The goal of technical writing is to produce documentation that effectively and efficiently communicates information the reader needs. Good documentation saves users time; bad documentation costs users time and reduces their productivity. Although you may not have written technical documentation before, you have probably had occasion to use a manual, online help, or some other form of documentation. From this experience, you may already have some thoughts about what makes good or bad technical writing, and what has or has not been effective at addressing your needs as a user.

This chapter gives you an overview of the most important topics in technical writing, but it is not a substitute for a good book or a course on the subject. The chapter's purpose is to review some strategies for user documentation and provide pointers to help you write successfully on technical subjects in a user support position.

TYPES OF USER DOCUMENTATION

There are many situations where members of a user support staff produce written materials. Although technical writing can have several purposes and can be in very different formats, they all must communicate their message clearly. The types of materials are summarized in Figure 7-1.

Brochures and flyers	Proposals, letters, and memos
Newsletters	E-mail messages
Handouts and training aids	Procedural documentation
User guides and manuals	Web pages
Online help systems	Troubleshooting guides

Figure 7-1   Types of technical writing

The following sections briefly describe each type of technical writing.

Brochures and Flyers. Brochures and flyers often promote various computer-related activities, such as staff training sessions, open houses, computer fairs, hardware and software product demonstrations, and guest speakers. This kind of documentation is primarily promotional and is intended to catch the eye of the reader and "sell" the event. User support staff are often involved in setting up these types of events.

Newsletters. Newsletters are an important way some user support groups communicate with their users. Today's powerful word-processing software or special purpose desktop publishing software can help you create newsletters with multiple columns and embedded images such as diagrams, pictures, icons, and charts. User support newsletters are especially popular in large companies where the support staff does not come in direct contact with other employees on a regular basis. An increasing number of companies now deliver newsletters online to their employees and customers.

Handouts and Training Aids. Handouts and training aids are primarily intended to summarize and promote recall of material covered in a training session. They may also be distributed online or in a computer documentation library to answer frequently asked "How to…" questions. These documentation pieces are usually short and address a single topic.

User Guides, Handbooks, and Manuals. User guides, handbooks, and manuals are more formal examples of written documentation. For some user support groups, these can be tens or hundreds of pages long, and are often printed in book format. They supplement vendor documentation and trade books with information specific to a company or computer facility. For example, a university or college may prepare a user handbook that explains what computer facilities and services are available, including how to access them, how to get remote dial-up communications software, ground rules for use and abuse, how to use popular software programs, and how to get help. In companies, corporate Information Services departments may publish similar guides for employees.

Software development companies and hardware vendors publish a variety of user guides and computer manuals that describe for purchasers how to install and use their products. These manuals may be organized in a tutorial format, which guides a user step-by-step through the features of a program, or they may be organized in a reference format. Some manuals combine tutorials with a reference guide. A tutorial format is convenient for new users, because it emphasizes the natural sequence of steps to learn the features of a product, beginning with the simplest tasks. However, a tutorial format introduces features as users need them for a particular task. This means that information about printers, for example, might be located at various places in a tutorial manual, as various printing needs arise. For experienced users, a reference format is probably more useful, because all the information on one subject, such as printing, is in one place.

Online Help Systems. Online help systems are increasingly common in today's software packages. They are often supplied on CD-ROMs that customers can use for self-training. In other cases, they are in the form of help files that install at the same time as the software itself. Some online help systems are well written and can effectively rival or replace printed manuals as a source of well-organized and accurate information. Writing online documentation is an art, however, because the information presented must be succinct. Writing for on-screen use is different from writing that will be printed on paper. Use of hypertext links and index searches in online documentation can provide users with powerful tools to locate needed information. Despite the increasing popularity and convenience of online documentation, however, some users still prefer to access large amounts of information in a printed form. It takes some end users a long time to feel comfortable with online documentation and to give up their dependence on printed materials.

Proposals, Letters, and Memos. Because businesses and organizations account for a significant portion of computer use, support staff need to be able to write proposals, letters, and memos. Support specialists who perform needs assessments for end users or departments frequently need to write the results of their investigations in the form of proposals. In addition, there is often a need to write memos, letters, performance appraisals, and other correspondence to colleagues, end users (both inside and outside the company), and supervisors.

E-mail Messages. The ability to communicate effectively via e-mail is becoming recognized as an important writing skill for user support specialists, especially those working at a help desk that communicates with users mainly by e-mail. E-mail messages from a help desk project an image of the company and should reflect good technical writing skills. Although internal e-mail messages may be somewhat less formal than messages intended for recipients outside the company, don't forget that even messages to coworkers and supervisors project an image of the sender. Supervisors may use e-mail messages as one measure of an employee's promotability.

Procedural and Operational Documentation. Procedural and operational documentation includes written procedure steps and checklists intended primarily for internal company use. The written descriptions of the steps to install hardware and software and the installation procedure checklists in Chapter 5 are examples of technical procedural documentation. Support specialists also use technical documentation to prepare problem reports in a help desk environment. Even for internal documents such as these, technical writing skills are essential. Procedural and operational documentation that is unclear, poorly organized, or incorrect, costs staff time, produces errors, and increases user frustration. Clear, well-organized documentation communicates information efficiently and reflects well on the writer.

Web Pages. Because an increasing amount of written materials ends up on the World Wide Web today, the ability to write for this medium is becoming more important. Web pages need to be organized and written so that users can locate information quickly and easily. This medium is another where the image of a company or organization is at stake. In general, materials designed for Web access must be very short, but contain hypertext links that lead readers to additional information. Web-based materials must be well written because Web users often do not have the patience to wade through a poorly written document to try to find the information they need. They tend to skim quickly and then click to go to another site.

Troubleshooting Guides. Finally, user support staff often write troubleshooting guides to help other employees solve problems. Troubleshooting guides can range from a chapter in a user guide, to a script to handle a specific type of problem, to a report in a problem-solving knowledgebase. Though this type of documentation is often internal, it still must be clear, concise, and well written.

In this chapter, all of these types of technical writing are considered forms of **documentation**. There are more similarities than differences among the various writing types. The following sections stress the similarities.

How Technical Writing Differs from Other Writing

Technical writing is different from other types of writing, such as personal letters, research papers, or novels. The principal areas of difference are in its style, the type of information it communicates, and its goals.

1. Technical writing uses short, declarative sentences, short phrases, and lists instead of long sentences that contain unnecessary words or phrases. In general, short, simple sentences are preferable to longer sentences. A simple sentence has one subject and one verb. Sometimes it is possible to use a compound sentence, which contains *and* or *but* as a connector and includes two subjects and two verbs. Limit the use of more intricate structures, such as a complex sentence, which has dependent or independent clauses, and a compound–complex sentence, which uses both *and* and *but* connectors in addition to clauses.

   You may wonder if simple sentences are as interesting as more complex and complicated ones. Remember that the purpose of technical writing is not to entertain, but to communicate information vital to the reader's productivity. Also, not all readers have good reading skills; they may have reading problems, or they may use English as a second language. In order to communicate effectively with the largest number of readers, keep sentences simple.

2. Technical writing often communicates a step-by-step sequence of events or tasks. Technical writers use a style and format that helps each reader understand the sequence.

3. The most important point should be at the beginning of a section or a topic discussion instead of at the end. Moreover, document writers should not try to entertain readers by calling attention to their own personalities.

4. Technical writing should be brief, but it shouldn't be cryptic, lacking information essential to understanding. Brief writing is short, but covers the information a user needs. To include more detailed information, it can contain **pointers** or cross-references to the location where a user can find more details.

5. Technical writers need to present information with an economical writing style. Readers of technical documentation usually want to open the document, find what they want to know, and get back to work. If they have to spend unnecessary time searching for buried information, then their productivity is reduced.

Because it fulfills very specific user needs, good technical writing follows these conventions. If it does not, it will not help computer users, and it will result in a higher volume of calls to user support.

7

How Technical Documents are Organized

The most successful technical documentation is organized in a logical sequence that begins with the most general information on a topic and then moves to more specific, detailed information. A common organization for technical documentation is:

Introduction
Purpose of document
Who the document is intended for
Why read the document

Body
Explanation and task steps
Common problems users encounter

Summary
Pointers to additional information

The introduction begins by addressing three questions. First, what is the purpose of this document? Second, who should read this? And third, why would anyone want to read this? In other words, the reader is going to want to know what information he or she will get from reading this document. Technical writers should answer these three questions immediately to save those readers for whom a document is *not* intended a lot of time.

The body of a technical document should include explanatory material. Most readers want a short explanation to help them understand why something works or why the information is important. Often, this can include a brief explanation of what the hardware or software is capable of and how it can help readers in their work. The explanation is often followed by a detailed description of the steps necessary to perform a task. Finally, the body should briefly describe common problems users are likely to encounter and how to recover from the problems. The summary should round out the discussion.

Some technical writers are tempted to include as much information as they can in a document. The material may digress from the main points to cover material that may be interesting to only a few readers, that isn't critical, or is very technical. It is usually best to omit less critical information or place this type of material in an appendix or attachment along with a pointer to it in the summary, so that readers will know it is there.

Documentation Planning

The steps writers take to plan user documentation writing projects are very similar to those trainers take to plan training sessions. As in training, planning is essential to producing high-quality documentation, regardless of its length or purpose. Most planning steps involve determining the characteristics of the audience and its needs, as shown in Figure 7-2.

- Who is the target audience?

- What does the audience already know?

- What does the audience need to know?

- What do you want the audience to be able to do when they finish reading your document?

Figure 7-2   Documentation planning steps

If you can answer these questions for a piece of documentation you plan to write, you will be well prepared to create a useful, well-targeted document.

Who is the target audience? To answer this question, you need to know readers' level of technical expertise. Writing a task description for new users requires different assumptions and techniques than writing for more experienced, technically sophisticated users. The audience definition should also include an estimate of their reading level. Most newspapers, for example, are written at a ninth to eleventh grade reading level, which is a good level to strive for in computer documentation for end users. Word processors often include tools to measure the reading level of a document.

What does the audience already know? To determine who the audience is, technical writers should attempt to find out the readers' background, including what they already know. A statement in the introduction about what the writer assumes the reader knows can help readers make an informed decision about whether the material is intended for them, whether it covers things they already know, or whether it may be over their heads.

When readers need to know specific procedures, it is sometime difficult to assess what skills they already have. In some situations, you may be able to assess skills using a questionnaire. But because that is not always possible, it is best to cover the most basic skills first, but with appropriate labels so that more skilled users can easily skip to what they need to know.

What does the audience need to know? Answering this question is one of the critical first steps in technical writing because it helps the writer define the purpose of the documentation. As with training (see Chapter 6), the purpose of technical documentation should be to move readers from what they already know to what they need to know.

What do you want the audience to be able to do when they finish reading your document? It is important to know what specific tasks you want the audience to perform after they read your document. This task focus will give direction to your writing and will help users know when they have successfully mastered the information. Is the documentation intended for information purposes only, or does the reader need to make a decision or be able to perform a task? Some documents guide users through specific step-by-step procedures, while others are for reference or troubleshooting.

When you fully understand the audience, their skill level, and their learning needs, you will be able to create a successful document. With a plan for the document, you can then begin the writing process.

THE TECHNICAL WRITING PROCESS

After writers have defined the audience, purpose, and overall organization of a document, they can then begin to write the document itself. Many writers use the seven-step process shown in Figure 7-3 to write a document.

1. Generate a list of important ideas or features to be covered.

2. Organize the list into a logical sequence to form an outline.

3. Expand the outline into a first draft.

4. Edit the draft one or more times.

5. Arrange for an outside review.

6. Revise the draft into its final form.

7. Proofread the document.

Figure 7-3   The technical writing process

Good technical writing follows this process. It may be tempting to take shortcuts due to time constraints, but remember that once a document is published, there is often little or no opportunity to change it. Even very experienced writers would never consider releasing their first draft to end users. They realize that the entire seven-step process is critical to producing quality documents.

1. GENERATE AN IDEA LIST

Writers often use a word processor to generate a list of ideas; others use paper and pencil. At this stage, writers **brainstorm** to generate as many topics as they can think of that might be useful to the reader. From among the potential topics, some become major topics, others become minor topics, and some are discarded.

2. ORGANIZE THE LIST INTO AN OUTLINE

Once they have a topic list that includes everything they want to cover, writers organize the topics into a logical order to form an outline. Most writers don't arrive at the final organizational structure of all topics on the first attempt. It is important to be flexible during the early organizational steps; writers often cut and paste to try out different sequences of ideas.

Most word processors have an outlining feature that makes it easy to rearrange topics. As writers begin to create the outline, other topics may come to mind that can be added. The most important question in creating an outline is "In what order does the reader need to know this information?"

3. Expand the Outline into a First Draft

After carefully creating an outline and checking it for logical flow, writers expand the outline into a first draft by explaining each point in the outline. In writing the first draft, writers use the features described below to make their documents readable and understandable. Although there are many techniques to help produce understandable documentation, these four are basic.

Paragraphs with topic sentences. The document should be organized into paragraphs, with each paragraph covering a different aspect of the topic. Each paragraph should have a topic sentence that introduces the topic in general terms. After the topic sentence, develop each paragraph with the details that support or expand on the topic sentence.

Transitions. Use transitional words like "for example," "therefore," and "as a result" to help show readers the relationship of one sentence to another. Other transitions useful for steps in a procedure are "first," "second," "next," "then," and "finally." Transitions help readers keep track of where they are in a sequence of information.

Defined terms. Good technical writers always define the terms they use. To introduce readers to a new term, define it clearly and boldface the term in the sentence that defines it, as you have seen in this book. When defining terms, be careful not to define a term using the term itself; use a synonym instead.

Formats. As they write the first draft, writers use formats to help readers understand information more easily. Different sized headings, for example, alert the reader to the overall structure. Many writers use italic type for emphasis, although it is best to use emphasis sparingly. Bulleted or numbered lists are useful to alert a reader to the structure of a long section. You'll learn more about formats in the next section.

4. Edit the Draft

After expanding the outline into the first draft, read and edit it. Most writers read through and edit a draft more than once, looking for particular problems on each pass. It is almost impossible for writers to do one edit pass and catch all the different types of problems. Therefore, they might perform one edit pass to delete extra words, because one of the goals of technical writing is to be brief. Consider, for example, the following short paragraph:

> Let's spend a bit more time discussing the relationship between the automatic call distribution (ACD) system and other help desk systems. Only the more sophisticated ACDs allow interfaces to other devices now, but it's clearly the wave of the future, not to mention a productivity enhancer.

The following version eliminates extraneous words while maintaining the meaning:

> Let's discuss the relationship between the automatic call distribution (ACD) system and other help desk systems. Today, only sophisticated ACDs can connect to other devices. However, future models will have this ability, which will enhance user productivity.

Eliminating extra words takes some practice, but is beneficial because tighter prose takes less time to read. Eliminate any words that are not critical to understanding the writer's meaning.

A second type of edit pass writers perform is a format consistency check. The purpose of a **format consistency check** is to make sure that headings and subheadings are in a consistent font and that indentation, centering, boldface type, italics, and underlining are used consistently. Check to see that these formatting features are not overused. Remember that the purpose of formatting is to help the reader understand the structure of the document. They should guide readers through the documentation without hindering understanding or becoming a distraction.

Another type of edit pass is a technical accuracy check. During a **technical accuracy check**, a writer goes through any procedural or technical steps in a document and tests them carefully with the hardware or software. If the documentation has been written about a beta or other prerelease version of hardware or software, it is important that a final accuracy check be made against the final version.

5. Get an Outside Review

The next step is to get an outside review of the draft—a second opinion. Another pair of eyes can often raise questions, spot inconsistencies, find unclear meaning, identify poor writing techniques, and locate other problems that the writer is too close to see. Getting outside criticism can be surprising, especially because writers who spend a lot of time on their first draft are satisfied that it is just about perfect. It can be especially painful if the reviewer doesn't share the same writing style and approach as the writer. But it is extremely important to get a second perspective on any written documentation, especially for documents that will get widespread distribution. This step serves the same purpose as a beta test of a training module. Over time, writers learn to set aside any defensiveness they may feel about their work and realize that the reviewer represents their potential audience. It is far better for a reviewer to find problems early than for the target audience to do so after publication.

6. Revise the Draft

After writers edit the draft and get feedback, they revise it to incorporate the corrections. If a writer is a perfectionist, one of the hardest parts of the writing process is to know when to stop. Although edit passes can serve a useful purpose up to a point, writers must learn when to quit. Fortunately for many technical writers, publication deadlines dictate when you are finished. Additional edit passes can result in very small incremental improvement in a document. At the end of each edit pass, a writer should ask whether the last pass resulted in a substantial improvement, or whether the improvements were only marginal; if they were marginal, that is the time to stop.

7. PROOFREAD THE DOCUMENT

After writing, editing, and revising a document, writers proofread it one last time to make sure that there are no small errors. Sometimes it is useful to have another person or a professional proofreader perform this task. Errors that proofreaders look for include:

Inconsistent capitalization and punctuation. Are proper nouns capitalized the same way? Are there any words that are capitalized that shouldn't be? Are commas used consistently in sentences and within large numbers?

Inconsistent font use. Are headings the correct font and size? Is all the body text in the same font?

Extra spaces between words and sentences. Is there the same number of spaces after every sentence? (Most typeset books and many desktop published documents use only one space after periods.) Is there only one space between words? You can use your word processor to search for two spaces and replace each occurrence with one space.

Incorrect page breaks. Are all the page breaks in logical locations? Are there any large white areas that should be filled with text?

The seven steps in the technical writing process help both new and experienced document writers ensure that their work is both well organized and understandable.

USING FORMATS TO SHOW STRUCTURE

After deciding on a structure for a document, writers must then decide how to successfully communicate the structure to the reader. The structure helps guide the reader through the parts of a document.

At the highest level, documents can be organized into chapters or modules. But within a chapter or module, writers often use different fonts, changes in the size of a font, boldface, upper case, centering, indentation, underlines, bullets, and numbering to help a reader understand the structure. They help the reader to understand what is important and what is less important. These devices also help with transitions from one topic to the next. They answer questions such as, "If I am not interested in this paragraph, where do I skip to start reading again so I don't miss anything?"

Although changes in font, case, indentation, centering, and other formatting can help alert a reader to the structure of a document, some writers get carried away with the power of a word processor and overuse these tools. Two fonts can be useful to help the reader deal with different types of material. But too many different fonts, too much boldface or italics, can be a distraction.

Format consistency is important. Use a consistent format for headings, paragraphs, and tables. Styles or style sheets in popular word processors can help make consistent formatting easy.

For technical manuals or other materials that will receive widespread commercial distribution, hardware and software companies and publishers hire a graphic designer to create a design for the interior of the book. For many smaller projects, however, preformatted templates, which are often created by professional designers, are sufficient.

Finally, when writers need to present a sequence of information, a bulleted or numbered list or a table is often more understandable than a long narrative passage. Lists and tables permit readers to locate quickly the information they need. It can be very difficult to find information quickly in a long narrative passage. Lists are most effective when they support a generalization or summarize information presented in narrative text.

TECHNICAL WRITING STRATEGIES

Some technical writing is a pleasure to read because it is well organized and readers can find the information they need quickly. If you analyze a successful document, some common strategies and approaches stand out.

Analogies. First, technical writers often use analogies to explain new material. For example, to explain the hierarchical structure of disk media, writers often use the **analogy** of an office filing system. They draw a parallel between the information in an office filing system and the information in a computer filing system. Analogies are useful because they relate something a user may be familiar with, an office filing system, to something they need to know about.

Repetition. Second, writers often use repetition for emphasis. Repetition is also a training strategy you encountered in Chapter 6. In both technical documentation and in user training, it is often useful to introduce a topic, explain it, and then summarize it. Repetition helps users learn new material and recall it later.

Consistent word use. Third, technical writers try to use words consistently. In creative writing, writers are taught to look for synonyms in order to avoid overuse of certain words and to inject variety in written work. In technical writing, however, consistent use of words can contribute to the reader's understanding. To vary word use unnecessarily can cause the reader to question whether there are possible subtle differences in meaning. For example, a writer on disk media may use synonyms like "disk," "diskette," and "floppy disk" interchangeably to refer to the same thing. In order to avoid confusion, it is best to choose one word to use consistently throughout a document. Many documentation departments and companies maintain a **style sheet** that lists their preferences for common terms so that all writers can use the same terminology. Sometimes a style sheet is a simple list of preferred terms and spelling conventions. In other cases, a style sheet can be a lengthy document that lists not only terms and spelling conventions but also preferred grammatical structures, product name usage conventions, and the like. Figure 7-4 shows a page from a publisher's style sheet.

Style Sheet *Page 3*

Item	Comments
check box (not checkbox)	
check mark	
checkbook	
choose	Do not use in steps
click (not "click on")	
click and drag (v.)	
click in	Use when positioning a pointer "in" a text box or placing the insertion point "in" a specific area
clip-art (adj.)	clip-art image, clip-art library
click-drag technique	
ClipArt	when referring specifically to Microsoft ClipArt Gallery

Figure 7-4 A page from a style sheet

Parallel structure. Fourth, the concept of parallel structure is important in technical writing. **Parallel structure** means that similar items are handled consistently throughout a document. Consistent formats for titles, headings, and subheadings are one application of parallel structure, as are consistent verb tenses and parts of speech. Parallel structure is also important in bulleted lists. See the example in Figure 7-5.

Not parallel	Parallel
Consider the following ways to measure help desk performance:	Consider the following ways to measure help desk performance:
• first: volume of calls	• call volume
• next: time it takes to respond	• call response time
• resolution time	• call resolution time
• how many calls are backlogged	• call backlog
• call aging	• call aging time

Figure 7-5 Parallel structure in a bulleted list

In the example on the left, note that few of the items in the list are worded the same way. For example, the word *time* appears first for some items, and last in another. The list on the right shows one way to rewrite the list using parallel structure. Notice that all the terms in the list are nouns, and their phrasing is similar.

Consistent verb tense. Finally, technical writers generally use a consistent verb tense throughout a document. Present tense is often preferable unless it is clear that the topic is something that happened in the past.

COMMON PROBLEMS IN TECHNICAL WRITING

There are some common problems that experienced technical writers learn to avoid. Their writing is clearer, more understandable, and easier to read if they avoid the ten problems summarized in Figure 7-6.

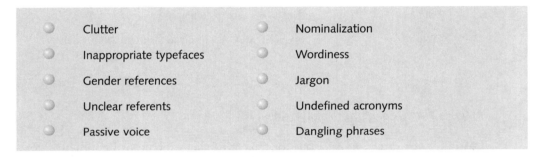

Clutter	Nominalization
Inappropriate typefaces	Wordiness
Gender references	Jargon
Unclear referents	Undefined acronyms
Passive voice	Dangling phrases

Figure 7-6   Ten common technical writing problems

Each of these common problems is described in the following paragraphs so that you can learn to identify them and edit them out of your own writing.

Clutter. The availability of powerful word processors and desktop publishing software means that even novice writers can produce very professional looking results. But all writers need to be careful not to include too many distracting design elements. Just because it is possible to include graphics, clip art, shading, word art, borders, and neon printer colors does not mean that you should use all of them. Use graphics to illustrate a point, not just for decoration. Use formatting sparingly and consistently, and only when it helps readers locate information or understand the subject. A document with simple formatting is often more effective than one with too many design features.

The most successful documents are those that include considerable white space where readers can rest their eyes. Include margins, insert spaces between paragraphs, and use a large enough font to be readable. The body text font size should be at least 9 points; don't reduce the size of the font just to make material that is too long fit within the space allocated to it. Rather, try to edit for conciseness.

Most body text should be left aligned. Large passages of centered text are difficult to read, as is **justified text**, which is aligned at both the right and left margins. Justified text, also called block-justified, sometimes contains large white spaces around words that can make text difficult to read.

Inappropriate typefaces. For many readers, serif typefaces are easier to read than sans serif. **Serifs** are fine lines that project from the top and bottom of a font's letters. These lines lead the eye from letter to letter across the line. The font you are reading now is called Bembo, and it is a serif font. **Sans serif typefaces** do not have the serifs; *sans* is French for *without*. Sans serif typefaces are often used for titles and headings, whereas serif typefaces are frequently used for body text.

Most word processors come with several **specialty typefaces** that are intended for special uses, such as invitations, brochures, or flyers. Script fonts fall into this category. Though specialty typefaces are interesting and fun, save them for informal use. Figure 7-7 shows a serif font, a sans serif font, and a specialty font. Which do you think is easiest to read?

This is an example of a 12-point serif typeface called Bookman Old Style.

This is an example of a 12-point sans serif typeface called Arial.

This is an example of 14-point script typeface called Brush Script.

Figure 7-7   Font examples

Most professionally produced books and manuals follow these guidelines on font use.

Gender references. In recent years, there has been a trend away from gender-related pronouns. *He, she, him,* and *her* are often replaced with gender-neutral words, such as *they, their,* and *it.* What this change in style means is that writers sometimes use a plural pronoun where they might have previously used a singular pronoun. Other gender-neutral words include *staff* instead of *manpower,* and *staffed* instead of *manned.* Use *chair* or *chairperson* instead of *chairman,* but be consistent. Don't refer to a male as a *chairman* and a female as a *chair,* instead, refer to everyone as a *chair.*

You can also use the phrase *he* or *she* (which is sometimes reversed, as you have seen in this book); some writers use the combined form *s/he,* but this solution is not usually preferred. Choose one of these strategies, but try to avoid gender-related words, unless they clearly fit. It takes some practice to use gender-neutral language, but the result is often clearer and less offensive than the alternatives.

Unclear referents. Another common problem in technical writing is the use of unclear referents. A **referent** is a word that refers to another word or concept. Consider this example:

> Windows 95 and Office 97 use pull-down menus. They are good examples of the power of the GUI interface.

The word "they" at the start of the second sentence refers (or is a referent) to a concept in the previous sentence. But does "they" refer to Windows 95 and Office 97, or to pull-down menus?

It is not clear. To clarify the second sentence, replace "they" with the intended referent:

> Windows 95 and Office 97 use pull-down menus. Both software packages are good examples of the power of the GUI interface.

Or:

> Pull-down menus are good examples of the power of the GUI interface.

Passive voice. Good technical writing uses the active voice instead of the passive voice. **Passive voice** is a grammatical structure that uses a form of the verb "to be" and the -*ed* form of the verb, such as...

> The new operating system was installed on Friday.

The same sentence is much stronger in active voice:

> A support specialist installed the new operating system on Friday.

Avoid passive voice whenever possible; it gives text a stilted, awkward tone, and is often unclear. Active voice makes text livelier and more interesting. Compare the examples in Table 7-1 and see how much easier the active voice sentences are to understand.

Table 7-1 Active versus Passive Voice

Passive Voice	Active Voice
The text is formatted by clicking the bold button.	Format the text by clicking the bold button.
The modem card is inserted into the PCMCIA slot.	Insert the modem card into the PCMCIA slot.
The file is read from the disk.	The computer reads the file from the disk.
Touching the disk media should be avoided.	Avoid touching the disk media.

Nominalization. In general, avoid **nominalization**, which is the use of -*tion* and -*ing* endings to create nouns. Verbs are easier to understand.

Table 7-2 shows examples of nominalization and their improved forms.

Table 7-2 Nominalization Examples

Nominalization	Improved Form
Development of batch files will take three weeks.	We will develop batch files in three weeks.
Perform an installation of the printer driver.	Install the printer driver.
The configuration of the system should take about an hour.	It should take about an hour to configure the system.

Wordiness. Avoid unnecessary words; find the shortest way to state your ideas. See Table 7-3 for examples of how to reduce unnecessary words.

Table 7-3 Reducing Wordiness

Too many words	Reduced
Call customer support to raise questions about the problem you are having.	Call customer support to ask about your problem.
Prior to the actual installation of the system...	Before installing the system...
Before making an attempt to install the card...	Before installing the card...
Put the computer in a location where it will not be in danger of being harmed by anyone who might be passing by.	Locate the computer where passersby will not accidentally damage it.

To make text easier to read, use short words whenever possible. Replace long words like *approximately* with a shorter word that means the same thing, like *about*, and replace *utilize* with *use*.

7

Jargon. Computer systems can intimidate users because of the amount of jargon used to describe and discuss them. Avoid the use of **jargon** words that are understood only by those experienced in the field. Instead, use simple, direct words that anyone can understand, unless the target audience will clearly understand the jargon. For example, it is convenient to write about the *boot process* for a computer system. In documentation for new users who have never heard that term, it is better to use a term like *start-up process*.

If you must use jargon terms, define them first so that you and the reader share a common understanding of the vocabulary. Writers often include a glossary at the end of a chapter or book, much like the Key Terms list at the end of the chapters in this book.

Undefined acronyms. Like jargon, **acronyms**, or series of letters that represent a phrase, can make technical writing difficult to understand. For example, I/O is an acronym for Input/Output; RAM is an acronym for Random Access Memory. Writers should always define the meaning of acronyms for the reader. The first time the acronym is used, spell out the words that the acronym represents, and then include the acronym in parentheses:

> Extended Data Output (EDO) memory is being replaced in some high-end systems with Synchronous Dynamic Random Access Memory (SDRAM). SDRAM is currently more expensive than EDO memory, but....

Some writers include acronyms in a glossary or a list where the acronyms are defined.

Dangling phrases. A **dangling phrase** is a few words (or a single word) at the beginning or end of a sentence that add little to the meaning of the sentence other than to make it longer.

> The accounting department is eager to get training on QuickBooks, generally.

> Generally, the accounting department is eager to get training on QuickBooks.

Either eliminate the dangling phrase, if it makes little difference to the meaning of the sentence, or look for a way to include it in the sentence:

> The accounting department is generally eager to get training on QuickBooks.

This may seem like a long list of potential problems. But most technical writers find that with practice over time, they become adept at avoiding these problems.

TECHNICAL WRITING TOOLS

Many word processors include tools technical writers can use to develop useful documentation. These include:

- An outliner to help organize work
- A spell checker to identify and correct spelling errors
- A thesaurus to help find the word that exactly expresses a concept
- A grammar checker to recommended changes in wording to improve readability
- A readability index to indicate the level of difficulty for the audience
- Desktop publishing features to help writers produce documents that appear more professional

Even with all these built-in tools, a good collegiate dictionary is also useful. Some other resources for technical writers are described in Chapter 13.

Be on the lookout for good examples of well-written documentation. Be critical of other documentation you read. Ask yourself what makes a piece of documentation useful and easy to read, and by the same token, what makes a piece of documentation difficult to use.

DOCUMENTATION EVALUATION CRITERIA

All technical writers have their own preferences and style. Although writers may disagree on specific styles, the ultimate measure of documentation is whether it effectively and efficiently communicates information the reader needs. For technical writers, *effectively* means readers get the correct information they need to master a topic or to perform a task. *Efficiently* means readers do not have to spend extra time searching for information or reading through irrelevant material to find what they need.

There are four general criteria that can be used as a checklist to evaluate written documentation.

1. Content
   Is the information accurate?
   Is the coverage of the topic complete?

2. Organization
   Is the information easy to locate?
   Are the transitions between topics identifiable?
   Can the user get in and out quickly with the right answer?

3. Format

   Does the layout help guide the reader?

   Is the format consistent?

4. Mechanics

   Are words spelled correctly?

   Is it grammatical?

   Is the writing style effective?

As you plan, write, and review your own written documentation, think of how it measures up to these criteria. The principles and practices you learned in this chapter apply to all the documentation forms a user support specialist may create. Regardless of a document's intended use, the purpose remains the same: clear communication that addresses readers' needs by giving them the information they need in a concise manner.

7

CHAPTER SUMMARY

- User support staff are frequently assigned technical documentation tasks to produce brochures, flyers, newsletters, handouts, training aids, user guides, computer manuals, online help files, proposals, memos, operating procedure documentation, e-mail messages, Web pages, and troubleshooting guides.

- The goal of technical writing is to produce a piece of documentation that effectively and efficiently communicates information needed by the reader.

- A technical writing task begins by defining the characteristics of the target audience, including their background and reading level. Each piece of documentation should be planned with a clear understanding of what the writer wants the reader to do or be able to do after reading the document.

- In technical documentation, short words and sentences are preferable to long ones. Information should be organized so it is easy to locate. The purposes of a document and its intended audience should be clearly stated so each reader can decide at the beginning whether to read the piece.

- The process of technical writing includes organizing ideas and topics into an outline, expanding the outline, and then carefully editing to eliminate extra words, tighten prose, and check for format consistency and technical accuracy. A review by an independent party is an important way to improve a document before the final revision.

- The layout of a document should help a reader understand the organization, know what is important, and be aware when transitions between topics occur. Formatting should be used consistently to enhance the information presented, not detract from it.

- Successful technical writers use strategies such as analogies, repetition, consistent word use, and parallel structure.

- Common problems to avoid in technical documentation include clutter, hard-to-read typefaces, gender references, unclear referents, and passive voice. Other problems include nominalization, wordiness, jargon, acronyms, and dangling words or phrases.

- Several software tools, including an outliner, spell checker, thesaurus, grammar checker, and desktop publishing features, are available to help technical writers produce well-organized, accurate, and professional-looking documentation.

- Finally, writers use four criteria to evaluate a technical document by reviewing its content, organization, format, and mechanics.

KEY TERMS

- **acronym** — A series of letters that represents a common phrase; for example, CPU is an acronym for central processing unit; use of acronyms where they are not defined or well known makes documentation difficult to understand.

- **analogy** — A writing strategy that relates an unfamiliar concept to one a reader is likely to know; for example, the CPU in a computer system is analogous to an office calculator in a manual system.

- **brainstorm** — A tool used by technical writers to generate a list of potential topics they think will be useful to readers; from a brainstormed list, the writer selects major and minor topics to include in a document.

- **dangling phrase** — A few words at the beginning or end of a sentence that add little to the meaning of the sentence other than to make it longer; for example, "Mohammed turned on the overhead projector, but the image did not appear, as everyone noticed." contains a dangling phrase.

- **documentation** — Technical writing targeted for end users in either a printed or an online format; includes brochures, flyers, newsletters, handouts, training aids, user guides, handbooks, manuals, online help systems, proposals, letters, memos, e-mail messages, procedural and operational documentation, Web pages, and troubleshooting guides.

- **format consistency check** — An edit pass through a document draft in which a writer checks to make sure that headings and subheadings are in a consistent font and that indentation, centering, boldface type, italics, underlining, and other formatting tools are used consistently.

- **jargon** — Words that are understood only by those experienced in a field; for example, the concept *hacker* would be better understood by a general audience as *unauthorized user.*

- **justified text** — A document format in which the text is aligned with both the right and left margins; justified text is commonly used in books and newspapers. Justified text created in word processors and desktop publishing programs can be difficult to read.

- **nominalization** — The use of *-tion* and *-ing* endings to create nouns in sentences where verbs are easier to understand; for example, "To accomplish capitalization, use the Change Case command" could be rewritten to avoid nominalization as "To capitalize words, use the Change Case command."

- **parallel structure** — A writing strategy that treats similar items consistently throughout a document; examples of parallel structure include consistent verb tenses and consistent wording and phrases in lists of items.

- **passive voice** — A grammatical structure that uses a form of the verb "to be" and the *-ed* form of the verb; for example, "The documentation was prepared by me" illustrates passive voice; "I prepared the documentation" is in active voice.

- **pointers** — References or cross-references in a document that describe where a reader can locate additional information on a topic of interest; often used in technical writing to reduce the size of a document by including directions to appendices, attachments, exhibits, figures, tables, and other materials related to the topic.

- **referent** — A word that refers to another word or concept; for example, in the sentence "Before you insert a CD-ROM, inspect it for scratches" the word "CD-ROM" is the referent of *it*; the referent of words such as *it, them,* and *their* should be clear.

- **sans serif typeface** — A style of type in a document in which there are no fine lines (serifs) added to each character; sans serif typefaces appear as simple, clean letters and are often used in titles and headings; compare with serif typeface.

- **serif typeface** — A style of type in a document in which each character includes fine lines that project from the top and bottom of each letter; serifs tend to lead the eye from letter to letter across each line, which improves readability.

- **specialty typeface** — A style of type in a document that is intended for special uses, such as notices, brochures, or flyers; the intent of specialty typefaces is to draw attention, although they may be difficult to read for general text; script typefaces are examples of specialty typefaces.

- **style sheet** — A list of common terms, formats, and writing conventions that describes the preferred use so that all writers use consistent terms and formats.

- **technical accuracy check** — An edit pass through a document draft in which a writer goes though any procedural steps to test them carefully with the hardware or software; the purpose of a technical accuracy check is to eliminate any errors in step-by-step instructions or other technical information.

REVIEW QUESTIONS

1. Explain why well-trained end users need documentation.
2. List several examples of end users documentation.
3. If vendor manuals are available, explain why a support organization might need to publish its own user guide.
4. Describe the difference in organization between a tutorial and a reference document. What kind of computer user would benefit from each type of organization?
5. Describe the advantages of online documentation over printed forms.

6. "Because e-mail is informal communication, good technical writing skills are less important for e-mail users." Do you agree or disagree with this statement? Explain why.

7. Explain the consequences of poorly written procedural, operational, and troubleshooting documentation.

8. How is writing that is accessible via the World Wide Web different from other kinds of technical writing?

9. List several questions document writers need to answer about their target audience before they begin to write.

10. Explain what the reading level of a document is and why it is an important concern.

11. Describe five ways in which technical writing is different from other kinds of writing.

12. Explain the basic organization of a technical document and the purpose of each section.

13. List the seven recommended steps in the technical writing process. What happens during each step?

14. Explain the role of brainstorming in the technical writing process.

15. What strategies can a document writer use to indicate transitions between topics to readers?

16. List several different kinds of edit passes a writer can make over a document, and explain the purpose of each pass. When should a writer stop editing a document?

17. Describe how consistent use of formatting features can help a reader understand and make effective use of a document.

18. List the four types of sentence structures and give an example of each. Explain which sentence types should be used predominantly in technical writing, and why.

19. How are analogies useful writing tools? Give an example of a useful analogy from your own experience.

20. What is a style sheet? Explain its purpose.

21. Show that you understand the following common writing problems by giving an example of each from your own experience: gender references, unclear referents, passive voice, nominalization, jargon, acronyms, and dangling phrases.

22. What are the differences among serif, sans serif, and specialty typefaces? When should each be used or avoided?

23. Describe several writing tools that are available to technical writers.

24. List four criteria a document writer can use to measure the effectiveness and efficiency of a technical document. Explain which of the four you think is the most important.

HANDS-ON PROJECTS

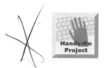 ## PROJECT 7-1

The following sentences and paragraphs contain many of the problems you learned about in this chapter. Rewrite the examples to make them clear and readable, using what you have learned.

a. From a one-page notice to inform employees of which machines they can use in a training room:

> Employees should be well advised that they should use only the first row of machines, the HP PCs. All other machines are used only for classes for training new users. If an employee doesn't do this, he will be asked to leave the training room.

b. From an e-mail message sent to all employees of a legal firm advising them to be alert for a new virus:

> This virus has been known to cause the destruction of files, and it is very important that you perform a search of your hard drive to try and attempt eradication of it using the search feature. Search for .EDT file extensions and delete them. Then the problem will be solved.

c. From an instruction sheet you will hand out in a training session on a new e-mail package the employees of Fred's Paint Store will begin using next month; this passage explains the capabilities of the package to users who have never used e-mail before:

> E-mail messages are stored on a central server, and you download it every time you open one, in effect. You can save it to a local disk if you want to keep it.

d. From a booklet that the user support department will distribute to employees of an insurance company to explain the capabilities of a new software claims management package:

> This is a new type of CMS (Claims Management Software) that every adjuster, regardless of his level, will benefit from, greatly. This Claims Management Software can: 1) organize claims information, 2) be used while you are on the telephone, 3) reports by claim type, and 4) generation of summary claims information.

7

PROJECT 7-2

Write an explanation of how to insert a 3.5" disk into a disk drive. Your explanation should be aimed at a person who has never used a computer before.

Exchange your explanation with another person in your project group and critique each other's draft. Did you include enough information for the user to insert the disk correctly? Did you include extra information that wasn't necessary to describe the disk insertion task?

If you can find a person who has not used a computer before, try out your explanation to see if he or she can perform the task using only your written documentation. Revise your instructions based on the peer and user feedback you receive.

PROJECT 7-3

The following article is for a technical newsletter intended for members of a professional computer organization. Your task is to rewrite the article, using what you have learned about technical writing in this chapter. You can correct any misinformation, format problems, and errors. Make the rewritten article an example of your best writing, ready for publication. Your instructor may be able to provide you with a copy of the article in machine-readable form.

Those darned ~*.tmp files

I always keep finding machines positively crammed with **~something.tmp** files. They take up way too much disk space and are annoying, positively. Many of these are caused by users turning off their machine before Windows if finishing doing its own house cleaning during shutdown. There are many time also where disabling quick save in MS Word also left behind several of those files each day and any application or hardware caused crash is going to leave this stuff behind.

I always have to periodically doing a search for all **~*.TMP** file and deleting all that aren't stamped with to-day's date. If you try to delete a temporary file that is in use, **FileManager** will give you a warning and then abort. So always "de-select" the **~*.TMP** files that have the today's date. If they're no good, I'll get them at a later date. I do this by when **FileManager** comes back with it's list, press **Ctrl-/** to select the whole list, then go through and hold **Ctrl** and **left-click** those files with the current date. Then by pressing **Del** and **OK** you can get them out of here. Depending on the size of your hard disk whether you want to cancel the "list contents has changed, new list" message that will appear after the deletions, I usually skip it and go back to what I was doing before. Usually, you can make this an automated process if you choose by going to the **AUTOEX-EC.BAT** file and finding the **SET TEMP=** line. Make sure that this **DOES NOT SAY** **"=C:\DOS"** or anywhere else that files might exist which are not temporary trashable files. If you find "=C:\DOS" or any directory where files would/could exist which you would not want to automatically delete, change it to something like **C:\TEMPFILE** as in **SET TEMP= C:\TEMPFILE.** (If you do this, be sure to go back and create such a directory with **FileManager** or **DOS** or whatever.

Now, add the following two lines to your **AUTOEXEC.BAT** file right after the **SET TEMP** line:

IF NOT EXIST

C:\TEMPFILE/NUL MD

C:\TEMPFILE

IF EXIT C:\TEMPFILE\~*.TMP

DEL C:\TEMPFILE\~*.TMP >

NUL

You can change the **C:** to the appropriate drive where you have the recommended five to ten Megabytes of free space for the temp files. The inserted lines will create the directory for the temporary files it has been deleted and will delete all **~*.TMP** files each time to boot the machine.

PROJECT 7-4

The following document is an excerpt from a computer textbook. It contains examples of many of the common problems described in this chapter. The line numbers are for your convenience to identify and refer to problems.

First, go through the document and note any problems that you find with it. If you are working as part of a project group, you may want to compare your list of problems with others in your group to see where members agree and disagree. Second, rewrite the document to correct the problems you identified. Your rewrite should make the document as clear and as easy to understand as possible. Your instructor may be able to provide you with a copy of the document in machine-readable form.

1   MANAGING DIRECTORIES AND DISKS

2

3   Introduction

4

5   There are many types of storage media today. Floppy disk are the most

6   common. It is the best of all the possible ways to save data. A hard

7   or floppy diskette is divided into various directories so that files can be

8   saved to them. Definitely, this is the most efficient way to manage a large

9   number of files stored on a disk.

10

11   Various DOS commands, especially those dealing with disks and

12   directories, produce you lots of computer numbers. To get a handle

13   on computer numbers, you need to get the big picture on bits, bytes,

14   megabytes, and gigabytes.

15   A computer may seem intelligent, but essntially it can "understand"

16   only whether power is on or not. To issue an instruction to a computer,

17   we need to go by 1 (on) or 0 (off). The two digits of 1 and 0 are the

18   foundation of binary (base 2) math. Binary math is based on bits, which

19   is a contraction of two words—binary digit. One bit can have the

20   value of either 1 or 0. Bits get a little large to move around, so

21   programmers combine 8 bits together to form a byte. Bytes can increase

22   in number: 1 byte can store a 1; 1KB (kilobyte) is the same as1024; 1MB

23   (megabyte) is 1048576; and 1073742824 equals 1GB. So, when you

24   hear that a diskette has a 360KB capacity, it can store 360 x 1024 = 374784 bytes.

25

26   Formatting of Disks

27

28   When you create a file you need to store it on a floppy. Before that,

29   it must be properly prepared to receive information (formatted). If you

30   have used a disk and it has some space on it, you can not cover this section.

31   If you have a brand new disk out of the box, procedue with 36 formatting it

32   this way:

33   1. Begin by inserting a disk in drive A. Make sure this disk is new, or

34   if it has been used, contains no file you are desirous of keeping. (Formatting

35   will destroy a disk's existing files, completely.)

36

37   2. Double-click the My Computer icon on the desktop.

38   3. Click 3-1/2" Floppy icon

39

40   3. On the File menu, click Format.

41   4. Click 1.44.

42   5. Indicate that you want a Full format.

43   6. Start the formatting process with the Start indicator. Wait for the

44   formatting to complete.

45

46   While it was being formatted, the disk was divided into a number of

47   concentric rings, tracks. Each track was separated into a number of

48   sectors. Each sector stored 512 bytes. A higher capacity disk contains

49   more tracks and sectors; that is how they stored more data, for your

50   information.

7

PROJECT 7-5

Write a one-page description of a simple computer task. It should include two or three headings and some procedural steps. Format it three different ways with different font and style variations. Show the three versions to three students and ask them to choose which one is easiest to read and why. Write a short summary of their responses and draw any conclusions about formatting that you learned from the exercise.

PROJECT 7-6

Find a piece of computer documentation, a memo, or other technical writing. It can be a published piece or something you've written. Apply the concepts and ideas you've learned in this chapter to critique the document; then rewrite it to correct any problems you discovered.

If possible, have a coworker or fellow student look over your work and make suggestions. Do you agree with her or his suggestions?

PROJECT 7-7

Find an example of online documentation. Analyze and critique it based on the information you learned in this chapter. Write a one-page summary of your findings.

CASE PROJECTS

1. SERGIO ESCOBAR'S INTERNET SEARCH GUIDE

Sergio Escobar is the supervisor of a computer facility used in a job retraining program. The computer facility has 18 Macintosh systems, which are used by trainees to improve their job skills and also as tools in their job search efforts. The Mac software includes a resume preparation program that is very popular with the trainees. Sergio has recently connected the Mac to a network to provide Internet access. However, the trainees do not have good Internet search skills and are frustrated that they cannot find employment information on the Internet.

Sergio posted a few URLs for various local and regional job banks, but he knows that information on the Internet changes daily. He also knows that if trainees knew how, they could use the Internet to research companies in preparation for job interviews. As a new support specialist, you are assigned to work with Sergio to prepare some basic documentation for the trainees on how to do information searches on the Internet. The document you prepare should include a description of how to use a search engine, how to enter a search, how to narrow a search, and helpful tips on Internet search strategies. It should include some examples that relate to job search strategies. It should be self-contained and designed to be used outside a classroom environment.

Your task is to write a short *Guide to Internet Searches* that Sergio can give to users of the facility he supervises. As a resource, look at the online documentation published by one or more companies that provide Internet search engines.

2. A COMPUTER FACILITY ORIENTATION GUIDE

As a user support specialist for a computer lab at The Career School, you have been assigned the task of developing a lab orientation guide aimed at new students or trainees who use the facility. Prepare a one-sheet (or two pages printed back-to-back) summary of information to new users of the lab. You can use the policies of a lab you are familiar with, such as a lab at your school. First, describe which classes and students use the lab. Orient your guide to those users.

Your orientation guide can include basic information about lab operating policies and procedures (such as scanning disks for viruses), use of resource materials, printing procedures, network login and logout, how to access popular software packages, and other general or technical information you think should be included. You may want to include short sections with information aimed at students in specific courses or training sessions.

As clues to topics you may want to include, think about what information a new student or trainee who walks into the lab would want to know. For inspiration, go to a lab you know and look at the postings on bulletin boards, whiteboards, walls, doors, machines, and tables. Rely on your own experience as a user of the lab or as a lab assistant. One of the goals of this writing project is to replace as much of the printed matter around the lab as possible with an information sheet that could be distributed in the lab.

3. TEMPLATES FOR ROCKY MOUNTAIN CONSULTANTS

Erica Allan is the supervisor of documentation for Rocky Mountain Consultants, a firm that provides consulting services to engineering companies. She recently received a request from several departments at Rocky Mountain to design a memo form that each department can adopt and use as their standard memo format. Erica would like to accommodate each of the departments but is short of staff she can assign to the project. And Erica feels strongly that, rather than design a template for each department, it would be more useful to give each department the tools it needs to develop its own memo template.

Erica would like you to develop an instructional document aimed at word processor users that describes the process for creating a simple template. (Use whichever word processor you have access to for this project.) Although each department wants a different and distinctive memo format, Erica suggests you use a simple memo like the one shown in Figure 7-8 as an example in your template write-up. Describe the fonts and format features to create a template that looks as much like the example as you can. Your document should describe the steps a user takes to create and store a template for the memo in the figure. Prepare a piece of documentation titled *How to Prepare a Simple Memo Template* that describes the process to users in Rocky Mountain Consultants.

Rocky Mountain Consultants
Document Preparation Department

MEMO

To:

From:

Copy:

Date:

Subject:

Figure 7-8   Sample memo format for the memo template documentation

CHAPTER EIGHT

COMPUTER FACILITIES MANAGEMENT

Computer facilities range from a single, standalone system installed in a small office or home (sometimes called SOHO—small office, home office) to a network of thousands of PCs in a large company or organization. They also include a laptop computer in a sales representative's hotel room and a mainframe computer in the Information Systems department of a large corporation or university. User support specialists are often assigned responsibilities for managing a PC facility, especially if they are the sole support providers in a small company. Even support specialists who are part of a large support staff in a corporation are often asked to consult with users about specific problems users encounter with their PCs.

Computer facilities management begins with the site preparation steps you learned about in Chapter 5, Installing End User Computer Systems. This chapter on computer facilities management is a continuation of some topics addressed in Chapter 5, and it introduces strategies for dealing with common facilities management problems.

AFTER READING THIS CHAPTER AND COMPLETING THE EXERCISES YOU WILL BE ABLE TO:

- Describe the major types of computer facilities
- List the most common facilities management problems
- Describe facilities management tools and procedures for dealing with problems end users often encounter

INTRODUCTION TO COMPUTER FACILITIES MANAGEMENT

A **computer facility** is the combination of the hardware, software, network, information, people, and operating procedures associated with the use of any computer system. It also includes the environment that surrounds the computer facility, including the furniture, space, and electrical power. Some computer facilities are centralized—that is, they are located at one site. For example, in a mainframe computer center, the hardware, peripherals, software, data, operating staff, and related facilities are located in the same place. Anyone who needs to use a mainframe computer facility comes to the central site, either physically or electronically via a terminal. Other computer facilities are decentralized; the computer equipment and related software and facilities are located where the people who use them are located. A standalone PC on an office desk or in a home is the most common example of a decentralized system.

The trend today is toward distributed computer facilities in which some parts of a computer system are centralized while other parts are geographically located where they are used. Networked systems are a good example of distributed systems. The network server or host is a central facility to which users in offices or classrooms may connect with their local client PC. The transition from centralized to decentralized and distributed computer facilities has also created significant demands on support organizations. With a less centralized user population, user support must find new ways to reach users in different locations.

External users who contact a support center via telephone or e-mail are an extreme example of decentralization. However, most of this chapter applies to support centers that provide support to internal users within a company or organization. Whether a computer facility is centralized, decentralized, or distributed may determine the nature of the problems support staff are likely to encounter. But no matter how large or how small a computer installation is, there is a common set of problems associated with every computer facility.

COMMON FACILITIES MANAGEMENT PROBLEMS

Support specialists and computer facilities managers must deal with many different types of problems. Some solutions are easy and some are not; some are more critical to system operation than others. Figure 8-1 summarizes some of these problems.

- Hardware problems
- Power failures
- Disasters
- Software problems
- Network problems
- Ergonomic problems
- User errors
- Crime and misuse

Figure 8-1   Common facilities management problems

Depending on their work environment, support specialists deal with these problems at some level. Each of these problems is discussed in the following sections.

MANAGING HARDWARE PROBLEMS

Most PCs today are fairly reliable, but as the number of PCs support specialists must manage increases, the likelihood that they will encounter at least some malfunctions or failures also increases. Although preventive maintenance procedures can increase the life expectancy of a computer system, electronic and especially electromechanical devices (those with moving parts, such as disk drives, tape drives, CD-ROMs, and printers), do fail.

 Some hardware vendors rate the devices they manufacture according to how long they are likely to operate before they begin to have problems. **Mean time between failure (MTBF)** is the number of hours an average device will operate before it fails. The MTBF is statistical and is based on device tests; some devices fail faster, some last longer. For example, a tape drive may be rated at 50,000 hours MTBF. The number 50,000 is like a life expectancy before the device may need repairs.

Some user support specialists have direct responsibility for hardware problem diagnosis and repair. They may perform simple tasks like changing a cable or swapping a monitor. But for most hardware repairs that include any substantial amount of problem diagnosis and parts replacement, companies today often outsource their hardware support, just as they may outsource their user support. So hardware maintenance is often not a major responsibility for support specialists and support groups in many companies. Instead of outsourcing the entire hardware repair function, a company may organize hardware repair as a separate group in its organization. This alternative is especially common among universities and other large organizations that have specialized staff devoted to computer hardware.

As the first person to whom end users turn when they have hardware problems, a support specialist needs to know enough about hardware to make simple repairs. For example, many support specialists can test and swap components, install memory, clear printer paper jams, and perform related tasks. A support specialist must also be able to recognize the difference between a real hardware malfunction and a configuration problem with the operating system or a temporary network failure. Often problems in other parts of a computer system can masquerade as hardware problems.

When companies outsource their hardware repair, they may contract with the vendor who originally sold them the hardware. In other cases, they contract with a third-party company that specializes in hardware repairs. Hardware repair companies range from local computer stores with service departments, to mail order and Internet hardware service providers, to national companies that are in the hardware service business.

When a company outsources its hardware service, it usually negotiates and signs a **service agreement**, or contract, with the service organization. The service agreement specifies such conditions as:

- The response time for service: how long after the company calls does the service organization have to respond

8

- The local availability of parts: many service organizations use overnight express shipments rather than stock a lot of spare parts in their own inventory

- Preventive maintenance and diagnostic services the service organization provides in addition to hardware repairs: reduces the frequency of downtime due to hardware failures

- The cost of the service contract

Hardware service organizations generally cover both parts and labor under a service contract, and most repairs occur on-site, at the company's offices.

Alternatively, a company can rely on a local computer store or service organization. Although local service companies will frequently negotiate a contract, they also provide service on what is called a **time and materials**, best efforts basis. In this situation, there is no contract that specifies response time and parts availability. The service provider charges an hourly rate (which is higher evenings and weekends), they charge for parts, and they make no guarantee about when or whether they will be able to make the repairs, because contract customers have a higher priority than walk-in business. Furthermore, the company with hardware problems usually has to take the hardware to the shop for repairs, unless the company is willing to pay extra for on-site repair.

Some businesses that do not want to incur the cost of a service agreement, but want to be able to make quick, cost-effective hardware repairs, purchase one or more backup systems to use in case a system fails. For example, when a company needs 20 systems in an office or training facility, it may actually purchase 21 systems. They use the 21st system as a backup and store it until they need it to replace a broken system that they can then send out for service on a time and materials basis. A **redundant system** (backup computer) adds to a company's up-front equipment cost, although if they purchase a large number of systems, one extra system is a small fraction of the total cost and is relatively cheap insurance. The concept of an inexpensive backup replacement has become popular with the development of RAID disk technology in recent years. A **redundant array of inexpensive disks (RAID)** provides large amounts of disk storage using a cluster of cheap hard drives. If one of the disks in a RAID system fails, it can be replaced. Combined with advanced operating system features, RAID technology permits the replacement to occur without interrupting normal operation.

MANAGING POWER FAILURES

A company's location can determine whether or not power failures are likely to affect computer equipment. In some parts of the country, power failures, including spikes and brown-downs, are more prevalent than in other locations. Obviously, uptime for the computer system in a hospital's critical care unit is more important than uptime in a school classroom. When preparing computer facilities for power outages, a support specialist needs to determine the likelihood of power outages and their impact on the organization. Beyond simple surge suppression units described in Chapter 5, which may be appropriate for home and small business PC installations, some companies invest in power conditioning equipment or uninterruptable power supplies.

Power conditioners input "dirty" power from the electric supplier and retransmit "clean" power to the computer devices. Dirty power is electricity that fluctuates beyond normal bounds in voltage, frequency, or other characteristics that can affect the operation of computer hardware. Power conditioners are capable of removing all but the largest power surges or spikes and can overcome some limited-duration brown-downs. Their goal is to protect the computer equipment from damage.

Uninterruptable power supplies (UPSes) usually include power conditioning circuits but also include a battery backup. The battery backup system begins operating when the electrical power supply is interrupted (or during a brown-down) and provides power to the computer equipment for a limited period of time. UPSes are designed to provide enough time for the computer equipment to be shut down correctly so that applications software and operating systems can empty memory buffers, close files, terminate operation and hardware can power down. Without a UPS, power loss can cause hardware or software to terminate abnormally, which may cause equipment damage or unpredictable problems when the system is powered back on later. The battery power in a UPS determines the amount of time the system can continue to operate and also the cost of the UPS unit.

Disaster Planning

Support specialists cannot prevent events such as power failures, floods, fires, storms, earthquakes, and sabotage from affecting computer services. But they can help plan a strategy to manage these unpredictable events by using risk management. **Risk management** is the use of a number of tools to reduce a company's risk due to these disasters and to be able to recover from them with minimal financial or customer service loss when they occur.

Some disaster management tools are listed in Figure 8-2.

Business interruption insurance	Backups
Engineering inspections	Access and security measures
Hot and cold site agreements	A disaster/contingency plan

Figure 8-2 Disaster management tools

Support specialists at sites of any size need to use at least some of these tools to protect their company's technology resources.

Insurance. A company can purchase **business interruption insurance** to provide additional financial resources at the time an unforeseen event occurs. The funds offset the cost of returning the business to an operational state and protect the company from financial ruin in case of a disaster.

Inspections. Companies can obtain **engineering inspections** to help identify the potential for damage to computer and other equipment. An engineering inspection may recommend that a company modify building structures to reduce the impact of a disaster on computer equipment. It might also recommend detection equipment to warn of a disaster.

Hot and cold site agreements are methods of creating redundancy that serve as backups to an existing system. They provide a way to get a computer installation operational quickly after a disaster. A **hot site** is a geographically distant location with operational equipment similar to the system it is designed to back up. In case a disaster occurs that makes a system unusable, recent versions of the user's software and data files are restored from off-site backup media onto a system at the hot site. A **cold site** is a similar facility, but includes only the space for equipment, not an operational backup computer. In conjunction with a cold site agreement, a company may contract with a hardware vendor to quick ship a new hardware system to the cold site upon receiving a call that the company's system has been damaged. Instead of purchasing a hot or cold site agreement from vendors, companies may sign mutual aid agreements to provide hot and cold site facilities to other companies. For example, a group of school districts may enter into a reciprocal hot or cold site agreement.

Backups. Copies of important programs and data maintained on separate media are called **media backups**, and are a critical component of any disaster contingency plan. They are absolutely necessary to get a computer system operational after a disaster, but many users do not back up their systems regularly. The discussion of operational procedures later in this chapter describes a plan for media backups.

Access and security measures. These measures are tools to deal with threats of sabotage. Large computer facilities often attract people who may be disgruntled with technology or with the way they have been treated by a bureaucracy. Their goal is to disrupt the business of the organization by damaging equipment, information, or facilities. For this reason, many facilities that have a large investment in computing equipment in a central location take steps to limit physical and electronic access to their facilities. Access management tools larger installations frequently use to prevent information and equipment loss include:

- Special entry locks
- Identification badges that function like keys
- Motion sensors and heat detection systems
- Camera systems that monitor facilities
- Metal detectors
- Physical barriers (walls and windows)
- Reception desks

In smaller facilities, locked doors are the primary means to control physical access.

The counterpart of physical security is electronic security. Passwords, Internet firewalls, callback modems, and other online security measures are common in installations of every size. These measures are popular with facilities managers who recognize that intrusions can be physical or electronic and can come from external or internal sources.

Vulnerable sites should develop procedures to handle telephoned bomb threats and other acts of sabotage. Telephone operators, help desk attendants, computer operators, and receptionists should be trained in emergency procedures.

A **disaster/contingency plan** is a useful planning tool for both large and small computer installations. These plans answer the question, "What steps will our organization take in case a disaster occurs?" A disaster/contingency plan should include these kinds of information:

1. A complete, up-to-date directory of all employees, including titles, home addresses, and phone numbers

2. A current list of all employees who need to be notified in case of a disaster, including addresses and phone numbers

3. A calling tree that specifies which people should call whom in the event of a disaster, to ensure the fastest possible response time

4. The location of all backup media for software and data stored off-site and whom to contact for access

5. A recent copy of all operational procedures and other site-specific documentation

6. A current inventory of equipment, software, and licenses

7. A list of any insurance policies, hot or cold site agreements, or reciprocal agreements for emergency services

8. A floor plan of the facility

9. Instructions for staff evacuation in case of an emergency

A disaster contingency plan is only effective if employees are aware of its existence and trained in its procedures. Therefore, support specialists should find the most effective way to communicate these plans to employees to ensure that recovery procedures can and will be carried out. Most organizations with disaster plans include a training component as part of the plan implementation.

MANAGING SOFTWARE PROBLEMS

User support specialists are often the first to learn about software problems, because they staff the facility that employees or customers call when problems occur. Some software problems are known bugs in an operating system or applications program. Others may occur in custom applications software developed in-house. In either case, the user support staff must establish procedures for dealing with software problems.

Many companies capture information about software problems when they are first called in to the support staff. The support staff usually keeps a problem log, making entries whenever a user calls with a problem. Alternatively, the support staff can use a **software problem report (SPR)** system that captures problem report data. An SPR system may be a manual paper-and-pencil system, or it may be a database on a network server. It records basic information such as the program in which the suspected bug occurred, a description of the bug, who discovered it, the urgency of the problem, and to whom the bug was referred for repair.

MANAGING NETWORK PROBLEMS

Because computer networks are combinations of hardware and software, the tools you learned about to deal with hardware and software problems also apply to management of network facilities. However, a network may include tens or hundreds or thousands of client devices with several different network servers and peripheral devices (such as printers) and additional layers of software that comprise the network operating system. This configuration of hardware and software means that facilities management for networked systems is often quite complex.

Networks pose their own unique administration, performance monitoring, media backup, security, and maintenance problems. Fortunately, the organization of hardware and software resources into a network also provides additional tools to deal with the added problems encountered in a network environment. These procedures are used to both maintain and troubleshoot networked systems.

Administrative procedures. In a network environment, administrative procedures involve tasks associated with user accounts and authorized access, disk space allocations, rights and privileges of resource use, and possibly accounting and billing procedures in an environment where users are charged for computer use. In a large company, a network administrator usually handles these tasks; in a small organization, they may be the responsibility of user support.

Monitors. Hardware and software tools that tell network administrators and user support staff how well a network is operating are known as **performance monitors**. Performance monitors collect information about key aspects of network operation, including:

- How many users are logged on
- How much access activity (often called hits) the server hard drive is taking from users
- What applications users are running
- CPU and memory use on the server
- The number of jobs waiting in the print queue

Performance monitors may collect and log performance data over time to give the support staff a statistical picture of how variables such as day of week and time of day affect network performance. Performance data over time can provide network facility managers with information on which to base capacity planning decisions such as when to purchase a faster server, when to add memory or additional hard drive space, or when to add an additional or a faster printer. Some performance monitors also include alarm and troubleshooting capabilities that can alert network staff to immediate and significant problems, such as a server that needs to be rebooted or a leg of the physical network that is no longer connected to the server.

Media backups on a network system can reduce facilities management costs and problems. For example, it is possible in many network environments to schedule automated backups of server software applications and user file space. Server media also provide a convenient way for users to back up the data files on their local hard drives. The backup software on a user's system can access the server hard drive as a backup medium instead of using a local tape or removable disk drive. And because network servers often operate 24 hours a day and 7 days a week, media backups can be scheduled at times when the user load on a system is at it lightest, such as at night or on weekends.

Access security in a network environment is often a more significant concern than on a standalone PC, because users can potentially access data and resources anywhere on the network and even from outside the network. However, many network operating systems provide additional security features that are more reliable than those available on a standalone PC. A network administrator plays a key role in the control of access to network facilities, because the administrator controls the user account management process.

Software maintenance is another significant management concern in a network environment. Maintenance is an area where the network not only poses management problems, such as how software on hundreds or thousands of machines gets upgraded but also provides the tools to solve the problem, such as applications software that runs from a single image on the server and installation procedures that can download software from a server to multiple client PCs. Network tools often make the software administration task easier than the task would be for a comparable number of standalone systems.

Although computer networks pose unique and challenging problems for facilities and network managers, their administrative, monitoring, backup, security, and maintenance tools make the tasks somewhat easier.

Managing Ergonomic Problems

Chapter 5 discusses ergonomic problems in the context of installing systems. In reality, ergonomic problems are ongoing; they occur during system use on a day-to-day basis. An installation that is ergonomically correct for one user may cause problems for a new employee who replaces the original user. Each ergonomic solution must be user-specific.

Although Chapter 5 addressed a number of health, safety, and productivity issues, strategies to address ongoing ergonomic concerns include training end users about potential workstation problems, questionnaires for end users to report problems they encounter, and site visits by support specialists to help identify and correct problem areas.

Managing User Errors

User errors are also a facilities management concern. User errors range from data entry errors to failure to make and keep adequate media backups. They can involve lapses in data security, such as leaving media out where others can remove or copy them. Unlicensed software can cause legal problems for a company or organization. Downloaded or borrowed software is a source of computer viruses that may infect not only the guilty user's computer but also every node on a network. Downloaded shareware can be improperly tested and can cause system problems or crashes.

Another category of problems users introduce can be traced to the misuse of powerful software tools such as spreadsheets, database systems, decision support systems, and presentation software. Although these are powerful tools when used correctly, they are just as powerful when used incorrectly. For example, a user may construct a spreadsheet to forecast product sales for the next several business quarters. If the user enters an incorrect formula during the design of the forecasting worksheet, the mistake may produce results that appear plausible, but are wrong. As use of the forecasting worksheet continues, the errors may compound over time, resulting in poor decisions about manufacturing targets and inventory levels.

Although there may appear to be significant differences between users who fail to make backups of important information, those who fail to check downloaded software for viruses, or those who make a mistake in a spreadsheet formula, each of these examples of user errors can have similar results: lost data, decreased productivity, or other problems for the company. An important computer facilities management task is to anticipate, plan for, monitor, and identify potential problems due to user errors. Unfortunately, there is no one, simple solution that will address all of the errors users can make. However, computer facilities managers and support staff can use several strategies to reduce user errors, including training, developer feedback, automated procedures and system audits.

Training for end users, which you learned about in Chapter 6, is one tool to reduce errors. Support staff should be on the lookout for patterns of mistakes users make, such as a data entry error that occurs repeatedly in the same situation. Problem patterns are useful for trainers who plan and develop corporate training programs.

Feedback to software developers often originates with support staff who observe patterns of problems users encounter. Software designers and programmers attempt to make the software they develop as robust as possible so it can identify and handle user errors as they occur. Software developers can often implement automatic software checks to verify that numeric values entered are within an appropriate range. They can also use tools such as batch totals and check digits to reduce the likelihood of invalid input or missing transactions. However, software developers need feedback from support staff on the kinds of problems users encounter.

Automated procedures are another way to address end user errors. The fewer steps an end user must perform manually, the less the chance an error will occur during a task. For example, it is preferable to automate media backups, virus scans, and disk defragmentation procedures, instead of relying on users to remember to run these programs. At a minimum, support analysts can send users reminders via e-mail or broadcast "messages of the day" to jog their memories to run important utility software or perform other routine operational tasks.

Audits are useful tools for support staff to identify particular kinds of problems. A **system audit** is an investigation by an independent person or group that tries to verify that proper operating procedures are followed and tries to identify potential end user problem areas. Audits may include the use of special utility software to identify the applications packages that are installed on a system. The purpose of audit software is to help verify that software licenses or site licenses are in place to document that each user is authorized to use the software installed on his or her system. Audits may also verify that proper operational procedures, such as media backups, virus checks, and preventive maintenance steps are performed on a regular basis. Some software packages include automated audit features. For example, spreadsheets can often detect common problems in the use of formulas or built-in procedures, such as references to blank cells or circular references.

User support specialists can play a significant role to help a company avoid problems caused by user errors; the same is true of computer crime and misuse.

MANAGING CRIME AND MISUSE

As you learned in Chapter 1, computer crime is the use of a computer system to commit an illegal act or the theft of computer equipment or services. There are several control tools available to support specialists to address these concerns. Many businesses, organizations, and schools have implemented some or all of these strategies to control this growing problem.

Access controls are important tools in the arsenal of a support specialist who is confronted with the potential for computer crime. Access controls include various user identification and authentication procedures, password entry to access system resources, and the granting of rights and privileges to categories of users. They also include the use of call-back modems and Internet firewalls to control access to company resources and information and to protect them from external threats.

8

Physical controls include locks, identification badges, and alarms that are physical barriers to access. Physical controls also include cabling systems designed to secure computer equipment (system unit, monitor, and printer) to an office desk. Cable tie-down systems are especially useful in computer training facilities and offices where a large inventory of computer equipment (and a sizable investment) is located in a central, easily accessible area. These facilities are often the target of computer thieves.

Inventory controls are part of an asset management system that provide facilities managers with information about the location, configuration, and value of equipment that is greater than a predefined minimum dollar amount. A minimum of $200, for example, means that support staff do not need to keep physical inventory of mice, diskettes, and consumable supplies. But the support staff responsible for inventory management may need to attach an inventory control label to more expensive equipment and enter the inventory number and equipment configuration into a database. Asset management procedures frequently require an actual physical identification of all items in the equipment inventory once a year. Based on the annual inventory, support staff can trace missing items and estimate the amount of loss or theft.

Information controls include procedures to limit access to valuable or confidential information. Access controls, described earlier, often function as information controls. Information controls might define which staff can access backup media or printed reports.

As end user computing has become widespread, many businesses and organizations have formulated policies for their employees and customers on the use and misuse of company computer facilities. These policies often define what is acceptable use, what is unacceptable use, and explain the penalties for unacceptable use. For example, a company may have a policy that prohibits or limits personal use of computers during business hours. Or a policy may state that limited personal use of company e-mail is acceptable, but that Internet access can only occur outside of regular working hours. Support specialists are often in a position to help companies formulate policies to limit computer crime and misuse and other facilities management problems.

FACILITIES MANAGEMENT TOOLS AND PROCEDURES

Computer facilities management tasks and responsibilities span a wide range of issues that concern user support staff. The last part of this chapter describes in detail some specific tools and procedures designed to help support staffs perform their responsibilities. Figure 8-3 lists some of these tools and procedures.

Media backup procedures	Preventive maintenance
Media defragmentation	Antivirus software utilities
Media maintenance	Use accounting and statistics
Computer supplies	

Figure 8-3   Facilities management tools and procedures

Facilities of any size, from a standalone PC in a home office to a large network installation, need to address these issues at some level.

MEDIA BACKUP PROCEDURES

One of the most difficult tasks for support specialists is to convince end users that media backups are important. Sometimes only after users have lost a significant amount of important data do they learn the lesson and make regular backups. Automated backups that run at a scheduled time can reduce the impact of power outages and hard drive crashes. As you learned earlier in this chapter, they are a way to work around users who are reluctant to or forget to make backups.

Utility software that writes media backups is usually packaged with backup hardware. Commercial and shareware packages that offer useful backup features are also available. Backup software copies files, usually from a computer's hard disk drive, onto the designated backup media. Some backup utilities write files on the backup media in the same format as they were stored on the original media. Other backup programs may compress the files so they take up less space on the backup medium. These files must then be decompressed if it is ever necessary to restore them from the backup media.

An important decision for a user or support person is how much to back up. The more files that are copied to the backup media, the longer the backup takes and the greater the amount of space required. Most backup utility software permits a user or support specialist to select a specific drive to back up and to selectively back up directory paths or folders. This features gives a user or support specialist control over the amount of information to back up.

For example, many users do not back up their operating system and program directories on a regular basis. Operating system and applications software files change less frequently than data files, and users should already have backups of software in the form of the original distribution media (floppy disks or CD-ROM). Some users make backups of their operating system and applications programs only when new hardware is installed or when a new application is installed on a system.

If the goal is to minimize the time to perform a backup and the amount of media space the backup takes, a user can opt to back up just the important data directories on a regular basis. Some backup utility software permits a user to choose the type of backup. Three options may be available.

- **Full backup:** backs up all files in the directory selected (and usually in all the subdirectories under the directory selected). Full backups ignore whether each file has already been backed up and whether it has changed since the last backup.

- **Incremental backup:** backs up only those files that have changed since the last time each file was backed up. An incremental backup does not take as much time or media space as a full backup, because the number of files that change on a regular basis is usually small relative to the total number of files.

- **Differential backup:** backs up only those files that have changed since the last full backup.

Other features in backup utility programs permit a user to back up only files that were created or changed before or after a specified date. That would permit a user to back up all the files created, for example, since July 1, 1998. Some backup utility programs also keep directories, logs, or catalogs of which specific files were backed up on each backup tape or disk.

Most users who perform frequent and periodic backups use more than one set of media (tapes or disks). If you use only a single backup tape, for example, each day's backup is written over the previous day's backup. But suppose something goes wrong during the backup procedure (a hard drive crash occurs), or suppose a file becomes corrupted and the corrupted version is written on the backup media. A user could risk losing the only good backup copy. A more conservative backup strategy involves the use of multiple sets of backup media, a rotation scheme, and off-site storage of one of the sets.

Table 8-1 shows a common strategy for managing three sets of backup media, the current set, an off-site set, and an old set that will rotate to become the current set in the following week.

Table 8-1   A Common Backup Rotation Scheme

	Age	Week 1 (this week)	Week 2 (next week)	Week 3	Week 4	Week 5
Status:						
Current set	0	C	A	B	C	A
Off-site set	1	B	C	A	B	C
Oldest set	2	A	B	C	A	B

Set C in this scheme is the current set this week. But next week, it is a week old, when the network administrator uses set A as the current set. Then, during week 3, set C is really out-of-date. But it will become the current set again in week 4.

The backup media recorded last week (set B in the example), is often stored off-site as a precaution. In case of fire, theft, or damage, an off-site backup of important files is an excellent facilities management strategy. Off-site may mean in a fire-proof vault at a nearby financial institution, or a contract where a support person takes the backup set home. Or it may be an arrangement with a media storage company. The important feature of off-site media storage is physical separation of the computer system and backups.

Companies that use a three-set rotation scheme described in Table 8-1 usually label the backup media so identification of media is easy. A network administrator might adopt a backup media naming convention such as **stdnn**. These letters mean:

> **s**—set letter (A, B, or C)
>
> **t**—type of backup (<u>F</u>ull or <u>I</u>ncremental or <u>D</u>ifferential)
>
> **d**—day of week backup was made (M, T, W, H, F, S, U)
>
> **nn**—sequence number (01, 02, 03, and so on)

Under this naming convention, a cartridge tape with a label **BDW02** is the second tape (02) in the differential (D) backup set B recorded on Wednesday (W). The network administrator also keeps a log of all backup tapes which shows the tape number and the date and time each tape was recorded.

Finally, just as it is important to make regular backups of important files, it is also important to have procedures in place to restore files. **File restorations** are necessary when a hard disk drive fails or when a user accidentally deletes one or more files and needs to recover them. A user support staff member may be assigned the responsibility to restore backup files based on requests from users. The file restore procedure sometimes involves using the same backup utility program that made the backup.

MEDIA DEFRAGMENTATION

Over time, as users create, expand, and delete files, the way files are stored on a disk changes. When a file is written on a disk, most operating systems try to write it in a space (a group of adjacent sectors) that is large enough to hold the entire file. If a sufficient amount of contiguous (adjacent sectors) free space is available, the file is written in that space, because that is the most efficient way to write files and manage disk space. If there is not enough contiguous free space, however, but there is enough *total* disk space available to hold the file, the operating system breaks the file into fragments that it stores at different locations on the disk. When this occurs, an individual file may be stored in several pieces at different locations on a disk. Part of the file is written on some sectors; other parts are written on sectors that may be located physically some distance away on the disk surface. As the number of separate pieces associated with a file increases, even small files may occupy more than one location on a disk. So the operating system does its best to accommodate a file in the space available.

That's the good news. The bad news is that, as the number of separate pieces of space a file occupies increases, the read-write head on the hard drive has to move more often and greater distances in order to read or update the file. The movement of the read-write head slows file access time and eventually affects the performance of the computer when it retrieves information.

The **defragmentation** process rewrites the files on the disk so that each file is in contiguous sectors. Then it regroups free space so it is contiguous (in one large chunk). The procedure can dramatically improve disk performance. The file fragmentation/defragmentation problem is illustrated in Figure 8-4.

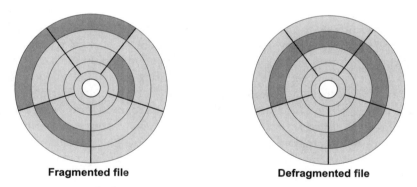

Fragmented file   **Defragmented file**

Figure 8-4   File fragmentation and defragmentation

Users or support specialists should periodically use a utility program to defragment their hard disks. In most instances, when fragmentation is minimal, the software will give a user the option not to run the program, a useful feature because the defragmentation procedure can take anywhere from a few minutes on a small hard drive up to several hours on a large hard drive. The defragmentation utility (sometimes called the defrag utility) may even be able to give the user an estimate of how long the procedure will take, based on the size of the hard drive, the extent of fragmentation, and the speed of the system. Although defragmentation procedures are generally reliable, as a safety precaution users should back up their hard drive immediately before they run a defragmentation utility program.

MEDIA MAINTENANCE

In addition to media backups and defragmentation, there are other periodic tasks a user or support specialist may perform associated with disk and tape devices. These tasks are important because they may affect either the amount of space available on a disk, the speed of access to information stored, or the reliability of information stored on magnetic tapes. Examples of common media maintenance tasks include recovering lost allocation units, erasing unused programs and files, and recycling tape cartridges.

Recover lost allocation units. Some operating systems occasionally lose track of the free space available on a disk. As files are created and deleted, sectors on a disk change status from used to free and back to used. In the process, the links between disk sectors can get corrupted. Usually this is not a major problem and affects primarily the amount of free space available on the disk. Operating systems that exhibit this problem usually provide a software utility to recover lost free space. For example, in DOS and Windows 95, the SCANDISK utility (and its predecessor CHKDSK) can identify and repair this and related disk storage problems. SCANDISK should be run on a periodic basis as part of general disk maintenance procedures.

Erase unused programs and files. When their hard disk gets full, some users just buy a larger hard disk. However, users who know about file and folder delete commands can take steps to make more free space available before their disk gets full. Periodically erasing unused files and folders can increase the amount of space available on a disk. Many users are reluctant to clean up their hard drives, however, because it is not always obvious which files are used for which purpose. Before you erase any files, make copies on backup media, just in case you need the files later, or in case something goes wrong during the file delete operation. In fact, most users should limit their disk cleaning activities to user data files. Furthermore, erasing program files does not necessarily remove all traces of programs from a system. Registry entries, .INI files, device drivers, and .DLL libraries are a few examples of remnants that can be left on a system after a program has been deleted. First, use an uninstall utility program, if one is available, instead of just erasing the directory that contains a program. Second, several companies sell utility software that is designed to inspect the software configuration on a disk and clean up any remnants of software that was partially erased.

Recycle tape cartridges. The magnetic tape used in tape cartridges and reel-to-reel tapes can become brittle if stored for several years. It is less likely to become brittle and unusable if it is periodically used (run through the tape drive). Tapes that have not been used for two to three years should probably be copied onto other tapes to reduce the risk of data loss.

Users often ask support specialists for advice about these and other media maintenance procedures. Experienced support specialists know that any substantial media reorganization or maintenance tasks, such as those described in this section, should be performed only after the media has been backed up as a precaution. Other suggestions for media maintenance are described in a section on preventive maintenance later in this chapter.

COMPUTER SUPPLIES

Another facilities management task that often gets assigned to a support specialist is the purchase of computer supplies. Alternatively, a support specialist may be asked her or his advice about where to find specific supplies or get the best price on them. Some support specialists manage an inventory of printer supplies (paper, labels, ink and toner cartridges and ribbons), media (diskettes, cartridge tapes, and removable hard disks), cleaning supplies (cloths and solution), and even computer parts (cables, tools, and batteries).

Sources of supplies range from local office supply stores to electronics specialty stores, and from mail-order companies that specialize in computer parts to suppliers that do business primarily on the Internet.

For many small businesses, convenience is a primary consideration in the purchase of supplies. Local office supply stores sell a variety of common computer items. Some offer free delivery within their service area as a customer service. However, for any company that uses a substantial quantity of supplies, there are significant opportunities to save money on volume purchases or through mail-order or Internet purchases.

PREVENTIVE MAINTENANCE

Although most personal computer equipment is primarily electronic and does not require a great deal of preventive maintenance, some moving parts (electromechanical) do require periodic attention. **Preventive maintenance** uses tools and procedures that reduce the likelihood of component failure and repair costs.

System unit. Most components inside the system unit either cannot be maintained or do not require preventive maintenance. However, in a dusty environment, the life of a PC can be increased by periodically vacuuming the inside of the case to reduce dust buildup on the components. Dust often accumulates inside the case because the electrical components attract dust particles. A vacuum cleaner with a plastic nozzle can be used on dust buildup and is preferable to cans of compressed air, which tend to blow the dust around, rather than sweep it up. Computer supply stores sell portable vacuums specifically built for preventive maintenance tasks. The system unit case and other plastic or painted parts can also be cleaned with isopropyl alcohol and a lint-free cloth, or with specially pretreated wipes designed for that purpose.

Finally, diagnostic software that tests electronic components in a system, such as keyboard, monitor, RAM, the data bus, peripheral adapter cards, and I/O ports, can sometimes identify components that operate marginally and may fail in the near future. Periodic use of diagnostic utility software, such as Norton Utilities, can alert staff to possible future component failure.

Disk drives. Although hard disk drives, CD-ROM drives, and removable hard drives contain moving parts that are more likely to fail than electronic parts, they should not be serviced by anyone other than a qualified technician. For the most part, there are no user-serviceable components in hard drives, CD-ROM devices, or removable drives, and when these components fail, they are replaced, rather than repaired. In the case of a floppy drive, a coating of residue builds up on the read-write head on a floppy disk drive. Under normal use, the residue buildup is minimal; in a heavy use environment, it's best to use a disk drive cleaning kit to occasionally clean the read-write heads. The kit contains a specially designed floppy disk with a cloth pad instead of disk media. The cloth pad is saturated with isopropyl alcohol or other cleaner provided in the kit, inserted in the drive, and used to clean the read-write head residue in a few revolutions of the pad.

Printers. The biggest enemies of most printers are paper dust and ink buildup. Even printer paper that looks clean carries dust particles. Printers that use continuous form paper are especially vulnerable to printer dust because it contains dust particles created during manufacturing when the edges are perforated and tractor feed holes are punched in the paper. A good preventive maintenance strategy for printers is to periodically use a vacuum cleaner to clean out the dust. The inside areas of a printer should also be free of ink and toner spills, because these chemicals attract dust particles that can cause problems for the moving printer mechanism. Replace worn-out printer ribbons because these also create dust residue inside a printer.

Another way to extend the life of peripherals such as printers is by **peripheral rotation**. In peripheral rotation, a heavily used device is periodically rotated with one in a lighter use environment. For example, a heavily used printer might be more likely to fail sooner than one that is less used. Before it has a chance to fail, it's often a good idea to replace it with a new one or one that has received less use, clean the used one, and place it in a location that is less demanding.

Keyboards. Vacuum a keyboard or spray it with compressed air periodically to remove dust and dirt particles from between the keys. A buildup of dust can make the keys stick or it can wear out the mechanism that makes contact with the membranes in the keyboard that send signals to the PC. Dirty keyboard keys can be cleaned with a lint-free cloth saturated with isopropyl alcohol. For especially dirty keyboard cases, a small brush such as a toothbrush saturated with isopropyl alcohol can be an effective cleaner.

Mouse parts. The rubber ball inside a mouse can become dusty and dirty with use and needs cleaning. Remove the mouse ball by twisting or pushing on the plastic mouse ball restrainer in the direction indicated by an arrow on the underside of the mouse. After removing the ball, clean it and the metal contacts inside the mouse cavity with isopropyl alcohol and a lint-free cloth. Be sure that the mouse ball rotates freely after cleaning and that the plastic restrainer has been properly reinstalled.

Display screen. Clean a computer screen regularly with a special pretreated cloth designed for that purpose, or with isopropyl alcohol and a lint-free cloth. However, preventive maintenance on a monitor is limited primarily to improved visibility. There are no user-serviceable parts inside a monitor. In fact, the high voltage components inside a monitor are dangerous. A monitor case should never be removed, except by a qualified repair technician.

Preventive maintenance can extend the useful life of many components of a PC system. Support specialists can often help end users understand important maintenance steps to increase both the life expectancy of the PC and its operating efficiency.

Antivirus Software Utilities

Computer viruses are a common problem in any facility that uses network technology, Internet access, remote dial-up to download software, and other computer-to-computer connectivity. They are also a problem when users exchange data on floppy disks. A **computer virus** is a program that can attach itself to other programs or to disk media. A virus can propagate (copy) itself from one disk to another disk and across a network connection. Some virus programs are benign; other than displaying a message on a display screen, they cause little harm. Other virus programs are more virulent. They can destroy programs and data on a computer system or network they infect. Standalone PCs that do not connect to a network, access the Internet, or read floppy disks from other systems are rarely infected by computer viruses.

Several software utilities are designed to manage viruses. They include programs to detect, remove, and monitor virus activity in a system.

- A virus detection program looks in common places such as executable files and the master boot sector on disks for virus signatures (evidence a virus is present). Because the number of viruses grows each month, virus detection programs must be continually updated to search for the latest virus signatures. Distribution of updated lists of viruses on the Internet is common.

- When a virus detection program has identified an infected disk, it alerts the user and perhaps automatically begins the removal process. In general, virus removal software is reliable, but in some cases the best removal procedure is to reformat a hard drive, reinstall the operating system and applications, and restore user data files from backup media. (This is yet another reason to make frequent backups.)

- A computer system that contains no detectable viruses can be monitored on a continuous basis for signs of virus activity. Virus monitoring software continually examines data and programs received via a network or dial-up connection, as well as any floppy disks used, to determine whether known virus signatures are present.

Many computer users install all three kinds of antivirus software on their systems and use them regularly as a precaution. Antivirus software is an especially important facilities management step for anyone in a network, computer lab, dial-up, software download, or floppy disk exchange environment. Symantec and McAfee are two software utility developers who distribute up-to-date antivirus packages.

Use Accounting and Statistics

Although there are no direct charges for the use of most PC systems and computer networks, some facilities charge an access fee. These situations include schools and colleges that often charge students for computer, e-mail, and Internet access, Internet Service Providers (ISPs) that charge a fee for Internet access and for storage of Web pages, and timesharing service bureaus that provide mainframe or minicomputer services and software for a fee. In some companies, fees are charged to individuals or, more often, to departments for computer use to allocate the costs of providing services to user departments. For example, an accounting department may purchase computer services (including hardware, software, network access, training and support services) from the Information Services (IS) department. Although no actual money may change hands in this example, the computer charges may be a paper accounting transaction that lets the IS department cover its costs and justify expenditures it makes to provide computer services to accounting and other departments. In other companies, computer services are treated as an overhead item in the budget, and there is no accounting for use of computer resources.

The facilities management aspects of their jobs sometimes surprise support specialists who provide services to internal users. This chapter should help you anticipate the kinds of questions you may get from users. Consulting with users on computer facilities management tasks often becomes among the most interesting and satisfying challenges in the career of support specialists.

CHAPTER SUMMARY

- Computer facilities can be classified as centralized, decentralized, or distributed. Each kind of computer facility poses facilities management problems for user support staffs. Common facilities management concerns and tools for support specialists include the following areas:

  - Support specialists perform simple repairs, but many hardware maintenance and repair problems are outsourced to a computer maintenance organization. Time and materials and redundant hardware are alternative ways to handle hardware problems.

  - Power failures (surges, spikes, brown-downs) can damage computer components. Power conditioners and uninterruptable power supplies with battery backup can address many power failure problems.

  - Although disasters can never be completely avoided, a contingency plan to manage the risks associated with disasters is an effective facilities management tool. Media backups, reciprocal site agreements, security measures, and a written disaster plan are tools to manage risk.

  - Software problem reports and logs of software failures are tools to identify patterns of problems that may be useful to software developers and those who plan training programs for users.

  - Network administrative procedures, performance monitors, media backups, and access security are common tools to address problems with shared network resources.

  - User mistakes are probably the rule rather than the exception; tools to address common mistakes include user training, robust software design, automated procedures to replace manual procedures, and system audits. These tools provide a range of solutions to reduce, but not eliminate, the impact of mistakes.

- Support specialists use a variety of access controls over electronic entry to a system, physical controls over facilities access, inventory controls for theft, and information controls based on a user's need to know to address computer crime. Computer viruses can be controlled with antivirus software. Many companies develop official policies that define appropriate computer use and misuse.

- User support specialists employ several operational procedures to help with computer facilities management tasks. These procedures include:

  - Regular media backups according to a fixed schedule that combines full and incremental or differential backups with off-site storage according to a backup media rotation scheme. Labeling conventions and backup logs help identify backup media when it is needed for a file restoration task.

  - Defragmentation of disk media with utility software that reduces read–write head movement and improves system performance.

  - Media maintenance to recover lost free space and improve access performance.

  - Purchase and management of commonly used computer consumables and supply items.

  - Regular preventive maintenance. Dust can be a serious problem for both electronic and electromechanical hardware devices. Regular cleaning of key system components can prolong the life of a computer system.

  - Antivirus software utilities. Computer viruses are common in situations where computers communicate via networks, modems, or exchange of floppy disks. Antivirus software is designed to detect, remove, and monitor virus activity in a computer system.

  - Access and security management. A variety of electronic and physical access controls are available to support staffs to ensure that access to computer systems is by authorized personnel only.

  - Use accounting. Software that collects, stores, and reports on computer resource use can be used to justify computer expenditures.

8

KEY TERMS

- **access controls** — Procedures and tools to limit electronic or remote entry into a computer system or network of computers; user accounts, passwords, and grants of access rights are common access control tools.

- **business interruption insurance** — A type of insurance policy that helps offset the cost of returning a business to normal operation after an unforeseen event such as a disaster; a risk management tool for some computer facilities.

- **cold site** — Similar to a hot site, except a cold site includes space and other facilities to accommodate an emergency backup computer system, but it does not include the operational equipment.

- **computer facility** — The hardware, software, network, information, people, operating procedures, and environment (furniture, space, and electrical power) associated with the use of a computer system.

- **computer virus** — A program that can attach itself to other programs or to disk media; viruses are transmitted over networks, via modem links, and through the exchange of infected floppy disk media; software utilities to combat computer viruses are a common facilities management tool.

- **defragmentation** — A process that rewrites the files on the disk so that each file is stored in contiguous sectors; defragmentation also reorganizes the free space on a disk so it is contiguous (in one large chunk).

- **differential backup** — A copy to alternative media of only those files that have changed since the last full backup was run; a differential backup takes less time to run and less media space than a full backup.

- **engineering inspections** — Investigations conducted by an engineering firm to help identify the potential for damage to computer equipment and facilities due to floods, storm damage, earthquakes, fires, and other kinds of disasters; an engineering inspection is often conducted as part of a computer facility contingency planning project.

- **full backup** — A copy to alternative media of all files (programs and data) stored on a computer system or in a specified directory on a system regardless of whether they were previously backed up.

- **hot site** — A backup computer installation maintained at a geographically distant location with computer equipment installed and operational; a hot site is for use in the event of a catastrophic failure of the equipment in a computer facility; compare with cold site.

- **incremental backup** — A copy to alternative media of only those files that have changed since the last backup; an incremental backup takes less time to run and less media space than a full backup.

- **information controls** — Procedures to account for and control the location and distribution of information in a computer system and among employees and customers.

- **inventory controls** — Tools and procedures to maintain records on the location, configuration, and value of equipment; inventory controls are part of an asset management system in many businesses.

- **mean time between failure (MTBF)** — The expected number of hours of operation before an average computer component is likely to fail.

- **media backups** — Copies of important programs and data written on separate magnetic or optical media; the purpose of media backups is to facilitate restoration of programs and data in case the originals are erased, lost, or damaged.

- **performance monitors** — Hardware and software tools that provide network administrators and user support staff with methods to track how well a network system is operating; performance monitors can alert staff to possible problems in the operation of a network.

- **peripheral rotation** — A heavily used computer component is periodically swapped with one in a lighter use environment; the goal of peripheral rotation is to increase the life expectancy of peripheral devices that get heavy use.

- **physical controls** — Tools used in computer facilities to limit physical access to equipment and information; physical controls include locks, identification systems, alarms, and physical restraints to secure equipment.

- **power conditioners** — Electrical equipment that inputs dirty power from an electric supplier and retransmits clean power to a computer system; a power conditioner can correct some problems with voltages, the frequency of the electric current, and the shape of the wave form.

- **preventive maintenance** — Tools and procedures used in a computer facility to reduce the likelihood of component failure in a computer system and to reduce the repair costs that result from parts failure; preventive maintenance steps are designed to clean and adjust equipment to prolong its useful life and enhance operational efficiency.

- **redundant array of inexpensive disks (RAID)** — A disk technology that provides large amounts of storage space with a cluster of cheap hard drives; if one of the disks in a RAID system fails, it can be replaced, often with no downtime.

- **redundant system** — Extra backup computer equipment identical to the hardware in a system that can be installed and pressed into service whenever the primary system fails.

- **risk management** — The use of a number of tools and strategies to reduce a company's financial and customer service risk due to interruptions in a company's ability to provide computer services; risk management often includes a disaster/contingency plan to address recovery from floods, fires, earthquake, sabotage, and storm damage.

- **service agreement** — A contract between a computer facility and a service vendor to provide hardware (and sometimes operating system) support, preventive maintenance and repairs; service agreements usually cover both parts and labor and guarantee response within a time period specified in the service agreement.

- **software problem report (SPR)** — Forms and procedures that capture and document problem report incidents; an SPR system may be manual or automated; may also be called a bug report system.

- **system audit** — An investigation by an independent person or group whose goal is to verify that proper operating procedures and safeguards are followed in a computer facility; a system audit often identifies potential problem areas that require corrective action.

- **time and materials** — An alternative to contracted hardware maintenance service in which a computer facility pays for hardware repairs based on time spent (labor) and the cost of replacement parts; time and materials repairs are performed on a best efforts basis with no time guaranty.

- **uninterruptable power supplies (UPSes)** — Electrical devices that include power conditioners and a battery backup to supply electricity to a computer system during power outages of short duration.

8

REVIEW QUESTIONS

1. List the individual components that go together to make up a computer facility. What are the differences between centralized, decentralized, and distributed facilities? What is the current trend?

2. List eight common computer facilities management problems.

3. "A user support specialist does not have to be a hardware repair technician." Do you agree or disagree with this statement? Explain why.

4. What kinds of conditions would you expect to find in a service agreement to outsource hardware diagnosis and repair services?

5. Explain the differences between a contract for hardware repair services and those on a time and materials, best efforts repairs.

6. What are the differences between surge suppressors, power conditioners, and UPSes? What factors determine which of these devices a computer facility needs?

7. Describe the purpose and contents of a disaster plan. Why are disaster plans described in the chapter as a risk management tool?

8. List six disaster management tools. What is the one tool every computer facility, no matter how large or small, should use? Why?

9. What is the difference between a hot and cold site agreement? Which provides more protection to a business?

10. Describe the information that you would expect to find in an SPR system. What are the purposes of this information?

11. List five tools that a network administrator can use to manage network facilities.

12. What information can a performance monitor provide to a network administrator or a support specialist? Give several examples.

13. Explain the following statement: "Computer networks cause complicated facilities management problems, but they also contain the tools to make the task less complicated."

14. Give some examples of common user errors and mistakes and explain why support specialists should be concerned about user errors. Describe several ways to reduce user errors.

15. What is the purpose of a system audit?

16. List four kinds of controls that are used in computer facilities to combat computer crime.

17. Describe eight facilities management tools and the specific problems they are intended to help solve.

18. Describe the differences between full, incremental, and differential backups. In what kinds of situations should each kind of backup be used?

19. Explain why off-site storage and media rotation are important media backup tools.

20. Based on the naming convention described in the chapter, what information can you discern about a tape labeled CFH03?

21. Explain how files on a disk can become fragmented, what problem fragmentation causes, and what can be done about the problem.

22. In addition to fragmentation, describe three media maintenance problems and their solutions.

23. What is the purpose of preventive maintenance on a computer system? Give three examples of preventive maintenance tasks a user support specialist could perform. What is the expected benefit of each of the examples you selected?

24. What is a computer virus? Describe three tools support specialists can use to combat virus infections.

25. List six tools a computer facilities manager can use to deal with access and security problems.

HANDS-ON PROJECTS

 PROJECT 8-1

Think about all the things that could happen to your computer system that would impact the operation of your school or business or organization for which you work. Make a list of the risks you would want to address in a service agreement that covers the hardware in your system.

 PROJECT 8-2

Visit a local computer store in your area. Find out if it has a service department. What do they charge per hour to work on computer hardware? At the hourly rate the service department charges, how many hours could it work on a $300 printer before it would be less expensive to buy a new one instead of repairing the old one?

While you're at the local computer store, find out what the warranty period is on a new computer system they sell. Also ask whether they will sell an extended service contract to cover a new system a customer purchases at their store after the warranty expires. What percent of the purchase price of the system is the extended warranty? Do you think an extended service contract makes sense? What kind of computer user should purchase one? Who should not purchase one? Write a brief description of your findings.

PROJECT 8-3

Ask your local electric utility if they recommend surge suppressors for computers used in their service area. Find out the characteristics and cost of a surge suppressor they recommend. Does the surge suppressor include insurance that would cover the computer equipment in case the surge suppressor fails?

 PROJECT 8-4

List the information you would include in a disaster/contingency plan for a small office/home office (SOHO) computer system. What problems in a large installation are not a problem in a SOHO installation?

 PROJECT 8-5

If you own a home computer, find out if it is covered under your homeowner's or renter's insurance policy. Is there a maximum value that is insured? Is there a deductible? If it is not covered, contact an insurance agent to find out how much it would cost to obtain insurance coverage for your computer. Write a summary of your findings and conclusions.

  PROJECT 8-6

Design a log or problem report form that could be used to report hardware, software or network problems in a computer lab at your school or in a training facility. What kinds of information would you need to collect on the report or log that would give support staff enough information to locate the equipment, begin to trace the problem, and contact the user with questions?

PROJECT 8-7

Should users who access only a few files on their hard drive on a regular basis do a full backup, an incremental backup, or a differential backup? Explain your answer in terms of the amount of time to do the backup, the amount of media space required to store the backup files, and the amount of effort required to restore a file that was accidentally erased. Write a memo to users to explain your recommendations.

PROJECT 8-8

A home computer user keeps one floppy disk to back up all her data files. Once each weekend, she reformats the floppy disk and then copies her data files onto the disk. She follows the same procedure every weekend. Write a note to the user that explains some problems with this backup strategy.

PROJECT 8-9

What preventive maintenance tasks should a support specialist perform during a regular six-month site visit to an office user's system? Make a facilities management preventive maintenance checklist for a typical office computer system.

8

PROJECT 8-10

Find out if your company or school has an official computer use and misuse policy. Make a list of things the policy says users can do and another list of things that are prohibited. In the list of things that are prohibited, put an asterisk next to any items that are illegal, rather than just policy.

CASE PROJECTS

1. BIZNET COMPUTER SYSTEMS

Kai Edmonds is a manager of support services for BizNet Computer Systems, a company that provides network computer systems for small businesses. She is aware of a number of BizNet's customers who have installed a network system but have very little experience with the tasks associated with keeping a business system up and running. Kai spends considerable time on the telephone answering questions about security concerns, media backups, disk performance, and other common computer management tasks.

Kai thinks BizNet needs some documentation to give its customers when they first take delivery of their networked system. The documentation she wants is a preventive maintenance checklist of tasks that small businesses should use to manage their systems for maximum performance and reliability. Beyond a simple checklist, Kai would like to provide clients with a brief explanation of how to perform the steps on the checklist.

Assume that BizNet sells Windows 95 clients that are attached to a Windows NT or Novell NetWare server (or make any other assumption that is consistent with the kind of network environment with which you are familiar). Write a preventive maintenance procedure checklist that explains briefly how to perform each task listed. Develop your checklist for BizNet clients who are not computer professionals.

2. MAINTAINING YOUR COMPUTER

To do this assignment, you will need an appropriate home computer system or access to one at your business. Do not undertake this case study unless you have permission to use a system for the purposes described in this case.

In this chapter, you learned about several software utilities related to system performance and reliability. They include system problem diagnosis, media backup and restoration, performance monitoring, media maintenance, disk defragmentation, and antivirus utilities. Find out which operating system and third-party utility software on your system fits into each of these categories. Learn about how the programs operate. Use the utilities on your system to get experience with the features of each of these categories of software. Use a word processor to prepare some notes on your experiences; describe any problems you encountered and the results of each utility you tried.

3. FRED'S PAINT STORE

In a case study in a previous chapter, Fred's Paints decided to purchase a laptop computer for each of several outside sales reps who sell paint to hardware and building supplies stores. Each of the sales reps has been using his or her laptop for several weeks. As a group, they like the ability to enter sales information and orders with their laptop system and send them via modem to Fred's for processing.

Unfortunately, last week one of the sales representatives experienced a hard disk crash on her laptop system. She suspects that the hard drive problem occurred when she accidentally dropped the carrying case containing the laptop at a customer's site. She could not recover the data on the hard drive, but the loss was not significant. She had sent all of her reports from previous days via modem to Fred's, so copies were available on the PC that receives the modem reports. However, she lost the order information from one large customer and some notes she had made on a prospective customer. Despite some embarrassment when she had to return to both customers and re-enter their information, she was able to recover from the disk problem in a few hours. Fortunately, Fred's purchased a backup laptop that she could use while hers is in the shop for repairs.

The support staff at Fred's Paints is considering a couple of alternatives to manage the risk that this problem could occur again. They feel it is a fairly common risk associated with laptops that are used extensively in a field situation. One alternative is to have the sales reps use their modems to call in each order immediately after it is entered. The cost of this alternative in added telephone calls is substantial compared to the twice-a-day calls that are made by each sales rep now. A second alternative is to develop a simple backup procedure that each sales rep can use to copy the order information from the hard drive onto a floppy disk. If the procedure is simple, the rep could run a backup after taking an order. Because each laptop has a built-in floppy drive, a backup procedure seems feasible. Furthermore, each sales rep stores the sales reports in a directory hierarchy named REPORTS on the laptop hard drives. The individual sales reports are named CUSTnnnn.TXT, where "nnnn" is Fred's internal account number for each customer.

Write a simple procedure that a sales rep can use to backup the relevant data in the REPORTS directory structure onto a floppy disk, using Windows 95. Remember that the sales reps have limited computer experience. Test your procedure to make sure that it works as you intend. Then, describe the procedure a sales rep would use to recover a file that he or she accidentally erased from a backup floppy. Also describe how the backup floppy disks should be labeled. Finally, discuss the problems associated with the use of floppy disks as backup media.

8

HELP DESK OPERATION

As you learned in Chapter 2, a company may provide support to its employees and customers via informal peer support, a user support group, a help desk, outsourcing, or other formats. Many companies have chosen to organize their user support as a help desk. The help desk provides a single point of contact for users who need technical support. To reach this contact, users might visit a physical location, telephone a hotline, or e-mail the help desk contact person to ask questions or request help with problems.

But a help desk operation, like other ways of providing support, can be costly. Therefore, businesses and organizations with a substantial investment in end user computer systems or with many external users continually search for cost-effective ways to provide technical support for users. This chapter describes a number of strategies and tools that help desks use to support end users in an effective and efficient way.

AFTER READING THIS CHAPTER AND COMPLETING THE EXERCISES YOU WILL BE ABLE TO:

- Describe a help desk and a typical help desk organization
- Describe the call management process
- Explain how hardware and software tools are used to manage calls
- Describe the concerns of help desk managers
- Describe help desk trends

WHAT IS A HELP DESK?

A **help desk** is a method of supplying user support that provides a single point of contact for a company's employees or customers. Why is a single point of contact important? In user support centers that have multiple points of contact, a support rep might not have the expertise to answer a particular question. He or she may have to refer the user to a different person or even a different department for an answer. But that person may not have the answer either. In extreme cases, multiple points of contact may disagree about the source of a problem or the strategy to resolve it. To avoid situations like these, many companies have formalized their user support function into a help desk operation.

Although the specifics of the support provided in telephone, face-to-face, and e-mail contact differ somewhat, there are similarities in the way help desks organize and provide support, and in the kinds of skills they require. Some provide a wide range of the support services like those you learned about in Chapter 2. Others focus on limited services. For example, a telephone support hotline for a popular software package may limit its services to questions about the specific product. The help desk in a large medical center, in contrast, may provide a more extensive array of services to its employees. The name of the help desk in a specific situation may include hotline, information center, lab assistance, support consultant, or any number of other titles. But the purpose is the same: to provide end users with a single point of contact for computer problems in order to keep them productive.

Companies structure their help desks differently, depending on whether their users are internal or external, the number of users and products they support, and the company goals and objectives for computer support. It is common for a company to structure its help desk into several levels (or tiers) of support, sometimes called a **multi-level support model** or frontline/backline model, shown in Figure 9-1.

| Level 1 Support | Level 2 Support | Level 3 Support | Level 4 Support |
| Customer | Call Screener | Product Specialists | Technical Support | Support Manager |

Figure 9-1   A multi-level support model

In this model, each level is staffed by a person with different skills. The Level 1 call screener (also called a call dispatcher or receptionist) is usually an entry-level employee. Higher levels of support staff require greater knowledge and experience. The Level 2 product specialist is a more experienced help desk employee; the Level 3 technical support is staffed by a programmer, product designer, or engineer; and the Level 4 support is staffed by a supervisor or manager.

Some support organizations have more or fewer levels. In general, help desks try to handle as many calls at the lowest possible level in the support hierarchy. They want to save their higher-level, more experienced staff resources for situations where their skills are necessary. Lower-level help desk staff members usually have someone to whom they can refer difficult problems and even difficult callers. You'll learn more about call management later in this chapter.

Regardless of the help desk structure, all help desks have the same goal: to provide customer satisfaction by effectively and efficiently resolving their problems and questions. To accomplish this goal, help desk staff use well-defined processes, tools, and strategies, which you'll learn about next.

THE CALL MANAGEMENT PROCESS

The **call management process** is a well-defined, formal procedure that help desk staff follow to solve user problems. Figure 9-2 shows the major steps in the process. Each of these steps is described in the following section.

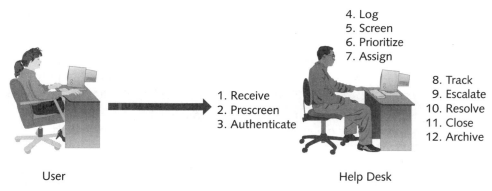

4. Log
5. Screen
6. Prioritize
7. Assign

8. Track
9. Escalate
10. Resolve
11. Close
12. Archive

1. Receive
2. Prescreen
3. Authenticate

User

Help Desk

Figure 9-2   The call management process

1. **Receive the call.** Whether a call is received in person or on a toll-free telephone line, the first step is to establish a relationship with the caller. Some support organizations have a specific script that recommends actual language to use when the call begins. For example, the level 1 help desk staff member may confirm the name of the support organization and provide her or his own name. The staff member may ask the name of the person who is calling. Other common call receiving activities include a warning that the call may be monitored (this is a legal requirement in most states), and an apology for any wait time. As you'll learn later in this chapter, some of these tasks can be automated.

2. **Prescreen the call.** Call prescreening is essentially a filtering process to determine how the help desk staff will handle the call. Before attempting to solve a problem, the level 1 employee may ask questions to determine if the call is a simple request for information that the call screener can provide. Many help desk calls fall into this category. For example, a caller may want to know when

the next version of a software package will be released and whether a known problem will be fixed in the new release. The caller may want to receive a marketing brochure on a product or find out where to buy it. Information request calls can frequently be handled quickly and easily at level 1 and then closed.

3. **Authenticate the call.** If a call is more than a simple request for information, many help desks or hotline services have an **authentication procedure** designed to answer the question, "Is the help desk authorized to handle this call or to provide information or services to this caller?" Call authentication may involve asking the caller for a part ID, model number, or a software license number. In other situations, the screener may ask the caller's name (and perhaps department), and query a database to learn whether the caller is a registered owner of a product or which help desk support services the caller has purchased. The staff member may have to obtain billing information from the customer (usually a credit card number) if the customer is on a pay-per-call basis. Like call prescreening, call authentication is a filtering process. The help desk staff member determines whether the caller has a legitimate claim to support services, and if so, at what service level. Once a staff member has authenticated a call, the call handling process can begin.

4. **Log the call.** The goal of call logging is to begin to document the call and its related problem. The help desk staff member may make an initial entry on a problem log, on a trouble report form, or in a call processing database. The staff member records only basic information about the caller. If caller information already exists in a product registration database, logging the call may be a simple matter of clicking a button that opens a new call and fills in the contact information automatically.

5. **Screen the call.** During call screening, the help desk staff member asks questions to categorize and describe the call. Calls are often categorized according to whether they are:

   - a request for information that could not be handled during prescreening ("Will the latest release fix my font problem?")

   - a question ("How do I get rid of commas in the numbers on my spreadsheet?")

   - a problem ("My printer works with every known software package in the world except yours.")

   - a complaint ("Your software is so full of bugs it locks up my computer every time I run it.")

   - a work order ("Will you please upgrade the operating system software on my machine so I can take a Windows 95 class?")

In addition to the call category, the support staff member enters a brief written description of the request, question, problem, complaint, or work order onto the problem log or into the call tracking database. An experienced help desk staff member learns to capture the essential facts of a problem report in a few key words or phrases.

6. **Prioritize the call.** Based on the call category and the nature of the problem or request, the staff member assigns the call an initial priority code. A **priority code** indicates how serious the problem is, how many users are affected, and perhaps the consequence of not addressing the problem immediately. Help desk staff may determine that the problem affects only one user and is therefore a lower priority than a call about, for example, a malfunction in a network that affects an entire department. During their training, help desk staff are usually given guidelines to help them prioritize calls. In other situations, a priority code may get assigned to a call automatically by a call management software package. The priority code is frequently based on the type of call, its severity, and company policy for that type of call. The service level a caller has purchased may also affect the priority in some help desks. Instead of assigning priority codes, some help desks distribute calls to support staff on a first-in, first-out (FIFO) basis.

The type of call and its priority often determine the queue into which a call will then be placed. A **queue** is a waiting line, like the line at the cash registers in a grocery store. Just as a grocery store may have separate lines or queues for regular and express check out, a help desk may have queues for different types and priorities of calls. The call queues in a help desk may be defined by product, call priority, or any other basis that the help desk uses to manage and assign calls to support staff.

9

7. **Assign the call.** In situations where help desk staff cannot respond to a call directly, they assign it to another help desk staff member who can provide the information, respond to the request, or solve the problem quickly and effectively. In some automated call management systems, the process of assigning the call simply moves it from one call queue to another.

New entry-level employees sometimes find it difficult to learn the best place to refer a call. As you learned earlier in this chapter, help desks prefer to handle as many calls as they can at the lowest possible level in the support hierarchy. Entry-level help desk staff learn quickly who among the experienced technical support staff have good problem-solving skills, give quick and correct answers, and can help deal with calls effectively.

8. **Track the call.** Whenever the essential facts associated with a call change, such as additional problem information, assignment of a new priority, or assignment of the call to a different staff member, the help desk staff update the call information record. **Call tracking** refers to the process of updating the information about a call as it is processed and as information is added to the call record. An automated system often records the date and time of each call tracking entry into a database to provide a complete record of what happened and when. Call tracking information is important input to measure the quality of call management, evaluate employee performance, and identify staff training needs.

9. **Escalate the call.** If initial attempts to resolve a problem are unsuccessful, most companies have policies and procedures to escalate a call. Call escalation is a normal process in which a call is transferred to a higher level of support that has a greater ability or resources to handle more difficult questions, as shown in Figure 9-1.

In some automated call management systems, the escalation process is automatic. For example, if a support staff member cannot resolve a call within a specified period of time, the call management software can often be programmed to automatically escalate it to the next level. If a call has been in the system for more than a specified number of hours, the system may automatically display it on a support manager's screen, where he or she can monitor it closely to make sure that staff members are progressing toward a solution.

10. **Resolve the call.** At some point in the call management process, a help desk staff member resolves the user's problem or question. **Call resolution** means that the user's problem has been solved or a complaint has either been noted or referred to product designers as a suggestion for the next product revision cycle. Call resolution doesn't necessarily mean the user or customer is completely satisfied, however. A small percentage of all calls, usually those that involve complaints about product bugs or features, cannot be resolved during the call management process. Obviously, one of the goals of a help desk is to minimize the percentage of calls that cannot be resolved satisfactorily, but the percent is rarely zero. Alternatively, call resolution may involve giving the customer authorization to return a product for replacement or a refund. The help desk goal, however, is a win-win situation where users receive the information or problem resolution they need and feel that the problem has been solved to their satisfaction.

11. **Close the call.** In **call closing**, the staff member may review the steps the help desk took to solve the problem. He may also get feedback from the caller about her or his satisfaction level. The help desk staff member usually terminates the call by thanking the user for calling and inviting the user to call back if there are further problems, or if the recommended solution to the problem doesn't work. In reality, the help desk hopes the user won't have to call back, but extends the invitation, anyway. Closing the call may also involve additional entries on a problem log or in a database to indicate the disposition of the call and how it was resolved.

Call closing can be a challenge. Some users either can't accept that their problem cannot be resolved in a reasonable way, or don't want to hang up because they enjoy talking technology with help desk staff. These cases fall in the category of difficult callers, which you'll learn more about in the next chapter.

12. **Archive the call.** Closed calls are often kept in the tracking system for some predefined period in case the user calls back. The help desk's policies may specify when the system should **archive** resolved calls by copying them to a database of completed calls. The system then deletes archived calls from the active call management system.

Call archives provide data that can be incorporated into a help desk knowledgebase. A **knowledgebase** is a database that contains instances of problems that have been successfully resolved and perhaps even those that were not. Staff members can then search the knowledgebase in future problem-solving situations to find problems with the same or similar characteristics.

These call management steps are examples of the kinds of activities that occur during call processing. Each company's support policies and procedures may dictate a somewhat different sequence of call processing events, based on business requirements, user expectations, help desk policies, and company resources.

HELP DESK TECHNOLOGY AND TOOLS

Automation has had a significant impact on the help desk industry in recent years. Three of the significant advances are help desk software packages, computer telephony, and the physical layout of the help desk work area.

HELP DESK SOFTWARE

The call management process collects, processes, and stores a large volume of transactions. Some help desks organize their transactions in a database, where tables contain information about customers, products, computer configurations, help desk staff, and perhaps an archive of solved problems. Transactions occur when links are established between a customer and a product (such as a product registration), or between a customer, a computer, and a help desk staff member (such as a problem incident report).

9

Commercial software packages are available to help both large- and small-scale help desks manage the volume of transactions. These packages have features that are useful to support both internal and external clients, including the following:

Log and track calls. Many help desk software packages include features to log and track calls. They often work in conjunction with a telephone system to manage call queues, set call priorities, and escalate calls when necessary. A call tracking system is useful even in a very small support center staffed by one or a few people. No one who needs technical support likes to "get lost in the system," and call management capabilities help support staff keep track of the volume of calls that need attention. As the number of help desk staff increases, and manual systems become cumbersome, some kind of automated call management system is almost a requirement

Contact information. Call processing usually involves contacts with people. Many help desk packages include capabilities to store, edit, and recall contact and location information about internal clients, external clients, help desk and information systems staff, and vendors. These packages often include a large contact database with names, job titles, phone numbers, e-mail addresses, fax numbers, and other information.

Product information. Many help desk callers request information, either for company-provided products or those from other manufacturers. Information about hardware, software, networks, and services help support staff respond to many questions about product features, limitations, new versions, configuration constraints, known bugs, product availability, and related information.

Information resource links. Most help desk software packages recognize that connections to information resources are critical for support specialists. These packages include external connections to e-mail and Internet resources as well as internal connections to online help files, product documentation, and problem archives.

Configuration information. Help desk software often includes features to document hardware, software, and network information about client systems. Although configuration information about external client systems is useful, it is difficult to collect and keep up-to-date, unless there is a service contract or facilities management contract that covers the systems. But configuration information is critical to help desk staff who support internal clients. Much of the configuration checklist information you learned about in Chapter 5 can be stored in a database. That way, support specialists who must troubleshoot or upgrade a system for an in-house client can easily access the information.

Diagnostic utilities. Some help desk software packages include diagnostic utility software to assist a support specialist with a specific system problem. **Diagnostic software** is useful to analyze the performance of a remote system and look for potential problem areas. Some utilities permit a support specialist to attach directly to a client's system, which can facilitate the problem diagnosis process.

Solutions knowledgebase. One of the benefits of research into artificial intelligence is the development of "smart databases," often called knowledgebases. Knowledgebases contain information about common problems and their solutions. Some knowledgebases can be purchased ready-made, and others can be built as user problems are solved and archived. The "smart" part of a knowledgebase is a set of search tools to help locate past problem situations that are similar to a current problem. Some products now incorporate search strategies based on research into artificial intelligence. Expert systems (sequences of IF-THEN rules), neural networks (automated learning systems), and case-based reasoning (pattern-matching strategies) are often incorporated into help desk knowledgebases to help support staff locate the specific information they need to solve a problem.

Product order entry. Help desk software manufacturers recognize that marketing is often an important help desk function; they know that a user request for information about a product can lead directly to an order for it. Therefore, many help desk software packages include an order entry capability that permits a support specialist to enter an order online. Product order entry integrates with other business systems, such as shipping and invoicing.

Customer feedback. Help desks can collect customer feedback to the company about its products and services. **Customer feedback** information includes the level of satisfaction with a specific call, the problem resolution, or with help desk services in general. It can range from complaints about features that don't work as advertised to suggestions for new product versions. The help desk staff needs a way to capture user feedback and route the information to product designers and engineers. This feedback is often a source of useful ideas for the next round of product feature planning. Other help desk software packages offer the ability to collect data for, as well as analyze and report information from, surveys that measure user satisfaction with help desk services. They are another form of feedback that helps identify strengths and areas for improvement in help desk services.

Inventory information. Another feature of many help desk packages is inventory control. This capability is designed to help the support staff manage a company's inventory of hardware, software, and spare parts, if that is a help desk responsibility. Computer equipment is often recorded in an asset management system, which may also be part of the help desk package. Since support staff are often involved in the purchase and installation of computer systems, help desk software is a convenient place to record system installation information. Because help desk staff can be involved in moving equipment from one office to another; they can make updates to the help desk database at the time of the transfer.

Service management. Companies often outsource hardware and peripheral maintenance to outside vendors. In addition to configuration and inventory information, some help desk packages include features to manage hardware service contracts. These capabilities can include warranty information, a service history, as well as reminders of when the next preventative maintenance or service is scheduled to be performed, and by whom.

Telephone system interface. Another useful software feature is an ability to interface with a telephone system. Because many help desk support organizations deal with a large volume of incoming and outgoing calls, integrated access to the company telephone system is important. Automated telephone systems are the subject of a later section in this chapter.

9

Statistical reports. Help desk software includes built-in statistical reports to meet the information needs of the help desk staff and management. Reports such as the number of unclosed calls by hour and day, the average length of time users spend on hold, the average length of calls processed (from receipt to closure), the productivity of staff members (call closure rate), inventory control reports, and frequently asked questions are examples of predefined reports that are common in help desk software packages.

Customizable interface and reports. Some help desk systems are customizable. They include features that let help desk staff modify the user interface, tool bars, menus, and data-entry forms. They may also allow staff to modify fields in the database tables and often include a report generator to let them prepare custom reports of database information. Custom reports let the help desk staff augment built-in reports with ones designed to address specific staff and management information needs. Some help desk packages include a programming language that staff can use to write macros or code to support extensions of the basic package.

Although no single help desk package necessarily offers all of these features and capabilities, many packages offer several of them. Selecting a help desk software package from among those on the market (and there are many) is often one of the most important product evaluation decisions a help desk staff makes.

The list of companies that sell help desk software packages is long. Some of the best selling packages are Clientele, Magic Solutions, ServiceCenter, Professional Help Desk, Remedy Help Desk, and Vantive. A monthly trade publication, *ServiceNews*, evaluates help desk software. Many of its reviews are online at **www.servicenews.com**.

The next three figures illustrate typical help desk software with a package named Clientele/IS, sold by Platinum Software. The Clientele/IS package is a commercial help desk program that includes several of the features you just learned about. Like many help desk software packages, Clientele/IS is customizable for specific help desk situations. Users can add, delete, or modify fields in the Clientele/IS database. A report generator provides custom reports beyond those built into the system.

Figure 9-3 shows the Clientele/IS main menu, tool bar, and search screen. From this window a support person can find contact and location information about people, departments, or an entire organization, information about computer equipment and software, and details about calls in queues.

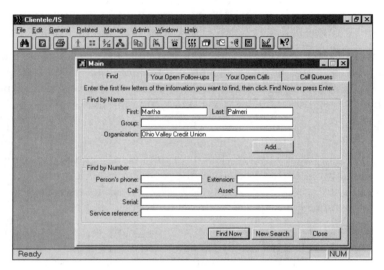

Figure 9-3   Clientele/IS main menu, tool bar, and search screen

Figure 9-4 shows an example of the calls in a queue that have not been closed. A help desk specialist can display the calls in his or her personal queue, or in a generic queue of unassigned calls, such as an engineering queue or a product information queue. Users of Clientele/IS can set up any queues that help them manage incoming calls.

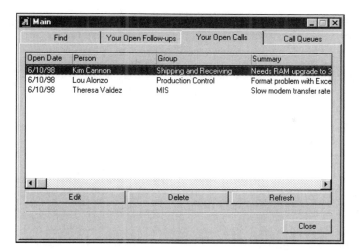

Figure 9-4   Clientele call queue

Figure 9-5 displays an example of the Clientele knowledgebase called the AnswerBook. The page shows the AnswerBook entry on how to clear a paper jam.

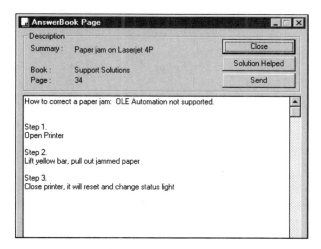

Figure 9-5   Clientele knowledgebase

Other help desk software packages have similar features and capabilities.

COMPUTER TELEPHONY SYSTEMS

Computer telephony is a relatively new name used to describe products that incorporate telephone and computer technology into an integrated package. Computer telephony is becoming increasingly popular among support organizations that make heavy use of both technologies to support help desk services. Whereas many small support centers rely on a help desk receptionist or a call dispatcher to respond to incoming telephone calls, an increasing number of help desk facilities invest in automated telephone systems.

Automated Call Distributors (ACD) are telephone systems that can answer calls, greet callers, provide menus to indicate the type of call, and route the call to a support specialist or to a queue. When integrated with a help desk software package, an ACD system can take call management a step further. When an appropriate support specialist becomes available, an ACD system can match the support specialist with the highest priority caller, signal the support specialist on her computer screen, and display information collected from the caller on the specialist's computer. It then routes the call to the specialist's telephone.

ACD systems can also collect information about the performance of the help desk operation, such as the average length of a phone call, the length of hold queues, the average amount of time on hold, and the average length of calls for each support specialist. They can also monitor calls by recording them for training and employee evaluation purposes. The major benefit of an ACD system is that it reduces the amount of employee time needed to respond to calls and route them to support staff. Because they increase the efficiency of help desk staff, they are help desk productivity tools.

PHYSICAL LAYOUT OF HELP DESK WORK AREAS

In most large-scale help desk operations, each support specialist works in a cubicle that is enclosed on three sides by carpeted wall panels. The walls are from four to six feet high, depending on whether visual contact with coworkers is desirable and depending on the need to reduce background and equipment noise. A typical cubicle is usually about eight feet long by eight feet wide.

Support specialists sit at a desk in the cubicle that includes space for one or more computer systems. One computer is the support specialist's own system on which he or she runs call management software, as well as the specific packages the specialist supports. There may be other computer systems in the cubicle, such as hardware and operating system platforms that are different from the specialist's own system. The support specialist uses these systems to replicate or reproduce a caller's problem. In some situations, problem replication systems may be located in a computer room where they can be shared among support staff. Mainframe access (where necessary) may be available through a terminal emulator on the support person's desktop, or through a separate terminal located in the cubicle. The work cubicle usually contains a reference library of information on specific products that the specialist supports.

To answer calls, most support specialists prefer a headset instead of a standard telephone handset. The headset permits considerable freedom of motion and can be easily unplugged when necessary to confer with a coworker or supervisor about a problem.

If workplace ergonomic issues are important for end users in general, they are even more important for help desk staff who provide telephone support. All of the ergonomic and facilities management concerns discussed in Chapters 5 and 8 apply to the design of workstations for help desk support staff as well. Job stress is a common complaint of help desk employees. The physical environment of the help desk work areas can either contribute to job stress or reduce it. The design of the work areas should reduce distractions due to excessive noise, motion, and other interruptions to the extent possible. Frequent and scheduled breaks are useful stress reduction tools.

MANAGERIAL CONCERNS: MISSION, STAFFING, AND TRAINING

From the moment you decide that you want to pursue a help desk position, you should be aware of the help desk management's perspective. Every decision a help desk manager makes affects the people who work there. Conversely, the more you know about his or her concerns and decisions, the better equipped you will be to focus your efforts on the tasks your manager thinks are important. Knowing the big picture will help you learn to play an important role in customer satisfaction and in the success of the help desk. It will also help prepare you to advance from an entry-level position to one with more responsibility and a higher salary.

There are three areas of management concern that directly affect your job: the help desk mission, staffing, and training.

HELP DESK MISSION AND JUSTIFICATION

Help desk organizations often develop a **mission statement**, which is a list of guiding principles that communicates help desk goals to staff, users, and management. Help desks also use their mission statements as a yardstick against which to measure whether their goals have been met. An example of a help desk mission statement follows; it primarily addresses internal employees but could be modified to apply to external customers or clients. The italicized terms highlight important concepts.

> The mission of the help desk is to maximize *operational efficiency* among the users in an organization by providing timely resolution to *technology use questions* and effectively *manage problems* to continuously *improve the quality* of help desk service to users, the *usability of information systems*, the *effectiveness of documentation and training,* and the *customer's satisfaction* with help desk services.

Two of the terms, *operational efficiency* and *usability of information systems*, directly address the end users' productivity. Increased employee (or customer) productivity is important because every help desk must justify its existence in the company. It must prove to its parent company that its benefits outweigh its costs. The remaining italicized terms emphasize objectives within the help desk operation itself.

Performance statistics and measures of customer satisfaction are one way to document and justify the value of help desk services. **Performance statistics** are data about the help desk operation. For example, the percentage of calls that are handled within two minutes of their receipt may be an important help desk statistic. However, especially in organizations where the help desk is treated as an administrative overhead budget item (an expense center), it is often difficult to justify expenses based on performance statistics or customer satisfaction when there is no revenue stream to offset the costs. That is one reason many hardware and software manufacturers now charge their customers for help desk services. Product vendors may offer several levels of help desk services, including a free level, a standard (fee-for-service) level, and a premium level for those customers who want and need very responsive service. Whereas the premium level of service may be more responsive than the free service or standard service, it also costs more to provide. It is important that help desk employees at all levels, even at entry-level positions, understand the importance of justification, because it affects help desk decisions that directly affect their jobs. To justify help desk operations, help desk managers often perform the kind of cost-benefit analysis you learned about in Chapter 4.

STAFFING THE HELP DESK

When you interview for a help desk position, you should be aware of the help desk manager's staffing concerns. Staffing a help desk begins with a mission statement. Based on the mission statement, a help desk manager writes one or more position descriptions: one if the help desk is new or small, several if the help desk has a multi-level structure. The position descriptions (like those you read in Chapter 2) are also based on an analysis of what a help desk staff member needs to know and be able to do. The mission statement, position descriptions, and the specific knowledge, skills, and abilities (KSAs) for a help desk operation are important first steps toward staffing a help desk.

Most help desk support staff members need a combination of technical skills and communications skills. A KSA analysis begins with a written list of both technical and communications areas:

- Technical skills
- Hardware, operating systems, and applications software familiarity
- Network background and skills
- Troubleshooting skills
- Communications and listening skills
- Ability to work in a project team
- Telephone skills
- Personal characteristics

In each category, detailed job-related requirements can be listed for a specific position. For example, a support position may require a person with KSAs to work with Intel-compatible hardware platforms in standard office configurations, Windows 95/98/NT operating system experience, working knowledge of Microsoft Office applications software, and so on. A position in a help desk that provides telephone support might emphasize communications skills and personal characteristics. A position that provides more advanced technical support would probably place greater emphasis on technical knowledge and troubleshooting skills.

When evaluating job candidates, managers screen applicants to narrow down the list of choices to those whose KSAs are the closest match with the requirements of the position. Screening prospective help desk staff members is a multi-step process. It begins with the development of a position description, like the examples in Chapter 2, which should include a clear definition of the duties and responsibilities of help desk staff members and a checklist of KSAs required to perform the job. The position description and KSA analysis form the basis for a classified ad (newspaper) or for a position order (employment or temporary worker agency).

Screening continues when the manager receives applications. Often a team of people who represent the help desk, help desk management, information services department (if applicable), and human resources screen resumes and applications to search for those who will be invited for an interview. The screening step often relies heavily on checklists of KSAs developed earlier.

Selection tools that help desk managers use include several kinds of interview questions and frequently a skills test. A **skills test** is a paper-and-pencil or verbal test that measures a prospective employee's knowledge and problem-solving ability. Many employment interviews include general questions about the applicant's educational and work background and experience. One particularly useful interview tool is the scenario question. A **scenario question** gives a prospective staff member a specific problem (or set of problems) that represents the kinds of problems help desk staff actually encounter. Scenarios can be a written exercise (when an applicant first applies), or a problem-solving exercise during an interview. Scenario questions often provide insights into an applicant's problem-solving skills, communications skills, and ability to perform in simulated stressful work situations. The scenario approach is often more effective than traditional interview questions in identifying staff who can perform well under pressure. Here is an example of a scenario:

9

Suppose as a new help desk staff member you are approached by a user in the manufacturing division who wants to bend your ear about ongoing network problems that affect the productivity of employees in manufacturing. The employee relates that manufacturing has experienced an increasing volume of network crashes on its server in recent weeks. The employee goes on to say that it takes forever to get the network restarted when it crashes, and the downtime affects the productivity in his department. The employee states that other manufacturing employees feel that they would be better off with the manual system they used to work with.

As a new help desk staff member, how would you handle this problem report?

Scenario questions can often be answered from a number of perspectives. Some applicants could treat this scenario as an opportunity to display their technical knowledge about networks. Others could discuss the problem-solving and communications process they would use to address the problem.

VALERIE GOULDS
MAINFRAME TECHNICAL SUPPORT ENGINEER
WALL DATA
KIRKLAND, WA

I've worked at Wall Data for a little over a year. Wall Data produces mainframe and AS/400 emulators that allow users to transfer information from a mainframe or an AS/400 to their PCs. I first started working at Wall as a part-time customer support intern while I was getting my degree at Bellevue Community College. After three months, I moved to the tech support position.

Screening. To get my current job, I had a strenuous interview with four managers and team leaders. They asked me questions on topics like memory management to get an overview of my technical knowledge. Then I was given scenarios to test my problem-solving skills.

Our mission. The overall mission of our help desk operation is to obtain 100% customer satisfaction. Wall has one of the highest customer satisfaction ratings in the industry, above 75%. We are constantly looking at our process and how to improve it.

Call management. We don't have a call distributor. Instead, customers reach a customer service rep who logs their information, then tries a tech support line for the appropriate team. We always work with the customer to establish an action plan so we both agree on the nature of the problem and how we will proceed.

Getting information: We use Scopus software for call logging and database searching to see how other technical support reps solved similar problems. We also have a knowledgebase and an extensive electronic library on our Web site where customers can search for information.

Our Group Structure: There are about 12 people in the mainframe group where I work. We work as a team to support our internal and external customers, which is very effective. We can also consult a senior-level engineer, who acts as a mentor to help step us through a problem so we learn from it. It's a supportive environment that encourages growth.

Difficult customers: Troubleshooting mainframe problems can be time consuming and frustrating, so we often have customers who are at the boiling point when they call us. I think the key to handling this type of customer is to actively listen to them, let them know you understand their frustrations, and let them vent. Then we can work together as a team to solve the problem. Sometimes, though, nothing works, and we just have to remember not to take it personally and to deal with the caller in a professional manner.

HELP DESK STAFF TRAINING

One of the most overlooked aspects of help desk operations is the training needs of the help desk staff itself. Many of the end user training methods and strategies you learned in Chapter 6 are effective for help desk staff as well. The problem is often how to schedule training time for help desk staff. Managers sometimes assume that help desk staff will pick up information about new products in the course of their everyday work. Sometimes that happens; other times it does not.

If a mission of a help desk is to provide quality service to users, help desk staff members need time to learn how to be productive with new technology. Successful help desk operations that intend to recruit and retain staff members invest in training both at the time an employee is hired and on-the-job to keep job skills up-to-date.

Training for new employees often includes:

- Orientation to the company
- Employee benefits information
- Specific job skill training
- Company policies and procedures
- Performance appraisal procedures

9

Of these training topics, information about company policies and procedures is especially important. New employees need to know not only specific job skills to function effectively as an entry-level help desk employee, but they also need to learn where to find answers to questions like, "What is the company's policy if a customer wants a refund?" or "What is the recommended procedure if a customer asks to speak to a supervisor, or the company president?" Although it is probably not possible to learn about every company policy or procedure, it is important to cover basic information about the company's general user support philosophy.

Company training programs for help desk employees should help keep support staff current with changes in computer technology and how changes impact their customer base. However, current knowledge and skills is a joint obligation. Company training programs are half of the solution; personal professional growth is the other half. Help desk employees are computer professionals who are expected to invest in their own continuing education. They should expect to attend conferences and workshops, read widely in trade publications and books, own a home computer, and make an investment in their own professional growth commensurate with the investment their employer makes.

It is also important to communicate to new employees when and how their job performance will be evaluated. A **performance appraisal** is a process to evaluate a help desk employee according to established criteria. The performance appraisal criteria should be related to the mission of the help desk and to a new employee's personal growth objectives.

For help desk staff who are interested in more information about help desk management, Chapter 13 on Information Resources includes some pointers to books that provide detailed information about the management perspective.

TRENDS IN HELP DESK OPERATIONS

Help desk operation is a relatively new field and is changing rapidly. Whereas many help desks in the past were based on walk-in or telephone support, the future of help desk services will undoubtedly rely to an increasing extent on electronic mail, the Internet, and remote diagnosis to provide help desk services. Help desks of the future will likely be more proactive and less reactive than current help desks. They will be better able to anticipate user needs and changes in user service requirements. As more help desk functions are automated in the future, help desk management can get higher-quality reports and statistical data that will alert managers to trends in the volume of calls, the kind of questions asked, the need for help desk staff with particular skills, and the kinds of problems users are likely to encounter.

CHAPTER SUMMARY

- Simply stated, the goal of most help desk operations is to provide customers with a single point of contact for information requests and problem resolution. Most help desk processes and procedures involve the effective management of user calls. Call management addresses the details of how calls are received, prescreened, authenticated to determine the caller's rights to various levels of service, logged for recordkeeping purposes, and screened to determine importance. They are then prioritized, assigned to an appropriate staff person, tracked as they move toward satisfactory resolution, escalated if necessary, resolved, closed, and archived in a database.

- Several tools are available to help manage calls. These include help desk software packages with features designed to automate many help desk call management tasks and procedures, computer telephony systems (including automated call distributors) which automate call routing and assignment tasks, and the physical arrangement of the help desk facility to improve staff productivity.

- Even new help desk employees will better understand their job tasks if they understand the help desk manager's concerns with mission, staffing, and training. Help desk operations often draft a mission statement that includes such objectives as increased user productivity, resolution of problems in the use of technology, and continuous improvement in the quality of help desk services. Help desk staff are recruited based on a combination of technical and communications skills. Training for new help desk staff members includes a job skills orientation and information about company policies and call handling procedures.

- Help desks of the future will continue to evolve. Increased automation of help desk functions and attempts to be more proactive to anticipate user problems will impact the staff and operations of future help desks.

KEY TERMS

- **archive** — A special database designed to store and retain copies of closed calls; in a manual call management system, this may be a file of closed calls.

- **authentication procedure** — A call management step that determines whether help desk staff are authorized to handle a call; usually includes checking product registrations and support services contracts.

- **automated call distributor (ACD)** — A computer telephony system that automates many of the first steps in call management, such as a greeting, menu options, caller authentication, call holding, queue management, and staff notification.

- **call closing** — A call management step that leads toward termination of a call; may include a review of the solution, mutual agreement that a solution has been reached, an invitation to call back, and final entries in a call management database.

- **call management process** — A well-defined, formal procedure that help desk staff members follow to handle calls, get the information users need or solve their problems, and close the calls.

- **call resolution** — A step in call management when the user's problem has been solved or information has been provided.

- **call tracking** — The process of updating call information as it is processed and as information is added to the call record.

- **computer telephony** — Integration of computer technology and telephone technology into tools designed to increase help desk staff productivity by providing a seamless interface between the two.

- **customer feedback** — Information collected from help desk callers about their level of satisfaction with a specific call, the problem resolution, or with help desk services in general.

- **diagnostic software** — Computer programs designed to help support specialists collect information and analyze problems with a computer system.

- **help desk** — An organization of user support services that provides a single point of contact for a company's customers or employees.

- **knowledgebase** — A database that staff can search for instances of past problems that have been successfully resolved.

- **mission statement** — A list of guiding principles that communicates help desk goals to staff, users, and management; often provides criteria against which help desk services can be evaluated.

- **multi-level support model** — A help desk structure that organizes support staff and services into several levels or tiers; sometimes called a frontline/backline model, the goal is to handle calls at the lowest possible support level.

- **performance appraisal** — The process of evaluating a help desk employee according to established criteria.

- **performance statistics** — Data gathered about the operation of a help desk; provides feedback to individual staff or to the help desk group on performance related to behavioral objectives and on customer satisfaction with help desk services.

- **priority code** — A designation assigned to a call that indicates how serious the problem is for users; help desk staff often work on high priority calls first, which are usually serious problems that affect a large number of users.

- **queue** — A waiting line or list into which incoming calls are placed when they cannot be answered immediately; there may be queues for specific products, customers, or levels of support.

- **scenario question** — A role-playing problem in a hypothetical help desk situation to provide insight into an applicant's problem-solving skills, communications style, and ability to perform in a stressful environment.

- **skills test** — A paper-and-pencil (or occasionally verbal) exercise designed to measure a prospective help desk employee's knowledge and problem-solving ability.

REVIEW QUESTIONS

1. What is a help desk? Explain the range of services help desks in different organizations may provide to users.

2. What is a multi-level support model for help desks? Describe some common levels of support.

3. At what support level do multi-level help desks try to handle most of the calls that come in to a help desk? Explain why.

4. What is the call management process? List common steps in the process and briefly explain the purpose of each step.

5. Why are help desk calls prescreened if they will be screened at a later step?

6. Explain several ways in which a help desk may authenticate a caller.

7. Why are call logging and tracking important aspects of help desk call management?

8. Describe the kinds of calls that are often encountered during the screening process. Give some examples of each kind.

9. What criteria does a help desk use to prioritize calls? How are priority codes used?

10. Explain the purpose of a queue in call management. List some common kinds of queues.

11. Why does a help desk need a call escalation procedure?

12. Explain the statement:"Our help desk tries to resolve every call to the 100% satisfaction of the caller. But we don't always reach that goal."

13. Give several examples of activities that occur when a call is closed. Explain why each is important.

14. Why do help desks archive completed calls in a knowledgebase? Explain the purpose of a knowledgebase.

15. Describe the features you would expect to find in a commercial call management software package. Do the aspects of call management you described have to be automated? Explain your answer.

16. Explain why customer feedback and performance statistics are important to a help desk staff.

17. Define computer telephony and explain why it is an important development in help desk technology.

18. What features does an ACD system provide?

19. Describe the physical layout of a typical help desk environment. Why are ergonomic and facilities management concerns important to help desk staff?

20. What is the purpose of a help desk mission statement? List some common objectives in a typical mission statement.

21. Explain the relationship between a help desk mission statement, position descriptions, and staff knowledge, skills, and abilities.

22. What decision tools do help desk managers use to screen job applicants and make staffing decisions?

23. What is a scenario question, and how is it used in help desk hiring?

24. List several topics you would expect to cover in an orientation for new help desk staff.

HANDS-ON PROJECTS

 PROJECT 9-1

Find a support specialist at your company or school, or one employed in a local business. Interview the specialist to find out how his help desk is organized and what services it provides. Ask about his career path and if he can provide you with his current position description. Write a summary description of the interview highlights.

 PROJECT 9-2

Arrange a visit to a company that provides primarily telephone help desk support. Study how the physical workspace for help desk employees is organized to facilitate their work. Find out if the company has a written call management process, if it uses a help desk software package, and if it uses a computer telephony system. Write a description of your findings. Draw a sketch of the physical layout of the help desk operation you observed.

PROJECT 9-3

Write a sample script that could be followed by an employee in a typical help desk environment. Your script should cover the first tasks in call management, including: receiving the call, prescreening the call, and authenticating the caller. Write another sample script that could be used to close a call. Incorporate in your scripts your own ideas on effective handling of calls and customers.

PROJECT 9-4

Suppose a help desk has a priority code system that includes the following codes:

Code	Meaning
U	Urgent
H	High priority
M	Medium priority
L	Low priority

Use the following criteria to assign a priority code to the given situations: a) severity of problem, b) number of users affected, c) availability of a reasonable workaround, and d) your own judgment.

1. A user calls with a question about how to format a chart in Excel.

2. The administrative assistant in the manufacturing division calls to report that the server in his building is down.

3. A user calls to report a suspected bug in the way a toolbar works in a software package, but she says the equivalent pull-down menu does work.

4. The president of the company calls to request the latest performance data on the help desk operation.

5. A bug is reported in the beta release of a software package; the production version is scheduled to ship next week.

6. Several calls are received from irate users that the accounting software package they purchased 12 months ago does not handle some end-of-year processing correctly.

7. A user calls to report that a diagnostic hardware utility has detected an error in her CD-ROM controller card.

Discuss your priority code assignments with another person or with your project group. Explore any incidents where you differ by more than one priority code. Write a summary of your conclusions.

PROJECT 9-5

Based on your experiences with checkout lines in grocery stores or fast-food restaurants, discuss whether it is preferable from a customer's point of view to have a few, longer queues or several shorter queues. Does either arrangement really make any difference? To whom? Relate your discussion to help desk call management. Write a one- to two-page paper that discusses the pros and cons of each strategy and summarizes your conclusions.

PROJECT 9-6

List the important pieces of information about a typical support call that you would expect to find in a call logging/tracking system. Use a word processor or database prototype feature to design a data-entry form that captures the information you identified to track a call.

9

PROJECT 9-7

Find information about a PC diagnostic utility program that is advertised in a trade publication or on the Internet. If you can obtain a copy of the program, try out its features. Make a list of the features of the software that you think would be especially useful to help desk support staff to help them diagnose hardware problems.

PROJECT 9-8

If you have had experience with a help desk that uses an ACD telephone system, write an evaluation of the user interface. Describe the first level of menus, and at least one other menu level. Evaluate the menus and menu navigation from a user's perspective. Write some suggestions on how the ACD interface could be improved.

If you work in a project group, compare your suggestions with those of members in your group. What are some common design principles the members in your group agree on for an ACD system?

PROJECT 9-9

If you work for a company or attend a school that has a help desk, find out if it has a help desk mission statement. Compare the mission statement with the sample in this chapter. List similarities and differences you find. Choose one of the mission statements and write some measurable criteria you could use to evaluate the performance of a help desk.

PROJECT 9-10

Write a one-page personal professional development plan for yourself or a typical help desk employee. Use the information resources in Chapter 13 to find professional growth materials you could include in your plan. Then compare your plan with ones developed by coworkers or fellow students in your project group. What useful ideas did you get from them?

CASE PROJECTS

1. HELP DESK PERFORMANCE AT VIRTUAL-SOFT

Beth Goldman, supervisor of Virtual-Soft's Help Desk service, gets weekly data from a help desk software package on her support specialists' performance. She would like to use the data to measure her staff members' productivity. Use a spreadsheet to analyze the data from last week shown in Figure 9-6.

Support Specialist	Calls Handled Per Week	Available Hours Per Week	Average Minutes Per Call
Susan	112	31.5	14.2
Jose	127	31.0	11.3
Sue	0	0.0	0.0
Barbara	87	25.1	15.9
Ekaterina	151	30.0	9.2
Shere-Kahn	63	24.2	13.6
Dennis	77	29.6	11.9
Kristen	63	27.1	10.6

Figure 9-6   Weekly help desk team report

Use a spreadsheet to analyze the help desk performance data in this table to determine who the most productive help desk employees are. Is there more than one right answer? Print your spreadsheet and explain your answer.

2. SELECTING A HELP DESK PACKAGE FOR SMARTCARD

You have been hired as a support specialist for SmartCard, a year-old designer and manufacturer of network controller cards. The volume of support calls is growing, and the company has asked you to research an inexpensive help desk software package.

Many help desk management software packages sell for several thousand U.S. dollars per seat (per each support specialist). One package with a considerably lower price tag is Manage-It!, a help desk management system distributed by Baron Software. In fact, a demonstration version of Manage-It! is available for download on the Internet. Anyone can evaluate this version for a limited time before making a decision to purchase it. The site address is **www.bssinc.com**.

If your company or school has facilities that permit you to download software, get a copy of Manage-It! Install Manage-It! on your system and learn to use its basic features. Although there is no tutorial or printed documentation with Manage-It!, there is an online help system. In most cases, the features in Manage-It! work like a database system. Practice using Manage-It! by entering one or more companies, contact persons, call categories, products, and parts. Then use the system to log some sample calls into Manage-It! Your instructor may give you some specific assignments to carry out.

Find information about at least one other commercial help desk software package in a trade publication or on the Internet. Compare the package you found with Manage-It! Write a description of some similarities and differences between the two packages.

9

3. RICHARD BLANK COLLEGE'S STAFF RECRUITMENT PROJECT

In Chapter 2, you learned about the position description for a Computer Network Support Tech (see Figure 2-6) at Richard Blank College. Suppose you are a member of the recruitment team that will select the best applicant for this position.

1. Based on the position description, make a list of knowledge, skills, and abilities an applicant for this position needs. Group your KSAs as technical knowledge and skills and communications skills.

2. Study examples of advertisements for help desk or related positions in a local newspaper. Note the format and contents of several ads. Then write a sample ad for the network position at Richard Blank College. Because newspapers charge by the line or the word for classified advertising, limit your ad to 75 words.

3. Write five questions that the recruitment group could use during candidate interviews. Include at least two scenario questions.

4. Write a model answer to one of the interview questions you designed that illustrates how you would answer the question if it was asked of you in a real job interview.

CHAPTER TEN

CUSTOMER SERVICE SKILLS FOR USER SUPPORT

As you learned in Chapter 9, communications skills are very important tools for help desk support staff. Whether they supply help to end users in person, via phone, fax, e-mail, or on the Internet, all successful support staff must be able to listen effectively, understand, and communicate solutions to user problems.

Communications skills are often more challenging for a new help desk employee to learn than technical skills or business skills and are more difficult to measure and evaluate. It takes practice to learn how to use communications skills effectively, and some people have more well-developed communications and customer service skills than others. But experienced user support specialists and their managers know that customer satisfaction with a call is directly related to how well a specialist listens to, understands, and speaks to the user. Support specialists who concentrate solely on finding the correct technical answer may be frustrated to learn that users are not completely satisfied with their support interactions. In this chapter, you'll learn about some practical listening, understanding, and speaking skills that user support staff can apply to almost any support situation to help solve user problems and achieve the goals of every support request: customer satisfaction and excellent customer service.

Many of the skills discussed in this chapter apply to telephone support, but can apply to support in other contexts as well. Good communication skills are essential in any support environment.

AFTER READING THIS CHAPTER AND COMPLETING THE EXERCISES YOU WILL BE ABLE TO:

- Describe the importance of communications skills and customer service
- Describe the reasons for careful listening
- Explain how to build and communicate understanding
- List and describe three important aspects of effective speaking in a support interaction
- Develop a call management strategy
- Explain strategies for difficult calls
- Describe other components of excellent customer service

COMMUNICATIONS SKILLS AND CUSTOMER SERVICE

Communications skills are essential elements in providing high-quality customer service. All user support specialists need to communicate effectively with users. Communication is a two-way process that involves both listening and speaking. To listen effectively, support specialists must also hear and understand, and their spoken communications must then reflect their understanding of a user's problem. Listening, understanding, and speaking are essential to solving user problems. A support organization that can solve user problems effectively and efficiently creates customer satisfaction and demonstrates that the support organization provides excellent customer service.

Help desks and support organizations frequently incorporate a customer service ethic into their mission statements. Many companies aim for 100% customer satisfaction 100% of the time. More and more support organizations realize that they need to emphasize customer service excellence. Why? First, satisfied customers are likely to be repeat customers. One of the most frequent reasons customers leave one hardware or software supplier for another is that they received poor service. Excellent service may be more important to customers than product features, price, convenience, or any other aspect of a business. Second, it usually takes longer to handle calls from dissatisfied customers than from satisfied ones. A dissatisfied customer is more likely to generate repeated callbacks, to require call escalation to a higher level support specialist, to return a product for a refund, and to evoke other activities that reduce support staff productivity.

A customer service ethic means that, in the pursuit of customer service excellence, support staff

- Provide users with the information, service, or solution they need, if there is any reasonable way to do so
- Explain to customers what they *can* do for them, if they cannot solve their problems
- Treat callers with respect
- Communicate to callers how long they are likely to be on hold
- Return calls when promised, even if to report that no progress has yet been made

Think of each caller as a valued customer. Always remember that user support is essentially a customer service job and that the goal of resolving all requests is to create satisfied customers. If callers are not treated as valued customers, they may not be customers for very long. If customers have a choice, where will they choose to shop? Probably where customer service is taken seriously. Even in telephone support, callers measure your attitude and react to the way you communicate and handle the call. Whether they intend to or not, support specialists inevitably communicate whether a call is an interesting one and whether they value the caller.

Think of each call as an opportunity to build customer satisfaction. To create customer satisfaction and help attain a company's customer service goals, support specialists must master the essential communications skills: listening, understanding, and speaking.

LISTEN CAREFULLY

In any support conversation, learn to listen before you speak. Listen initially to the caller's description of her question or problem to develop a thorough understanding of the problem.

 In the next chapter, you'll learn about a technique called active listening, which is a way to restate and clarify what you heard to reach a common understanding of a user's problem.

During the problem description, listen to two other features of the user's communication. First, listen to the *language* the caller uses to describe the problem. The language can frequently provide important clues as to whether the caller is a novice or an experienced user. It is often better for support specialists to target their own language level slightly below the level the caller uses to avoid language that is too complex or too technical for the caller to understand. Second, listen to *how* the caller describes the problem, which can give you further insight into the problem and the caller. What tone of voice does the caller use? Does the caller sound angry? Does he hesitate or struggle with the use of technical terms? Does she sound distracted? Subtle cues like these can provide you with valuable information about how to handle a call.

To build listening skills, look for learning opportunities in courses that emphasize communications skills. Unfortunately, many college speech courses cover public speaking but do not necessarily focus on listening skills. Look for courses in small group or interpersonal communications, which often place equal weight on listening and speaking skills.

10

BUILD UNDERSTANDING

Once you have listened to and heard the user's problem description, try to develop an understanding of the user's situation. Ideally, you will develop empathy with the caller. **Empathy** is an understanding of and identification with the caller's situation, thoughts, and feelings. A support specialist who can empathize with a caller understands the problem or question from the caller's point of view. One measure of empathy is whether you can express a user's problem in your own words. Empathy does not mean that you should take complete ownership of and responsibility for a problem but that you understand and can relate effectively to the user, who does own the problem. Try to understand, for example, why the problem is important to a caller, why a caller might want to know a particular piece of information, or perhaps why a caller is frustrated, upset, or angry. The following are examples of empathetic responses:

> "Clearly, we need to get this system running again so you can create the report. Here's where we'll start...."
>
> "It sounds like you've had a very frustrating morning, but I think I can help you with this..."
>
> "To help you close your accounting month on time, I can give you a workaround for this problem. Then, when that's finished, we can diagnose the problem you're having so it doesn't happen again."

As you develop understanding of the caller and the problem, communicate to the caller that you view him as a person, rather than as a phone call. One technique experienced support staff use is to visualize the caller. Think of someone in your own experience who sounds like the caller and then communicate with that image.

SPEAK EFFECTIVELY

In a support interaction, all aspects of your speech communicate your understanding of a situation, lead to successful call resolution, and influence the user's level of satisfaction with the call. Three important aspects are your call greeting, how you use call scripts, and your tone and style.

THE IMPORTANCE OF THE GREETING

If every trip begins with a single step, support communications begin with a greeting, which can affect the course of the entire call. The greeting is the icebreaker, and callers use it to form their first impressions of the support staff person, the support service, and ultimately the entire company that provides support. Most support providers train their staff members to use a standard greeting, which often includes the staff member's first name and the name of the company or other identification. A common greeting is: "This is Joel in Computer Support. Thank you very much for your call. How may I help you?" Practice using a sincere greeting with a tone that communicates interest and enthusiasm and avoids sounding stiff, overly rehearsed, or bored. The immediate "thank you" communicates to the caller that you appreciate the call and that it is important to you. If the caller gives his or her name after your greeting, write it down so you can use it during the call.

USE SCRIPTS APPROPRIATELY

Many support organizations supply their support staff with a script to help handle routine aspects of a call. A **script** is a prepared sequence of questions and statements that covers the important parts of a call. A script can include branches and decision points; support staff follow a path through the script that depends on the user's answers. Scripts can be a useful training aid for new support staff, as well as a tool to handle difficult technical problems and difficult callers. However, it should never sound to the caller like you are reading a script unless you make it clear that you are reading a piece of technical information to ensure it is communicated accurately. Scripts are also useful if a call evolves into an argument or other inappropriate communication. Reverting to a script can help you get the call back on track and make sure that the call is handled according to company policy.

Some help desk facilities maintain a database of frequently asked questions (FAQs) and prepared responses to them. When using prepared responses, the same cautions apply as to the use of scripts. Don't read lengthy responses, unless you make it clear that is what you are doing. Instead, restate them in your own words.

As part of a training program, a support specialist may be asked to learn or develop model answers to questions. Experienced support staff and supervisors are useful sources of information about what constitutes a "good" response to a FAQ.

USE TONE AND STYLE EFFECTIVELY

How you communicate with a caller is often more important than the content of the communication and has a direct impact on the caller's satisfaction with the support call. Which of these caller reports best illustrates the desired outcome of a support call?

> "The support specialists provided me with the minimum amount of information I needed, but I felt through the whole conversation that I was intruding on their time. They spoke rapidly and curtly, and weren't very pleasant."
>
> "The support specialist couldn't tell me what I needed to know, but explained why the information wasn't available yet, when it would be, and invited me to call back. I felt like a valued customer and that my call was important to them."

10

Help desk communications can be professional or casual, respectful or condescending, formal or informal, verbose or terse, and any number of other adjectives that describe communications. A communications style is the point between each of these extremes where support specialists choose to locate themselves. Often, as part of help desk training, support organizations will indicate the type of communications style they want their staff to use. They realize that style is important because it communicates the company's image. In reality, help desk staff members modify the company standard somewhat, depending on their experience, on user feedback, and on their own personalities.

Research studies have found that the words people use to communicate account for less than 10% of the information people receive. The tone, voice inflection, voice pitch, and other aspects of style account for nearly half. Nonverbal communication, sometimes called body language, accounts for more than half. In telephone support communications, where nonverbal cues are missing, communication tone takes on greater significance.

Use clear and succinct speech that is neither too fast nor painfully slow. Many inexperienced support specialists have a tendency to speak too fast, which is a natural reaction to stress. Practice speaking more slowly, but not so slow as to sound condescending. Match your speed to the proficiency level of the user. Remember, too, that shorter sentences are easier for a caller to follow than long ones. Avoid a rising inflection at the end of sentences, which sounds like you are asking a question or are unsure. Many of the suggestions about technical writing in Chapter 7 also apply to help desk communications style, including the use of gender-neutral language, and avoiding wordiness, long words, overly technical terms, acronyms, and jargon.

Avoid using empty phrases in support calls. New support staff, in particular, sometimes feel they need to continue to talk just to fill the pauses. Avoid empty phrases, such as "Now let me see… I think I've seen that problem before…. Let me think about where I have that information…." These phrases do not communicate useful information, although it appears that communication is occurring. Instead of empty phrases, learn to be comfortable with pauses.

Learn to phrase end user communications positively, rather than negatively. For example, instead of saying "The problem with your file occurred because you didn't follow the procedure described in Chapter 2 of the manual," use a positive statement, such as "I think the procedure on file handling in Chapter 2 describes a way to avoid the problem with the file you experienced. Let me find you the location. . . ."

While technically correct solutions are critical, they will not by themselves create satisfied customers. Successful support specialists use greetings, scripts, and their tone and style to communicate their willingness to help, their regard for the customer's value, and their company's concern for the customer's satisfaction. They also use effective speaking skills as part of a call management strategy, which is described in the next section.

JONATHAN VESTER
COMPUTER SUPPORT TECHNICIAN
WILSON TECHNICAL COMMUNITY COLLEGE

The technical support help desk at Wilson Technical Community College consists of two full-time employees—a network administrator and a computer support technician. I manage the help desk and handle all the technical support functions of the college. My responsibilities change from day to day and no two days are ever the same.

I have found that in order to be successful in my position, I have to be patient and have good communications skills. Listening is by far the most essential skill for this position. My job requires active listening and strong note-taking skills so that I have all the information I need to solve an employee's problem. When a staff or faculty member calls me with a computer problem, I listen closely to the problem description. If possible, I have them walk through a procedure from the beginning, making sure that they are going through every process correctly. I also have them read me every error message they see. If I don't know the solution to a particular problem, I will refer the user to someone that does or explain that I will need to call him back with the solution. I always strive to maintain the customer's confidence that I will solve the problem quickly or have another technician work with him when it is outside my skill area.

There are times when I have had to handle difficult callers. Older employees occasionally have negative attitudes about computer technology but respond eagerly when they understand how easy it is to fix a problem. It is always important to remember that there was a time when you knew less than the people you are trying to help. Remaining calm and logical will help the caller better than matching their frustration with hostility. Let customers know you are there to help them and that you enjoy solving problems. If they feel you don't have time or don't want to bother with them, they will not ask for help again.

DEVELOP A CALL MANAGEMENT STRATEGY

Support specialists who provide telephone support often have many calls waiting. At the same time they supply correct technical answers and excellent customer service, they must also handle calls efficiently. A **call management strategy** is a collection of tools, techniques, and approaches successful support specialists use to move through a call efficiently, from the initial greeting to the end of the call. Call management has four goals: 1) to provide the user with the information he or she needs; 2) to manage stress levels for both the caller and the support specialist; 3) to ensure that the call progresses from start to finish in an effective and efficient way; and 4) to make the user more self-reliant. Each support specialist develops and refines his or her own call management strategy. However, you do not have to invent your own call management strategy from scratch. Some resources you can build on and incorporate in your personal strategy include the following:

- Company policies on call management philosophy and expectations

- Call management strategies covered in support specialist training programs

- Observation and imitation of respected senior support staff members

- Your own communication experience and style

- Feedback from users, peers, and supervisors on call management strengths and areas for improvement

10

The following paragraphs contain some call management suggestions that many support staff find useful.

Ask goal-directed diagnostic questions. Each diagnostic question should be designed to move the call toward a successful resolution. Diagnostic questions can be embedded in a script or they can be based on a support specialist's experience. Chapter 11 suggests several critical questions to ask in a troubleshooting situation.

Be honest. It is generally better to be honest and forthcoming with users about product features, limitations, known bugs, and future product releases than to try to hide or cover up product problems and limitations. However, you must also abide by company policy on what information can be provided to users and what cannot. For example some manufacturers, as a matter of company policy, will not discuss future product features or availability dates. Many companies also have a policy that discourages communicating negative comments about a competitor's products.

Say "I don't know" when you don't. It is usually more productive to admit that you don't know an answer than to waste both your time and the caller's time trying to suggest possibilities you aren't sure of. It is a rare caller who expects a support specialist to know everything. However, never communicate "I don't know" with a tone that tells a user, "I don't know, and therefore your question is stupid," "I don't know, and I don't think anybody else does.," or "I don't know, and I don't care." If you don't know an answer, refer the user to a person or other information source where she or he can get the needed information. You can also promise to research the question and get back to the caller or escalate the question to the next level of help desk expertise.

Apologize. It is never a sign of weakness to apologize to users who feel that they have been done an injustice. One way to defuse a potentially difficult situation is to empathize with a user's situation and apologize for the perceived injustice, whether it is a caller who has spent a long time on hold, or received the run-around, or purchased a product ill-suited for his needs.

Say thanks. Thank the caller for calling. "Thanks for calling the Support Center" is a simple but effective way to communicate that the caller and the call are important. A "thank you" ends the call on a positive note, even if the call has been a difficult one.

Use call management not caller management. Be sure to distinguish between *call* management and *caller* management. Do not attempt to manage callers by issuing judgments about how well they communicate their needs, how they organize their files, or how they use their computers. Although you can suggest that users read a particular chapter in the manual, or reorganize the files on their hard disk, you should not make it a condition for helping them further. Do not communicate that you are upset if the user chooses not to take your advice. Callers who feel that a support specialist is trying to manage their work habits will rightfully feel resentful or manipulated and are more likely to be dissatisfied with the call.

Teach self-reliance. An immediate goal of each support call is to provide information or to solve a user's problem. A secondary, longer-term goal is to make users self-reliant. To create **self-reliance**, support specialists explain solutions so users understand the reasons for the problems and how to fix them. Specialists also help create self-reliance when they refer to relevant documentation where users can locate additional information about problems or questions. There is a built-in contradiction in user support: the support staff would like every user to call back (because their jobs depend on calls), but the staff hopes each user's problem gets solved so that he or she does not have to call back.

In reality, users will never become completely self-reliant. As computer use grows and systems become more complex, an increasing number of both new and experienced end users will continue to need a growing array of services from help desks and support staffs. Even power users and computer gurus occasionally need assistance. However, some users don't want to become self-reliant; they feel that the support staff's reason for existence is to solve user problems. Recognize that you cannot force users to change their behavior. Though absolute user self-reliance may never be completely achievable, it is an important long-term goal.

Successful call management ability is rarely an inborn skill among support specialists. It takes practice to develop your own call management strategy, and even then, some percentage of calls go awry, as you will see in the next section.

STRATEGIES FOR DIFFICULT CALLS

Although the majority of users are rational and polite when they call a support service, there are several kinds of difficult calls that require special handling strategies. You will probably not be able to change a user's behavior or attitude in the course of one call, so changing the user should not be a goal. Instead, focus on the specific problem, on getting the client the needed information, on providing excellent customer service in a respectful manner, and on getting on to the next call. To deal with difficult situations that might interfere with these goals, consider the strategies that experienced specialists use.

Callers who complain. Instead of simply describing their problem, some users complain about company products or services. They want someone to listen to their problems or concerns, and complaint processing is often an important function of help desk staff. Give users ample opportunity to voice their complaints. Don't switch into problem-solving mode too early in a call where a caller complains. Instead, use empathy: "I understand why someone who has experienced your problem would be concerned. . . . " Many support organizations use complaints as a valuable source of feedback and suggestions for future product and service offerings. Try to understand that most complaints are not directed at you personally, and avoid being defensive.

Calls from "power users." In this context, power users are those who are technically very knowledgeable, or think they are, or who believe they have personal connections with significant people in an organization that warrant special treatment. These callers often describe their powerful position early in a call in an attempt to establish how important they are and sometimes to cover their real lack of knowledge about their computer system. They may try to impress a support specialist to direct attention away from what they don't know. One strategy for handling these callers is to use inclusive language that makes them feel like a member of a team. Use pronouns like "we" to refer to the problem-solving process, such as "I think we can solve this problem. . . ." Use a tone or style of speaking that sounds authoritative because important, knowledgeable people like to talk with other important, knowledgeable people. Remember that your role is not to diminish their sense of self-importance but to solve the problem they called about.

10

Calls that get off track. Occasionally in the course of a call it becomes apparent that the call has taken a wrong turn and needs to get back on track. For example, a user might make a statement that contradicts an earlier statement. Or perhaps repeated attempts to isolate a problem have not succeeded. When this happens, try to refocus the call. Apologize to the user for the lack of a prompt resolution, summarize the basic call information, and offer to continue to work toward a solution. It is sometimes helpful to express confidence that, together, you will find a solution to the problem if you continue to work on it and that perhaps a different approach will be more fruitful.

Callers who are upset or angry. Angry callers are the most common kind of difficult call. Angry callers may be upset because of the way they have been treated. They may have been on hold too long, talked to too many support specialists, or explained the problem too many times. Or they may be upset because of real or perceived inadequacies in a product. They may also be angry due to circumstances that have nothing to do with the problem at hand.

The first principle for handling angry users is to let them vent their anger. Don't say anything during this period, and especially don't offer an explanation or go into problem-solving mode too early. Explanations to an angry person sound like an invitation to argue. The second principle is to reassure angry callers that the problem is an important one, and that you are willing to help them resolve it. The third principle to remember is that angry callers may continue to vent several times before they work through the anger. A polite question that refocuses the angry caller may be effective: "What would you like me to do to help at this point?" or "How can I help resolve this situation to your satisfaction?"

Remember to avoid defensiveness and don't sound patronizing. The caller is rarely upset with you personally. As with all calls, it is also important to continue to follow up on promises made to an angry caller to build trust and confidence.

Callers who are abusive. Abusive callers are those who are rude, use foul language, or make personal attacks on a support specialist. The goal is to first transform an abusive call into just an angry one and ultimately into a successful one. This goal is not always achievable. Some support centers have support staff who have training and skills to handle abusive callers; they pride themselves on their ability to defuse difficult situations. In general, handle abusive callers according to the support organization's policies and procedures for this type of call. For example, some support organizations instruct their staffs to terminate a call when abusive language is used. The support staff in other organizations invite the caller to use more appropriate and professional language: "We would like to work with you on this problem, but only when we can communicate about it in an appropriate and professional manner. Is that agreeable with you?"

Callers who won't talk. Usually callers who will not answer questions are confused, lack confidence, or don't understand the questions. They may be beginning computer users. To obtain the information you need from these callers, use very simple language, and avoid technical jargon. Try different kinds of questions. For example, if open-ended questions fail to initiate a conversation, switch to questions that can be answered yes or no, and begin with very simple questions, like "Is there a Start button in the lower-left corner of the screen?" Or, switch to discussing the problem-solving process, such as "I'll ask you some questions about what you see on the screen and you answer them if you can. Any information you can give me will help us solve the problem." Also give positive feedback when a reluctant user does provide useful information, such as "Now I think we are getting somewhere." Finally, if a caller continues to be reluctant to talk, suggest exchanging information via e-mail as a way to facilitate the problem-solving process.

Callers who won't stop talking or won't hang up. Some users have a hard time letting go of a problem. Even after the problem is solved, they may continue to explain how bad it was or continue to talk about related issues. To deal with excessive talkers, use behavior that indicates the call is over. For example, summarize the call and describe the conclusion. Thank the caller for calling. Express your belief that the problem is solved. Use very short answers that don't provide the caller with lead-ins to additional conversation.

 For additional information about difficult calls, including explanations of more types and suggestions for handling them, see an article by Kate Nasser, "How to Handle Difficult Callers," *Support Management* (January 1998): 16-24.

Handling difficult callers is never an easy task, but over time you can improve your skills with practice and patience. Beginning help desk staff can learn a great deal about difficult calls from experienced support specialists. Veteran staff are a good resource for company-approved and time-tested techniques for dealing with difficult call situations. Training sessions for new help desk employees often cover company guidelines for dealing with these situations.

COMPREHENSIVE CUSTOMER SERVICE

This chapter has emphasized that communications skills are essential to excellent customer service. Yet a comprehensive approach to excellent customer service is also based on specific values, attitudes, and actions.

First, customer service starts when each employee, from top executives to the newest help desk employee, recognizes that its customers are the primary reason for the company's existence. Each employee's job depends directly on customer satisfaction. Although help desk staff receive their paychecks from company management, the company is actually a conduit to transfer money from the customer to the service provider. Most support organizations' mission statements include the concept that each customer or client's productivity is the primary concern of the support staff. In a help desk environment, customer satisfaction is directly related to the extent to which each caller is treated as a valued customer.

Second, customer service excellence is based on whether support staff are willing to take extra steps to make sure customers are satisfied. For example, an excellent support organization keeps its customers apprised of the progress or lack of progress toward a problem solution. It actively seeks win–win outcomes for each call. It seeks agreement that problems have been adequately addressed and then conducts follow-up customer surveys to measure the extent of customer satisfaction.

Third, excellent customer service depends on adequate support resources. Customer service excellence rarely happens by accident but is based on advanced planning, adequate staffing, and a sufficient budget for help desk tools and information resources that encourage excellence.

 Excellent customer service does not necessarily mean that the customer is always right. Sometimes requests by even the most valued customers cannot be met for a variety of sound business reasons.

Although most of this book covers technical, problem-solving, and operational details associated with the operation of a help desk or support center, this chapter on communications and customer service is the most important one in the book. Why? Because you can perform all of the technical and operational duties of the support job adequately and still fail if you don't provide excellent service to your customers.

CHAPTER SUMMARY

- Communication is a foundation of excellent customer service, which is a goal in many company and support organization mission statements. Communication is a two-way process that involves listening, understanding, and speaking skills. Listening must be accompanied by a thorough understanding of customers and their problems.

- The most important communications skill for help desk staff is the ability to listen carefully to customers. In addition to a description of the caller's problem, help desk staff need to listen to the language level a caller uses so staff can gauge their responses to a similar level. Help desk staff need to listen for cues that indicate whether the user is frustrated, confused, or angry.

- Understanding a customer involves being able to restate her problem, but it also means an ability to empathize with the caller's situation and feelings and to understand why the problem is an important one for the customer.

- The ability to speak effectively includes skills with call greetings, the use of call scripts as aids, and the ability to use a tone and style that helps, rather than hinders, the progress of the call from start to finish. The appropriate tone is often more important than the content of a communication with users.

- Support specialists should develop a personal call management strategy. Goal-directed diagnostic questions, honesty, the ability to say "I don't know" and to apologize, to create user self-reliance, and to thank users for calling are components of a call management strategy.

- Difficult support calls include user complaints, calls from power users, calls that get off track, calls from angry or abusive users, and calls from users who either are reluctant to talk or who won't stop talking.

- Finally, a comprehensive approach to customer service includes not only communications skills but also company-wide recognition of the importance of each customer, a willingness to take extra measures to satisfy users, and adequate support resources to provide customer satisfaction.

KEY TERMS

- **call management strategy** — Techniques support specialists use during a call to move effectively and efficiently from the initial greeting to the end of the call.

- **empathy** — An understanding of and identification with a caller's situation, thoughts, and feelings; a support specialist who can empathize with a caller understands the problem or question from the caller's perspective and why the caller feels it is important.

- **script** — A prepared sequence of questions and statements that support specialists can use to handle parts of a call; may include decision points and branches to handle different situations.

- **self-reliance** — A goal of support service providers that seeks to increase user self-sufficiency and reduce a user's dependence on support services.

REVIEW QUESTIONS

1. Explain why communications skills are often more challenging to inexperienced support staff than technical or business skills.

2. What is the relationship between communications with end users and customer service excellence?

3. Explain the consequences of poor user support services to a company.

4. Why are listening skills important?

5. In addition to a description of a user's problem, what should a support staff member listen for in a call?

6. What is empathy? Explain why empathy is an important aid in understanding a user's problem.

7. Give three examples of speaking skills that affect the outcome of a support call.

8. How are scripts useful to inexperienced support specialists?

9. Explain the importance of tone and style in user communications.

10. Describe some components of a call management strategy. How can a new help desk staff member develop a call management strategy?

11. List the four goals a call management strategy is intended to facilitate.

12. What should a support specialist who doesn't know the answer to a question do?

13. Explain the difference between call management and caller management. Which one should a support specialist be concerned with and why?

14. What are some ways to make users more self-reliant?

15. Explain the role of a support specialist in handling customer complaints.

16. Give some strategies for handling angry or abusive callers.

17. Describe three ways support organizations can increase customer satisfaction.

HANDS-ON PROJECTS

 PROJECT 10-1

Chapter 9 provides a sample help desk mission statement. Review the mission statement and modify it to include a greater emphasis on excellent communication and customer services.

 PROJECT 10-2

This chapter describes several kinds of difficult callers, including two that are not always easy to tell apart: callers who complain and those who are angry. Sometimes there are few differences between the two. Work with others in your project group to compare your personal experiences with people who want to complain and those who are angry. Define some characteristics of complainers and angry callers that would help a support staff member distinguish between the two. Write a brief list of defining characteristics for each caller type.

PROJECT 10-3

Suppose that you work for a software company whose most recent product release has generated a number of calls complaining about numerous bugs. Write a sample script to diplomatically handle calls from users who call to complain about the product. Your company's policy is to record the complaint and pass it along to the software development group for consideration in their next release. Your script should communicate that the feedback is useful, and it should reflect an excellent customer service orientation.

PROJECT 10-4

Based on the discussion in this chapter and on your personal experience (or the experiences of your project group members), write a list of call management do's and don'ts that could be covered in a training session for inexperienced help desk staff members.

PROJECT 10-5

If you work for a company or organization that operates a help desk, invite one of the help desk staff members to talk with you or your project group. Ask the staff member to describe her experiences with difficult callers and the techniques she uses to handle them. In addition to those described in this chapter, what other kinds of calls does she find difficult to handle? What is the most common kind of difficult call in her experience? Write a report that summarizes the main points in the interview.

CASE PROJECTS

1. WRITEIT SOFTWARE COMPANY

You are a support representative for WriteIt Software Company, which develops customized software for businesses on a contract basis. You receive the following e-mail message from a large customer:

> We received the custom Visual Basic programs from your new programmer and installed them on our system last week. It was obvious from the first time we ran the programs that the programmer was new to your company. It was not clear the programmer had

> much prior experience with programming or with Visual Basic. The programs converted the information from our COBOL programs to our report formatter fairly well according to the specifications we provided her. But we discovered that all of the data conversion instructions were built into the Visual Basic programs. The programs lack the flexibility we need to handle all of the various data formats we have to convert. The programs should have been written with the conversion information in tables that are easily modified. The way they were written means we have to modify the programs every time we run them.

Write some examples of sentences that could be included in a reply to this e-mail that show empathy for the problem and a good customer service attitude, and incorporate some ideas about call management.

2. SCOTT SHIPPING CORPORATION

You have been working as an internal user support representative at Scott Shipping for six months and have been chosen by your manager to help coach a new employee, Gene Rosso. Like many companies, Scott Shipping records selected support conversations for training purposes. To give you some training and mentoring experience, your manager has asked you to examine this transcript of one of Gene's support call interactions and write Gene a memo with suggestions about how he can improve his communications skills with a stronger customer service orientation. Suggest alternative responses for Gene that improve the quality of the customer service interaction.

10

> **Gene:** This is the problem hot-line. Your problem please?
>
> **Caller:** This is Wes in Accounting.
>
> **Gene:** Oh, yes, I remember you. I've talked with you several times before. What's your problem?
>
> **Caller:** I'm having a problem printing a report this morning.
>
> **Gene:** What kind of problem?
>
> **Caller:** I've clicked on Print three times and gone down the hall to get the printout, but each time there is just a stack of about 50 sheets in the printer with a line or two on each one. But my report is not there.
>
> **Gene:** Oh, we've been hoping whoever was printing those reams of paper would call.
>
> **Caller:** I'm sorry, but I've never had this problem before. What am I doing wrong?
>
> **Gene:** What are you trying to print?
>
> **Caller:** The report is in a file named REPORT98.EXE.

> **Gene:** Didn't the training course you took cover printing .EXE files? .EXE files are programs, not reports. You can't print an .EXE file, you can only run them.
>
> **Caller:** Oh, I see. I forgot about that. I feel like an idiot.
>
> **Gene:** Yes, well, see if you can find a file on your hard drive named REPORT98 with a different extension and call me back.

3. CUSTOMER SERVICE AND PERSONALITY TYPES

A common personality test used in business and industry is the Myers–Briggs Type Indicator (MBTI). The test results determine where the test taker falls on four basic personality dimensions. The four dimensions of personality measured by the MBTI are Introvert (I)- Extrovert (E), Sensing (S)- Intuition (N), Thinking (T)- Feeling (F), and Judging (J)- Perceiving (P). Each person can be any of 16 combinations of these types.

Learn more about the MBTI personality test and the 16 personality types it measures. Learning resources include:

- Jean Kummerow et al., *Worktypes.* New York: Warner Books, 1997.

- Otto Kroeger & Janet Thuesen, *Type Talk at Work.* New York: Delacourt Press, 1993.

- The Team Technology Web site at
  www.teamtechnology.co.uk/tt/t-articl/mb-simpl.htm

- The American Education Network Corporation Web site at
  www.aenc.org/Temperament/personality/faq-mbti.html

Based on your understanding of the 16 personality types and your knowledge of help desk communications and customer service skills described in this chapter, work with your project group to identify which of the 16 MBTI types you think would be well suited to provide a strong customer service orientation.

If you have never taken the Myers–Briggs test or have not taken it recently, you may be able to take the test at your school's counseling department or at your company's human resources office. If you would like to take a shorter, online version, go to The Keirsey Temperament Sorter Web site at **www.keirsey.com/cgi-bin/keirsey/newkts.cgi.**

If the results indicate that you are a personality type not as well suited for help desk work as some other personality types, understand that the 16 MBTI personality types are not absolutes. Each person is actually a mixture of the eight types in the test. The MBTI test simply measures tendencies. Most people are more adaptive than the test often indicates.

Write a summary of your research into personality types and customer service orientation among help desk staff.

TROUBLESHOOTING COMPUTER PROBLEMS

As you learned in Chapter 2, one of the most critical and frequent tasks a user support specialist must perform is solving computer problems. "Computer problems" can cover a wide range; they can include requests for information, questions about how to perform a task, complaints about a product or feature, or a problem that prevents an end user from operating hardware or software. Some problems are relatively easy for support specialists to solve. For example, support specialists may recognize the problem as one they've seen before and already know the solution to, or perhaps they can locate the solution quickly in a database of problem solutions. It is probably fortunate for support providers that most support calls fall into one of these categories.

Some problems are more difficult to solve. A difficult problem may be one the support specialist has never encountered or one where the solution is not obvious. Despite attempts to find a quick solution, the problem-solving effort may fail. On occasion, a problem request may actually be the first in what will become a long series of reports about a problem with a new or recently modified product.

The purpose of this chapter is to describe methods and strategies that support specialists use to work on all problems, especially difficult ones. After examining these strategies, you will be encouraged to use these tools to develop a personal problem-solving strategy.

AFTER READING THIS CHAPTER AND COMPLETING THE EXERCISES YOU WILL BE ABLE TO:

- Define the troubleshooting process and the thinking skills required for successful troubleshooting
- Describe the tools used to troubleshoot computer problems
- Develop a personal problem-solving strategy

WHAT IS TROUBLESHOOTING?

Troubleshooting is the process of solving computer problems. Some people think of computer problem solving as a series of steps to follow to diagnose and repair a malfunction with computer hardware, software, and networks. However, it is unlikely that any one fixed sequence of steps will work to diagnose every computer problem; computer troubleshooting is often more complicated than that.

Troubleshooting is often not a sequential series of steps, but an **iterative process**, which means that troubleshooters follow a sequence of steps for a while, then loop back and perform similar steps, but down a different path. The process can include many starts and stops, as they pursue an approach, hit a dead end, switch to an alternative approach, make some progress, only to hit a snag, and start down another path. Figure 11-1 graphically compares a sequential process with an iterative process.

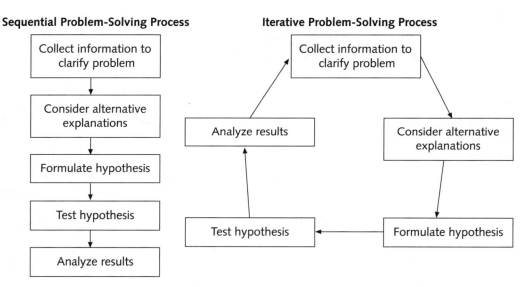

Figure 11-1   A sequential process versus an iterative process

An iterative process may seem repetitious, and in a way it is. Troubleshooting is not always a neat and orderly process. It is a creative process that requires flexibility and thought that will, more often than not, lead to a satisfactory solution.

Like woodworkers, troubleshooters use a variety of skills and tools in their work as they try to solve a difficult problem. They pick up one tool, work on one aspect of a problem with it, set that tool aside for a while, and pick up another tool, only to turn back to a tool or skill used previously. The tools a user support specialist uses in troubleshooting can be physical tools, like a diagnostic program or a database of information, or they can be thinking skills, like problem solving, critical thinking, and decision making. What are the similarities and differences among these skills?

Problem solving is often used in business and mathematics to describe a situation where there is a current state of events X and a future desired state of events Y, sometimes called the **goal state**. To solve a problem is to move from the problem state X to goal state Y. Figure 11-2 illustrates this problem-solving model as applied to a malfunctioning printer.

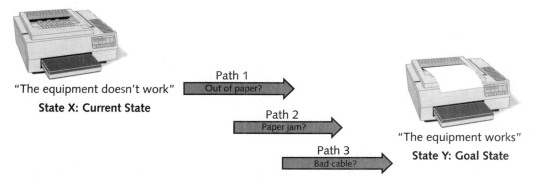

"The equipment doesn't work"
State X: Current State

Path 1
Out of paper?

Path 2
Paper jam?

Path 3
Bad cable?

"The equipment works"
State Y: Goal State

Figure 11-2   A problem-solving model

In computer problem solving, the troubleshooter wants to move from the problem state X (the equipment doesn't work), to the goal state Y (the equipment works again). The problem solver is looking for a path from X to Y that gets the correct answer efficiently. A person is a good problem solver if he or she is skilled in getting from X to Y quickly, accurately, effectively, or efficiently.

Problem solvers use a variety of thinking skills. For example, a problem solver may look for **analogies**, or ways in which the current problem is similar to other problems. Success in other problem-solving situations may involve an ability to recognize contradictions: if a network card doesn't operate in one computer, but works in another one, the problem is unlikely a defective network card. Several of the problem-solving situations in this chapter illustrate problem-solving methods and skills like these.

Critical thinking describes the cognitive skills a problem solver uses to analyze a situation, search for the underlying logic or rationale, and strive for alternative explanations of how the situation occurred or can be explained. To think critically is to use your experience, the power of logical thinking, the "mental models" of how things work, and various analytic tools to understand and explain a situation. Computer problem solvers rely on critical thinking skills in many situations to try to understand the possible causes for the observed behavior (or misbehavior) of a computer system.

Critical thinking skills include **creativity**, which is the ability to find a novel or innovative solution to a problem. A creative troubleshooter has the ability to see a problem from new and different perspectives. For example, a computer problem solver may discover a unique way to work around a difficult problem by thinking about how a similar piece of hardware or software operates.

11

Critical thinking skills also include the ability to design and test hypotheses. Troubleshooters sometimes formulate a hypothesis based on prior experience. For example, they may feel that a particular computer problem is due to a faulty power cable. They use their critical thinking skills to devise a hypothesis that allows them to test whether the power cable is indeed the cause of the problem. Critical thinking also involves metacognition. **Metacognition** is the ability to think about thinking. A good troubleshooter has the ability to step back from a problem-solving situation and study her or his own thought process. Metacognition is a critical thinking skill that can help a good troubleshooter become a better one.

Decision making involves selecting one alternative from among a number of alternatives based on some evaluation criteria. For example, business decisions can be based on criteria such as cost, output volume, quality, or employee morale. A good decision-maker is one who can define effective alternatives, weigh the pros and cons of each alternative against some pre-defined criteria, and reach a decision.

Decision making in computer problem solving is important when a support specialist is confronted with a number of alternative explanations for a problem. For example, when there are a number of diagnostic tests that can be run to gather information, the problem solver must decide which test is most likely to produce informative results. To select the wrong alternative could delay progress toward the correct solution and would reduce efficiency of the problem-solving process.

Troubleshooters routinely use skills such as problem solving, critical thinking, and decision making in their work. Computer support specialists share these skills and strategies with others who troubleshoot problems, such as auto mechanics, clock repairers, or engineers.

TOOLS TROUBLESHOOTERS USE

The tools successful troubleshooters use can be grouped into four broad categories. Think about the tools you have used to work on computer problems in your own experience to see how the tools fit into one of these categories, summarized in Figure 11-3

- Communication skills
- Information resources
- Problem-solving strategies
- Personal characteristics

Figure 11-3   Categories of problem-solving tools

These four kinds of tools are described in detail in the sections that follow.

COMMUNICATION SKILLS

Communication skills are an important tool category because most troubleshooting situations require at least some communication with an end user about a problem. A troubleshooter uses communication skills to get a basic description of a problem, to learn the user's perspectives on the problem, and to probe for additional information. When a problem has been solved, the troubleshooter needs to effectively communicate the solution back to the user. There are five principal types of communication skills used to troubleshoot computer problems; they are listed in Figure 11-4.

- Listening skills

- Paraphrasing

- Critical questions

- Probes

- Explanation

Figure 11-4   Communication skills for troubleshooters

Successful support specialists are adept at using these skills in almost every user support situation.

Listening skills. It is important to get a troubleshooting opportunity started on the right foot—to get as accurate a description of the problem as possible from the user's perspective. Therefore, the foremost communication skills every troubleshooter needs are listening skills.

Listen to the words the end user chooses to describe a problem. The danger of not listening, or of not giving the user enough time to explain the problem, is that a support specialist may jump ahead of the user and begin to work on the solution to a problem before he or she really understands the problem. When troubleshooters turn their attention away from what a user is saying to focus on the solution to a problem, they can miss important pieces of information, making the troubleshooting process less efficient and possibly causing frustration for the end user.

Listen to the user describe the problem symptoms. It may be useful for a support specialist to take notes about the symptoms. Listen for causal, If-Then statements of the form, "If I do X, the result is Y." For example, "If I try to adjust the monitor, the screen goes blank," or "When I click on Run, my system freezes up."

Paraphrasing. If basic listening skills are most important, active listening skills are in second place. In **active listening**, a listener is a participant in the communication process, not a passive receiver of information. The listener is as engaged in the communication process as the speaker. One active listening skill that is often extremely helpful is paraphrasing. When you **paraphrase**, you restate in your own words what you heard the user say about the problem. In describing a problem, a user might include unclear, unnecessary, or even contradictory information. Paraphrasing is especially helpful to resolve misunderstandings and get a clear problem description. As you paraphrase a problem statement, the user may correct the words you use. Table 11-1 shows some examples of how paraphrasing can help clarify the problem definition.

Table 11-1   Paraphrasing Examples

End User Description	Support Specialist Paraphrase
"I don't know what happened, but the program doesn't work."	"Let me make sure I understand. The program used to work, but now it doesn't?"
"No, I just got the program installed and it doesn't start up right."	"So you installed the program using the instructions in the manual, and when you double-click the program icon, the program doesn't start up?"
"The box on the screen asks for a file to open, but there are no files listed."	"The program starts to run and the Open Files dialog box appears, but there aren't any files listed in it?"

Critical questions. Another helpful troubleshooting tool is a list of critical questions designed to elicit important information from the user. These questions also challenge some assumptions a support specialist may make (sometimes incorrectly) about a problem situation. Five examples of critical questions are

1. What were you doing just before you first noticed the problem?

2. Have you ever had this problem before?

3. Has the system or component or feature you're talking about *ever* worked?

4. Is the problem repeatable?

5. Have you made any recent hardware or software changes to your system?

In their responses to critical questions, users often reveal information they wouldn't have thought to tell the support specialist. For example, a user may forget to say that a power outage occurred immediately before she noticed a problem with her color monitor. Another user may neglect to say that he had the same problem formatting floppy disks the last time he bought this particular budget brand of disks. Or, does it make a difference to you, as a support specialist, whether the failure to print from WordPerfect a user describes might be because she has *never* been able to print from WordPerfect? Is it useful information that the network access problem for a user only occurs from one computer lab on campus, and isn't a problem in any other lab? Or, would a support specialist find it useful to know that the sluggish speed of a system corresponded with the installation of Office 97?

In each of these example situations, responses to one of the five critical questions could provide important additional information a support specialist did not have, or force the support specialist to challenge some assumptions she or he may have made intentionally or unintentionally about a problem situation.

Every successful support specialist has a list of favorite critical questions. They are especially useful to break new ground if you've asked every other question you can think of and haven't arrived at a solution.

Probes. Follow-up questions intended to elicit more information on a problem are called **probes**. A good troubleshooter learns to ask effective follow-up questions. Consider the following situation; probes are shown in italics.

> **User:** I can't get the disk out of my disk drive. I can see it in there, but it won't come out. It feels like it's stuck.
>
> **Troubleshooter:** What size is the disk?
>
> **User:** Three-and-a-half inch.
>
> **Troubleshooter:** Did you push the Eject button?
>
> **User:** Yes. When I do, it sounds like the drive is trying to eject the disk, but it doesn't come out of the drive.
>
> **Troubleshooter:** You say it sounds like the drive is trying to eject the disk. *Do you mean the drive makes a noise?*
>
> **User:** Yes. A whirring noise.
>
> **Troubleshooter:** *Do you have a Macintosh computer?*
>
> **User:** Yes.
>
> **Troubleshooter:** There is a tiny hole next to the drive. If you unbend a paper clip, you can insert it into the hole, which should manually eject the disk.

11

Notice the importance of probes in this case. There was an initial misunderstanding about whether the Eject button was physical (on a PC), or a command on the screen (Macintosh). Through a series of probing questions and careful listening, the troubleshooter was able to determine a course of action to try to solve the problem. The user's use of the words "it *sounds* like . . ." describes the sound a Macintosh plays when it tries to eject a disk. A PC does not normally make a sound in this situation.

Explanation. Communication skills are also important at the termination of a troubleshooting session. An effective support staff member explains the problem's solution to the end user. If the solution is one the user can implement immediately, the troubleshooter can confirm that the solution did solve the problem.

For many users, a word of explanation is helpful and is more satisfying than a suggestion like "Click the Cancel button to fix the problem." One of the ways help desks can reduce repeated callbacks from users is to explain the problem at a level the user can understand. The user will then have some insight into the cause of the problem and into how the given solution fits the particular problem. Otherwise, a user may incorrectly assume that the solution to another problem is to press the Cancel button. Communication at the end of a troubleshooting process also provides important closure to the process. It permits the troubleshooter to check his or her perception with the user's perception that the problem is indeed fixed. Sometimes the two perspectives are different and communication can resolve the differences.

INFORMATION RESOURCES

It is unlikely support specialists have had prior experience with every troubleshooting situation they will ever encounter, so they must have access to information resources to consult when they need to research new solutions. Because new products come to market every day, support specialists' prior experience and the information they can recall instantly are less important than the ability to use information resources effectively to locate what they need to know.

Technical information about how computer systems work—and an understanding of some reasons they don't—are invaluable for a support specialist to bring to a troubleshooting situation. The more information support specialists know from experience, the more likely they will be able to find a quick solution to a problem. However, all troubleshooters encounter problems they have never seen before, or problems with hardware or software they have never worked with before. In this part of the chapter, you'll learn about some common information resources for computer troubleshooters.

Personal experience. All support people have a personal store of information they bring to each problem-solving event. This personal information is based largely on their background and previous experiences. One of the first steps in any troubleshooting situation is to search your personal knowledge for information about the problem or related problems. "Have I seen this problem before?" "How is this problem similar to the problem I worked on last week?" "How is it different?" "Now, what did I do last time the printer beeped three times and quit printing?" This type of personal knowledge search happens almost automatically.

One strategy successful troubleshooters use is to make notes after they have solved a problem. Notes can be informally organized in a loose-leaf notebook or recorded as formal entries in a problem solution database. Written troubleshooting notes can help avoid a situation in which troubleshooters too often find themselves: "I know I've seen this problem before, but I don't remember what we did to fix it." Notebooks with reminders of past problems solved become an important personal resource for troubleshooters and can be used even if a support center doesn't have a formal problem record keeping procedure. A notebook could be organized by symptoms, or equipment type, or in any other logical way that makes the information easy to find.

Scripts. Companies that sell computer support on a contract basis or that provide telephone help desk support often develop scripts or flowcharts to aid in the troubleshooting process. A **script** is a document that lists questions to ask and, depending on the user's response to each question, follow-up probes to ask. Often organized in the form of a flowchart, scripts are arranged in a logical sequence and cover all the possible (known) paths to solve a problem. Although scripts tend to be oriented toward common problems, they can contain valuable pointers to unusual problems.

Knowledgebases. Good troubleshooters have at their fingertips a variety of information resources to augment their personal experience. A **knowledgebase** is an organized collection of information, articles, procedures, tips, and previous problems with known solutions that can serve as a resource in a problem-solving situation. Knowledgebases come in a variety of forms from several sources.

1. **Vendor manuals**. Most hardware and software products come with tutorial or reference manuals. Support staff who provide technical support for specific products need to have easy access to vendor manuals for the products for which they are responsible. Vendor manuals often contain chapters on troubleshooting and frequently asked questions.

2. **Trade books**. Some vendor manuals are poorly written. As a result, a thriving trade book industry has grown up to fill the vacuum for well-written information about popular hardware and software products. Internet booksellers such as **www.Amazon.com** and **www.BarnesandNoble.com** have search capabilities to help users locate trade books for a specific hardware or software product. Most large computer stores have a large stock of trade books on computers, where you can browse the books themselves until you find one that is suitable. A troubleshooter's personal or professional library is a sometimes overlooked source of information about problems with products.

3. **Online help**. Most software products today, and some hardware products, come with online help. Sometimes the online help is no more than a convenient way to access the same information covered in product manuals. However, some online help systems include interactive troubleshooting wizards that provide useful insights into problem situations. Wizards are like online scripts or flowcharts to guide a user or support specialist through a series of steps to diagnose a problem.

4. **CD-ROM databases**. Some hardware and software manufacturers offer free or low-cost CD-ROM databases that you can search for information about a specific product or problem. For example, Hewlett-Packard sells a CD-ROM database called the HP Assistant. It contains technical specifications about HP products, user guides, and troubleshooting tools for HP personal computers, printers, scanners, and other peripherals. Microsoft provides a subscription CD-ROM database service with quarterly updates on its software products called TechNet. Other vendors provide comparable databases. Several trade book publishers now bundle a CD-ROM version of popular books shrink-wrapped with the book itself. These CD-ROM versions are especially useful because support specialists can search the book text for any keyword, such as a model number or a phrase that describes a problem.

5. **Faxback services**. Many hardware and software vendors operate fax services to provide users with low-cost technical information. Users of the service dial a toll-free number, respond to a series of questions asked by an automated call distribution system, and then key in their fax phone number. Technical product specifications, frequently asked questions (FAQs), and troubleshooting tips are then faxed to the caller.

11

6. **Internet Web sites**. Web sites maintained by product and service vendors are an increasingly popular information resource. Most sites provide product information and problem–solving suggestions; some include interactive troubleshooting assistance. One of the largest Web sites is **www.microsoft.com**, which offers troubleshooting information for Microsoft products. Figure 11-5 shows part of the Microsoft knowledgebase that many use for troubleshooting.

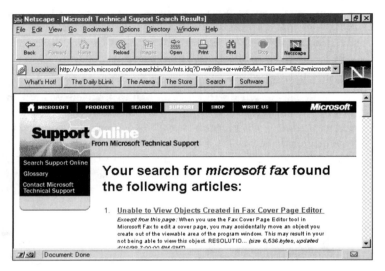

Figure 11-5   Microsoft knowledgebase

7. **ListServs and Newsgroups**. Another Internet-based information resource for support specialists is ListServs and Newsgroups. A **ListServ** is an automated e-mail service that distributes all (or selected) e-mail messages posted to the ListServ to every member who has subscribed to the ListServ. Some product manufacturers operate ListServs to provide their distributors with product information and a communications channel for technical problems. An active ListServ can be an excellent information resource but can also result in a high volume of mail in your inbox.

A list of ListServs can be found on the Internet at **www.lsoft.com/list_Q.html**. For example, Macintosh support specialists might be interested in a ListServ at **MacHrdwr@listserv.Dartmouth.edu**. Or, support specialists interested in adaptive technology for blind users could join the ListServ at **Blind-Dev@maelstrom. StJohns.edu**.

Newsgroups are Internet discussion groups where participants with common interests in a topic post messages in a bulletin board atmosphere. Participation is open to anyone who has an interest in the topic, and access is through a reader built into most browsers. Many support specialists find newsgroups an effective way to ask questions and to obtain and provide information. Most newsgroups provide new participants with a FAQ archive that can be a valuable resource for troubleshooters. Chapter 13 contains more details about information resources.

Most Web browsers maintain lists of current newsgroups. There are more than 30,000 newsgroups in operation today. Some are very general; others are highly specialized. For example, support specialists who work with spreadsheet users may be interested in the newsgroup **comp.apps.spreadsheet**. Support specialists interested in network firewall technology can find others with similar interests in **comp.security.firewalls**.

Colleagues. Coworkers are an important resource for many troubleshooters. When troubleshooters experience a "block" trying to solve a problem and they are not making any progress, a different perspective or "another set of eyes" on an intractable problem is sometimes necessary to break through the block. Many times, just describing a problem to a colleague results in new insights into the problem. When a problem is especially complex or of high priority, a meeting of the support work group may be called to address the problem.

When all else fails, a problem referral to a higher support level, called **escalation**, is a problem-solving option. Some companies deemphasize support levels and organize their support representatives into teams where mutual assistance and problem solving is encouraged; in these organizations, the whole team is responsible for solving problems, not just individual staff members.

Vendors and contractors. When you search for information and problem-solving resources, don't forget that product vendors are often an extremely useful information resource. A vendor may have seen a baffling problem before and be able to offer suggestions to resolve it. Some vendors provide e-mail access to their technical support staff.

There is a growing industry in the support field called **outsourcing**, in which companies provide problem-solving assistance for a fee. These companies sell their services on either a contract or a per-call basis. They can provide an important resource to augment the internal support services in a company. For example, a company could establish an internal help desk to handle most questions from its employees. It could also contract with a support service provider to handle calls on products that are beyond the expertise of the help desk staff, or to backup the internal help desk when the volume is greater than the support staff can handle.

 Stream International is an example of an external technical support provider. You can learn more about them at their Web site, **www.stream.com**.

PROBLEM-SOLVING STRATEGIES

Troubleshooters often apply one or more common problem-solving strategies. Figure 11-6 summarizes seven logical approaches to problem solving that are often effective in a variety of troubleshooting situations, even difficult ones.

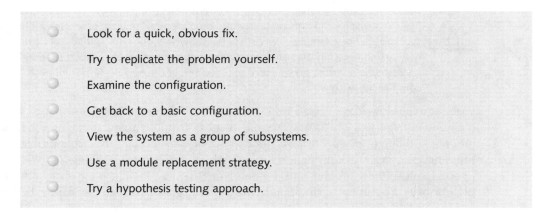

Figure 11-6   Seven problem-solving strategies

Each of these strategies is described in the following sections.

Look for a quick, obvious fix. Because most computer problems are not difficult to solve, probably the first problem-solving strategy in any situation should be to look for a quick, obvious fix. For example, if a monitor does not work, and you've tried to adjust it without success, consider the possibility that it may have become unplugged. Remember there are four possible ways for a monitor to become unplugged, shown in Table 11-2.

Table 11-2   Different Ways for a Monitor to Become Unplugged

	At the Monitor	At the Other End
Power Cord	Is the power cord plugged into the back of the monitor?	Is the power cord plugged into the wall outlet? Is the wall outlet working?
Signal Cable	Is the signal cable plugged into the back of the monitor?	Is the signal cable plugged into the video card on the back of the system unit?

Experienced troubleshooters sometimes find it amazing how often a nonoperational system is due to a custodian who accidentally unplugged equipment while moving furniture to clean the floor. The table illustrates another useful problem-solving tool: a diagram or checklist of possible alternatives reduces the chance that a source of the problem will be overlooked.

Another "old standard" in every support person's tool kit is, "If everything else fails, try rebooting the system." This advice falls into the category of looking for a quick, obvious fix, because rebooting the system can eliminate a number of stubborn problems (memory conflicts or hung peripheral devices, for example).

Try to replicate the problem yourself. A user may report that a problem occurs every time she performs a specific activity or series of steps. Although most users do not intentionally try to mislead a support person, their description may have omitted an important piece of information that you can only ascertain by trying to **replicate**, or repeat, the problem yourself.

Try to replicate the problem either on the user's system, if possible, or on your own support system. If you can't get the problem to reoccur on the user's system, it may be traceable to a mistake the user is making. If you can't get the problem to reoccur on a support system, a difference in the configuration of the two systems may account for the problem. Then you can begin to look at differences between the two systems (configuration differences, different software versions, and so on) to get to the root of the problem.

Examine the configuration. Some problems with computer systems occur because a particular combination of hardware, operating system, and applications software don't work well together. In technical jargon, they don't interoperate well. Examining the ways hardware and software are configured may lead to an understanding of the problem, or a solution.

For example, failure of an applications software package to work with a particular modem may be traceable to one of the following:

    a. At the time it was installed, the applications software package may not have been configured to work with that particular brand of modem.

    b. The operating system may not have been configured to work with the modem.

    c. The modem may be a different one than was originally installed, or the settings in the modem may have been changed.

    d. The configuration of the modem, operating system, and applications software may have changed since the last time the modem operated correctly.

Most hardware and software packages include a description of the configuration requirements (amount of memory, type of processor, disk space, video card requirements) needed to operate correctly. Comparing the configuration requirements with the actual installation configuration can often lead to solutions.

11

Get back to a basic configuration. Some problems occur when hardware or software interacts with other parts of a system. If a problem cannot be traced to a configuration problem, another problem-solving strategy is to remove components (hardware or software) to "pare a system back" to a basic configuration.

This strategy eliminates **variables**, or factors that can change, that can make a problem too complex to solve easily. For example, if a piece of hardware will not operate correctly when added to a system, a support technician may try removing one or more other components to see if the hardware component will operate correctly in a stripped down system.

In another possible scenario, a software package may fail to run when installed on a computer system connected to a network. One approach is to disconnect the system from the network and observe whether the program runs on a standalone system. In this situation, you are removing a variable (the network connection) to see whether that factor makes a difference. If the software runs on a standalone PC but not on a networked system, then examine the network configuration requirements for the software.

View the system as a group of subsystems. Computer systems are, first and foremost, systems. They are actually a group of subsystems linked together to form a complete system that is designed to perform a function. One problem-solving strategy is to consider the subsystems as a sequence of linked components, some hardware and some software.

For example, consider the problem of a user who wants to print a memo in the Courier font. But the memo prints in a different font. Where is the problem? Several subsystems are involved in the process of printing the correct font. These include:

- The applications software module that prepares output
- The operating system that adds control codes to the output
- The BIOS operating system component that sends data to the printer
- The parallel port where the printer is connected
- The cable from the port to the printer
- The software in the printer that translates data received from the computer into formatted characters

Some subsystems, such as the printer cable, may be less likely than others to be the culprit in this situation. However, a short in one of the signal lines in the cable may turn out to be at fault. There is not enough evidence yet to eliminate this possibility.

One strategy in this situation is to interrupt the sequence of events at some point (the midpoint is often a good place to start), and see on which side of the midpoint the problem occurs. In this example, you might select the point at which the printer cable connects to the parallel port as the midpoint. You could observe, perhaps with a different printer, whether the font problem is on the printer side or the system unit side. Another strategy is to start at one end of the sequence of subsystems and trace the problem either forward or backward. Used with the module replacement strategy described next, treating a system as a group of subsystems can help locate a problem.

Use a module replacement strategy. Hardware technicians frequently use **module replacement** as a tool to diagnose computer hardware problems. For example, if a CD-ROM drive fails to work correctly, the problem may be the CD-ROM drive itself, or a piece of hardware or software related to its operation. One way to determine if the problem is the CD-ROM drive is to disconnect it from the system where it malfunctions and connect it to a second system. If the CD-ROM drive works correctly in the second system, then the problem is not with the drive, and you can consider other options, such as the CD-ROM driver software, or signal cables that connect to the drive.

The module replacement strategy also works for software. In the case of malfunctioning software that used to work, the equivalent to rebooting a system is to reinstall the software package. Why reinstall a software package? Occasionally, the image of a software package stored on a hard disk becomes corrupted when some of the bits in the instructions are accidentally overwritten. The faulty software image loads into memory when the program runs, and the software fails to perform as it did previously. Reinstalling the software package is a way to replace the image (module) on the disk with a fresh image.

Try a hypothesis testing approach. In the hypothesis testing strategy, the troubleshooter formulates a **hypothesis**, which is a guess or a prediction, based on prior experience, about the cause of the problem. Then the troubleshooter carries out an experiment to determine whether the hypothesis is true or false.

For example, a user may report that she is unable to log on to a network server:

> **User:** I type my username and password, just as I usually do. The system gives me an error message that the username and password are invalid.

You may listen to the problem description and formulate some hypotheses that would explain the problem:

> **Troubleshooter** (to himself): This problem may be a hardware, software, or network problem. Where should I start? It is unlikely that it is a hardware problem, so I'll assume (hypothesis) that it is a network problem. If it is, then the user should not be able to log on from any other workstation. So I'll try an experiment to see if the problem is specific to a particular workstation.

In this case, suppose the user can, in fact, log on from another workstation.

> **Troubleshooter:** Ah, ha! If it is a network problem, it must not be on the server side. So I'll look at (hypothesis) the client side. If there is a problem with the client software, then no one else should be able to logon from the user's workstation. Let me try (experiment) to log on to my own account from the user's workstation.

In this scenario, suppose the troubleshooter was indeed able to log on to the server from the user's workstation using his own username and password.

> **Troubleshooter:** Interesting! We've apparently eliminated the network as a culprit. Maybe (hypothesis) the user is the culprit. Maybe she's forgotten her password (not likely). Let me try (experiment) to log on to the user's account from her workstation.

In this case, the troubleshooter's attempted logon was unsuccessful, too.

> **Troubleshooter:** OK! What now? Perhaps (hypothesis) the username and password are not in the user access database of valid usernames and passwords.

A call to the network administrator determines that the user access database does include the correct entries for this user.

> **Troubleshooter:** Hmmm! I assumed (hypothesis) that the problem was unlikely to be hardware. Maybe I should reconsider that assumption. Suppose I plug a different keyboard (experiment) into the user's system and try again. Ah, ha! Success. The problem is a defective key on the keyboard, and it is a key that happened to be in the user's password.

11

Although this scenario is oversimplified, the hypothesis testing method is at the heart of many problem-solving efforts. A troubleshooter's ability to formulate hypotheses and carry out experiments to test them is a valuable skill to build. It is a skill that is based in large part on the troubleshooter's experience with a number of different problem situations, the ability to devise a successful experiment to test the hypothesis, and the ability to think clearly and carefully about a problem situation. A component of hypothesis testing is critical thinking. The hypothesis testing strategy works best when a support specialist can think of several alternative explanations for a situation. Sometimes it helps to brainstorm alternatives with other support specialists in a team environment.

The problem-solving strategies described are critical tools in a troubleshooter's repertoire. They involve logical, organized, and critical thinking skills that should, eventually, lead to a satisfactory solution. Problem solving is a skill that can be learned, but it is practice and experience that build problem-solving expertise. Other factors that contribute to problem solving include several personal characteristics you will learn about next.

PERSONAL CHARACTERISTICS

Personal characteristics play an important role in the troubleshooting process. Some personal characteristics can contribute directly to one's success as a troubleshooter.

Some useful personal characteristics of successful support staff members are summarized in Figure 11-7 and described in detail in the sections that follow.

> They are patient and persistent.
>
> They enjoy the problem-solving process.
>
> They enjoy working with people.
>
> They are able to learn.

Figure 11-7   Characteristics of successful troubleshooters

To some degree, these characteristics are part of a support specialist's basic personality. However, personal experience, feedback from users, and coaching from other support staff can affect the degree to which a support specialist makes effective use of these characteristics.

Patience and persistence. Problem solving is often not easy work. It is sometimes frustrating to follow a strategy, reach a dead end, admit you've hit a wall, and try a different approach. A certain amount of frustration over an especially difficult problem is inevitable. But a successful troubleshooter finds ways to deal with frustration. One useful tool to restore patience and perspective is to take a temporary break from a problem. Go for a walk or work on a different project for a while. Perform a task where some progress is possible and then return to the problem where progress seemed impossible. Taking a break from the problem will give you a fresh look at the problem when you return, and you may then see other possible solutions you had missed. Experienced troubleshooters have encountered situations where a fruitful idea pops into one's head during a break or while working on another project.

Patience is important in two respects. Troubleshooters not only need to be patient and persistent with themselves, but they also need to be patient and persistent with users and clients. Successful support specialists are able to shield clients from their own frustrations. Expressing impatience with a customer solves no problem more efficiently and will only impair communication with the customer, a situation that will not help resolve the problem. Users may also lack persistence. They may be too willing to give up on a difficult problem and may need to be reassured that a problem is not insurmountable; that all possible approaches and resources have not yet been exhausted.

Enjoy the problem-solving process. Successful support specialists get enjoyment from the problem-solving process. Where users and clients may view the computer world as a never-ending sequence of technical problems and frustrations, support specialists tend to see challenges and opportunities. If you don't enjoy the challenge of solving problems for other people, you will probably not enjoy the work of a user support specialist as much as one who really enjoys seeing an apparently difficult problem conquered. Like physicians who complain that all they ever see are sick people, user support staff members are hired to solve problems for end users. If you don't really enjoy the challenge of solving problems and the excitement when one gets solved, you should perhaps consider a career in a field other than user support.

Enjoy working with people. There is a popular cultural image of the "techie," a technical person who just works with computer hardware and software, never comes into contact with people, and who talks in machine language. This image does not apply to user support specialists. Especially in the user support industry, the ability to work with all types of people is critical. User support specialists don't have to like every user they encounter. They don't have to treat each user as a personal friend in order to solve a problem. But they do need to communicate with users and to interact with them in a professional manner. If you don't enjoy working at a professional level with users, user support is not a field you'll likely enjoy for very long.

Ability to learn. Change is one of the constant features of the user support field. The hardware or software package you learned in school is not the one you will likely get assigned to support on the job. Last year's products you knew inside and out will become obsolete. Anyone with a serious commitment to the user support field must enjoy learning about new products.

Continual learning is an important job skill in a support position, whether it is written into a formal position description or not. Most user support specialists subscribe to one or more computer industry periodicals to keep up to date with changes in the computer applications field and with industry trends. Support specialists regularly attend training sessions or must teach themselves new software packages. They look for opportunities to learn from other support specialists. Some support organizations sponsor formal professional development opportunities, such as training sessions, and informal brown-bag lunches to encourage support staff to get together to exchange information about products and the computer industry.

WHAT IS A PERSONAL PROBLEM-SOLVING PHILOSOPHY?

The problem-solving approach in this chapter treats troubleshooting computer problems as a process, but not a process with a fixed sequence of steps that are guaranteed to work every time. You have learned about several problem-solving tools that you can apply to many trouble-shooting situations. Like a carpenter or auto mechanic, a support specialist reaches into a tool bag, grabs a tool, uses it, then picks up another tool, uses it, and so on. Either the trouble gets resolved, or the troubleshooter recognizes that she doesn't have the tools she needs to solve the problem.

The perspective on troubleshooting advocated in this chapter differs from two alternative approaches: The first alternative treats troubleshooting as a fixed sequence of steps one follows (1, 2, 3, ...) until the problem is solved. Sometimes a predefined sequence of steps moves a troubleshooter toward resolution, and sometimes it doesn't. A second alternative to the approach in this chapter might be described as a random, hit-or-miss approach to troubleshooting. It consists of trying various things in hopes of eventually hitting on something that works. Occasionally, the random approach resolves a problem, but often it doesn't. And sometimes troubleshooters using the random approach try things that make matters worse.

All support specialists are eventually confronted with problems they cannot solve easily. At these times, they need a personal approach to problem solving. A personal problem-solving philosophy includes an understanding of the strengths a support specialist brings to each problem. It is based on a recognition that selected tools and skills have been successful to solve past problems. It relies on information resources that have proved useful in past situations. It is improved by the metacognition process described earlier in this chapter, where a problem solver carefully examines his or her own thought processes. Without a personal problem-solving approach, a support specialist is more likely to use the random, hit-or-miss strategy instead of a logical, well-developed problem-solving strategy. He or she is more likely to get frustrated by difficult problems or to rely heavily on others when encountering a dead end. Successful troubleshooters recognize a dead end not as a stopping point but as an opportunity to get a fresh start, question assumptions, and try a different alternative with perhaps a different tool.

How do you develop a problem-solving philosophy? Each troubleshooter's strategy is ultimately based on her or his own experience, knowledge, skills, thought processes, access to information, and communication skills. You develop a personal problem-solving strategy by developing your own troubleshooting skills and by using the problem-solving tools described in this chapter. Think about the troubleshooting process. Recognize where your strengths and weaknesses are. Successful troubleshooters develop a sense of what works for them (a plan of attack), and what doesn't, and they try to take maximum advantage of their strengths. Finally, a problem-solving philosophy is not necessarily something a support specialist writes down. However, a personal philosophy about problem solving is something a support specialist thinks about a lot and works to improve. Chapter 12 provides some problems you can use to help develop a personal problem-solving philosophy.

CHAPTER SUMMARY

- Most computer problems are not difficult ones for support providers to handle. They are requests for information, complaints, or problems with which a support staff member has experience. This chapter describes troubleshooting tools and skills that are useful to solve more difficult problems.

- Troubleshooting is the process of solving computer problems. Rather than a series of sequential steps, troubleshooting is an iterative process, a creative process in which support specialists try an approach, and if it doesn't work, they try another.

- Troubleshooters use an assortment of skills in their work, including problem solving, critical thinking, and decision making. They also use several kinds of troubleshooting tools, including communication skills, information resources, problem-solving strategies, and personal characteristics. Troubleshooters apply these tools, skills, and resources to various aspects of a problem.

- Communication skills include listening to a user's description of problem symptoms, paraphrasing (or active listening) to verify one's understanding of a problem, and critical questions to get information from a user and force a support specialist to challenge assumptions that may block the path to a solution. The ability to ask probing questions and explain a problem resolution to a user are also useful communication skills.

- Information resources include a troubleshooter's personal experience with similar or related problems, prepared scripts that follow a logical path to a solution, and various knowledgebases. Vendor manuals, trade books, online help, CD-ROM databases, faxback services, ListServs, newsgroups, and Web sites are rich sources of information about problems. Coworkers, friends, and vendors are other information resources that may lead toward a problem resolution.

- Problem-solving strategies include several logical thinking processes that are often useful to troubleshooters.
  - Look for a quick, obvious fix.
  - Try to replicate the problem yourself.
  - Examine the configuration.
  - Get back to a basic configuration.
  - View the system as a group of subsystems.
  - Use a module replacement strategy.
  - Try a hypothesis testing approach.

- Personal characteristics that aid successful troubleshooters include patience and persistence, enjoyment of the problem-solving process, satisfaction in working with people, and the ability to learn new materials.

- The chapter challenges readers to develop their problem-solving skills, to think about the problem-solving process, and to develop their own problem-solving philosophy. The philosophy should include an awareness of their strengths and weaknesses when working with the problem-solving tools and resources described in this chapter.

11

KEY TERMS

- **active listening** — A communication skill in which a listener is involved and engaged in the communication process; paraphrasing is an example of an active listening skill.

- **analogies** — Ways in which the current problem is similar to other problems that have been solved; an analogy between similar problems may suggest a possible problem solution.

- **creativity** — A critical thinking ability that searches for innovative or unique solutions to a problem; alternative explanations for a problem situation or an innovative way to work around a problem are the result of creative thinking.

- **critical questions** — Specially designed questions to elicit information from a computer user that may force a support specialist to challenge some basic assumptions about the problem; critical questions permit a support specialist to move beyond a situation where thinking about a problem has reached a dead end.

- **critical thinking** — Cognitive skills used to analyze a problem, search for underlying logic or rationale, or find alternative ways to explain an event or situation.

- **decision making** — The ability to define and select from a number of alternative solutions to a problem and make a decision based on predefined criteria; decision making is an important skill for troubleshooters.

- **escalation** — A problem-solving tool where a difficult or complex problem is referred to a higher level support person or team for resolution.

- **explanation** — A communication skill in which a support specialist describes the solution to a problem so the user understands why the problem occurred and the steps required to resolve it.

- **goal state** — A desired outcome or objective; in troubleshooting, a common goal state is to diagnose or repair a computer system to return it to a normal operational state.

- **hypothesis** — An educated guess or prediction, based on experience, about the cause of a computer problem; based on a hypothesis, a troubleshooter may carry out a series of tests to determine whether the prediction is true or false.

- **iterative process** — A process that involves several paths or approaches to problems; steps are repeated in a loop until a fruitful path is found; troubleshooting is an iterative process in that it uses and re-uses a variety of tools and skills.

- **knowledgebase** — An organized collection of facts, information, procedures, tips, and prior problem resolutions that can serve as an information resource in a problem-solving situation.

- **listening skills** — The skills and abilities required to be a successful participant in the communications process; a support specialist uses listening skills to help understand and clarify the definition of a computer problem.

- **ListServ** — An automated e-mail service that distributes e-mail messages posted to the ListServ to every member who has subscribed to the ListServ.

- **metacognition** — The ability to rise above the level of ordinary thought to a level where a thinker examines her or his own thought processes; metacognition is a thinking ability that helps a troubleshooter gain expertise in problem solving through a critical examination of his or her problem-solving process.

- **module replacement** — A problem-solving strategy that replaces a hardware or software component whose operational status is unknown with one that is known to be operational.

- **newsgroups** — Internet discussion groups where participants with common interests in a topic post messages in a bulletin board atmosphere.

- **outsourcing** — An agreement with a computer services support organization to provide problem-solving assistance for a fee or by contractual agreement.

- **paraphrase** — A communication skill where a listener restates, in her own words, what she thinks she heard a user say about a computer problem.

- **probes** — Follow-up questions designed to elicit additional information about a problem situation; a sequence of probes often clarifies a problem situation.

- **problem solving** — An activity where there is a current state X and a goal state Y and alternatives path to get from X to Y; the objective of problem solving is to get from X to Y quickly, accurately, effectively, or efficiently.

- **replicate** — A troubleshooting tool that attempts to repeat a problem condition to see if it is repeatable in a different situation or environment.

- **script** — A predefined sequence of questions and responses that represents a method of solving a problem; a script is sometimes represented as a flowchart that shows the possible paths a problem investigation can take with sample questions, decision points, and solutions.

- **troubleshooting** — The process of defining, diagnosing, and solving computer problems; troubleshooting involves the use of several thinking and communications skills, information resources, strategies, and methods as aids to a troubleshooter.

- **variables** — Factors or aspects of a problem-solving situation that can change or be changed; support specialists often try to eliminate variables from a complex or difficult problem in order to simplify the problem so it is manageable and can be solved.

REVIEW QUESTIONS

1. Explain why some computer problems are more difficult to solve than others.

2. What is troubleshooting? Is troubleshooting a well-defined series of steps that always leads to a problem resolution? Explain why or why not.

3. Is troubleshooting an iterative process or a sequential one? Explain your answer.

4. Explain the goal of problem solving. Why is problem solving an important skill for a computer troubleshooter?

5. Explain why analogies are useful tools to solve computer problems.

6. What is critical thinking? Explain why critical thinking skills are important for computer troubleshooters.

7. Define metacognition and explain its role in troubleshooting computer problems.

8. Explain what activities are involved in decision making. Why is decision making an important skill for a computer troubleshooter?

9. Are problem solving, critical thinking, and decision making different names for the same skill? How are they related to each other? Explain your answers.

10. Describe the four categories of tools troubleshooters use when they work on the solution to a computer problem.

11. Explain why listening skills are important in the troubleshooting process. What is an active listener? What tools do active listeners use?

12. Describe paraphrasing. Give an example.

13. List the five critical questions described in this chapter. What is their purpose in the problem-solving process?

14. What is a probe? How is it used to help solve computer problems?

15. Why is the ability to provide an explanation an important skill and tool for support specialists?

16. Explain why information resources are an important tool for computer problem solvers. Give several examples of useful information resources.

17. What is a knowledgebase? Describe some of the different forms of knowledgebases. Why is access to several knowledgebases important in the search for a solution to a computer problem?

18. Explain the difference between ListServs and Newsgroups.

19. Explain the role of escalation in the problem resolution process. Why is it an important tool for troubleshooters?

20. What role can outsourcing play in solving computer problems?

21. Give some examples of problem-solving strategies. Are any of the strategies you described guaranteed to work? Why or why not?

22. What is the purpose of replicating a problem?

23. What is the goal of getting back to a basic configuration? Why is it sometimes a useful tool?

24. Describe the strategy discussed in this chapter of viewing a computer as a group of linked subsystems. What is the purpose of this strategy? What is the "midpoint"?

25. Describe how module replacement works as a problem-solving strategy for both hardware and software problems.

26. Explain how hypothesis testing works. Give an example of a problem situation, then formulate a hypothesis and describe how you would test it.

27. Describe several personal characteristics that are important for computer problem troubleshooters. Which characteristic do you think is the most important?

28. How does a computer troubleshooter develop a personal problem-solving philosophy?

HANDS-ON PROJECTS

PROJECT 11-1

Team up with another student or coworker and practice listening and paraphrasing skills. One student takes the role of the user; the other takes the role of a support person. The user describes a common problem with a computer system to the support person, who then paraphrases the problem description back to the user.

The user's role is important because he or she needs to listen for important parts of the problem that the support person omitted, that didn't exist in the original problem description, or that the support person modified. Continue the paraphrasing activity until the person in the support role can correctly paraphrase the original problem description. Then change roles.

11

PROJECT 11-2

Study the following problem description:

> My computer is hung up. I don't know what I did wrong. The screen is frozen. Nothing I try does any good. I press keys on the keyboard, and nothing happens. The mouse pointer won't move.

What additional information would you, as a support staff member, want from this user? Design several questions you could ask to get the additional information you would need to resolve this problem.

PROJECT 11-3

Write an explanation to a user who wants to know why the Office 97 applications software package will not operate on his PC, which is a 386 system that runs the Windows 3.1 operating system.

PROJECT 11-4

An applications package runs correctly on machine A, but the same package does not operate correctly on machine B. Make a list of basic computer system configuration information you would like to know in order to further diagnose this problem.

PROJECT 11-5

The chapter states that a computer system can be treated as a group of subsystems. List the major subsystems that go together to make up a complete computer system, and briefly describe each one.

PROJECT 11-6

Think about a difficult troubleshooting problem you've encountered in your recent experience—one where the solution was not straightforward and where the problem was not a simple request for information. The problem you pick might be one you experienced personally, or one you encountered on the job or as a lab assistant or while helping a friend.

Describe the troubleshooting tools, methods, and strategies you used in terms of the topics in this chapter. What subsystems were involved in the problem? Which specific aspects of the troubleshooting strategies discussed in this chapter did you use? Describe the communications tools, information resources, and problem analysis/diagnosis tools you used. Were the troubleshooting methods you used effective? How could you have improved the effectiveness of your troubleshooting strategy? Write a description of the troubleshooting event that answers these questions.

CASE PROJECTS

1. PROBLEM SOLVING: YOUR TURN

See how many of these problems you can solve working by yourself. Use books, manuals, online help, and so forth, as necessary). Don't work too long on a problem that seems difficult; ask your instructor for help. As you work on these tasks, make some brief notes that describe your findings. Some of the exercises require a Lab Exercise disk that you can get from your instructor.

1. A file, TESTFILE.NOT, on the Lab Exercise disk was accidentally erased. Can you recover it? Why or why not? If you can retrieve it, what is in the file?

2. Use the Lab Exercise disk that your instructor gives you as a boot disk to start your PC system. Does the system boot normally? Run the DOS utility EDIT to examine the file HUMOR05.TXT on the Lab Exercise disk. Describe any problems you encounter with the system. Make any modifications you need to the Lab Exercise boot disk so you can boot your system with it and run the EDIT utility.

3. Next, does the cursor work in the EDIT utility? Make any modifications you need to the Lab Exercise boot disk so the cursor works in EDIT when you boot from the Lab disk. Remove the Lab Exercise disk for the next exercises.

4. Unplug the keyboard from your system while it is turned off and reboot it. During the POST boot-up diagnostic tests, one of the devices tested is the keyboard. What message appears to alert the user to the keyboard problem? If you plug the keyboard back in again, will the system operate without rebooting? If necessary, plug your keyboard back in and reboot.

5. Use the operating system utilities on your computer to answer these questions about your system. For each question, indicate what utility tool you used to find the information.

   a. What model of processor is in your system?

   b. Does your system include a math co-processor?

   c. What type of bus architecture is used?

   d. How much total memory does your system have?

   e. How much memory is designated as "extended"?

   f. Where is HIMEM.SYS loaded in memory?

   g. Is the subdirectory C:\NET in the search path?

   h. How is the DOS environment variable TEMP defined?

   i. For the mouse on your system, what are the IRQ, COM port, and port memory addresses?

   j. What is the size of the hard drive, and how much free space is available on it?

6. If it is available, run the MS-DOS utility SCANDISK on your hard drive C:. What, if any, problems did SCANDISK find? If problems exist, what is the procedure you would follow to eliminate them? What precautions should a user take before running SCANDISK to eliminate lost clusters?

7. "I got the floppy disk you sent me, but I can't read it on my system. I don't understand why not." Give some examples of questions you could ask the caller to help determine the problem.

8. Use the copy of the MS-DOS PRINT.EXE utility program on the Lab Exercise floppy disk to print the ASCII file HUMOR05.TXT, which is also on the floppy disk. Explain the result and why it occurred.

11

9. There is a file ORDER.FRM on the Lab Exercise floppy disk. Erase the file. Describe any problems you encounter with this task.

10. Run the program INTERNET.COM on the floppy disk handed out in class. Describe the results. How would you explain what happened?

11. In previous versions of Microsoft Word, the Ins key would toggle from insert mode to overwrite mode, and vise versa. In Word 97 however, the Ins key does not perform this task. Can you find out how to get from insert mode to overwrite mode in Word 97?

 2. A Dual Boot PC for Dale Andrews

Dale Andrews, a software trainer, came into the support center late one afternoon after a long day of classes. He put his laptop computer on the table and said to anyone who was listening, "Help!" Dale explained to the support center staff that he teaches classes that require him to run a variety of software packages. Most of the classes he teaches use Windows 95 applications. In fact, he teaches classes for beginning and advanced Windows 95 users. However, he occasionally needs to teach classes that use Windows 3.1 and MS-DOS 6.2. Because his laptop boots automatically into Windows 95, he has had problems when he needs to use Windows 3.1 or MS-DOS 6.2.

A couple of members of the support staff suggested that Dale run Windows 3.1 and MS-DOS applications under Windows 95. They said most Windows 3.1 and MS-DOS applications should be able to operate in Windows 95 without any problems. However Dale responded that he liked to be able to run applications in the operating environment his trainees actually use. He said, "I don't think it is a good training strategy to demonstrate and train on Windows 3.1 software, for example, with references to the program manager, file manager, and program groups where those features either don't exist, or have a different name." Dale went on to say that he had invented a workaround, of sorts. He created an MS-DOS 6.2 boot disk that he uses to start up his laptop when he needs to teach a class using Windows 3.1 or MS-DOS. He installed both DOS 6.2 and Window 3.1 on his laptop and uses the special boot disk when he does a demonstration or training session that requires either operating system.

The workaround works, for the most part. However, Dale related that one day he accidentally left the DOS 6.2 boot disk in his office and had to delay the start of a training session to retrieve it. Dale said he had heard that it was possible to set up a PC so it could start in either Windows 95 or DOS 6.2 (and Windows 3.1). Several of the support center staff recalled that they had seen references to a dual boot option for Windows 95 PCs. But none could remember how to set up a system to provide the dual boot option.

Your task is to research the procedure that will solve Dale's problem. Find the steps required to configure a PC to dual boot into DOS 6.2 or Windows 95. If you have equipment you can use for this purpose, set it up with the dual boot option.

3. THE D'AMICO COMPANY: A FRIENDLIER SEND TO COMMAND

Jane D'Amico owns The D'Amico Company, which provides curriculum development consulting services to education boards across the midwestern United States. The consultants that work for D'Amico are former teachers, and although they use computers in their work, they are not always confident in their technical abilities. Jane likes to find ways to make it easier for the consultants to interact with their computers.

As you know, it is sometimes not easy to move or copy a file in Windows 95 from one folder to another. For example, to use the drag-and-drop method, you need to display at the same time both the file you want to copy and the folder you want to copy it to. The Send To command is useful if you want to copy a file to a floppy disk. However, Jane feels the Send To command would be more useful if a user could use it to copy or move a file to any path, even if it was not visible on the screen.

Research a utility program called *OtherFolder* that extends the capability of the Send To command. The utility is available on the Internet from **ftp://ftp.creativelement.com/pub/win95ann/AnyFoldr.zip**.

Install it on a system to which you have access. Test the capabilities of *OtherFolder* to solve the problem described above. Write a description of the problem, the *OtherFolder* solution, and about any problems you encountered with any aspect of the installation and use of the *OtherFolder* utility.

11

COMMON SUPPORT PROBLEMS

As you learned in Chapter 11, many problems that a help desk or computer support group handles are not particularly difficult or complex. You also learned about the problem-solving and troubleshooting process and some tools support specialists use to solve more difficult problems. In this chapter, you'll examine some real problem-solving situations and how support specialists solved them.

The chapter is not a comprehensive discussion of every kind of problem a support specialist might encounter; that would be an impossible task. However, there are some common problem types that experienced support specialists frequently come across. You will look at several problem examples and see how the user described the problem, what problem-solving strategies the support specialist used to resolve it, as well as his or her conclusions about the process. All the examples are taken from real-life support situations, including problems students have contributed from their own work experiences in classroom discussions of problem solving.

AFTER READING THIS CHAPTER AND COMPLETING THE EXERCISES YOU WILL BE ABLE TO:

- Describe the types of common end user computer problems
- Explain the problem-solving process support specialists use to solve several typical user support problems

COMMON END USER PROBLEMS

Although computer problems come in a variety of forms, most problems fall into one of several categories, shown in Figure 12-1.

○	Hardware problems	○	Documentation problems
○	Software problems	○	Vendor problems
○	User problems	○	Facilities problems

Figure 12-1   Common end user problems

In the first part of this chapter, you'll learn about these categories of common problems and study some examples of each kind.

HARDWARE PROBLEMS

Most hardware problems are related to one or more of three sources: installation and compatibility, configuration, and malfunctions.

Hardware installation and compatibility problems. Users encounter a large percentage of hardware problems when they first purchase a new hardware product, or upgrade an old one, and attempt to use it. The product may be incompatible with existing hardware or the user may not have installed it correctly. **Incompatible** computer components are those that cannot operate together in the same system. The following example illustrates the discovery of a hardware incompatibility at installation and the support specialist's solution:

> *Problem:* A user purchased a scanner for a computer system. The scanner was designed to plug into a parallel port. However, the user already had a printer connected to the system's parallel port. Fortunately, the scanner included a printer bypass option so the printer could be connected to the scanner, which in turn could be connected directly to the parallel port. Although the printer worked fine when it was plugged directly into the parallel port, it did not operate when it was attached to the scanner according to the instructions in the scanner documentation.
>
> *Solution:* A call to the scanner company's help desk revealed that the printer bypass feature does not always work reliably with all brands of printers. The scanner vendor recommended that the user purchase a second I/O adapter card with an additional parallel port so that each device (the scanner and the printer) could be plugged directly into its own port.

Hardware configuration problems. Incorrect configuration can be another source of difficulty. **Configuration problems** are caused when the hardware component settings are wrong for the particular computer environment in which the hardware must operate. Configuration problems were more common before the widespread adoption of Plug and Play standards than they are today. **Plug and Play standards** are rules that represent industry-wide agreement on methods that an operating system uses to communicate with hardware components. Using these methods, an operating system can recognize the components' existence and select options that permit the components to communicate with the operating system. Before Plug and Play, users and support staff frequently had to set small jumper pins and dip switches on hardware components to select various hardware options. They also frequently had to modify system startup files by installing special software drivers to get hardware components to operate. For example, whether a serial port on an older style communications adapter card was addressed as COM1, COM2, COM3, or COM4 often depended on how the jumper pins were set. Plug and Play standards have reduced the number of configuration problems users and support staff encounter.

But configuration problems have not disappeared, as shown in the following example:

Problem: A user purchased a new video graphics adapter card to increase the resolution of the display screen from 640x480 to 1024x768 pixels. The card installed easily and Windows 95 recognized on startup that there was a new piece of hardware in the system. The Windows Add New Hardware wizard went through the process of installing updated software drivers to support the new video card. However, when the user restarted the computer after installation, the video image was the same resolution as before.

Solution: A support specialist suggested that the user open the Windows 95 Display Properties Control Panel icon and change the settings for the display to 1024x768. Once the user changed the settings to match the new video card's capabilities, the screen image appeared at the higher resolution.

12

Although Plug and Play can help a user load the appropriate drivers, it does not always automatically adjust software settings to take maximum advantage of the new hardware's capabilities.

Hardware malfunctions. A small percentage of hardware problems are components that either have never worked or that no longer work. To avoid future hardware problems, the support staff may "burn in" a new system before installing a new system at an end user site. During **burn-in**, they operate the system nonstop for a 48- to 72-hour period to give any component that is marginal or temperature sensitive an opportunity to fail before installing it. Defective components will usually fail during the burn-in period. After the burn-in, the probability that a component will eventually fail is small. Electromechanical devices that have moving parts (disk drives, CD-ROM drives, and printers) are much more likely to develop problems than are electronic components (CPUs, memory, bus slots, and expansion cards). Companies that make utility software, such as Norton Utilities by Symantec, often include hardware diagnostic tools that can help support specialists with system burn-in and common hardware malfunctions. Although some malfunctioning components can be repaired, the hourly cost of electronic shop labor today means that vendors often replace rather than repair them.

To solve hardware problems, support specialists should be sure to consider the following: 1) Look for possible interaction problems between hardware and software; 2) Examine any applicable README files for updated compatibility information; and 3) Check vendor Web sites for updated drivers and software patches. These resources often lead to installation and incompatibility solutions.

SOFTWARE PROBLEMS

Most software problems are related to one or more of four sources: installation and compatibility, configuration, bugs, and performance.

Software installation and compatibility. Many software problems appear during the installation of new software products or upgrades, even though software installations are generally easier today than they were in the past. Ten years ago, a user would often have to create a subdirectory for the new software, copy files from the distribution media to a system's hard drive, and configure software drivers and options to match the specific system hardware. The potential for mistakes during this manual procedure was substantial. Nowadays, software installation processes are automated, and users can avoid common problems that once plagued both users and support specialists. **Installation software** can automatically create subdirectories with correct path names, examine the hardware configuration to determine whether the hardware and software are compatible, and automatically set configuration options in the software to match the hardware.

However, in spite of flexible installation programs, support specialists still deal with installation problems. Not all software installs automatically, and support specialists are occasionally asked to install older software, as in the following example:

Problem: A support specialist installed a software package that was designed to run in an MS-DOS environment on a Windows 95 PC. The support specialist investigated how to run a DOS application in a Windows 95 environment using a feature called DOS-compatibility mode. Unfortunately, the DOS program did not operate correctly in this mode because the program bypassed some of the operating system features and performed its own input and output operations. The program appeared to be incompatible with Windows 95, even in DOS-compatibility mode.

Solution: The support specialist called the software vendor and learned that to run the older program on a Windows 95 PC successfully, he had to set up the computer as a dual-boot system so that it could run both MS-DOS 6.2 and Windows 95. In a dual-boot environment, the user chooses which operating system to use at boot-up time.

The dual-boot solution meant the user could continue to run a valuable DOS application on a Windows 95 PC. Although the dual-boot option is not a solution in every case of incompatibility because dual-boot systems can also *create* problems, in this case it solved the problem without undesirable side effects.

Shareware software downloaded from the Internet can be another source of compatibility problems. Although many shareware programs are written to current industry standards and are designed to be compatible with operating systems and other applications, some shareware programs may produce conflicts with other software. A **conflict** is a state where two computer components use systems resources (CPU, memory, or peripheral devices) in different and incompatible ways. Conflicts often make systems inoperable or do not allow them to operate normally (for example, performance may be slow).

Software configuration problems. Some software problems are related to the way the software is configured to run on a system. Configuration problems result when software options are not set for the specific operating environment or hardware. These problems may occur when users install or upgrade new hardware or software or attempt to use a software feature for the first time, as in the following example:

Problem: A Windows 3.1 user purchased a new ink-jet printer to replace a dot matrix printer in her system. When she tried to print reports from her accounting software, however, she discovered that a few garbage characters would print at the top of each page, and then the sheet would eject. She contacted a customer support specialist in her department and learned that she would need a different printer driver to replace the dot matrix printer driver. Unfortunately, the documentation that came with her new printer described how to install a printer driver for Windows 95, but did not mention Windows 3.1. She called the support specialist again and explained the problem.

Solution: The support specialist researched the problem and found that a Windows 3.1-compatible printer driver for the new ink-jet printer was available from the accounting software vendor's Internet Web site and could be downloaded for free. The driver was also available on a floppy disk for the cost of shipping. After the support specialist downloaded the Windows 3.1 version of the printer driver and updated the accounting software configuration to use it, the printout problem disappeared.

12

Software bugs. Major errors in a software program, or **bugs**, are due to coding mistakes programmers make when they write the software. Bugs occur more often in custom-written programs and programs written for a limited market segment than they do in mass-market programs. In all software, bugs occur for the most part in infrequently used features of a program. Many bugs are eliminated during the testing period that occurs before a software product is released for sale. However, even the most popular software products can have known bugs several years after their initial release.

Mass-market software vendors sometimes release new versions, new releases, updates, patches for existing versions, or even new products to fix bugs and provide new features.

- A new **version** of a program contains major new features and is usually the result of a substantially rewritten program.

- Users of a previous version of a program may be able to purchase an **upgrade**, which provides the features of the new version at a lower cost to owners of the previous version.

- A new **release** of a program contains some new features that have been added to an existing program.

- An **update** is a release that fixes known bugs in a previous version or release.

- A **patch** is a replacement for one or a few small modules in a larger system that fixes one or more known bugs.

Although there are no industry standards on how to number software releases, some software companies use the software version number to indicate the release type. For example, version 2.0 is the first release of a new version, version 2.1 is an update with new features, and version 2.11 (or 2.1.1) is a bug-fix release or update of version 2.1 but does not include major new features. Other vendors add a service release letter to a version number. For example, version 2.5A is the first (A-level) patch of release 2.5. A service release is a replacement for a small section of a program that repairs a specific software bug. The following example illustrates how one user obtained a patch:

> *Problem:* A user experienced a spreadsheet formatting problem that only appeared in very large dollar amounts.
>
> *Solution:* When the user contacted the software vendor's help desk, the user learned that the problem was a known bug, that it had been repaired, and that a patch could be downloaded from the vendor's Web site or requested on a floppy disk. The help desk staff provided the user with instructions on how to download the patch and explained that the fix would self-install when the user double-clicked on the downloaded file.

Before installing any patch, a support specialist should make sure that the patch is for the version of the software that is installed on a user's system. In addition, any software upgrades, new releases or patches that are installed on a system should be documented in the site installation notebook described in Chapter 5.

When users install a patch to repair a problem, they must remember to reinstall the patch if they ever need to reinstall the software from the original distribution media. In general, new software releases or versions incorporate all bug fixes that have been reported and fixed prior to the new release. For example, version 2.1 contains all patches released for version 2.0. However, the documentation for some patches may include a note that patch 3.4A must be installed before patch 3.4B can be installed.

In some cases where there is no patch for an existing software bug, a support specialist or software vendor may be able to suggest a workaround for a problem. A **workaround** is a method or feature to accomplish the same result a user wants, but it bypasses the bug in the software. For example, there are usually several ways to give a command in a GUI environment: keyboard commands, menu commands, mouse clicks, and shortcut keys. If a menu option does not work correctly, there may be a keyboard workaround.

Software performance problems. When a computer system works at some level, but not as efficiently as it should, it has **performance problems**. These are often a combination of hardware and software problems. For example, a user may report that the hard disk drive light comes on more frequently and stays on longer on her PC than it used to and that the system seems sluggish. The response time from choosing the Save command to the completion of the Save activity has become longer and longer. The user may suspect that the problem is due to hardware—perhaps the hard disk drive is beginning to fail. However, performance problems are usually related to how the software, the operating system in this case, is managing the hardware. A support specialist might investigate alternative explanations such as the following before concluding that the hard drive is the problem:

- The hard disk drive may be almost full; the operating system may not have adequate unused space to write temporary files on the hard drive during its file management tasks. The user may need to back up and delete infrequently used programs and data files.

- The hard disk may be fragmented; files written on the disk in small chunks may take longer to read and write than files in contiguous sectors on the disk. A defrag utility can often fix this problem.

- The hard drive may have wasted space because links to free space are lost. ScanDisk can reclaim lost space due to improperly linked allocation units on a disk.

- The system may not have enough RAM to run the software and is using the hard disk as an extension of RAM to accommodate large amounts of data. The system may need more memory to run the software efficiently.

Closely related to software problems is the user's ability to operate the software, as you will learn in the next section.

USER PROBLEMS

Many support problems are caused by users. Although most users try to be well informed and do their best to use hardware and software correctly, even the best-intentioned users can introduce problems into the support picture.

Mistakes. All end users, including computer professionals, make mistakes. Systems analysts may not understand all aspects of a business process and may design a software system incorrectly; programmers may make a mistake in the code they write and introduce a software bug; and a professional data entry operator types the wrong keystroke every few thousand characters. Even support specialists make an occasional mistake. What can be done about user mistakes? Well-designed computer systems anticipate potential user mistakes, alert the user, and provide corrective action. But despite the best efforts of software developers, users occasionally press a wrong key and end up in a part of the program where they didn't want to be. It is easy for users to press one sequence when they meant to press the other. Some inadvertent key sequence errors can have drastic consequences. For example, in some word processors, if a passage is selected (highlighted) and the user presses a key, the character representing the pressed key replaces the entire selected passage. If users don't know how to recover from this situation, they can easily lose some of their work and not understand why.

Although user mistakes account for a significant percentage of common problems, support specialists need to consider carefully how to handle these problems from a customer service perspective; some users do not like to be told that they made a mistake. Chapter 10 covers some strategies for handling interactions with difficult users.

Misunderstandings. Other user problems stem from misunderstandings about product features or limitations. Users may expect a product to be able to perform tasks for which it was not intended, as shown in the following example:

Problem: A number of companies now advertise free e-mail service along with a software package that operates on a PC with a modem. The software on the local PC usually dials the e-mail provider's central computer, uploads and downloads e-mail messages addressed to the user (along with advertising, which is how the service can be offered without cost), and lets the user read and create messages. Many users of these services, who are confused about the difference between e-mail and the Internet, contact the free e-mail service provider to inquire how to view Web pages from their e-mail software.

Solution: Users may misunderstand that the connection between their PC and the e-mail server is not an Internet service, and that e-mail software does not provide free Internet access. Support staff at the e-mail service refer these users to an Internet Service Provider (ISP).

Wrong products. Users frequently purchase the wrong product to accomplish a task. They may purchase a software package or hardware peripheral that is incompatible with their existing system. A common problem occurs when users of an older model PC system hear about a new software product they would like to purchase. They may not understand that the software requires a later model processor or more memory than their system has. Or users with Windows 95 systems may inadvertently purchase the Macintosh version of a software package because they have not read the packaging carefully.

Users may also purchase software without an understanding of its capabilities and limitations, or without knowledge of alternatives, as in the following example:

> *Problem:* A Macintosh user who wanted to create a newsletter bought a collection of clip art on a CD-ROM from an office supply store because the packaging included an illustration of clip art embedded in a newsletter. The user assumed the software was capable of producing a result like the newsletter illustrated on the package. When the user installed the clip art on his system, he called the support number in the documentation to complain that the software did not produce the newsletter form he wanted.
>
> *Solution:* The support specialist suggested that the user return the software to the store.

The same problem often arises with the purchase of new hardware. For example, a user may purchase a 56K modem to dial an Internet service. However, prior to the summer of 1998, there were two different 56K modem standards. A user may unintentionally purchase a modem that isn't compatible with the standard her ISP uses.

Poor training. Some problems arise because users are poorly trained or do not read the documentation that came with the hardware or software. Many calls to support centers can be easily answered by referring to the user manual, a tutorial, or online help, but users often do not want to take the time to search for information. **Quick start behavior** is a name support specialists give to the natural tendency among users to want to get a new hardware component or software package operational as soon as possible. Many vendors now include a very brief quick start guide, or "Getting Started with . . ." manual, in an attempt to get users to at least read something before they begin to use a new product. Lack of adequate training ultimately translates into waste and lost user productivity. For example, the Macintosh user described earlier who wanted to produce a newsletter did not realize that his word processor included most of the features he would need to produce a reasonably complex newsletter. He actually had the software he needed but did not realize it.

Forgotten information. In other cases, users just plain forget how to perform a task or don't remember how to find the information they need. For example, local area network administrators report that the most common call they receive is from users who have forgotten the password to their accounts.

 Caution users against writing their passwords on paper. For users who are forgetful and need frequent reminders of their passwords, one strategy is to suggest that they keep a written note in a nonobvious place that contains a word or phrase that will remind them of their password but does not include their actual password.

Those who use computers infrequently are especially likely to forget information. Cheat sheets are an effective aid to help users remember how to perform common tasks.

DOCUMENTATION PROBLEMS

Another source of computer problems can be traced to documentation problems. The readability of some vendor documentation has improved in recent years. However, poorly organized and inaccurate documentation is still the direct cause of much user misunderstanding and contributes to the volume of calls a help desk receives. Inaccurate documentation may have both misstatements and omissions of information users need.

The best user documentation includes a quick start guide, a tutorial guide that takes a user step-by-step through the major features of a software package, a reference manual that contains information organized by topic, a troubleshooting guide, and online help that users can search by keyword and that includes wizards to assist them with common problems. Chapter 7 suggests ways to improve documentation that a support staff prepares.

VENDOR PROBLEMS

Calls to a help desk or hotline are often related to vendor performance. Some vendors consistently oversell their products; they promise features that are not actually present in the final product. Vendors may also release a beta software version for widespread use that contains known bugs that can put user data at risk. Some vendors are also notorious for delivering new products much later than they were promised. **Vaporware** refers to hardware or software products that appear in ads or press releases but do not actually exist. A company may announce products that don't yet exist in order to study market reaction or to confuse its competitors. A help desk that handles calls from external customers and clients should establish a policy for its support staff on how to handle calls from disgruntled customers about vendor product performance. Chapter 10 describes some customer service and communications skills that are useful to handle such calls.

FACILITIES PROBLEMS

A relatively small percentage of support calls involve facilities problems. Support calls related to viruses, backup media, security, and ergonomics issues fall into this category. Chapter 5 discusses solutions to several ergonomic problems, and chapter 8 deals with common tools and strategies for other facilities management problems that a support specialist may have to solve.

Networks are a frequent source of problems support specialists encounter. Because network problems are often traceable to hardware (including hubs, routers, bridges, and gateways), software, operating systems, or other categories of problems discussed earlier, they are not a unique problem category. However, network problems are often among those that are most difficult for a support staff to handle because they frequently involve the interaction of hardware and software components. Furthermore, an increasing number of end users are connected to a network via the Internet, a company intranet, a dial-up modem, or a local area network that supports client-server applications. Although network problems account for a large percentage of all support calls, most turn out to be related directly to hardware, software, or some combination of the two.

EXAMPLES OF END USER PROBLEMS

As support staff solve problems, the solutions become common knowledge among them. They use this ever-expanding bank of knowledge to solve new problems. The purpose of this section is to describe several additional examples of common support problems. You or your coworkers or fellow students may have experienced some of the problems in this section, or ones like them; in other cases the problems may be new to you. The greater the variety of problems you learn about, the better the knowledge and experience you will have at your command when you tackle new problems.

PROBLEM 1: SOUNDS LIKE TROUBLE

Problem: A user in a remote branch office sent me an e-mail message that she had lost the sound in her system. I started the troubleshooting process by asking about her basic configuration and some critical questions, such as "Has this problem ever happened before?" and "What program were you running when you noticed the sound was lost?" She wrote back that the system is a 486 PC running Windows 95, that the sound had been working fine, and that she couldn't remember exactly which program she was running when she first noticed the sound no longer worked. She also mentioned that two other employees had access to her system.

Problem-solving strategy: My first reaction was to try some quick, obvious fixes. I suggested that she:

- Reset the sound card in the expansion slot.

- Try the sound card in a different expansion slot.

- Check all the connections and cables to the sound card.

- Check the Windows 95 device manager to see if there were any IRQ conflicts between the sound card and other devices.

She responded that she checked these items, but that the sound still didn't work. I discussed the problem with some support colleagues, describing what we had already tried. They came up with a couple of other suggestions.

- Make sure that the volume is turned up on the speakers.

- Make sure that the volume is turned up in the Windows 95 media player.

- Check that the speakers are connected correctly.

- If the speakers require electrical current, make sure they're plugged in.

She checked all these possibilities and reported that there was still no sound. I asked her if there were any changes made to her system recently. She wrote back that apparently one of her work colleagues had downloaded a shareware version of an antivirus program from the Internet about the time the sound problem first occurred. The colleague said that, after several attempts, he couldn't get the antivirus program to work correctly on the system, so he uninstalled it. The fact that some new software had been installed on her system got me

12

thinking in a different direction. I looked on the Internet and found a Web site for her brand of sound card. They listed about 20 different models of cards, one of which was hers. So I e-mailed back the Web address where she could download the latest version of the software driver for her particular card. Later that day, I received a message that she had downloaded the sound card driver, installed it in Windows 95, and now her sound works again.

Conclusion: I'm not certain of the diagnosis, but I think the shareware program may have affected the driver software her sound card used. Once she reinstalled the driver, the problem was fixed.

I was pleased that I solved the problem. I used communications skills to get information from the user, which was not easy using e-mail. I also used critical questions that opened up a different avenue of investigation. I used several information resources, including my support colleagues and the vendor's Web site on the Internet. I used several troubleshooting strategies, including looking for a quick, obvious fix, some hypothesis testing, and module replacement. [*Based on an incident described by Billie Brendlinger.*]

PROBLEM 2: THE PROBLEM WITH MODEMS

Problem: I was at a customer's site to troubleshoot an Internet setup on their Macintosh computer. I had previously installed terminal emulation software and configured the customer's machine for Internet access. I had also trained the user to log in and run the software to access the Internet. When I left after the installation, everything appeared to be in working order.

After using the system for about a week, the user called our help desk, saying that she had an occasional problem with Internet access from her Mac. The modem usually dialed the ISP's computer successfully, but occasionally it would report than it couldn't get a dial tone.

Problem-solving strategy: On my follow-up visit, I asked a series of questions about her telephone service, including whether she had any features added to her basic phone service, such as caller ID, call waiting, or other services. The user assured me that her telephone was a standard line with no frills. I checked the modem with the terminal emulation software, and the diagnostic check indicated that the modem was correctly connected. Since the setup had worked after the original installation, I suspected the modem connection was OK, but I was glad to get the confirmation.

Then I decided to unplug the modem and connect the telephone handset directly to the phone line. My hypothesis was that there was something wrong with the telephone service that was affecting the modem. When I picked up the handset, I heard a blip-blip-blip-blip sound, then a long pause, and finally a dial tone. The blips did not sound abnormal, but my phone doesn't make that sound. Then I recalled that I had heard the blip sounds before at a friend's house. I realized that it is the sound that the telephone company's voicemail system makes when the customer has a message waiting. I recalled that my friend used to check her voicemail messages first, clear them, then dial out with the modem. If there were no voicemail messages waiting, there were no blip sounds.

Conclusion: I advised the user to always check for voicemail messages before dialing the Internet phone number. I also found a setting in the terminal emulator software that controls the amount of time the software listens for a dial tone before it gives up. I set the time to 20 seconds in case the user forgot to check for voicemail messages.

The problem was an interesting one, and I was glad I was able to solve it. I learned that users don't always know the answers to the questions I ask. In this case, the user's answers threw me off track. I also used my personal experience to identify the voicemail sound on the phone line. The rest of the process was eliminating variables (when I replaced the modem with the telephone handset) and hypothesis testing. [*Based on an incident reported by Jaime Chamoulos.*]

PROBLEM 3: GIVE CREDIT WHERE IT IS DUE

Problem: I am a support person in an online ticket sales company. A computer operator is responsible for running an electronic data interchange (EDI) software package to process credit card transactions. The program uses a modem to send batches of credit card transactions to a credit card processor. The credit card processor then authenticates each transaction and processes it with the financial institution that issued the credit card.

The computer operator was frustrated and unhappy with the EDI software because the program would not process batches of transactions correctly, so she had to call in each transaction individually. She had called the software vendor about the problem. The vendor said the problem was likely on the credit card processor's end. So the operator called the credit card processor; they pointed the finger back at the software package. I was assigned the task of finding the cause of the problem.

Problem–solving strategy: Before I contacted the software company again, I wanted to make sure I understood how the software was supposed to work and that I understood what the real problem was. I considered that the problem could be with the EDI software program, the credit card processor, or the computer operators procedures.

I started at the top of the list and arbitrarily assumed that the problem was with the software program. I decided to install it on my own computer, read through the manual, and use the computer operator's notes to learn how to process batches of transactions. Although the software documentation was not extensive, I eventually pieced together enough information so that I understood how the program worked. The simple test cases that I constructed seemed to work fine. I decided to write up some better documentation for the computer operator based on the software manual, her notes, and a couple of calls I made to the software company to clarify some points in the batch processing procedure.

Then the computer operator and I sat down and went through the process of building a batch of transactions with some actual data. We used my expanded documentation as a guide. The batch file we sent seemed to process okay, but we did not receive an expected confirmation that the transactions were received or accepted. According to the software manual, the credit card processor should have returned a report file to us to indicate a normal termination of the batch process along with the status of each transaction. The next day, I called the credit card

12

processor to see if they could verify that the transactions we sent had indeed been received and approved. They had been, so we knew that the expanded procedure documentation was accurate. We could now transmit batches of transactions.

However, we now had a new problem: Why didn't we receive the confirming report file from the credit card processor? I tried to display the report file from within the EDI software, but nothing happened. I poked around the system and eventually found the report file. It was there, after all. I used a file diagnosis utility to examine the report file. My examination revealed that the report file actually did contain all the information that successful batches of transactions had been sent and received, including the ones we had sent the previous day. But somehow the program could not display the report file. Then I noticed some corrupted data at the beginning of the file that was in a different format from the remainder of the file. I made a backup copy of the old report file as a precaution and then deleted the original report file. The next day, we ran a batch of about 200 transactions. The credit card processor received the transactions, processed them, and returned the report file successfully. I figure the corrupted data in the report file was probably due to an error the computer operator made because she didn't really understand all the steps to transmit batches. Once I removed the corrupted data, the report displayed correctly.

Conclusion: I used a lot of trial-and-error and hypothesis testing on this problem. I also tried to replicate on my own system the problem the operator experienced. To this day, I'm not sure I understand the exact error the computer operator made. She was very frustrated and obviously needed better documentation. Based on the documentation I prepared, she has been able to process batches correctly ever since I worked on this problem. [*Based on an incident described by Mark Gauthier.*]

PROBLEM 4: THE OVERDRIVE LOCKUP

Problem: I had installed a Pentium Overdrive processor on a 486DX machine in order to improve its performance. After installation, the system would occasionally lock up and not boot.

Problem-solving strategy: I reread all the documentation that came with the overdrive processor. The booklet indicated that I might need to change a jumper or a dip switch on the motherboard. So I called the company that manufactured the motherboard and asked their advice. The first support person I talked with said the jumper settings were fine. He suggested that I change some CMOS settings. The changed settings did not seem to affect the lockup problem.

I called the motherboard manufacturer back and asked to talk with someone who had experience with overdrive processors. This support technician had me change the CMOS settings back to the way they were set prior to the first call. I described the configuration of the 486 system and mentioned to him that it was using a translation software utility to enable it to access a hard drive larger than 504 MB, which was the maximum size the version of the BIOS in the 486 would support. He said the translation software should not make a difference. He suggested that I comment out (put the command REM in front of) a couple of power saver definitions in the WIN.INI file. That did not solve the problem either.

On my third call, I explained the problem to the call dispatcher and was referred to a higher level of tech support. This person suggested that I make a couple of changes to the way the hard drive was defined in the CMOS and reinstall the hard drive translation software. I asked whether reinstallation of the translation utility would wipe out the data on the hard drive. He thought it probably would.

At this point, I decided it was time to reassess my troubleshooting strategy. I felt that I had just been trying things for the sake of trying them, and that I did not have a consistent strategy. I tried to think of other plausible alternatives that would explain the lockup problem. My inclination was to try to rule out the hard drive translation software as a potential problem. So I called the tech support staff that supplied the translation utility to ask if they knew of any conflicts that might occur between the Pentium Overdrive processor and their hard drive translation package. They immediately replied that their translation package does not work with overdrive processors. I asked if there was a workaround and learned that there was not. After I removed the overdrive processor from the 486 system, the lockup problem disappeared.

Conclusion: Although I did not successfully meet the initial goal to upgrade the processor in the 486 system, I was pleased that I had the patience to keep working on the problem until I discovered the incompatibility problem. I learned that it is very important to be patient and persistent with technical support staff and to follow up with repeat calls until a problem gets resolved. I also feel it is important to avoid a random, hit-and-miss approach to problem solving. I thought it was important to pause when I hit what appeared to be a dead end, examine the assumptions I was making, and look at other alternatives. [*Based on an incident described by Nancy Todd.*]

PROBLEM 5: THE PATH NOT TAKEN

Problem: The call came into the support center late one afternoon. A user said that one of his PC systems could no longer access my company's vertical market software. The rest of our support staff was in a training seminar for the afternoon, so I had to solve the problem on my own. As a new member of the support staff, I was a little nervous. The user on the phone said that he had been able to run the software successfully earlier in the day, but he had lost the desktop icon to run our software package.

Problem-solving strategy: After asking a few questions and paraphrasing some of his statements, I clarified that the icon for our software was actually still on the desktop but that double-clicking on it produced no results. I asked several other questions, including the critical question, "What were you doing on the system when the icon stopped working?" The user responded that he had been cleaning up some unwanted files.

My first thought was that perhaps the user had accidentally deleted the .EXE file associated with the icon. I led him through the steps to see if the .EXE program file was still in the correct subdirectory and it was. My next thought was that perhaps the shortcut path from the icon to the .EXE file had been destroyed. After checking the shortcut properties, we confirmed that the path was in place. Then I wondered if the user had somehow deleted the path to some of the files the program needs to operate. I wasn't sure how to check that, but I knew that some of the files were on a server and that each client machine defines the drive mappings to the network drives when it boots up. I explained my reasoning to the user and suggested that he quit all applications and shut down his system, just as if it was the end of the day. We waited a few seconds and then rebooted his system. After the reboot, everything worked fine. Apparently, he accidentally erased the drive mappings during his system housekeeping.

Conclusion: I was pleased to be able to handle the call, which was one of my first as a support specialist. I used several troubleshooting strategies, including communications skills to listen to the user's definition of the problem, paraphrasing, and critical questions to give me the information I needed to formulate a hypothesis. I also used a mental image of the sequence from the icon to the disk files to troubleshoot the problem. [*Based on an incident reported by Andra Heath.*]

PROBLEM 6: THE NONRESPONSIVE NETWORK

Problem: I am the network support assistant for an economic think tank. One afternoon I received a call from a staff member who reported that something was wrong with his workstation. He said it was very sluggish. I walked down the hall and looked at his workstation, which was running Excel. The user was in the process of saving a worksheet on the file server, but the server had not yet responded to the save command.

Problem-solving strategy: I canceled the save operation. Before I investigated the problem further, as a precaution, I tried to save the user's worksheet on the local hard drive instead of on the file server. This time the save operation worked fine, so I thought it was unlikely the user's PC was the problem. My attention immediately turned to the server.

I went to the computer room where the server is located and found that the display screen was blank. I noticed that the power lamp indicators were lit on both the server and the display, however, so I eliminated the likelihood of a power supply problem. I used a workstation we keep in the computer room to monitor network activity to try to log in to the server, but the attempt failed. Then I tried to reboot the server. It did not appear to boot, but I couldn't tell much because the display screen was still blank. I thought that perhaps there was a problem with the monitor, but I wasn't sure. However, I felt that I needed to fix the problem with the monitor first, so I could get feedback on the situation with the server. I disconnected the monitor from the server and borrowed a monitor and cable from the nearby workstation. After I plugged in a different monitor, the server still didn't appear to boot and the display screen was still blank. So the monitor was probably not related to the problem.

Since I was focused on the blank monitor screen, my next thought was to replace the video card in the server. So I pulled the video card from the nearby workstation and replaced the one in the server with one I knew was operational. When I rebooted the server, the result was the same blank monitor screen. At this point, I stopped to think about the subsystems that were involved in the display screen problem. I sketched on a notepad the monitor, the cable, the video card, the motherboard, and the power supply. Since the power supply lamp was lit, and since I had replaced everything else, I looked at the motherboard. I could not see any visible problems with it. I decided to set up a substitute server. First I returned the borrowed video card and monitor back to the workstation. I then removed the hard drive from the inoperable server and installed it in the workstation. Finally, I crossed my fingers and rebooted the substitute server. It came up OK. The motherboard apparently was the problem.

Conclusion: I received a call from the repair shop the next day that confirmed my suspicion that the server motherboard was damaged. It had several burned-out components and needed to be replaced. I obviously relied heavily in this situation on a module replacement strategy and on my knowledge of how the subsystems in a computer are linked together. The incident confirmed for me that users are not always capable of diagnosing the problem, which turned out to be with the server and not with his workstation.

This chapter's purpose has been to describe some common sources of problems support specialists are likely to encounter in their work and to provide some examples of several problem types. One theme that runs throughout the discussion of troubleshooting and problem solving in Chapters 11 and 12 is the important role information resources play in the pursuit of solutions to problems. In Chapter 13, you'll learn about some resources that can help you become a more effective troubleshooter and support specialist.

CHAPTER SUMMARY

- Although computer problems vary widely, there are a few categories of problems that account for most user contacts with help desks, hotlines, or support centers. The common categories include hardware problems, software problems, user problems, documentation problems, vendor problems, and facilities problems.

- Common hardware problems include difficulties with installation of hardware components, compatibility of new or upgraded components with other hardware in a system, hardware configuration problems, and actual malfunctions that require repair or replacement.

- Common software problems include difficulties with installation (although these problems are less common today than they were with earlier generations of software), incompatibilities with other software packages or with hardware, or configuration problems that prevent the software from operating correctly. Other software problems may be due to bugs or performance problems.

- User problems are caused by mistakes all users make, misunderstandings about how a system operates to perform a task, the purchase of the wrong products to perform a task, poor training, failure to read product documentation, and forgotten procedures or passwords.

- Other problems include difficulties with documentation (such as poor organization, and incorrect or incomplete information), vendor problems (such as a tendency for some vendors to oversell their products, misrepresent product features, deliver software with known bugs, and deliver products later than they were promised), and facilities problems (such as problems with security viruses, backups, and ergonomic issues).

12

KEY TERMS

- **bugs** — Errors in a computer program that occur when a programmer writes incorrect coded instructions during program development.

- **burn-in** — A 48- to 72-hour period during which a new computer is operated nonstop in an attempt to discover obvious problems and identify any marginal or temperature-sensitive components.

- **configuration problems** — Difficulties caused when the hardware or software settings are incorrect for the computer environment in which a component must operate.

- **conflict** — A state where two computer components use systems resources (CPU, memory, or peripheral devices) in a way that is incompatible with another component.

- **incompatible** — Describes computer components that cannot operate together successfully in the same system. See also **conflict**.

- **installation software** — Special-purpose utility software that aids in the installation of other software packages; installation software is often able to detect and correctly configure software for most operating environments.

- **patch** — A replacement for one or a few small modules in a software package that fixes known bugs; a patch is usually designated by adding a digit or letter to a version number (for example, a patch to version 1.5 becomes version 1.51 or 1.5A).

- **performance problems** — A category of computer problems where a system is operational but does not operate as efficiently as it can or should; performance problems often involve the interaction of hardware and software.

- **Plug and Play standards** — A computer industry agreement between hardware and operating system vendors; the standards specify the communication methods an operating system uses to recognize and incorporate hardware components into an operational system.

- **quick start behavior** — A tendency among computer users to forego reading the installation manual and get a new hardware or software component installed and operational as rapidly as possible.

- **release** — An updated version of a software program that contains some new features the original program did not have.

- **update** — A bug fix release that repairs known bugs in a previous version or release of a software package.

- **upgrade** — A new version of an existing program that is sold at a lower cost to owners of a previous version of the program.

- **vaporware** — Hardware or software products that are described in ads or press releases but that don't really exist.

- **version** — A new release of a software package that contains significant new features and is usually the result of a substantially rewritten program.

- **workaround** — A procedure or feature that accomplishes the same result as another feature that does not work due to a bug or other malfunction.

REVIEW QUESTIONS

1. Describe the common categories of support problems that account for most of the calls to a help desk or support group.

2. Why do problems occur during hardware installation? Give an example of a hardware installation problem.

3. Define hardware incompatibility. Give an example.

4. What is a hardware configuration problem? Give an example.

5. How do Plug and Play standards reduce the occurrence of hardware configuration problems?

6. What is a hardware malfunction? Why are hardware components usually replaced rather than repaired?

7. Describe the hardware burn-in procedure and explain its purpose.

8. Which computer components are more likely to fail, electronic devices such as memory chips or electromechanical devices such as disk drives? Explain why.

9. What is the purpose of installation utility software? What problem is it designed to solve?

10. What is a software incompatibility problem? Give an example from your own experience.

11. Describe software configuration problems. Give an example of one that occurs with operating systems and one that occurs with applications software.

12. Explain why a new printer driver was needed when the user in the chapter purchased an ink-jet printer for a Windows 3.1 system.

13. Explain why software bugs occur. Give an example of a bug you have encountered.

14. Explain the significance of a software package whose version is 6.22.

15. What is a workaround? When is one useful?

16. Define a performance problem and give an example.

17. Why are so many computer problems traceable to user mistakes? Describe a recent mistake you made as a computer user. Do you think it is a common mistake?

18. What is the difference between a user mistake and a misunderstanding?

19. Explain several different ways a user can end up purchasing the wrong computer product. Include both hardware and software examples.

20. Describe quick start behavior and what support specialists or vendors can do about it.

21. What are some strategies for dealing with users who forget important information?

22. How can poor documentation affect the kind of calls a support center receives?

23. Do you agree or disagree with the statement, "Network problems are not a unique category; all network problems are basically hardware or software problems"? Explain your reasoning.

HANDS-ON PROJECTS

The Hands-on projects in this chapter provide an opportunity to gain additional experience with troubleshooting and problem solving. The projects vary in difficulty from easy to challenging. They require a variety of problem-solving skills and information resources to find the answers. Use them as practice to build your troubleshooting and problem-solving skills. But do not spend too long on any one project. If you run into a roadblock and can't find the answer, ask your instructor or colleagues for assistance.

PROJECT 12-1

Learn about the Year 2000 (Y2K) problem on microcomputers. Find out about specific tests that a support specialist can run to determine whether the BIOS on a PC will handle dates after December 31, 1999. Also find out about ways to test whether the BIOS in a PC handles the February 29, 2000, leap year correctly. Write a one-page documentation sheet for end users that they can use to test their own PCs to determine Y2K readiness.

PROJECT 12-2

A user would like to use the advanced statistical functions and features in the Excel spreadsheet program because she does a lot of statistical work in her job. She has a book that explains how to use these features. She clicked on the Tools menu in Excel but did not find the Data Analysis menu item the book she was reading had described. She also tried to use some of the built-in statistical functions that are supposed to be included in Excel according to her book, but she got an error message, #NAME?, wherever she entered one of the function names. Describe the steps the user would need to take in order to be able to use the statistical functions.

PROJECT 12-3

Find out if there is a utility program on your Windows 95 system named MSInfo32.exe. If you can find it, where is it located? Use the MSInfo32 help system to learn about the features of the program. Write a brief description of its purpose and to whom it would be useful.

 PROJECT 12-4

A user received some software installation disks from Microsoft that were marked "Distribution Media Format (DMF)." The user wanted to make backup copies of the installation disks as a precaution but discovered that the DMF diskettes could not be copied with DISKCOPY or other utilities. The user learned that the DMF format has some advantages. First, 1.7MB of space is available in the DMF format, which reduces the number of diskettes required by Microsoft to distribute its software. Second, since the disks cannot be copied with standard utilities, the DMF format reduces the number of illegal copies that are made. However, the user wonders if there is any way to make backup copies of her original installation disks. She says the software manuals used to warn users to "make backup copies of the distribution disks before installing the software." That warning still makes good sense to her. Is there a way to copy DMF format disks? Research this issue and write a documentation sheet for other users based on your findings.

12

 PROJECT 12-5

An e-mail message from a user says, "I am just beginning to use Excel spreadsheets after using Lotus 1-2-3 spreadsheets for several years. Whenever I enter a number in a cell, Excel adds a decimal point, even if the number format I use doesn't include a decimal point. It just doesn't look right to have an integer number like 5280 displayed as 5280. with the decimal point. Is this a bug in Excel? How can I fix the problem?" Research the problem and write an e-mail response to the user with the information you found.

 PROJECT 12-6

A user asks your advice about how to automatically load an ASCII text file into NOTEPAD. He says that he knows Windows 95 recognizes certain extensions. For example, it recognizes a .TXT extension as a text file and when the user double-clicks the file, Windows will automatically open it with NOTEPAD. An .XLS extension indicates an Excel worksheet and Windows 95 will automatically open it in Excel. The user says he regularly receives ASCII text files from an information clearinghouse with an extension .RPT. He would like to be able to double-click on the file and open it automatically with NOTEPAD. Describe the procedure that will let him tell Windows 95 that any file with an .RPT extension is a NOTEPAD file.

PROJECT 12-7

A user who is away from her office for much of the day wants to keep a simple log of contacts and short notes about client meetings she has throughout the day. She would like to include the current date and time for each entry in the log. She says a work colleague has an icon on her laptop that automatically opens NOTEPAD and inserts an entry in the file that contains the current date and time. Then it is easy to make an entry about a meeting with a client. She would like you to set up her laptop with a similar feature. Write a documentation sheet listing the steps she should take to accomplish this task.

CASE PROJECTS

1. FRED'S PAINT STORE

The help desk at Fred's Paints has analyzed the database of calls it received in the past month to identify the top ten most common calls. As part of a project to write model answers for help desk staff to answer frequently asked questions, they would like you to research and write documentation that can be sent to users on disk space management. Specifically, the help desk staff finds that many calls with disk space complaints come from users who say that they have run out of space on their hard drives. Most of these calls come from active e-mail users and users who frequently download information from the Internet. Other calls come from users who have used their PCs for several years, and often the systems were purchased with smaller hard drives than those available today. In each of these cases, the hard drives on their Windows 95 PCs are now full, and they want to be able to do something short of replacing the hard drive.

Your task is to investigate common ways the space on a hard drive gets filled up. As one resource, you may want to compare your ideas, experiences, and findings with those of your coworkers or students in your project group. Then write a document for support staff to provide to end users that describes the reasons why the drives become full and the procedures you recommend to free up disk space. Organize your document as a checklist, but include any explanations and precautions you feel are necessary before a user embarks on a procedure to reclaim disk space on a hard drive.

2. MEDIA CRITIC

Your town's public library has a variety of lecture series on topics of interest to its residents. One series is for computer users. They have asked you to participate in a presentation on resources for computer users. They would like you to critique locally available radio and newspaper problem-solving resources.

Many local radio stations carry programs aimed at computer users. Some feature local experts; others are nationally syndicated programs. They invite listeners to phone or e-mail the program about problems they are having with their computer system. Similarly, local newspapers frequently publish advice columns specifically for computer users. They often offer advice to users who write or e-mail their problems.

Consult your local newspaper to identify radio programs or newspaper columns intended for computer user audiences. Your instructor may be able to help you identify programs or columns in your local area. Listen to a couple of computer-oriented programs or read several newspaper columns that answer questions for computer users. Based on the categories of common problems described in this chapter, analyze the kinds of questions users ask. Are some categories more common than others? Do you agree or disagree with the answers provided? How could the answers be improved? Evaluate their technical accuracy, communications style, and alternative explanations or solutions. Write a short paper that analyzes the categories of questions, answers provided, and your evaluation of the program or column.

12

3. EVELYN TONOLO'S COMPUTER UPGRADE

Evelyn Tonolo is a teacher in the English department at Willagansett Community College. She teaches courses in literature, including a very popular course in films as literature. As a help desk staff member at Willagansett CC, you received the following e-mail from Evelyn.

```
To: helpdesk@wcc3.edu

From: etonolo@wcc1.edu

Date: 1-Sept-98

Re: Computer Upgrade

I've read in one of the academic journals to which I subscribe that
an increasing number of films will be available during the 1998-1999
academic year on a new type of disk media called a Digital Video Disk
(DVD). I would like to be able to obtain and view videos distributed
in the new format. If possible, I want to upgrade the PC in my office
to be able to play the DVD films. Otherwise, I need to ask my depart-
ment chair for a new computer.
```

My current system is a 133 Mhz Pentium with 16 MB RAM, a 1 GB hard drive, and a 12X CD-ROM drive. I currently run Windows 95 but could upgrade to Windows 98 if that would be desirable. Could you please tell me whether my PC can be upgraded to play DVD disks? What is involved in the upgrade and approximately what would it cost?

Thanks very much for your advice!

Eve

Your task is to investigate Digital Video Disk drives, collect the information you need to answer her questions, and respond to Evelyn's e-mail.

4. RALPH'S IRKSOME IRQS

A neighbor, Ralph, who knows you work with computers, drops by after work one evening. He explains that he just purchased a new sound card, CD-ROM drive, and speakers for his Windows 3.1 system. Ralph says he had no problem installing the new hardware in his system unit, but now he gets a message on his screen that says something about a device conflict because a device is already in use. The computer store employee where he purchased the new hardware said something about device IRQ conflicts, but Ralph tells you that he doesn't really understand what they are or whether they can be fixed. He'd like your help.

Explain how you would determine whether an IRQ conflict exists in Ralph's Windows 3.1 system, and if one does, write a summary of the steps you would take to identify the problem and fix it.

INFORMATION RESOURCES FOR USER SUPPORT

As a user support specialist, you will bring to any job a wealth of information. In your coursework, you have probably learned a great deal about hardware and software systems, and, in earlier chapters in this text, you learned about the major user support topic areas that a potential employer will expect you to know. You will use this information to help users solve problems. But chances are you won't be able to answer every question or solve every problem. No support specialist can; there will always be new problems, and the rapid introduction of hardware and software products means that all specialists have to use information resources to find answers to difficult problems and to keep their knowledge current.

In this chapter, you will examine the major types of information available and learn how to find information you will need to keep up-to-date. You will then learn about some representative print, interactive and informal resources you can use to find information.

AFTER READING THIS CHAPTER AND COMPLETING THE EXERCISES YOU WILL BE ABLE TO:

- Understand the role of information resources in a user support organization
- Understand the types of user support information available
- Use effective search strategies to locate information resources for user support
- Use common information resources to respond to user questions

THE ROLE OF INFORMATION RESOURCES IN USER SUPPORT

Information plays a central role in user support organizations. Most users contact a help desk or user support center because they need information. The specific information they need may range from information about a product or service to information about how to solve a specific problem they have encountered. At its most basic level, a user support specialist's job is to collect, process, search, store, and distribute information.

User support specialists have always accessed information resources as they provide users with information or diagnose problems with computer systems. However, many of the resources support specialists use are now available to end users, including online help systems, CD-ROM databases, Internet search facilities, and so forth. Does widespread access to information resources mean that user support specialists are becoming obsolete? Probably not; support specialists often have a more finely tuned ability to find information, read and understand it, and separate what is important from what is not. They also have more skills that help them interpret the information and apply it to a particular situation. In addition, they are paid for the time it takes to find information; end users often do not have the time to find the specific information they need. In spite of increased accessibility of information to everyone, the role of the support specialist is as important as ever.

Few support specialists know everything necessary to perform the tasks described in this book. If you are preparing for a career in end user support, the best background you can expect to bring to a position is an interest in user support problems, a basic knowledge of computer technology, the ability to work with users, and a knowledge of where to look and how to search for information. Wouldn't it be ideal if you knew everything you needed to know from day one, or if someone could offer a course or training program that would package everything you needed to know in one place? It's a nice thought, but it isn't going to happen. The most significant difference between an experienced support specialist and an inexperienced one is her relative ability to locate and use information effectively and efficiently. An experienced specialist can find the desired information with a reasonable expenditure of effort.

TYPES OF USER SUPPORT INFORMATION

Information is available in a variety of forms to both users and support specialists. Some of the more popular formats are print publications, interactive resources, and informal resources.

PRINT PUBLICATIONS

Print publications include books and magazines in the following categories:

Technical documentation: User guides and reference manuals supplied by hardware and software vendors

Technical specifications and "white papers": Publications distributed by vendors to provide product information and briefings about solutions to technical problems

Trade books and textbooks: Books on specific hardware or software products for those who want to learn to use computer products

Trade publications: Periodicals that include

- *Computer magazines* sold in computer stores, newsstands, or by subscription

- *Controlled circulation periodicals* distributed free to those who make purchasing decisions

- *Computer-related journals* published by various professional organizations and associations for their members

Printed information has advantages and disadvantages. People whose work takes them away from their desks periodically prefer its portability. Readers often prefer printed material because they can grasp the entire work, understand its organization, and can navigate easily among sections. Many computer users find printed materials easier to read than on-screen displays, especially if they have a low resolution monitor. However, print is a very expensive and highly perishable medium. Especially in the computer field, where changes occur very rapidly, some printed items are obsolete before they are published! To overcome this problem, software packages frequently come with README files on the distribution media with late-breaking information.

INTERACTIVE RESOURCES

Interactive resources include a wide range of computer-accessible information, including the following:

13

Online help systems: Designed to augment technical documentation in a form that users can access easily as they use a software product

CD-ROM databases: Include technical and troubleshooting information about a vendor's products

The Internet: Includes several types of information available primarily on the World Wide Web that is accessible by search engines, which you'll learn about in the next section

Other Internet resources: Include Internet newsgroups, frequently asked questions (FAQs), ListServs, and chat rooms, which you'll learn about later in this section

Many print and interactive information sources either contain advertising or are published by manufacturers or product distributors. **Controlled circulation periodicals**, for example, are distributed free to qualified subscribers, but contain advertising. So readers should always be aware that they are not reading a completely unbiased source of information. In fact, controlled circulation periodicals often highlight a single product or products from a limited range of vendors. However, for owners of products supplied by a specific vendor, they may provide just the information some users need. As long as readers are aware of the information source and its possible biases, controlled circulation and vendor-specific information resources can be useful support tools.

Interactive and online materials (including CD-ROMs, help systems, and Internet knowledge-bases) are usually easier to search for a specific piece of information than printed materials. Some computer book publishers now package a CD-ROM version along with the printed version to overcome this shortcoming. However, CD-ROM databases share a problem with print media: Although they are more interactive because they are searchable, the information on a CD-ROM tends to become obsolete rapidly. Weekly, monthly, or quarterly trade periodicals often contain more up-to-date information than CD-ROMs, trade books, textbooks, and vendor manuals. A number of trade publications now offer readers Web-based updates between publication dates and archival access to previous articles. Web sites can provide up-to-the-minute changes in products and services, as long as their owners keep them up-to-date.

 In order to compensate for the perishability of printed information, many textbook publishers now maintain Web sites to provide students and instructors with updated information. This book, for example, has a Web page that you can access on the Internet through the Course Technology home page: **www.course.com**. It contains updated Web addresses for any sites listed in this book that have changed since publication.

Although Internet access is far from universal, computer users and most support specialists today find the Internet to be an exceptionally rich information resource. It is especially useful because many product vendors now use the Internet to distribute software and other information. This gives users and support specialists the latest information in an easily searchable form in a timely way, and at the lowest possible cost.

Although Web pages are exceedingly useful sources of information, they can be relatively static, like the pages in a book. Some Web pages never change and do not provide interactive or search capabilities. As is often the case, information on a Web page that hasn't been updated for several months may be obsolete. However, Web pages that are actively maintained provide a vehicle to disseminate up-to-date information worldwide instantaneously.

Beyond the Internet's information content lies a network of personal and professional contacts that can be a very fruitful resource for support specialists. These contact networks include:

- Subject-specific **newsgroups**—Internet special interest groups whose members exchange information and opinions on a variety of specific topics

- **Chat rooms**—online conferences where participants can read and write messages with special chat software

- ListServs—e-mail lists of subscribers to whom contributions are disseminated; ListServs are organized by topic and may be public or private and moderated (filtered for content) or unmoderated

- Electronic mail links to insiders in a vendor company

All of these Internet resources provide a second level of information assistance to those who need information.

 Newsgroups and home pages often include frequently asked questions, or FAQs, to provide new users with questions and answers that summarize previous discussions or common requests. Although FAQs are designed to protect newsgroup "old-timers" from basic questions from novice members, FAQs can be a good resource for support staff looking for answers to common user problems.

Experienced Internet users use bookmarks in their Web browsers to keep track of Internet sites that provide useful information. A **bookmark** is a shortcut to a URL to which a user expects to return. Bookmarks eliminate the need to type lengthy URLs, which is a difficult and error-prone task.

INFORMAL RESOURCES

In addition to printed and Internet sources of information, most successful support specialists develop a personal network of information resources. In many organizations, news about new software bugs, common troubleshooting experiences, and industry rumors spreads by word-of-mouth. In addition, support specialists often maintain a private e-mail list or limited focus ListServ to keep in touch with both internal and external colleagues who have common interests or who have been proven resources in prior problem situations.

Many cities have active user groups and professional associations that are attractive to employees in the support industry. Platform-specific user groups are common for Windows/Intel and Macintosh systems. Professional associations with local chapters include the ACM (formerly the Association for Computing Machinery) and the Association of Information Technology Professionals (AITP, formerly DPMA). Large associations and professional groups that cover a wide area of interests in the computer field sometimes encourage the formation of smaller special interest groups, or **SIGs**, for members who share a specific common interest. For example, the ACM has a SIG devoted to those with special interests in artificial intelligence.

A well-informed user or support specialist has access to a variety of information resources and knows where and how to search for the information necessary to make him- or herself and end users more productive.

13

EFFECTIVE SEARCH STRATEGIES

If the Internet is—or will become—an important tool in your information resources tool kit, it is necessary to learn how to access Internet information effectively. The primary search tool is a **search engine**, software that allows users to search Web sites using specific words related to the information they want to find. Some common search engines include Yahoo!, AltaVista, and Excite. There are also other ways to search the Internet for information. For example, many companies that sell hardware, software, and network products have home pages. A feature of many home pages is a site map. The **site map** is like an index to a Web site that describes the kinds of information users can find there. A site map is a list of **hyperlinks**, which are words or graphics users can click to view a topic on another page. Some sites have their own built-in keyword search or query features. Another way to locate Internet information is through the subject matter index on a search engine's home page. For example, the home page for the search engine Yahoo, at **www.yahoo.com**, lists several categories of information, as shown in Figure 13-1. Users can **drill down**, or follow the hyperlinks to locate specific information that interests them.

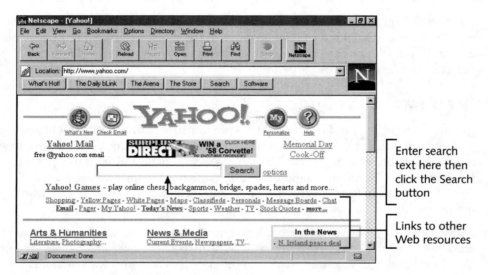

Figure 13-1 Yahoo search engine home page

Web sites like Yahoo that started off as search engines, but that now provide links to many other Web resources, are often called **portals** because they act as doorways to the vast amount of information now available on the Internet.

Each search engine has its own unique search tools and methods. Most users and support specialists try several search engines and eventually find one they like and stick with it.

Here are some general strategies that are common to many search engines.

> **Natural language searches.** Many search engines permit users to enter a **natural language query**, a question in the form of a sentence or phrase users might use in everyday speech, such as, *How do I use a search engine?*

> **Keyword search.** In a **keyword search**, a user enters one or more words to indicate the subject of the information sought. For example, to locate information on a specific model of Canon printer, a user might enter *Canon BubbleJet BJC 4300.*

Include or exclude keywords. An include or exclude feature lets a user list several related keywords with an inclusion symbol (+) or an exclusion symbol (-) to include or eliminate specific words from the search. For example, to locate information about IOMEGA (the company), but not about the ZIP disks (one of its major products), a user could enter:

+IOMEGA -ZIP

This means that the Web page references the search engine finds *must* contain the word *IOMEGA*, but *cannot* contain the word *ZIP*.

Exact phrases. To find references that contain an exact phrase, enclose them in quotes. For example "hard disk drive" would find references that contain exactly that phrase, but would not find references that contain only the phrase *"disk drive."*

Languages. A search engine may allow users to limit a search to specific languages. For example, a user could specify a search for items that are in English or French.

Domain limitations. Some search engines permit other limitations, such as a limitation on the domain of the search. For example, a user can specify a search limited to the World Wide Web or can also include newsgroups and so on.

Case sensitivity. Most searches are not sensitive to upper- and lowercase letters. This means that if you type the search string *windows*, it will find the same references as it would if you typed *WINDOWS* or *Windows*. However, a search engine may include an option to limit searches to references that contain exact case matches.

Wildcard search. The asterisk wildcard symbol (*) is used in a **wildcard search** to help users broaden a search to make sure that all forms of a root word are included. For example, the search string *troubleshoot** would locate references to troubleshooting, troubleshooter, troubleshooters, and so on.

AND searches. An **AND (&) search** provides a way to narrow a search by using AND as a conjunction between two simple keywords. For example, a search for *Works & spreadsheet* would locate references that contain both the word *Works* and the word *spreadsheet* somewhere on the Web page. AND searches are called narrowing searches because they reduce the total number of references located compared with a search for either word by itself. Some search engines use AND and others use & as the symbol for an AND search.

OR searches. An **OR (|) search** provides a way to broaden a search by using OR as a conjunction between two simple keywords. For example, a search for *Microsoft | IBM* would find all references that contain Microsoft, plus those that contain IBM. The OR search includes references that contain both but also those that contain *either* one. Some search engines use OR and others use | as the symbol for an OR search.

Figure 13-2 shows the AltaVista search engine and a search request for the exact words *"technical support jobs"*.

13

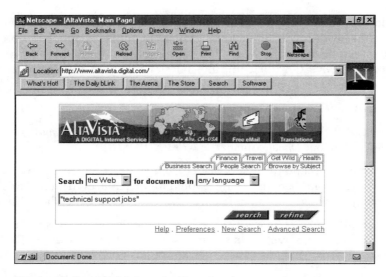

Figure 13-2 AltaVista search engine home page

To learn more about Internet search engines, including a list of popular ones, their Internet addresses, their strengths and limitations, and more about how to construct effective searches, there are several Web sites with relevant information. For example, see CMP Media's NetGuide at **www.netguide.com/guide/internet/searching.html**.

As with any tool, you need to practice using a search engine to become proficient at searches. The Internet is a rich resource of information, but locating the information needed is a job skill that is worth developing for a support specialist.

INFORMATION RESOURCES FOR USER SUPPORT

The information resources in the sections that follow are organized in the same way as the topics in this book: by user support task. These resource listings are not exhaustive, but they provide examples of information resources and references to some that others in the support field have found useful. This section is not a buying guide; no endorsement of the products or services listed is implied. Over time, you will probably develop your own resource list. It's a good idea to keep it in a handy location and in a format that is easy to update.

This listing contains the most recent version of each resource at the time this book went to press. Some of the print resources have dates as far back as the early 1990s. For periodicals, dates older than a year or so would likely indicate dated information. For books in particular areas, however, such as documentation, the information is still timely today.

The information resources in each section are grouped by the type of resource.

End User Computing

Print

Ralph M. Stair, Jr., and George Walter Reynolds, *Principles of Information Systems: A Managerial Approach*, 3rd ed., Cambridge, Mass.: Course Technology, 1997.

> Stair and Reynold's text is an introduction to computers and information systems in businesses and organizations. It includes information on end user computing and end user computing tools to supplement the information in Chapters 1 and 2 in this book.

Barbara McNurlin and Ralph Sprague, Jr., *Information Systems Management in Practice*, 4th ed., Englewood Cliffs, N.J.: Prentice-Hall, 1997.

> McNurlin and Sprague's book is aimed primarily at those who manage information systems in businesses and organizations. Chapters discuss the management of end user computing and end user computing technologies.

Internet

Ziff-Davis' job search: **www.jobengine.com**

> A service by computer periodical publisher Ziff-Davis for those looking for employment in the computer industry. Allows users to post a resume and also contains a search engine for employers to find resumes of those looking for work.

State of Oregon employment Web site: **www.emp.state.or.us**

> There are many job search Web sites on the Internet. This one is state-specific to Oregon. Many state human resources departments have similar services. Use an Internet search engine to locate one for your state.

Product Evaluation

Print

PC Today is a monthly publication that reviews hardware products and trends. It frequently contains articles that compare competing products. An interesting monthly feature, MarketWatch, tracks the latest trends in the prices of hardware components, with graphs of 18- to 24-month trends. Address: 120 West Harvest Drive, Lincoln, NE 68521; phone (800) 544-1426. Web address: **www.pctoday.com**.

Hardware and software product evaluation articles are frequently published in several trade publications, including *PC Week*, *InfoWorld*, *Byte*, *PC Magazine*, and others.

INTERNET

The following Web sites have information on benchmarking popular computer products:

Bapco home page	**www.bapco.com**
Ziff-Davis benchmark operation home page	**www.zdbop.com**
Standard Product Evaluation home page	**www.spec.org**

The following are Web sites with links to hardware and software suppliers that do business via mail order or directly over the Internet:

PriceScan home page	**www.pricescan.com**
ComputerESP home page	**www.uvision.com**
Ziff-Davis Computer Shopper NetBuyer home page	**www.netbuyer.com**
PriceWatch Corporation home page	**www.pricewatch.com**

The following Web site has an extensive library of downloadable freeware and shareware demonstration and evaluation versions of software:

CNET Download home page	**www.download.com**

User Needs Assessment

PRINT

Many popular textbooks on systems analysis and design cover user needs assessment. However, these books usually assume that the prospective system will be built or programmed from scratch. The following resources assume the system will be purchased, not built.

Joseph Beckman, *The Small Business Computer Guide.* Boston: Digital Press, 1995.

Shelley O'Hara, *10 Minute Guide to Buying a Computer.* Indianapolis, Ind.: Alpha Books, 1994.

Sterling Software, *Selecting and Implementing Packaged Software: Executive Briefing.* Sterling Software Applications Development Division, 1997.

> The Sterling publication is an example of an industry "white paper." Sterling Software is in the applications software business, but the publication contains some useful strategies to minimize risk when selecting software. Sterling Software, 6620 Chase Oaks Blvd., Plano, TX 75023.

SYSTEM INSTALLATION

PRINT

Most documentation on system installation is published by hardware, software, and network vendors. For popular products, however, trade publications such as these are designed to supplement vendor documentation:

Rob Tidrow, *Windows 98 Installation and Configuration Handbook*. Indianapolis, Ind.: Que Education & Training, 1998.

Susan Plumley, *Documented NT Server: A Start-To-Finish Network*. New York: John Wiley & Sons, 1997.

Jess Curry, Jr., and David Bonner, *Up and Running: The Small Business Computer Implementation Cookbook*. Englewood Cliffs, N.J.: Spectrum Books (Prentice-Hall), 1984.

END USER TRAINING

PRINT

Elizabeth Regan and Bridget O'Connor, *End-User Information Systems: Perspectives for Managers and Information Systems Professionals*. New York: Macmillan, 1994.

> This is a good book on the development of end user information systems. Although the book focuses on development, Chapter 15 covers training end users.

Geoffrey Moss, *The Corporate Trainer's Quick Reference*. Homewood, Ill.: Irwin, 1993.

> Moss' book is full of information for technology trainers about the pros and cons of various training methods and delivery systems. It also provides suggestions for trainers about effective uses of training methods and materials.

Technology Training is published by Ziff-Davis, 10 Presidents Landing, Medford, MA 02155; phone (888) 950-4302, Web address: **www.ittrain.com**.

> This monthly controlled circulation periodical includes articles of interest to end user trainers and managers of end user training programs. Many companies with computer-based training modules and other products aimed at the training industry advertise in this publication.

Syllabus, Syllabus Press, 345 Northlake Drive, San Jose, CA 95117; phone (800) 773-0670, Web address: **www.syllabus.com**.

> This is a monthly controlled circulation publication of Syllabus Press, which also operates a LISTSERV. To join, send e-mail to **syllabus-request@lists.best.com**. Include in the message: subscribe [your e-mail address].

> *Syllabus* contains articles about the applications of technology to training and education, with special emphasis on higher education. It frequently includes articles on

13

distance education, the impact of technology on curriculum, and the use of the Internet as a delivery vehicle in training and education.

T.H.E. Journal (Technological Horizons in Education), 150 El Camino Real, Suite 112, Tustin, CA 92780-3670; phone (714) 730-4011, Web address: **www.thejournal.com**.

> *T.H.E. Journal* is a monthly controlled circulation publication that includes a variety of articles that describe computer applications in education and training. A number of companies that sell educational software, as well as hardware such as projection systems, multimedia systems, and security devices, advertise in *T.H.E. Journal*.

Oregon Education Association, *Technology Issues for Educators.* Tigard, Ore.: Oregon Education Association, 1997.

> This publication summarizes legal issues that educators and trainers should know about. It discusses fair use of copyrighted materials in classrooms.

OTHER

Courses

Several companies provide contract and customized training courses for various purposes. For example, Microsoft licenses companies to be Authorized Technical Education Centers that are qualified to offer courses in a specialized Microsoft curriculum. Many of these courses can lead to Microsoft certification for those who pass a test. An example of an authorized training center is Global Knowledge Network, PO Box 2055, Nashua, NH, 03060-9982; phone (800) 332-5656. Global Knowledge Network offers courses nationwide that cover many Microsoft products.

Videos

KeyStone Learning Systems is an example of a company that markets training videos. They offer a broad product line of videos at progressively graded levels for popular operating systems and applications software. Videos and computer-based training are especially good ways for small companies with limited training budgets to train employees at a reasonable cost per person. Address: 2241 Larsen Parkway, Provo, UT 84606; phone (888) 288-3658. Web address: **www.klscorp.com/iwm**.

Seminars

TechLink Training, PO Box 226, Fanwood, NJ 07023, is a company that offers seminars specifically designed to train help desk employees; examples of seminar topics include Managing a Customer Support Help Desk and Customer Service Excellence.

A company that offers specialized training for support professionals is Pink Elephant, 3430 South Service Rd., Burlington, Ontario, L7N 3T9; phone (888) 273-PINK, Web site: **www.pinkelephant.com**.

END USER DOCUMENTATION

PRINT

Microsoft Corporation, The *Microsoft Manual of Style for Technical Publications*. Redmond, Wash.: Microsoft Press, 1995.

> Microsoft's style guide is an excellent resource for technical writers, whether about Microsoft products or others.

Lyn Dupre, *Bugs in Writing.* Reading, Mass.: Addison–Wesley, 1998.

> Dupre's book describes a number of common problems technical writers experience and offers suggestions for writing improvement.

Carol Perry, *The Fine Art of Technical Writing.* Hillsboro, Ore.: Blue Heron Publishing, 1991.

> Perry's book is a short but complete introduction to technical writing. For a writer who needs to improve quickly and wants some basic suggestions, Perry's book is a good place to start.

William Strunk, Jr., and E. B. White, *The Elements of Style,* 3rd ed., New York: Macmillan, 1995.

> This classic book is a must-read for any writer. It discusses the mechanics of writing but is not specific to technical writing.

Smart Computing, Sandhills Publishing, 120 Harvest Drive, PO Box 85380, Lincoln, NE 85380; phone (800) 424-7900, Web address: **www.smartcomputing.com**.

> This is one of the best written of the regular computer periodicals aimed at the general population of computer users. The magazine prides itself on clearly written articles that address issues of interest to general users. It avoids jargon, acronyms, and highly technical explanations and information. It is both a good resource for end users and an inspiration to technical writers. It is also an excellent resource for new users and "technophobes." It is widely distributed in computer stores and newsstands.

13

FACILITIES MANAGEMENT

PRINT

ergonomic news, Penton Publications, 1100 Superior Ave., Cleveland, OH 44114-2543; phone (216) 696-7000.

> This bimonthly publication includes articles on ergonomic issues associated with computer use. Many companies that make ergonomic devices to solve specific workplace problems advertise in this controlled circulation magazine.

Patrick Bultema, *How to Design and Write Effective Customer Satisfaction Surveys.* Colorado Springs, Colo.: Help Desk Institute, 1993.

SC Magazine, West Coast Publishing, 498 Concord Street, Framingham, MA 01702-2357; phone (508) 879-9792, Web address: **www.infosecnews.com**.

> This controlled circulation monthly publication covers topics related to security in computer facilities and on the Internet.

Information Security Handbook for Enterprise Computing, AXENT Technologies, 2400 Research Blvd., Suite 200, Rockville, MD 20850; phone (800) 298-2620. Web address: **www.axent.com**.

> This is an example of a "white paper" published by a company that markets security software products. It contains several useful suggestions for creating company-wide security policies, procedures, guidelines, and standards. It also contains a description of the AXENT Technologies product line.

INTERNET

Michelle Weil and Larry Rosen's Web site: **www.technostress.com**

> This Web site is based on a book entitled *Technostress: Coping with Technology @WORK @HOME @PLAY* by Michelle Weil and Larry Rosen. The Web site includes a quiz to assess stress levels and tips for adjusting to the stress of working with technology.

HELP DESK OPERATION

PRINT

Donna Knapp, *A Guide to Help Desk Concepts.* Cambridge, Mass.: Course Technology, 1999.

Francoise Tourniaire and Richard Farrell, *The Art of Software Support: Design and Operation of Support Center and Help Desks.* Englewood Cliffs, N.J.: Prentice Hall, 1998.

Barbara Czegel, *Running an Effective Help Desk*: *Planning, Implementation, Marketing, Automating, Improving, Outsourcing.* New York: John Wiley, 1998.

> Czegel's book is one of the best-known books on help desk operation. It is primarily of interest to help desk managers, but support professionals can find useful information, too.

Navtej Khandpur and Lori Laub, *Delivering World-Class Technical Support.* New York: John Wiley, 1997.

Noel Bruton, *Effective User Support: How to Manage the IT Help Desk.* New York: McGraw-Hill, 1996.

Microsoft Corporation, *Sourcebook for the Help Desk,* 2nd ed. Redmond, Wash.: Microsoft Press, 1997.

Ron Muns, *The Help Desk Handbook.* Colorado Springs, Colo.: Help Desk Institute, 1993.

Ralph Wilson, *HELP! The Art of Computer Technical Support*. Berkeley, Calif.: PeachPit Press, 1991.

> Wilson's book was one of the first publications aimed at the user support profession. It is still one of the best sources for ideas on the communication and problem-solving interaction between users and support specialists.

Help Desk Institute (HDI)

> A professional organization that addresses issues and concerns of interest to managers and employees in the help desk industry. HDI publishes books and periodicals and sponsors seminars and conferences for members. It also has local chapters in major U.S. cities. Help Desk Institute, 650 Townsend Street, San Francisco, CA 94103-4908, phone (800) 248-5667. Web address: **www.HelpDeskInst.com**.

> Examples of Help Desk Institute print publications:

> Karen Eberhardt, *Customer Service Skills for Technical Support Professionals*, 1992.

> Karen Eberhardt, *Managing Stress: A Guide for Customer Support Professionals*, 1992.

Service News, United Publications, 106 Lafayette St., PO Box 995, Yarmouth, ME 04096; phone: (215) 788-7112, Web address: **www.servicenews.com**.

> This is a monthly controlled circulation periodical aimed at help desk professionals and managers. It covers the latest trends in support centers, training and certification, hardware maintenance, and help desk software tools and utilities. Each issue reviews one or more help desk software packages. The Web site includes a collection of previous articles and information useful to help desk employees. A buyer's guide to products and services is published annually.

Support Management, Target Communications Corporation, 535 Connecticut Avenue, Norwalk, CT 06854; phone (203) 857-5656, Web address: **www.supportmanagement.com**.

> This bimonthly controlled circulation periodical is aimed at managers in the information technology support and services industry. It frequently includes articles on help desks, end user training, third-party maintenance and service providers, and Web-based support alternatives.

Call Center, Telecom Library, 12 West 21 Street, New York, NY 10010; phone (800) 677-3435. Web address: **www.CallCenterMagazine.com**.

> This monthly periodical covers all types of call center operations, including computer help desks.

CTI magazine, Technology Marketing, One Technology Plaza, Norwalk, CT 06854; phone (800) 243-6002. Web address: **www.ctimag.com**.

> CTI is a controlled circulation monthly magazine, free to qualified subscribers, that covers the computer telephony industry. Includes articles on current products and services useful to help desk operations.

13

INTERNET

Viewz Online Magazine Web page: **www.viewz.com/techguide/softhard.htm**

> A Web site that includes links to home pages and support sites of major hardware and software vendors.

Microsoft OnLine Support: **www.microsoft.com/ithome/itcycle/helpdesk/default.htm**

> This Web site is part of Microsoft's Internet online support services. Contains useful information and links to help desk resources.

Clientele Products Division of Platinum Software Web page: **www.clientele.com**

> This site provides access to the Web site for Clientele Software. Clientele help desk products were described in Chapter 9 of this book. An evaluation CD-ROM can be requested at the site.

TROUBLESHOOTING

PRINT

Kim Komando, *1001 Komputer Answers.* Foster City, Calif.: IDG Books, 1995.

> Komando's book is based on her popular national radio program that answers caller questions about the operation of PC hardware and software. The book includes a CD-ROM with the complete book text that can be easily searched to locate information.

Gina Smith and Leo Laporte, *101 Computer Answers You Need to Know.* Emeryville, Calif.: Ziff-Davis Press, 1995.

Technical Support, monthly periodical of NaSPA (Network and System Professionals Association), Web address: **www.naspa.net**.

Balfer Interactive Web page: **www.HelpMeNow.com**

> A Web site with a wealth of online information about computer topics. The response time to e-mail questions is advertised as 24 hours but sometimes takes longer. Visitors can ask questions about Windows 95, Windows 3.1, DOS, Internet, Web Publishing, HTML, and Macintosh topics.

Indiana State University: **sckb.ucssc.indiana.edu/kb**

> A large collection of 4,500 technical questions and answers, plus an online forum for information you can't find in the question listing.

Cermak Technologies Web page: **www.cermak.com/techguy/index.html**

> A large collection of 12,000+ articles and technical questions for hardware and software problems. A search facility assists users with access to articles that address specific problems.

Troubleshooting Hardware

Print

Mark Minasi, The Complete *PC Upgrade & Maintenance Guide*, 8th ed. San Francisco: Sybex, 1997. Includes searchable CD-ROM.

Linda Rohrbough, *Upgrade Your Own PC.* Foster City, Calif.: IDG Books, 1996.

Scott Mueller, *Upgrading and Repairing PCs*, 8th ed. Indianapolis, Ind.: Que Education and Training, 1997. Includes searchable CD-ROM.

Jim Boyce, *Keeping Your PC Alive.* Indianapolis, Ind.: New Riders Publishing (NRP), 1994.

Other

HP Support Assistant

> This is a CD-ROM database of technical specifications and troubleshooting information for Hewlett-Packard computer products, including peripherals, network components, and desktop PCs. Both technical and user manuals are included on the CD-ROM. The service is one of a number of self-help services offered by Hewlett-Packard. It sells by subscription. Web address: **http://hpcc923. external.hp.com/cpso-support/guide/psd/selfhelp-js.html**.

Troubleshooting Operating Systems

Print

Mary Campbell, *DOS Answers: Certified Tech Support.* New York: Osborne/McGraw-Hill, 1994.

Peter Norton and Robert Jourdain, *Peter Norton's PC Problem Solver.* New York: Brady, 1993.

Peter Norton, Inside PC: Upgrading and Repairing Windows 95. Indianapolis, Ind.: SAMS, 1997.

Internet

Infowest Global Internet Services Web page: **www.32bit.com**.

> This is a Web site devoted to questions about Microsoft Windows 95, Windows/NT, and Windows CE operating systems.

13

TROUBLESHOOTING NETWORKS

PRINT

Ed Tittel and David Johnson, *A Guide to Networking Essentials.* Cambridge, Mass.: Course Technology, 1998.

> Tittel and Johnson's book is intended to prepare the reader for the Microsoft MCSE exam on Networking Essentials. It is good background material for support specialists who want an introduction to network concepts and operation.

Kelley J.P. Lindberg, *Managing Small NetWare Networks.* San Jose, Calif.: Novell Press, 1996.

Debra Niedermiller-Chaffins et al., *Managing NetWare Systems.* Indianapolis, Ind.: New Riders Publishing (NRP), 1994.

James Nadler and Don Guarnieri, *NetWare Answers: Certified Tech Support.* New York: Osborne/McGraw-Hill, 1994.

Network Computing, CMP Media, 600 Community Drive, Manhasset, NY 11030. Web address: **www.cmp.com/domesticpubs/netcompufiles/netcomp.htm**.

> This twice monthly controlled circulation publication is aimed at network administrators and support personnel. It includes articles of interest to network and Internet professionals. CMP Media's Web site includes links to a variety of information resources useful to support professionals.

NT Systems, Miller Freeman, 600 Harrison St., San Francisco, CA 94107; phone (888) 847-6188. Web address: **www.ntsystems.com**

> This monthly controlled circulation magazine includes articles on hardware and software use in Windows/NT networks. It publishes an annual buyer's guide to NT vendor products and services.

TROUBLESHOOTING APPLICATIONS SOFTWARE

PRINT

Mary Campbell, *Excel Answers: Certified Tech Support.* New York: Osborne/McGraw-Hill, 1994.

Microsoft, *Office 97 Resource Kit.* Redmond, Wash.: Microsoft Press, 1997.

> Microsoft publishes a number of resource kits for their applications and operating system software. They contain a wealth of technical information and troubleshooting tips on Microsoft products.

Internet

Microsoft Corporation Web Page: **www.microsoft.com**

> Microsoft's home page address is a popular entry point for many Microsoft products and information resources. The technical support area for hardware, software, and support questions is at **www.microsoft.com/support**. While the Microsoft Web site is indispensable, it contains a large amount of information and is difficult to navigate. Microsoft continues to try to make the site more accessible in an attempt to get support specialists the information they need and to reduce their volume of telephone calls.

End User Applications Development

Print

Elizabeth Regan and Bridget O'Connor, *End-User Information Systems: Perspectives for Managers and Information Systems Professionals.* New York: Macmillan, 1994.

> Part 4 of this book is "Planning and Implementing End-User Information Systems."

M. C. Thommes, *Advanced Spreadsheet Design Using Lotus Macros.* Danvers, Mass.: Boyd & Fraser, 1994.

Other Resources

Print

Information Week, CMP Media, 600 Community Drive, Manhasset, NY 11030; phone (800) 292-3642. Web address: **www.informationweek.com**.

> This weekly publication contains articles on products, services, stock market data on technology companies, and computer industry trends for managers in business and technology. Several articles are available on the Web page, and subscribers can sign up for a daily news update via e-mail.

Beyond Computing, IBM Magazines in affiliation with Forbes; Phone (800) 753-3380. Web address: **beyondcomputingmag.com**.

> This bimonthly controlled circulation periodical targets information system professionals; it is probably of greatest interest to managers of help desks. Aims to identify and follow trends in the strategic use of business systems.

13

INTERNET

CIO Insider Web page: **www.cio.com/CIO**

> This is an Internet version of a trade publication, *CIO (Chief Information Officer)*. It contains articles of special interest to information systems managers and others interested in the strategic application of information technology to businesses.

whatis.com Inc. Web page: **www.whatis.com**

> This Web site is a reference tool for user support staff and trainers who need definitions for common computer and Internet terms and acronyms. It includes a glossary as well as information about hardware and software, how the Internet works, and other cyberculture tips.

The information resources listed in this chapter are intended as examples where user support specialists can locate information that supplements this book. As with all information, this chapter itself will become increasingly obsolete as time elapses between when this book was published and when you read it. Please use the Course Technology Web site at **www.course.com** to update the information in this book and to locate additional resources to help with your career in user support.

CHAPTER SUMMARY

- Information is the raw material a help desk gathers, processes, stores, and distributes to end users to answer their questions. Information for both users and user support specialists comes in a variety of print and interactive formats. Printed materials include technical documentation, books, and trade publications. Interactive materials include online help, CD-ROM databases, and World Wide Web and other Internet facilities.

- Information resources vary with respect to their timeliness, bias, interactivity, cost, and ease of access.

- User support specialists need to learn how to conduct effective and efficient searches that find the correct information with a reasonable time expenditure. To do this, they need to master and use the principal search strategies discussed in this chapter.

KEY TERMS

- **AND (&) search** — A search that narrows the list of matching references by combining two or more keywords with an operator that represents AND. Example: *Syquest AND Iomega* finds only references with *both* terms.

- **bookmark** — A shortcut to a URL or home page address that a user wants to visit in the future.

- **chat rooms** — Online conferences where participants can read and write messages with special chat software; users must be connected to the Internet during a chat session to participate.

- **controlled circulation periodical** — A printed trade magazine that is distributed free to qualified subscribers who influence purchasing decisions; these publications are supported by advertising revenue.

- **drill down** — To follow a sequence of hyperlinks from a top level to progressively lower levels in a hierarchy of information; at each lower level, the information displayed gets more specific to a user's needs.

- **hyperlinks** — Graphics or highlighted words on a Web page; users can click on a hyperlink to load and view a different page; also used in online help systems.

- **ListServ** — E-mail lists to which contributions are disseminated to all those who subscribe; ListServs are organized by topic and may be public or private and either moderated (edited for content) or unmoderated.

- **keyword search** — A search strategy in which users enters one or more primary terms to indicate the subject of the information they seek.

- **natural language query** — A search strategy in which users input a question in the form of a sentence or phrase that might be used in everyday speech to indicate the information they seek.

- **newsgroup** — Internet special interest groups that exchange information and opinions on a variety of specific topics; many Web browsers facilitate searches and permit access to newsgroups.

- **OR (|) search** — A search that broadens the list of matching references by combining two or more keywords with an operator that represents OR. Example: *DVD OR CD-ROM* finds references with *either* term.

- **portals** — Web pages that let users navigate the many hyperlinks as a primary means of accessing Internet information.

- **search engine** — An Internet tool used to search Web sites and home pages to locate information based on matches to keywords.

- **SIG** — Special interest group; a small group in a large professional association where users with specific common interests can organize to share information; some SIGs meet occasionally, publish newsletters, and maintain Web sites.

- **site map** — An index to a Web site that provides an overview of how the pages on the site are organized; intended to help users navigate the site to locate the information they need quickly.

- **wildcard search** — A symbol in a search string that means "match anything"; a wildcard search uses the root form of a keyword and a wildcard symbol (a common one is *). Example: a wildcard search for **print*** matches print, printer, printers, printing, and so forth.

13

REVIEW QUESTIONS

1. Explain why widespread user access to information resources will probably not reduce the need for user support specialists.

2. List three popular forms of information resources available to support specialists. Explain the advantages and disadvantages of each form.

3. Describe the common forms of printed information resources support specialists frequently use.

4. Describe several forms of interactive information resources for user support. Explain why they are called "interactive."

5. What is a controlled circulation periodical? Who can subscribe to them?

6. Why do book publishers sometimes include a CD-ROM of a book along with the printed text? Compare the CD-ROM format with the printed format.

7. Explain why information in the computer industry is described as "perishable."

8. What is a static Web page? What is the problem with them?

9. What is a search engine? Name two examples.

10. Why would a user of a Web browser be interested in a bookmark feature? Explain why they are productivity tools for support specialists.

11. Describe several informal information resources you think would be useful to support specialists who are new to their jobs.

12. What is a site map and why would you use one?

13. What is the difference between a keyword search and a natural language search? Give an example of each.

14. How do include and exclude keywords help a user control the results of a search?

15. Explain the use of a wildcard symbol in a search. Give an example and explain the result.

16. Explain the difference between an AND and an OR search. Why would a user need these tools?

17. Explain the drill down process with hyperlinks.

18. What are FAQs and who is their intended audience?

HANDS-ON PROJECTS

PROJECT 13-1

If you have access to a CD-ROM database, such as Hewlett-Packard HP Support Assistant or Microsoft TechNet, or another similar product, learn about the information stored on the

CD-ROM and the search capabilities available to access it. Write a summary of your findings and an evaluation of how useful the information would be to a support specialist.

PROJECT 13-2

Find a trade book on a particular hardware or software topic in your personal library or in your school or business computer library. Look at the organization of the information presented.

- How does the format of the trade publication differ from textbooks with which you are familiar?

- Are some chapters or sections of particular interest to support specialists? How could chapters on product installation, troubleshooting, or tutorials for beginners be incorporated into a training program?

- Does the table of contents give an accurate picture of the organization of the material?

- Is there an index? Does it contain enough detail to allow you to easily locate information you might need in the book? Does the index list terms you would be likely to use to look up information?

Write a summary of your findings and your own evaluation of how useful the book would be to a support specialist.

PROJECT 13-3

13

Find a controlled circulation computer publication in your library or computer lab. Your instructor may be able to help you identify them, or use the lists in this chapter as a starting point. Locate the card to request a subscription to the magazine. (Alternatively, look at the subscriber qualification information on their Web site). Analyze the information the publisher wants to know about subscribers. Are the questions asked of subscribers related to the advertisers in the magazine? Write a summary of your findings.

PROJECT 13-4

Use the Internet to learn about the special interest groups (SIGs) available to members of the ACM. How many are there? List the ones you think would be of interest to a user support specialist. If you could join one SIG, which one most closely matches your personal interests in the computer field?

 PROJECT 13-5

Use the Microsoft Web glossary to find the definition of the term *hyperlink*. Microsoft's support home page is **support.microsoft.com/support.** Make a list of the steps to access a word in the glossary starting from their home page.

 PROJECT 13-6

Use the search engine AltaVista at **www.altavista.digital.com** to perform several searches. Start with the advanced search option in AltaVista. Find the number of references for a Toshiba laptop computer model *Toshiba 430CDS*. How many Web references were located? Then find the references for *Toshiba 430CDS* and *PC card*. How many references were found with the AND search? Next, find the references for *Toshiba 430 CDS* or *PC card*. How many references were found with the OR search? Explain the difference between an AND and an OR search. Finally, repeat this experiment with the simple search options in AltaVista. Write a short report of your conclusions.

 PROJECT 13-7

Use the Internet to find a supplier who sells inkjet refills and replacement cartridges for a Canon printer model BJC 4300. Write a note to a user that provides the supplier contact and price for these supply items.

 PROJECT 13-8

Use the Yahoo Internet home page at **www.yahoo.com** to find a map of your home location. While in the Map section of Yahoo, use the FAQs to find out how to print a map. Write a description of the procedure to print a map.

CASE PROJECTS

1. FRED'S PAINT STORE

The computer support specialists at Fred's Paint Store you first met in Chapter 2 would like to put together a list of information resources they could use to respond to user questions. Each support specialist has agreed to research some resources in one of the categories described in this chapter. Select one of the categories that is of interest to you. Research information resources in the category you chose. See if you can find at least one resource of each of these types:

- Vendor manual or literature

- Trade book or textbook

- Trade periodical (magazine)

- Online help system

- Internet Web addresses to useful sites

- Other materials you can locate

Write a description of the resources you found.

2. EVALUATING LISTSERVS AND NEWSGROUPS

13

If you have access to the Internet at your school or business, research the availability of ListServs and newsgroups. Join one of each in a subject area that interests you for a trial period (it doesn't have to be a subject area related to computer support). Write a short paper that summarizes your experiences with these Internet resources. Discuss the procedures to join and withdraw from membership. Describe some pros and cons of ListServs and newsgroups as information resources.

3. Valley Publishing Company

Linda Lane, supervisor of user support at Valley Publishing, is interested in improved diagnostic software tools for her support staff. She is aware of several diagnostic utility products that advertise in trade publications:

- First Aid 97 (CyberMedia)
- Norton Utilities (Symantec)
- PC Care (AMI)
- WINProbe 95 (QuarterDeck)

These products all include features to diagnose various hardware, operating system, and performance problems with PCs.

Linda would like you to begin an assignment to help the support group learn more about software products in the diagnostic utilities category. First, are there software vendors that sell diagnostic utilities the group should consider in addition to these? Second, one of Linda's concerns is that for whichever product is eventually selected, she would like to have good technical information and support available to her support staff on the Internet. She would like you to find and evaluate the Web pages for the diagnostic utility products you identified. She has questions such as: Do these companies provide technical support on their Web pages? Is their Web site easily navigable and does it include a site map? Can you reach their support staff via e-mail from their Web site? Does their Web site include frequently asked questions (FAQs) for new users?

Research these questions about diagnostic utility software vendors and write a memo to Linda with the results of your research.

INDEX